SAN DIEGO PADRES

Royals

TORONTO BLUE JAYS

ST. LOUIS CARDINALS

Braves

expos

Win! Twins!

DETROIT TIGERS

American Baseball

AMERICAN BASEBALL

Volume III

*From Postwar Expansion
to the
Electronic Age*

DAVID QUENTIN VOIGT

Foreword by
Clifford Kachline

*The Pennsylvania State University Press
University Park and London*

Library of Congress Cataloging in Publication Data

Voigt, David Quentin.
   American baseball.

   Vol. 1 foreword by Allan Nevins; v. 2 foreword by Ronald A. Smith; v. 3 foreword
by Clifford Kachline.
   Vol. 1–2 are reprints. Originally published: Norman : University of Oklahoma
Press, 1966–1970.
   Includes bibliographies and indexes.
   Contents: v. 1. From gentleman's sport to the commissioner system—v. 2. From the
commissioners to continental expansion—v. 3. From postwar expansion to the
electronic age.

   1. Baseball—United States—History—Collected
works.   I. Title.
GV863.A1V65   1983   796.357′64′0973   83-2300
ISBN   0-271-00331-6   (v. 1)
ISBN   0-271-00334-0   (pbk. : V. 1)
ISBN   0-271-00330-8   (v. 2)
ISBN   0-271-00333-2   (pbk. : V. 2)
ISBN   0-271-00329-4   (v. 3)
ISBN   0-271-00332-4   (pbk. : V. 3)

Printed in the United States of America

With the publication of Volume 3 of Voigt's *American Baseball*, Penn State Press
reissues Volumes 1 and 2 in order to complete the series.

The team logos depicted herein are the property and trademarks of their respective
Major League Clubs and have been reproduced with the permission of Major League
Baseball.

To my in-laws, Clair and Dorothy Erb, and to the memory of William and Ethel Voigt.

Contents

Foreword

Placing events into some proper perspective can often be a difficult task. For those of which we have no firsthand knowledge, such as those that occurred before we were born or were aware, we must depend upon and interpret versions supplied by other people. Even happenings in our lifetime can sometimes present interpretive problems because of elements of secrecy or because of the inevitable differences of interpretation that are possible and that occasionally lead to the courts.

One's own relative position in life can likewise affect perspective. Many senior citizens mourn "the good old days" and can find little, if anything, today that approaches the quality of yesteryear. By contrast, the younger set generally believes that almost everything now is bigger and better than ever before, and particularly anything associated with sports.

In this latest in his series of baseball histories, David Voigt seeks to order and illuminate the events that marked the game's past three and one-half decades. Like all authors, he encountered occasional barriers because of the secretiveness (sometimes understandable) that enveloped events. While his interpretations may not always be shared by readers or by the baseball establishment, they provide provocative and enlightening reading.

Most baseball historians today would agree that the 1946–82 period produced more dramatic and significant milestones than any era in the sport's history. And why shouldn't this be true? After all, the lives of people in almost all places have been reshaped and enhanced at a far more accelerated pace since World War II than in all previous recorded history. While critics have long maintained that baseball is slow to accept change, advances in technology and an increased interest in human independence and self-control combined to force many major changes in our national game.

Baseball's reshaping began in October, 1945, when Branch Rickey signed Jackie Robinson for the Brooklyn Dodgers's Montreal farm team in the International League. Not since 1898 had any blacks been permitted to participate in organized baseball. It wasn't until April of 1947, of course, that Robinson broke into the major leagues, but the Montreal contract was the formal breakthrough. Within ten years of Robinson's Dodger debut, blacks were an integral part of all but two major league teams. It was quickly evident that, as some observers have put it, fans attending major league games had seen "only half of the great players" in the all-white, pre-Robinson days.

Franchise shifts and expansion likewise forged a new dimension. For fifty years major league baseball was played in only twelve U.S. cities, those ranging from Boston in the east (and north) to St. Louis in the west (and south). The Braves's sudden move from Boston to Milwaukee a few weeks before the start of the 1953 season opened the floodgates. Five other teams quickly penetrated what might be termed virgin territory, including two that went to the west coast. By 1962 both leagues were operating with ten teams, and the boom was on. Politicians played a prominent role in the transformation of old order by promoting the erection of municipal stadia and arranging favorable tax situations in several cities to induce teams to transfer. A new breed of owners and the pressures their methods exerted on magnates from "the old school" similarly figured in the transformation.

Technology, in the form of television in particular, also greatly reshaped professional baseball. By delivering major league games into homes everywhere free of charge, the tube hastened the demise of minor league ball in a vast number of cities, though, at the same time, it fattened the coffers of the big league teams. The money that television represented spurred many changes, including salary escalation, divisional setups, and schedule revisions involving the World Series and other games. Two other products of technology—artificial turf and domed stadia—likewise introduced important changes.

Player acquisition and control underwent a drastic overhaul. Vast farm systems dominated for years before the demise of the minors and the adoption of a universal draft of high school and college talent prompted radical revisions in player procurement. Unionization came to baseball and—keeping step with the national trend toward greater individual freedom—broke the shackles of the "lifetime" reserve clause in favor of free agency, salary arbitration, and player work stoppages or strikes.

Despite all of these "external" upheavals, baseball on the field continued in much the same fashion as it had during the first seventy years of major league activity. New heroes and heroics emerged regularly. The ability of millions to watch via television the same performances that previously could be witnessed only by those attending games conceivably magnified the individuals and events to a greater degree than was deserved—yet it is doubtful that any period in baseball history produced more notable performances than the 1946–82 span. Certainly the achievements of Jackie Robinson, Stan Musial, Don Larsen, Willie Mays, Al Kaline, Hank Aaron, Reggie Jackson, Pete Rose, and others will be remembered as long and as vividly as those of any other generation.

It is this vast panoply of personages and events that David Voigt skillfully recounts on the following pages, bringing up-to-date his scholarly series on the history of The National Pastime.

Clifford Kachline
Historian, National Baseball Hall of Fame

Photo Credits

The photographs in this book are from the collections of Jim Rowe, the major league baseball clubs, the Commissioner, the Hall of Fame, the *New York Times,* and *The Sporting News;* all of these sources graciously permitted the reproduction of their photographs in this work. Photos are listed by page numbers and letters that indicate position on the page—alphabetically arranged, reading first left to right, then top to bottom.

Atlanta Braves: 235a, 307i
Baltimore Orioles: 149a, 151ab, 301c, 307d
Boston Red Sox: 63a, 120a, 176ab, 199a, 245c, 307a
California Angels: 227c, 307e
Chicago Cubs: 56b
Chicago White Sox: 76b, 85b, 251b
Cincinnati Reds: 162abcd
Cleveland Indians: 56c, 73abc
Detroit Tigers: 176cd
Houston Astros: 121b, 227e, 240a, 341a
Kansas City Royals: 255b
Los Angeles Dodgers: 28bc, 31b, 35a, 45a, 129b, 137a, 159abcd, 245a, 301ab, 351b
Milwaukee Brewers: 202abc
Minnesota Twins: 245b, 255a, 307h
Montreal Expos, 255c
The National Baseball Hall of Fame and Museum: 94ab
New York Mets: 147abc, 227a, 307c
The *New York Times:* 101abc
New York Yankees: 10abcd, 13bcd, 18a, 63b, 120b, 196abcd, 242a, 301d, 307f, 351a
Oakland Athletics: 185abcd, 189a, 227df, 307b
Office of the Baseball Commissioner: 311ab
Philadelphia Phillies: 76a, 169abc, 240b, 255d
Pittsburgh Pirates: 28ad, 152ab, 227b
Jim Rowe: 6ab, 13a, 31a, 56d, 63c, 85a, 139abc, 149b, 251a
San Diego Padres: 307g
San Francisco Giants: 56a, 121a, 129a
The Sporting News: 209a

Acknowledgments

John Donne's admonishment that "no man is an island, entire of itself" should serve as a watchword for every member of the growing tribe of baseball historians. Twenty years have now passed since my doctoral dissertation acceptance spurred me on to write a history of major league baseball; since that time, I have drawn upon the works of hundreds of baseball aficionados: players, fans, officials, umpires, talent scouts, journalists, sportscasters, novelists, academics, gifted amateurs, and collectors. These people have helped to forge this book. While footnotes and bibliographic references identify many such creditors, there are others whose names are omitted, but whose valuable contributions are gratefully acknowledged.

I have amassed many debts over the years that have been spent writing this volume of *American Baseball* and those that preceded it. I extend enduring gratitude to my classmates at the Milton Hershey School, for sparking my interest in the sandlot game, and to the late Professor Allan Nevins, for his consistent encouragement and assurance that baseball history is a worthwhile scholarly undertaking. Likewise, for piloting my doctoral dissertation on major league baseball in the 1880s through shoals of doubters, professors Nelson Blake, Donn Hart, Paul Meadows, and the late Earle Bell have earned lasting appreciation.

I especially wish to thank the following people, who have rendered priceless help in the research and the writing of this volume:

Former Hall of Fame baseball historian Lee Allen and his worthy successor, Clifford Kachline, have fortified me with their aid and support. Many members of the Society for American Baseball Research have furnished promising leads for my work; among them, special thanks are extended to John Thorn, John Holway, and Robert Davids. As one baseball historian among many, I acknowledge our debt to the Popular Culture Association, especially to the association's founder, Professor Ray Browne, and to the North American Society for Sports History, whose *Journal of Sports History* is a valuable tool for all scholars of the diamond. All members of NASSH have provided valuable assistance, but special thanks go out to Ronald Smith, Steve Riess, Richard Crepeau, Robert Barnett, and Marc Onigmann.

Other individuals and groups who have offered sterling support are Professor Kevin Kerrane, Brandy Davis, the public relations staffs of the twenty-six major league clubs, the league presidents, the Commissioner of Baseball and his staff, the Major League Players Association, and the Major League Umpires Association.

Finally, my warmest gratitude goes to the entire staff of The Pennsylvania State University Press.

Introduction: American Baseball at Mid-Century

S canning America's decade of the 1950s from latter-day

The Nation—Problems Amidst Plenty

perches, social critics differed sharply in their judgments. To some it was the "Fabulous Decade" or the "Nifty Fifties"; to others it was the "Nightmare Decade" or the "Haunted Fifties."[1]

In truth the decade fitted both extremes. To historian Eric Goldman it was a time of sweeping social revolution in which more Americans laid claim to the fruits of equality and individualism. No longer were such values to be the domain of middle-class white males; downtrodden minorities now served notice that they, too, would participate in the abundant life.

What most Americans sought, along with marital happiness, was material abundance; this included comfortable housing, cars, television sets, and other things. Advertising helped to persuade millions to acquire mass-produced goods, to find fun through commercialized leisure outlets, and to quest after ever higher material standards. Masses of people came to know a standard of living unprecedented in human history.

The increasing availability of material goods stirred personal and social ambitions, while the G.I. Bill of Rights spurred a college attendance boom that saw millions of young Americans enrolling, trusting that their degrees would serve as passports to satisfying careers. The "knowledge revolution" that ensued contributed much to the spread of equalitarian and individualistic sentiments and fostered higher aspirations. To get ahead, to be somebody, became each man's motivation—and the inspiration of women as well. To protect their newly won jobs and purchasing powers, Americans increasingly joined unions and protective associations.

Indeed, Americans needed protection from the nettles in the land of plenty. Fear of recession, of eroding inflation, of war, and of hostile repression was rife and drove many into conformist shells, prompting latter-day critics to label Americans of the 1950s "the silent generation." Taught that the great external fear was the Soviet Union and its minions, Americans accepted the cold war as a reality. In truth, except for the Korean War, which revived the military draft, no major threat from the international arena disturbed American goals. General Eisenhower's presence in the White House radiated assurance that under his guidance the nation would move into the uplands of abundance.

Still, as more Americans grasped at material delights, there were signs that the new lifestyle was blighted. So much stress on individualism, on putting one's self first, placed unbearable strains on marriages, communities, and the national morale. Similarly, all-out equalitarian demands triggered social upheavals that eventually reshaped these social institutions. In new suburban wonderworlds, psychic and social tensions challenged marital togetherness, prompting a new generation of muckrakers to expose the harried lives of affluent Americans. To read of "cracks in picture windows" or "split-level traps" was to glimpse the seeming hollowness of American life. Books about "organization men" in "gray flannel suits" carried bleak messages of petty, striving behavior and toadying conformity. Yet these, like exposés of seductive ploys used by advertisers to create demands for goods, carried sobering messages that titillated briefly, but were mostly ignored. After all, who wanted to dwell upon the sham of the abundant life? It was far easier to dismiss such bleak concerns, but by doing so, Americans of the 1950s allowed such problems to grow and fester, and later to threaten the stability of the affluent society.[2]

The Leisure Boom

In the postwar era, Americans banished their concerns by immersing themselves in leisure pursuits. With working hours in 1950 averaging just under 41 a week, most of the 150 million Americans enjoyed weekends free from work, as well as annual vacations. With half of the population now clustered in metropolitan areas, Americans were spending $11.3 billion a year on commercialized leisure pastimes which reflected a great diversity of individual tastes and interests and were loosely classified as participant or spectator activities. Television viewing became the most popular outlet, kindling a new interest in the various sports. Thus, the 1950s saw the marriage of television and sports, a union that put both partners in the national spotlight.

From dim beginnings, television in the 1950s became the catalyst that forced the expansion of major sports into all regions of the land, making gods of athletes by putting them "on stage" and in time enriching them with more cash and glory than any generation of athletes had ever known. Television, however, played no favorites among the sports. What counted was viewer appeal, measured by statistical ratings. While baseball was the early favorite, producers turned to football, basketball, hockey, bowling, tennis, golf, and others as opportunity beckoned. What ensued was a broad exposure to sports that turned Americans into sports generalists. In time this would make baseball's claim to being the national pastime a shop-worn myth, as watching *sports* on television became the national pastime.[3]

Such a prospect in 1950 was beyond the ken of baseball men reveling in their newfound prosperity. Major league attendance had outpaced the nation's population growth since 1946, reaching almost 21 million paid admissions in 1948, the year the Indians attracted a record 2.6 million paying fans. Also sharing in diamond glory were the minor leagues, whose leagues and teams outnumbered those of previous eras.

This was the high-water mark of baseball's traditional format. Beginning in 1950, attendance slumped below 20 million and averaged fewer than 16 million over the next five seasons. For the majors, losses were succored by television income, but many devastated minor leagues died.[4]

Other pro sports—football, basketball, and hockey—now gained in popularity and posed vague threats to baseball's pre-eminence. In company with baseball, these sports composed the "Big 4" of professional athletics. In 1950 they co-existed peacefully as each sport's season succeeded another's in orderly fashion, lending a comfortable rhythm to the calendar. As the decade wore on, however, these sports cut into baseball's long season. By 1959 hockey's Stanley Cup playoffs competed with baseball's April opening, while football's preseason exhibition games challenged baseball in the fall. These were the first shadows of overlap which later became the bewildering "squeezing of the seasons."

Among these competitors, pro football became baseball's most formidable rival. Born in the 1920s, the National Football League grew slowly, stunted by meager publicity and a dependence upon major league parks. After World War II the league's adolescence was blighted by the rival All-American Football Conference, which challenged the NFL up to 1949. The death throes of the Conference affected the outcome of the 1950 National League baseball season: Dodger president Branch Rickey lost money investing in the AAC's football Dodgers, prompting him to sell Sam Jethroe and Irv Noren, whose absences contributed to the loss to the Phillies that year.[5]

Still, the victorious NFL gained strength over the 1950s. With its new platooning strategy and exciting passing game, the NFL dominated American football and, with 12 teams scattered coast to coast, drew fans from urban areas unexposed to major league baseball. As patrons flocked to the games, network television money poured in, so that by the decade's end the major leagues faced a formidable challenge from the NFL.

Meanwhile, basketball become the fastest growing spectator sport at the grassroots level. In the early 1940s the game shed its slow, set-shooting style of play for a dazzling running game, marked by accurate one-handed shooting. Catching on in schools and colleges, the new style triggered a postwar basketball mania. As college stars then turned professional, the struggling Basketball Association of America gave way in 1949 to the sturdy National Basketball Association. The NBA dominated American basketball in the 1950s just as major league baseball and football ruled over their games. By 1960 the 8-team NBA was profitably entrenched and had television money behind it, so that baseball was faced with another strong rival.

Such rivals cut into baseball's grassroots support. As football and basketball programs dominated school and college athletic programs, baseball became a second-ranked sport. A diminishing supply of baseball recruits resulted, forcing major league owners into costly bidding wars and producing the "bonus baby craze" of the 1950s.

At least professional hockey provided no competition. This speediest of team sports, nearly all of whose players were Canadians, was organized into the National Hockey League, a 6-club circuit that gained popularity from its newly adopted fast-breaking and passing styles. Fans were dazzled by hockey's non-stop, often brutal action. Although ripe for expansion, conservative NHL promoters stood pat until the late 1960s, when they made their move. Although largely at the expense of pro basketball, the extended hockey season also cut into baseball's domain.

Baseball's Fitful Fifties

Major league owners of 1950 could still feel smugly secure about their game. Attendance was up and television money enhanced profits. Problems like the admission of black players or the challenge of Mexican League baseball nagged, but these were surmounted. Militant players had been mollified by the grant of a pension plan and a toothless company union. Also, anxieties stirred by Congressional anti-trust probes into baseball's reserve clause and league radio and television policies were still shielded by a 1922 Supreme Court decision.

Thus, baseball's traditional format held firm in 1950. The time-honored east-west alignment of 11 cities, stretching from Boston to St. Louis, afforded a marvelously balanced 154-game schedule that had each team playing each rival 22 times. This allowed long home stands and four western road trips for each team, the latter easily accomplished by Pullman train, with a few adventuresome clubs opting for air travel. As in the prewar past, each season began with a long spring training period in the southlands, featuring many exhibition games played against rivals and minor league teams to help cover expenses. The championship season began in April and, with time out for the July All-Star game, action continued until October when the World Series climaxed the long season.

One of the comforting delights of baseball was the seeming timelessness of its rules. However, that year much bombast centered about the recodification of playing rules, the first in half a century. Although there were few obvious changes, many subtle shadings were contained in the 40-odd pages that few players and managers studied. Nor did teams hold meetings about rules. Such concerns were for umpires, the familiar men in blue, whose presence still invoked time-honored ritualized hostilities.[6]

The major rule change of 1950 was a redefinition of the strike zone as the area from a batter's armpits to the top of his knee. Most rule changes, however, dealt with records which spelled out qualifications for batting champions or winning pitchers: in 1954, for example, a batter was no longer charged with a time at bat if his fly ball scored a run after the catch.

A rule prescribing minimum dimensions for new parks hinted at changes to come. As of June 1, 1958, this rule required that all new playing fields maintain minimum distances of 325 feet from home plate to the nearest left and right field fences. Four hundred feet was the minimum distance from home plate to the center field fence.[7] Meanwhile, the same old, idiosyncratic parks housed the fans of 1950. Most of these dated back to the steel and concrete building boom of the 1910s, but Sportsman's Park in St. Louis and the Polo Grounds in New York were wondrously old, in spirit as well as structure. Racism lingered at Sportsman's Park long after Jackie Robinson's debut, while the Polo Grounds, with the shortest distances down the lines of any park, offered inviting targets for "Chinese" homers. The newest and most capacious parks of this era were Yankee Stadium and Cleveland's Municipal Stadium, built in 1923 and 1932 respectively.[8] Most of the parks stood within cities. The owners, unrestricted by conforming rules, tailored their parks' boundaries to suit the offenses of their own teams. Thus, the old parks defied classification, and the stadiums of the 1950s still expressed a morality of "rugged individualism."[9] Among the odd configurations were the horseshoe shape of the Polo Grounds field; Fenway's "green monster" left field wall; Shibe's raised right field barrier, constructed to block the views of outside free loaders; and Chicago's Comiskey Park, whose 1912 blueprints included a retractable roof which was rejected as too expensive.

Newly erected light towers indicated the popularity of night baseball in every park but Wrigley Field. By 1950 Senator owner Clark Griffith had triumphed in his fight for unrestricted night games, providing a boon to poorer clubs. Now most games were played at night to the apparent satisfaction of fans. If traditionalists worried about night ball's damage to batting or pitching performances, such fears were laid to rest by studies which showed little difference between night or day performances.[10]

As the decade wore on, however, falling attendance alerted owners to the inadequacies of the old parks. Not only were they uncomfortable, but they lacked parking spaces for autos, and their deteriorating neighborhoods repelled fans. Commissioner Frick urged the construction of new, all-weather parks in 1958, but the owners claimed the costs were too high for private means.

Meanwhile, owners tried to update the old parks. Yankee Stadium introduced its "electronic" scoreboard in 1950. The 73' by 34' scoreboard required two operators to operate some 5,000 keys, which spelled out illuminated messages in non-glaring colors. Cincinnati's Crosley Field later boasted a more versatile scoreboard that flashed the batting averages of players. Elsewhere extensive painting and upkeep was undertaken, but some owners allowed deterioration to run its course. Griffith's scoreboard in Washington was so unreliable that umpires still used hand indicators. Straitened circumstances forced owners Bill Veeck and Connie Mack to sell their parks to National League tenants, and enterprising owners like Lou Perini, Walter O'Malley, and Horace Stoneham soon abandoned old grounds for greener pastures elsewhere.[11]

Inside some of the parks fans were escorted to seats by comely usherettes wearing long-skirted, "new look" uniforms. This eye-catching change was just one of the departures from earlier eras: a greater variety of food was hawked by concessionaires, bustling activity was seen in bullpens where relief pitchers plied their skills, and changes were noticed in playing style. That familiar path leading from home plate to the pitcher's mound disappeared in the 1950s, as did the old custom of fielders leaving their gloves on the playing field or wadding them into hip pockets as they batted.

Since 1949, gloves had grown in size, becoming veritable ball traps rather than hand protectors. The gloves of the 1950s had two breaks—at the palm and at the thumb—which eliminated the old single pocket and pushed fielding averages to .979 by 1979. Some players now defied the ancient taboo by making graceful one-handed catches. As gloves grew larger, rule makers of 1956 set limits on their dimensions; widespread evasions forced a second ruling in 1959, which was no more successful. Even as purists protested the big glove trend, some players wore golf gloves in batting practice as protection against blisters.

Bats also changed, becoming lighter and more narrowly tapered at the end. Such "whippy" bats accounted for prodigious homer production in the 1950s, but the continuing "big bang" style produced more broken bats and strike-outs. Obsessed with the homeric style, some players illegally "doped" bats, embedding nails or cork in the barrels in hopes of smiting balls harder.[12]

Not suprisingly, the spate of homers stirred charges about livelier balls. Similar accusations in past eras had proven true. Though the Spalding Company still denied the charges, two University of Wisconsin professors now showed that Spalding's balls varied by size, cover thickness, resiliency, yarn, weight, and seam width.

The popularity of the "big bang" style overrode this paper controversy. The fans delightedly cheered the long hits, scrambling after balls that flew into the stands. Because such balls were treasured keepsakes and fair game for fans, clubs now used as many as 1,000 dozen in a season. In 1957 President Eisenhower ceremonially tossed out the supposed 10 millionth major league ball, manufactured by Spalding.

Meanwhile batting helmets slowly freed players of the ancient terror of being hit by pitched balls. These had been tried in past eras and judged too cumbersome, though some batters chose to insert protective linings in their caps. Now these gave way to light, impact-resistant plastic that promised better protection.

By 1955 Branch Rickey had patented a plastic helmet with a protective flap which covered the side of the head facing the pitcher and had sent his moribund Pirates to the field thus armored. Predictably they were jeered, one writer quipping that miners' lamps should be added to show them the way out of the cellar. The helmets, however, proved their worth when a Pirate base-runner, hit on the helmet by an errant throw, escaped injury. The gear was soon ruled compulsory.[13]

Slower to change were the familiar flannel uniforms with baggy knickers and numbered shirts. Rickey experimented with shorts in the minors, bucking a formidable taboo. Then, in 1959, Bill Veeck's White Sox appeared with their surnames displayed on their shirt backs.

Although equipment and uniform changes displayed an interest in the new and different, baseball in this decade reflected a national conservative trend. Reacting to cold war tensions between America and Russia, baseball officials adopted a patriotic stance. For players this meant performing military duties, though critics complained that some joined reserve units to escape full-time conscription.

In 1952 baseball was drawn into the propaganda war with Russia when a young people's Communist League organ in that land attacked the American game. The article described "beizbol" as a brutal sport played by enslaved players under capitalist-masters. Indeed, the article argued that the game was a stolen version of the Russian folk game of "lapta"! Widely reprinted, such claims were ridiculed and one of American baseball's most fiery defenders, Eddie Stanky, proudly called baseball "the big game of a free people."[14]

However, some native critics found much fault with the game. Sports historian Herbert W. Wind derided the banality of baseball, blaming television for running the game and turning owners into profiteers, players into mercenaries, and fans into entertainment seekers. Fed up with baseball's mindless homer strategy, Wind chose football as the best of the outdoor spectacles.[15]

To baseball's defense sprang Harold Rosenthal, who called the 1950s the game's best decade and cited franchise moves, sparkling performances, television's stimulating influence, and awesome feats (such as the Giants's Miracle victory and Don Larsen's World Series no-hitter) as solid proof for his claim.[16]

In truth, much changed and much stayed the same. Billy Herman judged that the game of the 1950s was "pretty much the same game [but] played with better bats and balls in smaller ball parks." When faulting the parks, he alluded to shortening fences for more homers which came in godsplenty—1,263 by the National League in 1955 for a new seasonal record.[17]

As always, some critics complained of games lasting too long, of coddled players, and of antiquated parks. Indeed, several thought it high time that baseball disenthrall itself from the natural elements— this included bug swarms like the invasion of "Green Bay Flies" that once postponed a game at Cleveland.

A perennial protest, sounded every decade since the 1920s, damned Yankee domination. The Yankee tyranny was now even more oppressive; in this decade no American League team but the Yankees won a World Series. New Yorkers won six, enough to maintain American League supremacy.

The National League teams faced their own tyrants; the Dodger dynasts won five pennants and two world titles, while the Giants and Braves each took a world title. If such successes sobered American partisans, National League victories in annual All-Star games also awarded bragging rights to the older circuit. At one point the Americans held a 12–4 edge in these contests, but the Nationals reeled off four straight wins, and by 1956 they narrowed the gap to 13–10. The Americans still led at decade's end, but the Nationals were closing fast.

The surging National League humbled the junior circuit in other ways. Offensively, the Nationals led in homers and base stealing— explaining why National attendance exceeded American. For its offensive superiority the National League had black players to thank. Rickey deserves credit for bringing forth Jackie Robinson as the first of the "Negro Vanguard." Then, as tremulous American owners waited, more venturesome National clubs signed on the most talented black and Latin American players. By the end of the decade, such players were the new stars in the baseball firmament.

In another tradition-shattering move, the Nationals were first to abandon an established franchise to move to a more lucrative site, thus destroying the myth which held that baseball's success depended on maintaining permanently stable franchises in old, established communities.

Expansion talk was rife throughout the postwar era, and rightfully so. Population growth and changing settlement patterns created promising opportunities in western and southern regions. In 1946 Clarence "Pants" Rowland petitioned for major league status for his Pacific Coast League, vainly hoping to protect his sites from carpetbagging major league "vultures."[18] While Rowland's petition was denied, major league owners hungrily eyed his Los Angeles and San Francisco territories. A Congressional subcommittee suggested in 1951 that the major leagues' restricted membership opposed "free play of competitive forces." This perhaps persuaded owners in 1952 to rescind their old rule requiring unanimous consent of both major leagues in the event of a franchise shift. The new policy helped sick franchises, like the Browns, Braves, and Athletics; but when the franchise shifts of the 1950s took place, the choicest sites went to the more enterprising Dodgers and Giants, who snared the coveted west coast cities.

Certainly the Browns could have fared better had owner Bill Veeck had his way. An imaginative promoter, Veeck revived the dying Browns and boosted their attendance. Unfortunately his effort was too small to avert bankruptcy. When Veeck then petitioned in 1952 for permission to move to Milwaukee, his request was blocked by Brave owner Lou Perini, who held city territorial rights; when Veeck proposed occupying Los Angeles or Baltimore, he was turned down by his own vengeful colleagues.

Perini's luck was different. His colleagues approved his petition to move to Milwaukee. One month before the start of the 1953 season, Perini heralded the coming expansion era by undertaking the first franchise shift in fifty years. This move was closely monitored by other owners, who soon waxed green-eyed with envy. The rechristened Milwaukee Braves settled into a new $6.6 million county-financed stadium and attracted a record 1.8 million fans. They proceeded to draw crowds of close to 2 million a year for the next seven years.

The first returns on the "Milwaukee Miracle" persuaded American owners to free the moribund Browns and A's. At the close of the 1953 season, the Veeckless Browns were moved to Baltimore where they, too, played in a new, publicly financed stadium and drew many spectators their first year. After a honeymoon season, however, attendance fell to modest proportions and the presence of the new Orioles added to the Washington Senators's straitened circumstances.

Soon after this ill-considered move the Americans blundered again. Late in the 1954 season the once-proud Philadelphia A's were sold by the Mack family. When the new owner, Arnold Johnson, asked to move to Kansas City where $3 million of local tax money had refurbished a minor league park, permission was granted. Like the Orioles, the Kansas City A's enjoyed a short honeymoon, followed by years of disappointing attendance. Worse yet, revelations of collusion between owners Johnson and Del Webb of the Yankees embarrassed the American League. For the remainder of the decade a spate of player trades between these clubs strengthened the Yankees.[19]

Thus, as the Americans occupied marginal sites, the Nationals scored the coup of the decade by staking out the lucrative west coast sites. The prime mover behind the coup was Walter O'Malley, owner of the Dodgers. Although his team was victorious and drew a profit in Brooklyn, O'Malley recognized the greater attendance and television potential of Los Angeles.

At the same time Giant owner Horace Stoneham faced problems with his deteriorating Polo Grounds site. Up against falling attendance and limited television revenue, Stoneham accepted O'Malley's suggestion to join the west coast move and transplant the Dodger-Giant rivalry to Los Angeles and San Francisco. O'Malley's political acumen brought off the coup. Pleading a decline in attendance at home, O'Malley urged city officials to build a new ballpark and offered to contribute $5 million to the cause. Then, when officials delayed, O'Malley burned his bridges by selling his holdings and announcing that he would quit Brooklyn after the 1957 season. O'Malley meanwhile carried on delicate negotiations with baseball-hungry Los Angeles politicos: he sought a land grant for a proposed new park at Chavez Ravine, a $2 million city grant for access roads to the park, and temporary quarters for his team at the Los Angeles Coliseum.

Stormed at by angry Brooklyn fans and harried by opposition forces in Los Angeles, O'Malley was sorely tried. His coup "caused a bitter political, legal and perhaps moral controversy," but the pro-

Dodger forces in Los Angeles prevailed—although O'Malley was given only land for a stadium and funds for access roads. Nonetheless, the Los Angeles Dodgers proved an immensely popular attraction; the combination of record attendance and television money justified the move and enabled O'Malley to build Dodger Stadium, the last baseball arena to be financed by private capital.[20]

The westward moves of the Dodgers and Giants rocked the foundations of the major leagues. Outcries by incensed fans prompted renewed Congressional investigations and fueled demands for big league clubs in other urban regions. The owners retorted in 1958 that they would welcome expansion, and even a rival major league if it met certain criteria. Branch Rickey and William Shea saw an invitation here to launch their rival Continental League in 1959, promising New York fans a new team and a new stadium in Flushing Meadows.

The Continental League confronted the majors with their most formidable challenge since the Federal League. Moreover, the threat of anti-trust action ruled out time-honored counteractions formerly used against interlopers. Compromise was now a far better solution; the majors quashed the threat by absorbing the more promising Continental sites into an expanded major league format. Thus, the price of carpetbaggery was a drastic alteration in major league structure.

If expansion was the antidote to Continental interlopers, there was no effective nostrum against charges that baseball was becoming a commercialized entertainment. Truthfully, it always had been, but owners still wallowed in the myth that theirs was a sporting venture.[21] Oddly enough, that dying myth now exposed owners as carpetbaggers who might coldly abandon traditional sites for siren dollars, and especially television revenue, which some now suspected had come to control the game.

As the 1950s passed, so did baseball's old order. Although controversial pre-expansion moves evoked lamentations from fans in abandoned cities, there were joyous cheers from fans at the new sites. Still, the decade ended amidst a confusion as to where the game was heading. That expansion, television, and profits sent baseball along uncertain paths was clear; but towards what new equilibrium, none could say.

 I *The Postwar Era*

1

The Postwar Campaigns: The American League

The Power Struggle of 1946–1948

Like many American League fans in that heady springtime of 1946, clubowners basked in the nation's war victory and looked for a return to baseball normalcy. After three seasons of ersatz baseball, this seemed possible, and rapid demobilization returned many former stars to their familiar flannels.

Not surprisingly, many observers touted the Yankees because of returnees like Joe DiMaggio, Tom Henrich, Charlie Keller, Phil Rizzuto, and Joe Gordon. Also, the club's new owners were optimistic enough to ready Yankee Stadium for night baseball. On May 28th the first night game was played at the stadium, drawing 50,000 fans despite the bad weather.

Yankee rivals were grimly defiant. The Tigers looked for support in slugger Hank Greenberg and a pitching staff of Dizzy Trout, Virgil Trucks, and Hal Newhouser. Returning Red Sox stars like

Ted Williams, Rudy York, Bob Doerr, and Dom DiMaggio, excited Boston fans.

What followed was a nightmarish season for the Yanks. Disciplinary problems in the spring vexed manager Joe McCarthy and worsened his failing health; he eventually submitted his resignation. Bill Dickey succeeded McCarthy and lasted until September, when John Neun finished the season. By then the team was 17 games behind, hitting poorly, and going nowhere.

As the Yankees foundered, manager Joe Cronin's Red Sox surged. In mid-May the Sox won 15 straight, and at mid-season their 54–23 record far outclassed pursuers. Leading the attack was Williams, who went on to bat .342 and smite 38 homers. So devastating was "the Thumper" that the Cleveland manager, Lou Boudreau, devised a defensive strategy of stacking infielders on the right side and giving the left-handed slugger the gaping hole between second and third. Others adopted the "Boudreau" shift, but to little avail. Williams's teammate John Pesky batted .335 and led the league in hits, Dom DiMaggio hit .316, and three Sox each drove in one hundred runs. With solid pitching from Dave "Boo" Ferris, Tex Hughson, and Mickey Harris, the Sox never looked back. Only in early September did they slump; then rallying swiftly, they clinched the pennant on the 13th and finished 12 games ahead of the Tigers.

The 1946 triumph was Sox owner Tom Yawkey's first return on the dollars he had lavished over the years, trying to build a winner. Now, with the league's best batting and fielding team, he eyed a world title. Unfortunately, Williams injured his elbow in a meaningless exhibition game and managed only five singles in the Series. Still, the Series was hard fought and went to the limit. After Boston took the opener in St. Louis, the combatants swapped victories until the final game. In the eighth inning of that game, Enos Slaughter of the Cardinals stunned the Boston defense with a daring show of base running; scoring from first on a single, Slaughter sank the Sox.

Despite this loss, experts picked the Sox to repeat a strong season in 1947. Hoping to strengthen his team, Yawkey met with Yankee president Topping to discuss swapping Williams for DiMaggio. This mind-boggling proposal had logic on both sides. What a right-handed hitter like DiMaggio might do against Fenway Park's short left field wall was balanced by what Williams could accomplish against Yankee Stadium's short right field wall. Negotiations broke off, however, when Yawkey demanded that the Yankees throw in Larry "Yogi" Berra.[1]

Yawkey would have rued the day that the trade had gone through because Williams won a Triple Crown, leading the league in batting (.343), homers (32), and RBIs (114). Still, his heroics failed to offset a pitching collapse.

Few bettors picked the Yankees that year. The new manager, Stanley "Bucky" Harris, had not won since 1925 when he served as "boy manager" of the Senators. Except for first baseman George McQuinn, the daily lineup was much the same. The infield had McQuinn, George "Snuffy" Stirnweiss at second, Bill Johnson at third, and Phil Rizzuto at short. With Keller crippled by back injuries, Harris heralded an outfield of Henrich, DiMaggio, and Johnny Lindell. Although the catching was average, the versatile Berra was a promising newcomer.

Improved pitching held the key to success. Over the winter Joe Gordon was dealt to Cleveland for big Allie Reynolds. Rookies Frank "Specs" Shea and Vic Raschi joined Chandler, Bill Bevens, and reliefer Joe Page on the staff. That year Reynolds won 19, Shea 14, and Chandler 9. Only Bevens flagged, but his failure was offset by Page's relief work. Appearing in 56 games, Page saved 17 and won 14. In the stretch drive, young Raschi won seven, as did Louis "Bobo" Newsome, an aging castoff acquired late in the season.

Regrouping under the genial Harris, the Yanks led early and went on to win the flag by 12 games. DiMaggio led the attack with a .315 average, 20 homers, and 97 RBIs. Only McQuinn joined DiMaggio in the .300 class, but the team led the league in batting, homers, and pitching effectiveness.

With the Yankees and Dodgers due to meet in the 1947 World Series, baseball seemed back to normal and the rematch between these Gotham powers met all expectations. Opening at home, the Yanks took the first two games, the first on a big rally in the fifth inning and the second by a 10–3 romp. At Ebbets Field the Dodgers battered Newsom to win the third, 9–8. In the fourth game the Dodgers became part of Series folklore by ruining Bevens's ragged bid to become the first no-hit pitcher in Series history. With two out in the ninth inning and the Yankees ahead 2–1, Cookie Lavagetto doubled on Bevens's second pitch to drive in the winning Dodger runs. The victory knotted the Series, but the Yanks rebounded with a 2–1 win. Returning home and needing one more, the Yanks fell behind 8–6 when, with two mates on base, DiMaggio sent a drive to left center that looked like a homer. Instead, little Al Gionfriddo in left field made one of the most spectacular catches in Series history

Cardinal outfielder Enos Slaughter (*left*) dashed American League hopes in the Series of 1946 by scoring the winning run against the Red Sox; but lefty Joe Page, star Yankee reliefer (*right*), helped the Yankees defeat the Dodgers in 1947 to regain the heights.

to save a Dodger victory. It tied the Series, but the Yankees took a 5–2 triumph the next time out, highlighted by reliefer Page's five innings of shut-out pitching.

After two memorable Series encounters, what could baseball do for an encore? The Yankees, back now on top, seemed likely to stay there, especially after acquiring lefty Ed Lopat from the White Sox. This heady pitcher, who delivered six different pitches off the same motion, was joined by another lefty, Tom Byrne, back from the minors where he had been sent to learn control. Receiving was young catcher Berra, and bonus baby Bobby Brown joined the infield. Such infusions gave the world champs an invincible appearance.

Their opponents were also retooling. Ex-Yankee manager

McCarthy was lured out of retirement to skipper the Boston Red Sox. Owner Yawkey purchased pitchers Jack Kramer and Ellis Kinder and infielder Vern Stephens from the impoverished Browns.

Meanwhile, owner Veeck assembled a powerful team at Cleveland which included the league's first black players. Larry Doby was signed to join Dale Mitchell and Allie Clark in the outfield. Shortstop, playing-manager Lou Boudreau anchored a veteran infield of Ed Robinson at first, Joe Gordon at second, and Ken Keltner at third. The great Bob Feller headed the pitching staff, along with Bob Lemon, a converted infielder, and Gene Bearden, an ex-Yankee prospect. Behind them was stellar catcher Jim Hegan. Playing in the league's most capacious park, the Indians, backed by Veeck's zany promotional schemes, drew hordes. Veeck's best ploy came in July when he signed legendary black pitching ace, LeRoy "Satchel" Paige. With Paige and Doby as turnstile attractions, the 1948 Indians drew an unprecedented two million fans.[2]

Never before was there a tighter race than the 1948 American League struggle. Throughout the campaign, the Yankees, Indians, and Red Sox grappled. Williams hit a league-leading .369 with 25 homers and 127 RBIs for the Sox. Yankee DiMaggio, slowed by a foot injury, hit .320 and led the league in homers and RBIs. Cleveland's .282 team batting powered the best-balanced attack, paced by Boudreau, Doby, and Gordon.

In September only 4½ games separated the first place Red Sox from Connie Mack's fourth place A's; in time the A's faded and the Indians appeared doomed. On the 12th Boston led the second-place Yanks by three, then the race tightened, and by the 18th the Indians had battled back. As late as the 25th a three-way tie ensued for first place, and soon afterward the Indians led by two. At this point Boston won its last four, eliminating the Yankees along the way. Coupled with two Cleveland losses, Boston's streak tied the Indians and forced the first postseason, tie-breaking playoff in league history.

League rules called for a single game to decide the winner. Boston won a coin toss and the right to host the game. However, a strange lassitude gripped the Sox pitchers and no starter volunteered to pitch the crucial game. Forced to choose, McCarthy named veteran Denny Galehouse, a spot starter, who earlier had worked effectively against Cleveland. Boudreau countered with Bearden, whose knuckleball had earned 19 wins. Bearden won easily, 8–3, with Boudreau getting four hits, including a pair of homers. Watching Bearden, Williams glumly remarked, "He'll be lucky to have another winning season."[3] The slugger's prophetic words were of little comfort to Sox fans; a temporary solace was provided by the success of the Braves, winners of the National League, who met the Indians in the World Series. The Braves's best shot came on opening day when Johnny Sain outpitched Feller 1–0, in a game tainted by a controversial umpire call on Feller's eighth-inning pickoff attempt. The runner scored the only run. The Indians went on to easily win the Series, four games to two.

The Great Yankee Tyranny, 1949–1961

Each baseball season since 1946 had seen new champions emerge, but this brief sniff of competitive balance ended when the majors returned to their traditional dynastic format. Equalitarian hopes were now dashed by the emergence of the most awesome dynasty in major league history.

Finishing third in 1948, the Yankees looked like bland imitators of their prewar forebears. Their presence, however, was intimidating, and a 1928 description of the Yankee mystique still held: "The team has something that every great person has. . . . It has a certain intangible . . . a confidence, almost cockiness that it is the best team on earth. It has poise, aplomb, insouciance—a calm faith in itself that . . . is radiated to the other team and the enemy crowd."[4]

As much as any man in the Yankee organization, general manager George Weiss fanned this mystique. Since joining the club in 1932, Weiss built a Yankee farm system that matched Rickey's. So productive were his farms that the team seldom spent money for players, but, instead, profited from the sale of surplus talent.

Like Louis XI, the "Spider King of France," this empire-builder was unimpressive in appearance. The shy, gnomish Weiss shunned publicity and worked alone. This workaholic harassed his underlings endlessly with demands, yet excelled as a judge of playing talent. Weiss beat down salary demands and coldly dismissed faltering performers. His ruthlessness nearly cost him his job in 1947: at the team's victory celebration, owner MacPhail fired Weiss, who was later reprieved when Dan Topping bought out MacPhail, boosting Weiss's salary and widening his powers.

After the 1948 loss, Weiss sacked Harris and hired Charles "Casey" Stengel. The critical press reacted with mixed emotions. Although Stengel once starred as a player, he had been a failure as a manager. After nine unsuccessful years of managing in the majors, he had sunk to the minors where his teams won three pennants in twelve years. Now came the offer of a lifetime, but the 58-year-old Stengel only reluctantly accepted a two-year contract to skipper the Yankees.

Events quickly showed Weiss's wisdom, for the colorful Stengel proved an artful juggler of his 25-man squad, having learned from McGraw how to win games by playing percentages and platooning his men. Stengel commanded more good talent in the spring of 1949 than he had ever known. At hand was the brilliant pitching trio of Raschi, Reynolds, and Lopat, the reborn Byrne, and the veteran reliefer Page. Backing the staff was the hard-hitting Berra, who headed a four-man catching corps.

Stengel solved a chronic first base problem by stationing Henrich there and testing a string of rookies. The tough, durable Joe Collins stood out among this group. The otherwise solid infield had the league's top shortstop in Rizzuto and youngsters Jerry Coleman at second and Bobby Brown at third, all backed by able veterans Stirnweiss and Johnson. The outfield of DiMaggio, Lindell, and Keller was battle-tested, but aging and injury prone. Stengel platooned here, inserting newcomers Gene Woodling and rookie Hank Bauer, a World War II Marine hero.

As Stengel came to know his team, he learned that the natural leader was the great DiMaggio. Indeed, this tall, quietly commanding player was the most popular Yankee since Ruth; already a legendary star, he was the game's best-paid player. Accommodating DiMaggio had posed no problem for McCarthy, who regarded him as the epitome of Yankee class, or for the genial Harris, who had accepted his leadership. With Stengel, however, a clash of personalities ensued: Stengel resented DiMaggio's charisma, and DiMaggio chafed at Stengel's meddling—especially at his ill-considered attempt to post him at first base. Stengel once dared to send a substitute to replace DiMaggio in center field, but DiMaggio sent the player back with a withering rebuke: "Go back to the bench and tell that crooked-legged SOB that DiMaggio will let him know when it is time to make a change in center field." Henceforth, the two leaders carefully skirted each other, and their coolness continued until DiMaggio retired at the close of the 1951 season.[5]

While he played, the injury-hobbled DiMaggio was the greatest player Stengel ever managed. Stengel learned by his absences that he could not be replaced. In 1948 DiMaggio played in great pain from a bone spur in his heel, a condition only aggravated by an operation. The still-crippled DiMaggio missed spring training and

the first months of the 1949 season. The pain lessened in June and DiMaggio, wearing a special shoe, entered the lineup in a crucial series against the Red Sox at Fenway Park. DiMaggio later recalled this performance as the most satisfying of his career, but others saw it as a baseball miracle. He singled and homered in the first game to key a 5–4 win; his two homers in the second capped a 9–7 win; and his homer in the third carried the Yanks to a sweep of the series.[6]

His incredible debut staved off the onrushing Red Sox, who threatened to tear the league apart. Even so, the Sox rebounded with an awesome offense that included a league-leading .282 team average. Heading the attack was Williams with another MVP performance, Dom DiMaggio with a 34-game hitting streak, Stephens with 159 RBIs, and pitcher Mel Parnell with 25 victories.

To offset such power, Weiss eyed big John Mize, the slugging though aging first baseman of the Giants. The Red Sox also sought him but the Yankees won the auction. Weiss used the waiver system to evade a rule banning inter-league trades during the season and acquired Mize, whose big bat keyed the Yankee stretch drive.

The Yankees needed every gun to win. On Labor Day they led the Sox by 1½ games. The Sox downed the Yankees twice at home on the 24th to deadlock the race; moving on to Yankee Stadium they rang up another win. With two games remaining, the Sox needed one to clinch the flag. On October 1 at the Stadium, in a game dedicated to DiMaggio, the Yanks overcame a 4–0 deficit to win 5–4 on Page's pitching and Lindell's homer. Then, with the league title on the line, the Yanks carried a 5–0 lead into the ninth, but Boston scored three and had the tying run at the plate. Raschi forced Birdie Tebbets to foul out and the Yankees won the flag by the narrowest of margins. It was a second straight single game loss for McCarthy's Red Sox.

Luck rode with the Yankees that year. The rescheduling of earlier rained-out games can be credited with the staging of the final showdown at home. Also, reliefer Page was blessed; of his 60 appearances, the Yankees won 47. Finally, DiMaggio's inspired half season produced a .346 average, 14 homers, and 67 RBIs.

Opposite: Pitchers Vic Raschi (*upper left*) and Ed Lopat (*lower right*) guided the Yankees to five straight world titles in the years 1949 to 1953. Later acquisitions, slugger Roger Maris (*upper right*) and catcher Elston Howard (*lower left*) helped to extend the Yankee tyranny.

Following such a struggle, the World Series had to be anti-climactic, even with the Dodgers again opposing. After the two teams swapped shut-outs, the Yankees reeled off three straight wins to land the title. External events of the following year brutally burst baseball's idyllic postwar bubble. The Korean War began in June, 1950, and American troops entered the fray on behalf of South Korea. The war affected all institutions: the big fear for baseball was the loss of players to the draft. Revived in 1948, the military draft lasted until 1973, affecting the pennant races and the careers of a generation of players.

Stengel fretted over his 1950 lineup. Outfielders Keller and Lindell were gone, and the arthritic Henrich was spending his last season as a part-time first baseman. DiMaggio's heel bothered him so much that he offered to quit rather than collect his $100,000 salary under false pretenses. Topping assured the star that he was needed, so DiMaggio joined Woodling, Bauer, Cliff Mapes, and the promising rookie Jackie Jensen in the outfield.

Stengel improvised at first base by platooning Henrich, Collins, Mize, and veteran Johnny Hopp. Johnson and Brown were adequate at third, but medical school limited Brown's service to 95 games. Rizzuto's arm ached at short, but he batted 617 times and hit .324, his best ever. Coleman at second was pressed hard by rookie Billy Martin.

The pitching was also shaky. Raschi again won 21, but the staff was buffeted so that Lopat's 3.47 ERA led. Page had an off year, winning 3 and saving 13; but with Berra in charge, the catching was among the league's best.

Thus weakened, the Yankees joined another hot race. Three rivals contended all season, and at the finish only six games separated four contenders. Boston mounted a fierce challenge on the strength of an incredible .302 team batting average—by far the best of the era. Their pitching, on the other hand, yielded nearly five runs a game, accounting for a slow start. Frustrated by his team's 32–30 record, McCarthy quit, but under Steve O'Neil the team stormed into contention.

Cleveland's assault was powered by 169 homers and superb pitching, but the surprise team was the Tigers. Managed by ex-Yank Red Rolfe, the lineup included a corps of crafty pitchers and three Yankee castoffs; the team batting average of .282 matched the Yankees's.

Opposite: Fiery second baseman Billy Martin (*upper left*), switch-hitting slugger Mickey Mantle (*upper right*), and 236-game winner lefty Whitey Ford (*lower left*) made a legendary winning manager of Casey Stengel (*lower right*).

Other changes marked this midcentury season: 88-year-old Connie Mack neared retirement while the lowly Browns, who beat out Mack's lowly A's for seventh place, made headlines by hiring a psychologist to inspire the players. However, when the campaign ended, the psychologist was gone and the Yankees with 98 wins were back on top, victors by three games over the Tigers.

Still, it was a tight squeeze with a dramatic finish. DiMaggio again performed superbly in the stretch; playing against medical advice, he overcame a slump to bat .301 with 32 homers and 122 RBIs. Rizzuto, Berra, and Bauer also topped .300, but big Mize's clutch hitting was indispensable. Irate over a low salary offer from Weiss, Mize nearly quit; but placated, he turned tartar and homered in five consecutive games during the last part of the season. Inserted mainly in clutch situations, his 277 at bats produced 25 homers and 72 RBIs. Yet another hero was a slim, blond, left-handed rookie pitcher who joined the staff in July. A sensation in the minors, brash "Whitey" Ford offered to pitch for nothing if given his chance. When he got it, he won nine of ten decisions.

In the World Series the Yanks met the youthful Phillies, who had narrowly edged the Dodgers for the National League pennant. A Yankee sweep resulted, but the games were close—the Phils sorely missed drafted pitcher Curt Simmons.

That winter the Yanks also felt the blast of the draft; Ford, Coleman, and Brown were called to serve. To plug the gaps, Stengel conducted an "instructual [sic] school" for twenty promising rookies until Commissioner Chandler ruled it an illegal ploy. Nevertheless, Stengel had seen enough to settle on Mickey Mantle, Gil McDougald, and Tom Morgan. Morgan was a promising pitcher and McDougald came as a versatile infielder with an oddly effective batting stance.

Mantle was the prize. The sturdy 19-year-old from Commerce, Oklahoma, was touted as the next DiMaggio. Taught to switch hit by his father, the young infielder was both powerful and fast, though he suffered a potentially deadly bone disease of the leg, the result of an ill-treated football injury. The disease, now under control, kept him out of the draft, so Stengel pursued his plan to turn him into an outfielder. That spring Henrich and DiMaggio coached the sensitive youngster, who could be set to weeping and bat-smashing by only brief frustrations. Early in the season he was sent down for seasoning, but was back for the stretch drive.

A new DiMaggio was sorely needed. The ailing original now was determined to quit at 37. Unable to pull the ball, his prowess and pride faltered. Although, despite frequent benching and a sub .300 average, he drove in 71 runs. Topping begged him to sign one more $100,000 pact for 1952, but the proud player refused: "I'm finished. I can't play any more. I'm never going to put that goddamn uniform on again."[7]

Pitchers Byrne and Page left, creating a gap in the bullpen which Stengel met partly by using Reynolds, who added seven saves to his 17 wins. Otherwise, the great pitching triumvirate was intact; Raschi won 21 for a third time, and Lopat matched him and added a 2.91 ERA. In addition, rookie Morgan won nine and catcher Berra netted his first MVP award.

The start of the 1951 race was tight, as the Red Sox, White Sox, and Indians challenged. Late in July the soon-to-depart Brown sparked the team to 17 wins in 20 games, sending the Yanks to first. After that only the Indians gave hot pursuit. Managed by ex-catcher Al Lopez, the Indians boasted a trio of 20-game winning pitchers in Feller, Mike Garcia, and Early Wynn. They pressed so hard by September that Weiss again turned to the National League for help. For $50,000 and pitching prospect Lou Burdette, the straitened Boston Braves sent Johnny Sain to the Yankees. It was a case of mortgaging the future for the present; Burdette went on to win over 200 games and haunt the Yanks in future World Series play. For now, however, Sain pitched effectively and proved valuable as a coach.

On September 28 the Titanic Yankee-Indian struggle was decided indirectly in a memorable double-header between the Yanks and Red Sox. Reynolds pitched the opener, gaining his second no-hitter of the season; DiMaggio clinched a sweep in the nightcap with his last seasonal homer. Meanwhile, the Indians lost to the Tigers and then collapsed, losing the race by five games.

By then attention had riveted onto the National League race, as the incredible Giants battled from far behind to tie the Dodgers. In the final game of the playoffs, Bobby Thomson struck the homer that sent the Giants to the World Series. Momentum seemed to ride with the Giants, who won the Series opener and two of the first three games. Reynolds, pitching stoutly and forcing Willie Mays to hit into three double plays, tied the Series with a 6–2 victory that saw DiMaggio hit his last homer. Lopat followed with an easy 13–1 win, which cost dearly when he injured his arm; and the Yankees closed out the Series the next day with a third straight win, reliefer Bob Kuzava dramatically snuffing out a Giant rally. With Giants on every base, Kuzava threw three pitches, each resulting in a long fly caught by a Yankee outfielder. Two runs scored, but these weren't enough, as the Yankees towered 4–3. By winning this Series, the Yanks took another step toward a majestic record.

Indeed, the New Yorkers now threatened to erase the team's old record of four consecutive world titles. The 1951 win notched three in a row, but any more must come without DiMaggio. To fill that gap, Weiss traded Jensen to the Senators for veteran outfielder Irv Noren and called up rookie Bob Cerv. Both were needed, as Mantle was slow to shake off an injury sustained in the Series. Injuries that year to Martin and Berra also told. By June, however, the wounded were back, the pugnacious Martin sparking the team by brawling with rival hotheads like Jim Piersall of the Red Sox and Clint Courtney of the Browns. They took first place on June 14, but Lopez's Indians hung so close that Weiss again sought help, obtaining the fading pitcher Ewell Blackwell from the Reds. In September the Yanks and Indians met before 73,000 Cleveland fans who disappointedly watched the Yankees score a decisive victory. Thereafter both rivals posted identical 19–5 records, with the Yankees winning by two games.

Now they faced a grimly determined Dodger team in the Series. It was the fourth "subway" series between these rivals and the Dodgers were winless. What followed was a classic struggle that lasted seven games, the two rivals exchanging wins until the end. Opening at Brooklyn, the Dodgers won, but the Yanks rebounded on Raschi's three-hitter. The Dodgers took the third at the Stadium; then Reynolds evened matters with a four-hitter. The Dodgers earned a 3–2 extra-inning victory and returned home on an upbeat note.

Down 3 games to 2 and playing in Brooklyn, the Yankee "miracle in the making" seemed dead. Still, Raschi won a tight 3–2 game on a Mantle homer, and in the decisive seventh game Stengel used his three pitching aces to stay the Dodgers. Kuzava, the 1951 hero, again came to the mound with the bases loaded and one out to preserve a precarious Yankee lead. This time Kuzava squelched the threat by getting Duke Snider and Jackie Robinson on infield flies, but it took a diving catch by Martin to keep Robinson's ball from falling safely. Finally, Kuzava blanked the Dodgers, allowing his team to tie the old record of four consecutive world titles.

Now came the acid test of the 1953 campaign. To meet it, Stengel stood pat with his veterans, confident that Ford's return would provide the extra boost, but all the previous races had been agonizingly close and this clincher promised to be the same. The Yankees broke fast, winning 11 of their first 14 to take an early lead. In June the team won 18 straight, the league's longest skein since the war. After that they drove Stengel wild by losing nine straight, but the chastened team recovered. Entering September 8½ games up on the second-place Indians, they held this advantage to the end.

Throughout the season, the team's relentless efficiency inflamed jealous rivals. A memorable brawl occurred in St. Louis when the Brown's catcher Courtney was jostled by a hard-sliding Yankee. Courtney later spiked Rizzuto and sparked a brawl, prompting frustrated Browns fans to bombard the Yanks with garbage.

Despite all the anti-Yankee hostility, when it came to play they were unstoppable. Facing the Dodgers in the Series, the Yankees took charge with two quick victories at home. The Dodgers stormed back at Ebbets Field to tie, but the Yanks took the fifth game and then ended the Series at home with a 4–3 victory, powered by hits from Bauer and Martin. Tough Billy Martin's 12 hits in 24 at bats set a Series record, and, finally, the victory nailed down Stengel's miracle—an unmatched record of five straight world titles.[8]

The American League's face changed in 1954: The Browns became the Orioles and owner Veeck was out of baseball. Some saw Veeck's ouster as a baseball version of the witch hunts that Senator Joe McCarthy was launching at the time. Whatever the circumstances, Veeck was indeed purged, and before the year had ended, Philadelphia fans watched with mixed emotions as their franchise moved to Kansas City.

Although such moves seemed un-American to some fans, the reassuring presence of Yankee enforcers was still there. Unfortunately, there were chinks in that team's armor. For demanding more money, pitcher Raschi went to the Cardinals in return for veteran outfielder Enos Slaughter. Others added to this gap: Mize and Brown retired, Martin's draft number was up, and Mantle was ailing again. To plug these spaces, Weiss reacquired Byrne, purchased pitcher Jim Konstanty from the Phils, and gained a pitcher and infielder from the A's. The A's deal was the first of several eyebrow-raising trades between these clubs; later dealings incited conflict of interest charges. The Yankee farm system also now supplied promising rookies in pitcher Bob Grim and infielders Andy Carey and Bill Skowron.

Yankee right-hander Don Larsen delivers the last pitch (a strike) to register the first no-hitter pitched in a World Series. It happened in the fifth game of the 1956 World Series against the Dodgers.

Thus fortified, the Yanks broke fast and rolled to 103 wins, Stengel's best record so far. They triumphed because of good pitching, Grim winning 20 and Sain posting a league-leading 22 saves. Moreover, four Yanks batted above .300 and Berra won the MVP award.

Incredibly, such production yielded only a second-place finish, eight games behind the awesome Indians. Since assuming the reins of the Indians in 1951, manager Lopez had never bettered second place, but this year's team was invincible. Lemon and Wynn each won 23 games, while Garcia won 19 and held the league's best ERA. Almost as successful were second liners Art Houtteman, who won 15, and Feller, who took 13. Reliefer Ray Narleski saved 13 contests.

Backing the pitchers was an offense headed by batting champ Bob Avila and homerics Vic Wertz, Al Rosen, and Larry Doby, who helped power the team to a league-leading 156 homers. They led in September by 6½ games when the challenging Yanks came to town. Before 86,000 fans, Lemon and Wynn each downed the Yanks, effectively ending the race as the Indians went on to win a record 111 games.

It seemed impossible for this team to lose the World Series, but the Giants beat the Indians in four straight games. In the opener,

Giant outfielder Willie Mays spiked a Cleveland rally by catching Wertz's 460' drive; then, pinch-hitter Jim Rhodes homered for the Giant win in the tenth. Rhodes, however, didn't stop there; his pinch homer won the second game and his pinch single gained the third. This unbelievable humiliation signalled the coming dominance of the National League.

While rebuilding the Yankees in 1955 Weiss summoned quiet Elston Howard to be the first black Yankee. He hired rookie pitchers John Kucks and Tom Sturdivant to replace Reynolds and Lopat. Moreover, in this major overhaul, Weiss engaged in a 17-player deal with the Orioles that brought pitchers Bob Turley and Don Larsen to New York.

This rebuilt team carried the Yankees to four consecutive pennants in the years 1955–1958. The team broke fast in 1955 and engaged the Indians, White Sox, and Red Sox in a four-way struggle. Martin returned from military service in September to shore up the infield, while Larsen, recovering from arm trouble, won six of his seven games. The re-armed Yankees caught the Indians in mid-September and on the wings of an eight-game winning streak, won the pennant by three games. Leading the team were Berra with another MVP performance; Ford, the league pitching leader; and Mantle, whose 37 homers established him as a superstar.

Any hopes for another skein of Series victories were dashed by the Dodgers, who turned on their tormentors. The Yanks won the first two games at home, but then lost all three played at Ebbets Field. Returning home, Ford kept the Yankees in contention, but the Dodgers won the finale 2–0, as Johnny Podres outdueled Byrne in a game highlighted by a rally-busting outfield catch by Dodger outfielder Sandy Amoros.

The Yankees rebounded in 1956 with vengeance. With McDougald playing brilliantly at short, Weiss coldly released Rizzuto in an ill-considered announcement before a capacity Old Timers Day crowd at the Stadium. Few fans complained; their fickle eyes were on Mantle, the superstar who stirred the nation by winning a Triple Crown on a .353 average, 52 homers, and 130 RBIs. With Ford leading all pitchers in ERA and the offense pounding a record 190 homers, the Yanks outlegged Lopez's Indians by nine games.

Then came the last and most dramatic of the famous subway Series duels between the Yanks and Dodgers. Opening at Ebbets Field, the Yanks lost the first two games, but rallied at home to square the Series. The fifth game was played at the Stadium on a beautiful fall day before a crowd of 64,000. The fans saw a perfect game pitched by Larsen, whose no-windup delivery and matchless control baffled Dodger batters. It made a legend of Larsen, who never again in nine seasons approached stardom. To many fans that masterpiece ended the Series, but the Dodgers squared matters the next day, only to fall 9–0 in the finale on Kucks's three-hitter.

The Yankee domination continued, to the detriment of the American League. So attractive were the pin-striped tyrants that their games accounted for forty percent of American attendance. This enraged rivals, but no more so than Weiss's suspicious dealings with the Kansas City A's, which brought stars like third baseman Clete Boyer, pitchers Bobby Shantz and Ryne Duren, and others to New York in exchange for second stringers, 16 of whom played with the 1958 A's.

Yankee jealousy flared anew in 1957 over a tragic accident that ended the career of the brilliant Indian pitcher, lefty Herb Score. Score was pitching against the Yanks at Cleveland when McDougald smashed a liner that struck him in the right eye. The nearly blinded Score was never again effective, nor was the deeply regretful McDougald.[9]

The spirited Yankees sometimes hurt themselves, as when Mantle and Martin injured each other in childish horseplay. Weiss blamed Martin, and when Martin was later involved in a night club brawl, Weiss dealt him to the A's.

Still, none of this affected the 1957 race, which the Yankees won easily, taking an early 15-game lead. Thereafter, though playing only .500 ball, they were still good enough to win by eight over the White Sox—a team now managed by Lopez. The cocky 1957 Yankees were ripe for a fall and they received their come-uppance at World Series time. Matched against the Milwaukee Braves, the first of the carpetbagging clubs, the Yanks seemed to be playing their familiar scenario when they took the opener before 70,000 home fans. Then one of Weiss's castoffs, pitcher Lou Burdette, intervened: Burdette turned back the Yankees 4–2 in the second game and spun 1–0 and 5–0 shut-outs in his next two outings. The Braves took the Series 4 games to 3; the victors taunted their victims and fired the Yankees with a vengeful resolve.

Amidst a mounting chorus of Yankee hatred, the 1958 Yankees responded with even greater effort. They caught the wrath of bereft Dodger and Giant fans who resented the Yankee attempt to claim the entire New York territory. Elsewhere, the team was lustily booed on the road. Such outbursts shook the 68-year-old Stengel.

Despite such tensions, the team seized an early lead and never looked back. They held a lead of 17 games by August and, despite a late season slump, coasted to a 10-game victory over Lopez's White Sox.

Matched against the Braves in the Series, the Yankees saw an opportunity to avenge their 1957 drubbing. This hope faded, however, when the Braves took the first two games at Milwaukee. At home the Yanks gained the third, but then Warren Spahn tossed a two-hit shut-out to put the Braves within one win of the title. Again the Braves's taunts were infuriating. In the next match Turley fired a shut-out to keep hopes alive, and in the sixth game, played at Milwaukee, Turley's relief work saved a ten-inning game for the Yankees. Now came the decisive contest; this time the Yankees fell upon Burdette, driving him to cover with a four-run rally in the eighth to complete a magnificent comeback. It was now the Yankees's turn to taunt, and Stengel managed this withering understatement: "I guess we could play in the National League."

Sadly, that was Stengel's last hurrah. His team collapsed in 1959 under slumps, injuries, and assaults from the downtrodden. Late in May, the Yankees occupied the cellar for the first time in a generation. Fans blamed Mantle for this turnabout and booed him unmercifully. In a desperate move to rally his forces, Stengel shifted to a conservative "hit, bunt, and run" style. Weiss worked yet another trade with Kansas City, landing pitcher Ralph Terry, an ex-Yankee, and outfielder Hector Lopez. Sparked by Lopez, the Yankees rallied, but three losses to the White Sox late in June stifled hopes.

The year belonged to the White Sox, a team inspired by the return of maverick owner Bill Veeck. Gaining control of the club from the Comiskey estate, Veeck was in his third stint as an owner. Under his command Comiskey Park took on a new look and hopeful fans were treated to ingenious sideshows and giveaways. Meanwhile, Al Lopez's skilled hand kept a veteran team in contention. Fine relief pitching from Gerry Staley and Turk Lown propped a shaky staff that was backed by catcher Sherman Lollar, a Yankee reject, who led the team in homers and RBIs. Offensively, the team relied on the speed of shortstop Luis Aparicio and on timely hitting from second baseman Nelson Fox. Thus enforced, Lopez wrested a second pennant from the Yanks; rumor had it that Topping eyed him as Stengel's replacement.

Still, there was no Series victory in the cards for Lopez. His 1954 dream team had lost to the Giants; now the transplanted Dodgers did him in. The Dodgers had invaded Los Angeles the previous year and finished a dismal seventh, but they rebounded in 1959 to tie Milwaukee and snatch the pennant with two consecutive playoff victories. They divided the first two World Series games played in Chicago, then delighted 277,000 Los Angeles fans by winning two of the three games played at the laughably asymmetrical Coliseum. Returning to Chicago, the Dodgers ended the Series with a 9–3 victory.

The Dodger victory ushered in the expansion era. Baseball leaders had long ignored population shifts to newer urban centers whose citizens lusted for big league ball. By 1960 the handwriting was on the wall—either expand the majors or face competition from the threatening Continental League. Consequently, the majors finessed the Continentals by absorbing some of their clubs; both major leagues adopted the expanded ten-league format.

Oddly, the American League's 1960 season, the last to follow the eight-club format, saw the old guardsmen giving way to youth. That year Ted Williams played his last game. The 42-year-old still batted .316 with 72 RBIs and 29 homers, including a farewell blast in his last at bat in Boston. Williams's passing left a lonesome gap, as did the parting of Stengel and Weiss. Both were forcibly retired after the Yankees lost the hard-fought 1960 World Series to the Pirates.

Ironically, these oldsters endeavored to pump young blood into the 1960 Yankees. In the last major trade with his Kansas City vassals, Weiss dealt Bauer and Larsen and others for Joe De Maestri and Roger Maris. The key acquisition was the slumping Maris, whose rebirth as a power hitter sparked the last phase of the Yankee tyranny.

Sacking Stengel certainly made more sense than dumping Weiss. Stengel reportedly lost control of the team in 1960; when he was hospitalized in May, the Yanks rallied under Coach Ralph Houk and launched an eight-game winning streak. This zenith was needed to stave off the young Orioles. In mid-September the two teams tied, but the Yankees took charge, beating the Orioles four times and finishing with a flourish. The victory opened another five-year skein of league titles.

This win was blighted by Series losses, beginning with a Pirate victory in 1960. In a memorable struggle marked by a strange cadence, the Pirates opened with a victory on Bill Mazeroski's homer.

Then, after six grueling games, Mazeroski nailed down the title with a ninth-inning homer. Between those losses the Yanks packed victories with herculanean scores of 16–3, 10–0, and 12–0. Only a freak of ill luck, in the form of a bad bounce, opened the doors to a Pirate rally, setting the stage for Mazeroski's heroic belt.

As Stengel's successor, Houk led the Yanks into the expansion era. The 42-year-old coach was a rarely used Yankee catcher, but years of coaching and minor league managing stamped him as a leader. That "the Major" was tough, umpires, rivals, and his own players well knew.

A special expansion draft was held to stock the newly enrolled Los Angeles and Washington teams for the 1961 10-team race. Under its rules, newcomers drafted players from the rosters of the eight teams. Although stars were protected, every team lost reserve strength. Houk, less the platooner than Stengel, liked a set lineup—as did his men, who unleashed a devastating offensive.

Leading the attack, Maris and Mantle together accounted for 115 homers and 270 RBIs. As others weighed in, the Yankees broke the old homer record in August and went on to set an all-time mark of 240. That year the nation's eyes fixed on Maris and Mantle, "the M&M boys." Their target was Ruth's seasonal homer record of 60, and going into September each had a chance. Then injuries slowed Mantle, leaving Maris alone in the full glare of national publicity. Harried daily by booing fans and prying reporters, Maris nearly buckled under strain. At the end of 154 games he had failed to notch 60, but the expanded 162-game schedule allowed him to finish with 61. It was a new season's record, but Commissioner Frick ordered that an asterisk be placed after Maris's attainment, indicating that Ruth's old 154-game mark still stood. Denied his full measure of glory and soured by the mean-spirited Yankee fans, Maris's future effectiveness was impaired.

Nevertheless, 1961 was a glorious year for the Yankees. Dogged by Detroit until September, they swept a series from the Tigers and closed out the season on a long winning streak that produced a total of 109 wins, the postwar high for a Yankee team. Meeting the Reds in the Series, they won easily, four games to one. Ford's pitching highlighted this dull Series. A 25-game winner during the season, he extended a string of scoreless World Series innings to a record 32, erasing another of the great Ruth's records. As Ford quipped, "It was a tough year for the Babe."[10]

2

The Postwar Campaigns: The National League

A saving myth of baseball celebrates the competitive balance among teams. Holding that any team at a given time has an equal chance to win a championship, the myth treats all monopolistic dynasties as sinful aberrations. As a device for deluding fans, the myth is useful, but any believer lives in a fool's paradise. In fact, baseball annals record the cold truth that monopolistic dynasties have won most of the pennants. From Harry Wright's Red Stockings of the early 1870s to the Yankee-Dodger mini-dynasties of a century later, each decade has passed with some powerful team lording over the others. Furthermore, when a tyrant fell, most often it was a successor dynasty that wrenched control. In truth, pennant monopoly is the norm in major league baseball; those brief periods when a different champion is crowned each year are exceptional.

The Dodger Dynasty

The Allied victory in World War II offered a brief hope for world peace and freedom; similarly, the National League's first postwar season revived the myth of competitive balance. While the American League enjoyed three sunny seasons before succumbing to the Yanks, the Nationals also sustained a short respite prior to submitting to the Dodgers. Indeed, the two dynasties were strikingly similar. Both originated with a pennant victory in 1947 and endured into the 1960s—the Yankees falling in 1964, the Dodgers toppling two years later.

If measured by number of pennants won, the Yankees were by far the more successful team, capturing fifteen league pennants and ten world titles. On the other hand, the Dodger empire was more durable, innovative, and profitable. The team was much stronger than their amassed total of ten league titles and four world championships indicates. During their glory years, five seasons passed when they lost league pennants by the narrowest of margins, including three given away in postseason playoffs. Hence, unlike their lordly rivals, the Dodgers knew the anguish of unexpected defeat; they learned to bleed, and then to rise and fight again. Because of their indomitable spirit, theirs was considered the more human dynasty.

The 1946 Dodger training camp was packed with returning service men, promising strength for upcoming duels with the St. Louis Cardinals. The Cardinals had known the best of these matches, winning consecutive pennants from 1942 to 1944. With a mixture of returning veterans and promising youngsters, the Cards were touted to win in 1946. With hurlers like Max Lanier, Howie Pollet, Harry Brecheen, and Murray Dickson, Cardinal manager Eddie Dyer had the makings of the finest staff in baseball. Proven hitters like Enos Slaughter, Harry Walker, Dick Sisler, and Terry Moore contended for positions in the outfield. The infield of Red Schoendienst at second, Marty Marion at short, and Whitey Kurowski at third was battle-tested—and at first base stood the incomparable Stan Musial. This year Musial won the batting title with a .365 average, the second of seven titles captured before his 1963 retirement at age 43. Departing with a lifetime average of .331, Musial joined DiMaggio and Williams in the Hall of Fame; collectively, they composed the great triptych of the postwar era.

Such were the Cardinals of 1946; yet behind a glittering facade lurked a dying organization. Under the miserly ownership of Sam Breadon, salaries were limited to $14,000. The players rightly complained; Lanier and Fred Martin jumped the club for the outlawed Mexican League. Musial reluctantly refused a five-year, $195,000 offer to join them. Such rumblings lowered morale, but more crippling was the loss of general manager Branch Rickey to the Dodgers. The old Cardinal dynasty had been Rickey's handiwork; while he labored in St. Louis, this master recruiter and rookie developer kept the flow of talent coming. Now serving the Dodgers, his inspired philosophy of seeking quality in quantity developed the strongest National League power since McGraw's Giants.[1]

Indeed, his Dodgers just missed crashing through in 1946. By combining the talents of prewar stars like Peter Reiser, "Pee Wee" Reese, Billy Herman, Dixie Walker, and Kirby Higbe with those of newcomers Carl Furillo, Bruce Edwards, and Hal Gregg, the Dodgers tied the Cards and forced the first postseason playoff in league history. It was decided that the team winning two of three games would take the league pennant; the Dodgers won a coin toss to earn the home field advantage in two of the games. Manager Durocher chose to play the opener in St. Louis for the advantage of hosting the last two games; unfortunately, his gamble backfired.

When play began at Sportsman's Park, both teams were tired and hurting. For his starting pitcher, Durocher had chosen young Ralph Branca, a talented right-hander who was destined for a place in baseball infamy as the loser of crucial games. Branca lost this one; yielding three runs in the early innings, his own team could only pull in two. Then Durocher's strategy failed completely at Ebbets Field, as the Cardinals crushed the Dodgers 8–3 to gain the pennant.

Cardinal pitcher Brecheen won three games against the Red Sox in the World Series, including the decisive seventh when he came in to relieve Dickson. Slaughter and Kurowski led the game attack, Slaughter scoring the winning run in the 4–3 victory on Walker's two-out double in the eighth. With bold élan, Slaughter raced from first base to home, as a flabbergasted Boston infielder delayed a throw to the plate. It would be 18 seasons before a Cardinal team again scaled such heights.

As the Cardinals sank, Rickey's genius sent the Dodgers soaring. Rickey defied baseball's unwritten racist policy in 1946 by signing black star Jackie Robinson to a Dodger contract. After Robinson's successful debut at Montreal, Rickey promoted him to the big team in 1947. Fearing a stormy reception, Rickey labored to ease Robinson's ordeal, but it still took spartan courage for Robinson to survive. Even some Dodgers demanded his ouster, but the protest was defused when two of the harder cases, Walker and Higbe, were eventually traded. Nevertheless, Robinson faced teams like the Phillies and Cards, whose bench jockeys sang raucous songs, screamed epithets like "shine" and "black bastard," and sometimes deliberately injured him. Commissioner Chandler and, belatedly, league president Frick defended Robinson. However, when Chandler suspended Durocher shortly before the start of the 1947 season, Robinson had to adapt to a new manager, the sympathetic Burt Shotton, along with learning to play first base.[2]

Following a slow start in 1947, Robinson came on to bat .297 and pilot the league in stolen bases. Outfielders Walker and Reiser both topped .300 and stout pitching was received from Branca, Joe Hatten, and Vic Lombardi. The Dodgers took the pennant by five games over the Cardinals, and although they fell to the Yankees in the World Series, they did so only after a hard-fought, seven-game struggle. The loss stung, but Robinson's success enabled Rickey to fortify the team with more black players.

In 1948 Rickey brought in Roy Campanella, the black catcher who would star in that role for years. Campanella was part of an infusion of new blood that met Rickey's demanding expectations. Gone now were malcontents like Walker and Hugh Casey, surplus pitchers like Lombardi and Gregg, spare infielders like Spider Jorgensen and Ed Stanky, and the ill-starred Pete Reiser.

Some were dealt to Pittsburgh for pitcher "Preacher" Roe and infielder Billy Cox. Although Roe was so lightly regarded that he had to beat out Dwain Sloat for a place on the team, he soon became the ace of the staff. At third base, Cox anchored an infield that included the great Reese at short, Robinson back at second, and rookie Gil Hodges at first. Rookie center fielder Ed "Duke" Snider joined a revamped outfield, with Furillo as the only holdover.

Pitching remained, however, a chronic problem. Although Rickey worked hard at pitcher development, he never developed a great mound corps. Perhaps, as one critic suggested, the thorn was his stubborn insistence that each pitcher master an elbow-straining overhand curve. At a time when pitchers relied more on the slider, such conservatism was faulted.[3]

Durocher was back at the helm and Dodger hopes that year were bright. Then, the team foundered in the early going and Durocher quit, shocking Dodger fans by joining the hated Giants. Rickey recalled Shotton, who rallied the team and drove them to a third place, 7½ games behind the winning Braves.

The Boston Braves were the Cinderellas of 1948. Overshadowed by the Red Sox, the Braves were owned by contractor Lou Perini, who sought to revive the profitless, declining franchise. Under man-

ager Bill Southworth, a former Cardinal skipper, the Braves now mounted a formidable offense. Led by outfielder Tommy Holmes's .325 average, four Braves topped the .300 mark and the team posted a league-leading .275 team average. This outstanding batting was sorely needed, since the pitching staff had only three dependable starters in Johnny Sain, lefty Warren Spahn, and Vern Bickford. So unreliable was the pitching that the slogan "Spahn and Sain and two days of rain" became a part of baseball folklore. Nevertheless, the poor-pitching Braves took the flag by 6½ games over the Cards. That was the end of the line. Although Sain delighted home fans with a 1–0 shut-out in the Series opener, the Indians speedily dispatched the Braves.

Landing the 1948 pennant was a Pyrrhic victory for the Braves; the dying embers of local interest were only briefly kindled. When the team failed to repeat their performance, disillusioned fans turned away, thus hastening the day when the Braves became baseball's first breakaway franchise in half a century.

As Boston foundered, Brooklyn saw the dawning of an empire. From 1949 through 1959 a Dodger dynasty held sway, winning six league titles, narrowly missing three more, and routinely outdrawing all rivals at home and on the road. This dominance was Rickey's glory, but 1949 was his last year as Dodger president. A victim of palace politics, he was forced to sell his interest to Walter O'Malley in 1950. From Brooklyn he moved to Pittsburgh to spend his waning strength trying to enliven a sick franchise.

Rickey's Brooklyn years had been his finest. His struggle against racism succeeded so well that in 1949 he returned Dodger spring training operations to Florida where the team occupied a model training facility at Vero Beach. Yet the ultimate tribute to Rickey's battle against racism was reflected in his protégés. In 1949 Robinson led the Dodgers to victory and won the MVP award for leading the league in batting and stolen bases. Now he was joined by other black stars. Rickey brought in Don Newcombe in May to shore up the pitching. This hard-throwing right-hander led the staff with 17 victories. Backing Newcombe was Campanella, who batted .287 with 22 homers and 82 RBIs.

Opposite: Slugger Duke Snider (*bottom left*) and pitcher Don Newcombe (*top right*) helped the Dodgers rule the National League during the 1950s; but by the decade's end the Pirates, led by outfielder Roberto Clemente (*top left*) and second baseman Bill Mazeroski (*bottom right*), pressed hard.

Still, winning the 1949 pennant was a hard feat. Like the American League race, this battle came down to the wire. Under constant pressure from Dyer's Cardinals, manager Shotton raged over losses and berated injured players for lack of guts. In the end, the Dodger balance made the difference; while they stood second to the Cards in pitching and batting, they led the league in homers, stolen bases, and fielding. Not until the last day was the contest settled, and then the Dodgers defeated the Phillies to clinch a narrow victory.

At World Series time, the Dodgers again faced the Yanks. Newcombe pitched the opener and later judged it his best game, though he lost 1–0. Then Roe, leading the league in ERA, blanked the Yankees 1–0. The Dodgers lost the next three, as Snider—following a sensational season as a regular—established a Series record by striking out eight times.[4]

O'Malley was determined to expunge the memory of Rickey, so when the Dodgers suffered agonizingly narrow losses in 1950 and 1951, he blamed Shotton, Rickey's appointee. Consequently, Shotton's insecurity affected morale and the team faltered, enabling the Giants, Braves, and Phillies to move into contention. Finally, the hungry young Phillies seized the lead in July and held on desperately.

Many fans felt that the spectacle of the Phillies perched atop league standings was as believable as a Socialist presidential victory. After all, the Phillies had not won a flag in 35 years and their record for futility was unmatched. However, owner Robert Carpenter took over in 1946 and spent nearly $2 million in bonuses for promising youngsters, like pitchers Robin Roberts and Curt Simmons, catcher Stan Lopata, and outfielder Richie Ashburn. These rookies developed rapidly and carefully, and under the handling of manager Eddie Sawyer, an ex-college professor with no major league playing experience, the team became a contender. The "Fighting Phillies" of 1949 finished strong and might have won but for key first baseman Eddie Waitkus's unfortunate off-the-field accident.

Waitkus recovered and in 1950 steadied the young infield of Mike Goliat at second, Granny Hamner at short, and Willie Jones at third. Behind these players ranged a solid outfield of Ashburn, Dick Sisler, and Del Ennis. Roberts led a good pitching staff, winning 20; Simmons gained 17 before being called for military duty; and reliefer Jim Konstanty took 16 and appeared in 62 games, often as a savior. The hard-hitting Andy Seminick caught this staff and was backed by Lopata.

During the postwar era, no National League hurler topped Warren Spahn (*left*) in victories, while Harold "Pee Wee" Reese (*right*) of the Dodgers was considered the league's classiest shortstop.

Dubbed the "Whiz Kids" by an adoring local press, the young Phillies led by 7½ games on September 20, with only 11 left to play. Then the Dodgers mounted a blistering counterattack, winning 13 of 16, while the Phils won only three. Thus, when the swooning Phils, ahead by only two games, came to Ebbets Field to play the last two games of the season, Dodger hopes soared. After the Phils lost the first of these, 35,000 fans jammed the little park to watch Newcombe battle Roberts.

With Simmons gone, manager Sawyer had over-pitched Roberts in a desperate bid to avert collapse. Now Roberts faced a must-win game. What followed was a classic duel between two great hurlers. The Dodgers nearly triumphed with the game tied at 1–1 in the ninth, but a clutch throw by outfielder Ashburn nailed Cal Abrams at the plate as he tried to score on a single. This was the high tide of the Dodger surge; Sisler homered in the tenth with two on base for a 4–1 Phillies victory.

The Dodger defeat handed O'Malley an excuse to sack Shotton, replacing him with Chuck Dressen. Meanwhile, the Phils had little time to savor victory. In the Series they fell to the Yankees in four straight games.

In both victory and defeat the Phillies looked like a one-shot phenomenon, unlikely to repeat. The Dodgers, on the other hand, regrouping under Dressen, had every reason to hope that their 1950 surge would carry them to the 1951 flag. So it happened, as they tore up the league most of that year. On the strength of Robinson's batting, sluggers Campanella and Hodges, and Roe's brilliant 22–3 pitching, in August the Dodgers led the second-place Giants by 13½ games. Should the cakewalk continue, an early September clinching loomed.

The Giants, however, mounted their charge. The offensive, which baseball folklore would remember as "the little miracle of Coogan's Bluff," was headed by ex-Braves Al Dark and Eddie Stanky. Dark captained the Giants, but Stanky was the team's holler guy. Fired by this pair and inspired by team mottoes "Let 'er rip" and "Just keep it going," the Giants netted 37 of their last 44 games, enough to deadlock the shocked and slumping Dodgers at the end. Indeed, the Giants almost won the flag by beating the Braves, as the Dodgers fell behind 8–5 in their game at Philadelphia. The Dodgers rallied in the eighth to tie, but in the 12th only Robinson's diving catch of a liner—an effort that stunned him temporarily—could keep the team alive. Then, the doughty Robinson homered in the 14th to win the game.[5]

Now the two rivals—whose meetings over the years so often resembled dockyard brawls—met in a climactic playoff series. Playing at Brooklyn, the Giants took the opener 3–1 with Jim Hearn beating the luckless Branca. In game two, however, Clem Labine pitched a six-hit shut-out at the Polo Grounds, and the Dodgers romped 10–0. The stage was now set for the most memorable game in recent history. Through seven innings Sal Maglie of the Giants and Newcombe of the Dodgers engaged in a tense duel. The Dodgers broke through in the eighth, scoring three runs on four singles, a walk, and a wild pitch. A weakening Newcombe retired the Dodgers with a 4–1 lead; this was the score when the Giants batted in the last of the ninth. Hitting first, Dark fouled off seven pitches before singling. Then Don Mueller singled, and after Newcombe retired Irvin, the big pitcher complained of a tired arm. Robinson snarled, "---- your arm, man! Stop being a crybaby and get this man out of here."[6] Only "the man," Whitey Lockman, doubled, bringing in Dark while Mueller slid safely into third, though injuring his ankle. Newcombe was finished, as Dressen called on his bullpen and was advised that only Branca seemed ready. The fresh pitcher faced Bobby Thomson, a .292 hitter who had hit twice already in the game. After taking a strike, Thomson told himself to "watch the damn ball," and on Branca's next delivery he drove a line-drive homer into the short left field stands to win the game.[7]

Thomson's dramatic October blow was witnessed by some fifteen million television viewers and heard by eighty million radio listeners. The radio fans heard announcer Russ Hodges break all rules of decorum, as he screamed ". . . The Giants win the pennant! The Giants win the pennant. . . . And they're going crazy. . . ."[8] Indeed, no other emotions could describe the crowd reaction; one observer compared the uproar with VE day in Paris. The noise was deafening: fans pummeled each other and one excited couple openly made love in a box seat, but few took notice. In the Dodger bullpen, Carl Erskine sadly shook his head and said: "That's the first time I ever saw a big fat wallet flying in the grandstand."[9]

That this "little miracle" went no further is mostly forgotten now amidst the legendary aura surrounding that game. Reality arose in the form of the imperial Yankees, who defeated the Giants in six games in the World Series.

For failing so dramatically in 1950 and 1951, the Dodgers were branded "choke" artists by fans, rivals, and writers. No Dodger suffered so much as young Branca, who joined Fred Merkle in the annals of diamond failure. Although Merkle starred for a dozen years after his ordeal, the 25-year-old Branca was never again effective. During the winter a fall from a chair injured his pelvis. Winning only twelve games over the next four seasons, Branca's career ended in 1956.

The Dodgers bravely shouldered their shame and came back stronger than ever. Returning with the same lineup—with the exception of outfielder Andy Pafko and the addition of rookie pitchers Billy Loes, Ben Wade, and Joe Black—the 1952 Dodgers launched a face-saving drive that produced 153 homers, a .262 team average, and the league's best fielding. They slipped to second in May, then rebounded as the Cardinals and Giants pursued. To slow the Dodger momentum, the Cards resorted to racist taunts, but Robinson replied in kind and Black answered with brushback pitches. Young Black was superb that year, winning fifteen and saving as many on an ERA of 2.15. Only Roe was better; mixing an occasional spitter with his repertoire, he won eleven and lost two.

By September the Dodgers led by five over the menacing Giants. Early that month the Giants took two from the Dodgers at Ebbets Field, and then prepared for the kill as they hosted at the Polo

Grounds. The Dodgers met the challenge. Roe beat the Giants 5–1 in the first game, pretending to throw spitters, but actually (he claimed) tossing only five. In the next outing reliefer Black used his fast ball to intimidate the Giants, while his mates romped to a 10–2 win. Thus the Giant threat ended, as the Dodgers clinched the flag on September 23.

Still, the Yankee nemesis could not be exorcised. The Dodgers took three of the first five World Series games and returned home needing a single win to clinch. The Yanks rallied to take the sixth game, and Kuzava's hitless relief stint in the finale nailed down yet another Yankee World Series victory.

The 1953 Dodgers, still wearing the choker label, destroyed all opposition by winning 105 games and another pennant. This time they added black players Jim Gilliam, an infielder, and outfielder Sandy Amoros. Gilliam developed so rapidly that Robinson was shifted to third, forcing Cox onto the bench. Now the growing number of dark Dodger faces may have resulted in a "tipping point" notion that some felt sent Amoros to the minors. The sullen Cox, while accepting black veterans like Robinson and Campanella, loudly objected to the presence of that "nigger kid" Jim Gilliam. Such protests illustrate the tortuous pace of racial integration in baseball. While they gained in numbers, blacks had to "prove" themselves: Joe Black's frustration at his inability to develop additional pitches sapped his confidence, and he became a conspicuous failure among a team of super-achievers.

That year the Dodgers mounted a bludgeoning offensive. Their .285 team average was the highest of the era. Furillo's .344 led the league, while Campanella hit .312 with 41 homers and led in RBIs at 142. Supported by the league's leading fielders and homer hitters, life was sunny for Dodger pitchers.

No rival could stand the pounding. Deprived of the military-drafted Mays, the Giants were never in contention, though the reborn Braves were. Playing now in Milwaukee before huge crowds, the Braves came alive on the pitching of Spahn and Lou Burdette, and the heavy hitting of Joe Adcock and young Ed Mathews. They still finished a distant second, 13 games off the pace.

For the fifth time the Dodgers were set against the Yankees, a team looking for an all-time record in Series competition. A Dodger victory now would have settled old scores, but the Yankees held firm. The Yanks won the first two games at the Stadium, but at home the Dodgers tied, with Erskine fanning a record 14 Yanks in

Future Hall of Fame member Jackie Robinson steals home safely in this 1952 game against the Chicago Cubs.

one game. The Yanks took the next two and landed a fifth straight world title, leaving the hapless Dodgers to wear their perennial choke tag.

The traditional remedy for such failure is to fire the manager, but Dressen was too popular to be dumped without cause. When Dressen's wife, however, asked that he be given the security of a multi-year contract, O'Malley sprung his trap. Summoning a press conference, he explained his policy of not granting extended contracts; consequently, Dressen was freed to seek his security elsewhere. Soon O'Malley announced his new pilot; an obscure Dodger farm club manager named Walter Emmons Alston would assume Dressen's duties in 1954. When told that Alston was arriving in town under an assumed name, jaded reporters wondered why the precaution was being taken. As one wag headlined the appointment: "Alston (Who's He?) To Manage Dodgers."[10]

To follow the steps of men like Durocher, Shotton, and Dressen was a tough assignment for this quiet man. That he succeeded and lasted twenty years under O'Malley defied all prophecy. Alston's first year was nearly his last. His tough disciplinary code galled veterans; they also resented his decision to sell Roe and Cox to the Orioles and invest money in bonus baby Sandy Koufax, a wild but promising left-handed pitcher. Such talent transfusions were necessary; Robinson and Campanella were fading and the Giants again were threatening.

Mays rejoined the Giants that year and resumed his brilliant career. He led the league batters in 1954 with a .345 mark that included 41 homers and 110 RBIs. With Mueller and Jim "Dusty" Rhodes weighing in, Giant homer production matched the 186 tallied by the Dodgers. Ultimately, pitching made the difference. Durocher's acquisition of Johnny Antonelli was a deal that paid off handsomely in 21 victories; with Reuben Gomez, Sal Maglie, and Hoyt Wilhelm supporting, the Giant staff posted the league's best ERA. In a close race, the Giants won 97 to finish five up on the struggling Dodgers.

While losing to Durocher was painful enough, watching the Giants destroy their American League opponents in the World Series was sheer torture for envious Dodgers. Moreover, the Giants did it with élan, beating the Indians in four straight games. The losers had recently minted an American League record by winning 111; the underdog Giants now cut them down with brilliant plays. In the opener at the Polo Grounds, the Indians threatened to break open a tie game with a late-inning rally when Mays made an astonishing catch. Then Rhodes bought the game with a homer in the tenth. The next day Antonelli outdueled Early Wynn in a close match, Rhodes driving in two on a pinch single and a homer. Down by two, the shakened Indians now lost at home, as Gomez and Wilhelm pitched and the irrepressible Rhodes delivered a two-run pinch hit. The next day 78,000 stunned Clevelanders saw the Giants erupt for seven runs to close out the Series.

Perhaps their rival's success shocked the Dodgers out of their "World Series" complex. Time was running out on this seasoned team. In 1955 it was obvious that there would be few tomorrows for veterans like Robinson, Reese, Campanella, and Furillo. The "Boys of Summer" were aging; newcomers like Don Hoak, Don Zimmer, and Sandy Amoros were pressing from behind, along with young pitchers like Koufax and Karl Spooner.

Still, it was the veterans who carried the team to an easy 1955 victory. With a 13-game lead, the Dodgers headed the league in four important categories: while they took batting and homer honors, the pitchers led in strike-outs and ERA. Rebounding from a horrendous year, Campanella batted .318 with 32 homers and snatched a third

MVP award. Furillo and Snider were equally formidable, and Newcombe led the pitching staff with a 20–5 log.

There were warning clouds. Robinson slumped badly, young Spooner's promising career ended with arm trouble, and Koufax battled wildness. These warnings were blown away by a rampaging start that saw the team win 25 of its first 29 games to take a big lead which they never surrendered. Their clinch on September 8 marked the earliest end to any race in league history. This was Alston's greatest triumph and Durocher's darkest hour; when the Giants collapsed that year, Durocher was sacked.[11]

For a sixth time the Dodgers faced their Yankee tormentors. The old doleful script appeared to unfold when the Yanks won the first two at home. The Dodgers unleashed a volley of 34 hits at Ebbets and swept the next three from the Yanks by scores of 8–3, 8–5, and 5–3. Needing one more to clinch their first Series victory, the Dodgers succumbed to Ford's masterly pitching upon their return to the Stadium.

For the decisive game Alston staked his reputation on the arm of young Johnny Podres. An inspired choice it was; Podres responded with a 2–0 shut-out, Hodges batting in both runs. Nevertheless, Alston was wise to insert Amoros as a defensive outfielder in the sixth. In that inning Amoros ended a Yankee rally with a remarkable catch of Berra's opposite field drive and turned one out into a double play. Thus, astuteness and luck combined to realize Brooklyn's 15-year dream; "This Is Next Year!" rang a joyous headline.[12]

That glory year of 1955 marked the summit of Dodger power. The aging team mounted in 1956 one last effort. In two hard-fought battles, the Dodgers prevailed: first, in a fierce struggle against the rising Braves, the Dodgers overcame a mighty pitching effort and the league-leading bat of Hank Aaron; second, the Dodgers controlled the Reds, who came on behind a barrage of 221 homers. This they did with a weak team average of .258.

Defense and pitching kept the Dodgers in contention. Newcombe turned in his best season with 27 wins, but help was still needed. Alston gambled, purchasing the 39-year-old Sal Maglie from Cleveland. Maglie's Brooklyn reputation was that of a hated Dodger killer, but now he was welcomed as a savior. The pitcher responded with 13 victories, including two crucial September triumphs over the Braves. Backed by Maglie and Newcombe, the Dodgers amassed 93 wins, enough to edge the Braves by a game and the Reds by two.

This paper-thin victory margin was provided by the Braves, who lost two of their last three games to the Cardinals.

That autumn the last battle was fought between the Brooklyn Dodgers and the New York Yankees. Such meetings were by now so frequent that Gotham fans regarded them as a birthright. That they would soon end, that for a mess of pottage the Dodgers would quit Brooklyn, still sounded like the message of scaremongers.

Forebodings of drastic change to come hung over the 1956 World Series, lending a strange feeling of finality to the proceedings. Brooklyn excitement mounted, as the Dodgers took the first two games. At the Stadium the Yanks quickly tied the match. The fifth game matched Maglie against Larsen, the latter having been brutally pounded in a game at Ebbets. What followed was an Olympian event: Larsen pitched a perfect game, an attainment worthy of some divine intervention. The Dodgers won the next game to tie the match, but the Yankees romped 9–0 to officially end the Series.

Skeptics looking for more tangible signs of a coming baseball millennium found one in the 1957 collapse of the Dodger empire. The Milwaukee Braves, the first franchise transplant, started the revolution. As harbingers of the coming expansion era, the Braves's move to Milwaukee excited the envy of ball club owners like O'Malley, whose move westward was a shrewd and timely relocation. Clearly, the team was declining; Robinson was gone, and Reese, Campanella, Furillo, Newcombe, and others were tottering. A general overhaul was needed; this was a process that victory-sated Brooklyn fans would not easily abide, but one that could be carried out with great profit in Los Angeles, where thousands hungered for baseball.

This formula had enriched the Braves for the past three seasons. Perini's rebuilt team climbed to second in 1953, temporarily slipped to third, and then rose again to challenge the Dodgers in 1955 and 1956. Sensing the Dodger weakness, the 1957 Braves regrouped under the astute management of Fred Haney and readied for the kill. Shrewd trades and promising rookies bolstered the team at every position. Ex-Yankee pitcher Lou Burdette now won consistently and, in company with Juan Pizarro and Don McMahon, supported the great Spahn.

The infield was as strong as this pitching corps. Frank Torre and slugger Joe Adcock contended at first base; on second was the veteran Red Schoendienst, a Cardinal castoff; at short was scrappy Johnny Logan; and at third stood the heavy-hitting, fully matured Ed Mathews. The outfield was the league's best, with Aaron in right,

Billy Bruton in center, and Wes Covington in left. To back this trio
Haney could call on veterans Andy Pafko and Bobby Thomson, or
on rookie Bob "Hurricane" Hazle. Summoned to the Braves midway
in the 1957 season, Hazle became the "phenom" of the year, batting
.403 in 134 at bats.

Unleashed by Haney, the Braves dominated the league and delighted the more than two million fans who whirled Milwaukee turnstiles for a league record. Their team won 95 games that year, easily
outpacing the Cards and the Dodgers. Leading the attack were
Aaron, who batted .322 and led the league in homers and RBIs, and
Mathews, who added 32 homers as the Braves led the league
clouters. Spahn led all pitchers with 21 wins, while Bob Buhl and
Burdette notched 35.

The Braves lost the Series opener to the haughty Yanks at Yankee
Stadium, but recouped behind Burdette's seven-hitter. When action
shifted to County Stadium in Milwaukee, the Yankees, sneering at
the "bush" antics of the local fans, thrashed the Braves 13–2. But a
strange incident in the next game turned the tables. The Yankees
were leading in the tenth when Brave batter Nippy Jones pointed to
a blotch of shoe polish on the ball as evidence that he had been hit
by a pitch. Awarded first base, he scored on Logan's double. Mathews then homered to win the game and tie the match. Burdette won
again the next day with a 1–0 shut-out. The snakebit Yanks squared
the Series at home with a 3–2 win, but Burdette returned to win his
third victory and the Series.

Soon after this Yankee humiliation, New Yorkers received the
shocking news that the Dodgers and Giants would presently depart.
More than any event, that move spelled the end of baseball's old
order. Bereaved Brooklyn fans of 1958 had only the bitter solace of
the failure of their prodigals in their first season at Los Angeles.

Meanwhile, the Braves seemed about to establish a new dynasty.
Fielding the same lineup, though with added pitching from rookies
Carlton Willey and Joey Jay, Haney drove his charges to another
flag. The Braves broke open a close race in July and marched on to
92 wins; the total was three less than that of 1957, but eight better
than the rising Pirates. A league-leading batting average of .266
provided punch, Aaron showing the way with a .326 average, 30
homers, and 95 RBIs. Again, Spahn led the league's pitchers; his 22
wins were trailed by Burdette's 20.

Installed as favorites against the Yankees, Spahn and Burdette
spun a pair of home victories to put the Series flag in sight. When

Spahn won the fourth game in New York, a Brave victory seemed certain. Then the Yankees surged; they rocked Burdette in the fifth game, went on to tie the Series, and won the finale at Milwaukee. The crestfallen Braves were jeered for snatching defeat from the jaws of victory![13] The team never recovered. In 1959 they lost to the Dodgers, a team that had been left for dead in 1958, but whose resurrection compared with those of the 1914 Miracle Braves or the 1951 Miracle Giants.

Surprisingly, it was the 1959 Giants, playing in a small minor league park in San Francisco, who challenged most of the way. Powered by Mays and Orlando Cepeda, the Giants contended until late September when they swooned, losing seven of eight to finish third. Into the fresh breach rushed the Cinderella Dodgers, a team virtually rebuilt, with such exceptions as Hodges and Snider. The boys of summer were vanishing; Campanella suffered a paralyzing accident, Erskine quit rather than endure an aching arm, and others simply wore out.[14] Doughty Duke Snider hung on, even when robbed of his left-handed power by the Coliseum's terrible 440' right field boundary.

Few baseball fans expected the 1959 Dodgers to contend. With so many gaps to fill, only the team's pitching appeared sound. Don Drysdale and Podres were proven winners, Koufax was improving, and rookies Roger Craig and Larry Sherry offered added support. Help also arrived from the strong farm system, which sent Charlie Neal, Don Zimmer, and Maury Wills to join Hodges and Gilliam in the infield. Rookies Don Demeter and Ron Fairly joined an outfield strengthened by the acquisition of Wally Moon from the Cards. Like Snider, Moon batted left-handed, but acting on Musial's wise advice, he tailored his swing to avoid the right field death trap.

The Dodgers struggled all season, avoiding extinction by winning key games. They caught fire in September, winning 13 of 18 games to match the Braves. This was the third deadlock in league history, and again a playoff decided the outcome. Marked for defeat, the lightly regarded Dodgers carried the team's added burden of having lost in both previous playoffs. Still, Sherry's relief pitching won the opener at Milwaukee; then six Dodger pitchers labored for twelve innings at the Coliseum before a key hit by Furillo earned the game and the pennant.

The 1959 World Series was a new experience for the Dodgers. Instead of facing pin-striped Yankees, as in seven previous outings, their opponents were the Chicago White Sox. However, the Sox opened like Yankees, using two homers by Ted Kluszewski and Early Wynn's eight-hit pitching to take a crushing 11–0 victory. Next, reliefer Sherry starred in three straight Dodger victories, including two played before Coliseum crowds of more than 90,000 each day. After the White Sox won another, Sherry nailed down the clincher in relief of Podres. An amazing one-man performance, Sherry accounted for all four Dodger wins, two by saves and two by victories.[15]

Unfortunately, this Cinderella team collapsed in the dust of the 1960 race. Alston rebuilt when they failed, dropping Hodges and Snider for newcomers Tom Davis and Frank Howard.

The Pirates and the Reds

As the Dodgers faltered, the Braves, now managed by wily old Chuck Dressen, took heart. In 1960 Braves Spahn, Burdette, and Buhl delivered good pitching, while Aaron, Adcock, and Mathews conducted a league-leading homer barrage. Yet, for all their pyrotechnics, the Braves finished second, checked by the surging Cards and Pirates. The Cardinals received stout pitching from Ernie Broglio and Larry Jackson, but the offense was weak and the best the team could earn was third place. This opened the way for the Pirates to win their first flag in more than 30 years.

Since the war the Pirates had been league doormats. In the years 1950 to 1955 the team finished last five times, including a horrendous 42–112 log in 1952. As recently as 1957 they were last, throwing a cruel blow to Rickey's efforts to build a winner. Many of the 1960 Pirates were Rickey foundlings.

The 1960 Pirates were managed by Danny Murtaugh. This humorous, tobacco-chewing Irishman was one of the most respected and best-loved managers of this era. Murtaugh got sound defense and good hitting from infielders Bill Mazeroski, Dick Groat, and Don Hoak. The situation at first base, however, was a nightmarish reminder of the manager's playing days with the futile Phillies. Whether played by Dick Stuart (whose efforts earned for him the sobriquet of "Doctor Strangeglove") or by Rocky Nelson, the opposing teams benefited from this weak spot on the field.

The Pirate pitching staff luckily had good starters in Vern Law and Bob Friend, and an exceptional relief pitcher in Elroy Face. Catcher Smokey Burgess atoned for his immobility with timely hitting. Otherwise, the club's main strength was a superb outfield— Roberto Clemente, Bill Virdon, and Bob Skinner—which made only four errors throughout the season. And future Hall of Famer Clemente batted .316 with 94 RBIs. In a year when league power was up for grabs, Murtaugh drove a balanced club to 95 victories, seven games ahead of the Braves.

The arrival of the Yankees to begin the World Series reminded some gray-haired Pittsburgh fans of the drubbing the bombers had handed the 1927 Pirates. These Yankees gave a similar display of window breaking in the opener, but the Pirates survived an early homer assault and won 6–4. The Yankees snatched the advantage the following day, blasting the Pirates 16–3. Moving to New York, Ford now held the visitors to four hits, as his mates ran the score to 10–0. With Face pitching stoutly in relief, the Pirates salvaged the next two games with scores of 3–2 and 5–2. Returning to ancient Forbes Field with a 3–2 lead in games, the Pirates were crushed 12–0 behind a 17-hit barrage and Ford's stingy pitching.

The Pirates took a four-run lead in the deciding game, but were then silenced by Yankee relievers; the Yanks battered Law and Face for a 7–4 lead. Then, Murtaugh was favored by a strange quirk in the bottom of the eighth. With a Pirate on first, Virdon hit what looked like a hard double-play grounder to short, but the ball bounced crazily and struck the shortstop in the throat, incapacitating him. Before the inning ended, the Pirates had scored five times to lead 9–7. The Yankees still battled back to tie, but in the bottom of the ninth lead-off Pirate Mazeroski blasted the second pitch over the left field wall to win the Series. As he passed third the fans mobbed their new hero, exulting over one of the most memorable moments in Series history.[16]

Experts picked the Pirates to repeat in 1961, the last season under the eight-club format. Once again they led the league in batting, Clemente winning the title with a .351 average. The team fell, however, to sixth on a miserable 75–79 record; an error-prone infield and Law's arm trouble were blamed for the failure.

Into the gap moved the Dodgers, as pitcher Koufax won 18 and showed signs of attaining long-promised stardom. Still, even though the Dodgers bettered their 1960 mark by seven victories, the total was too little to stave off a hungry interloper. The Cincinnati Reds had not won a pennant since 1940, and a sixth place finish in 1960 seemingly confirmed their impotence. Yet the 1961 Reds finished first in a tight race; theirs was one of the rare underdog triumphs that renews a tired old myth claiming that a team is never beaten until the last out.

Cincinnati's rise resulted from the joint efforts of general manager Gabe Paul and field manager Fred Hutchinson. Paul promoted trades that landed pitcher Joey Jay and second baseman Don Blasingame, giving Hutchinson the strength he needed. Blasingame tightened the infield of Gordon Coleman at first, Ed Kasko at short, and Gene Freese at third. A regular outfield of Frank Robinson, Vada Pinson, and Wally Post was supported by Gus Bell and Jerry Lynch—the latter one of the finest pinch-hitters in baseball history.

Pitching weakness had sunk past Reds squads, but this year Hutchinson worked a minor miracle with Jay. Jay, never a big winner, responded now with 21 victories. Veterans Jim O'Toole and Bob Purkey added strength, while sturdy relief pitching by Jim Brosnan and Bill Henry saved 32 games.

Cincinnati batters averaged .270 and smote 158 homers. Outfielder Robinson led the offensive attack, hitting 37 homers and driving in 124 runs, while Pinson hit .343 with 87 RBIs. Thus, the balanced Reds won 93, four better than the Dodgers's sum.

The Reds were still no match for the Yankees, whose homers in the expanded American League set a record of 240. Against this juggernaut—even minus the injured Mantle—the best the Reds could manage was Jay's 5–2 win in the second game. The Yanks swept all three games at Cincinnati and closed out the Series with a 13–5 bombardment. However, the old era of Yankee domination was ending, and in the dawning expansion era, the National League would assert its powers with a vengeance.

Profile: Jackie Robinson, Equalitarian

Among the divisive problems of the American country, none is more enduring and festering than the rift between its black and white citizens. America's racial turmoil has continued to be a most visible front throughout the past century. Although federal and state policies barring discrimination have been enacted and the integrationists have dominated the political scene, confrontations between blacks and whites have still sorely tried the nation.

From the beginning of baseball's postwar era, the struggle for black equality rocked the foundations of the game. For the better part of a century, baseball propagandists touted "the national game" as a repository of democratic energy. Spokesmen in 1946 still sang of poor boys using baseball as a path to cash and glory, citing examples of children of immigrants becoming heroes of the diamond, while sportswriters and popular historians portrayed the game as a social lighthouse showing the way to creative democracy.

Of course, baseball's long history of segregation mocked such claims. Blacks were expelled from the majors when the segregation

Opposite: Jackie Robinson's driving determination is evidenced by these panels, showing him stealing home against the Yanks in the 1955 World Series. That year the Dodgers won their first Series.

barriers of the 1880s were erected. Furthermore, when these outlawed players organized their own leagues, white historians and journalists ignored their deeds. Thus denied, the black leagues comprised an "unknown chapter of baseball history," and their records were rendered "invisible."[1]

Recent historical inquiry into the black leagues reveals an excellent brand of baseball, fully comparable to the white majors. In 1920 Andrew "Rube" Foster organized the Negro National League, bringing order to the chaotic structure of black baseball. The Eastern Colored League was later organized, and for nearly a decade the black major leagues flourished. The great feats of pitchers like "Smoky" Joe Williams, of outfielders like Oscar Charleston, and of sluggers like Mule Suttles drew large crowds to games played in rented major and minor league parks. Although the gifted Foster had died by 1930 and an economic depression threatened, the black majors still compared favorably with their white counterparts. Up to 1948 some 400 exhibition games played between white and black major leaguers showed the blacks winning at least 268. Such feats, however, prompted Commissioner Landis to ban these games, allowing only meaningless but profitable matches between all-star teams of black and white players. Still, black performances were of such high calibre that historian John Holway recently suggested an asterisk be placed after Babe Ruth's homer records to indicate that his slugging was never tested against the great black pitchers of his day.

Unfortunately, the deeds of the great black players are largely lost. In a sad footnote to this lost chapter of baseball history, a major league council in 1969 belatedly honored a few black heroes by voting into the Hall of Fame. When the duty was performed, the committee disbanded; their acts only mirrored the grudging acceptance of black equality in American life.[2]

The end of World War II found blacks still barred from major league play. Although managers John McGraw and Connie Mack tried to circumvent the policy, their efforts to smuggle in blacks ran afoul of the "unwritten law." That testament so established the discriminatory policy that few writers challenged it. Bill Veeck, Jr. learned how strongly entrenched the law was in 1943 when he tried to purchase the moribund Phillies and stock the club with black stars. He was publicly scolded by the editor of *The Sporting News* and privately rapped by Landis. Landis also rebuked Leo Durocher for openly advocating integration, and stubbornly ignored singer Paul Robeson's eloquent appeal to "Have a Heart." Right up to his death in 1944 Landis would utter no further word on the subject, insisting that owners had rights to hire or bar any players.[3]

The Commissioner's passing signalled an end to this racist policy. Outside of baseball, integrationist sentiments were knocking down discriminatory institutions, as the blacks gained more political and economic power. Meanwhile, some enlightened citizens sought to batter away absurd racial theories and to expose the social evils of discrimination.

Such voices failed to reach a cabal of baseball leaders, whose ranks included the league presidents and owners Sam Breadon, Philip Wrigley, Tom Yawkey, and Larry MacPhail. In 1946 they composed a secret manifesto which opposed baseball's integration.[4] Some owners defended this policy in July before a Congressional subcommittee; blaming outside agitators for stirring up trouble, they argued that the admission of the few qualified black players would cripple the profitable black leagues. Among the agitators were the two black newsmen in 1945 who tried to use the new laws to forcibly integrate the Brooklyn Dodgers. President Branch Rickey had viewed the prospective players and rejected each as overage. While Rickey had told the newsmen, "I'm more for your cause than anybody else you know," he had added that baseball integration is "a matter of evolution, not revolution."[5]

Rickey's hopeful declaration was backed by Commissioner A.B. "Happy" Chandler. Soon after his 1945 election, Chandler was visited by Ric Roberts of the *Pittsburgh Courier*, a black newspaper. Roberts was astounded by Chandler's views on blacks playing in the majors: "I'm for the Four Freedoms. If a black boy can make it on Okinawa and Guadalcanal, hell, he can make it in baseball. Once I tell something, brother, I never change. You can count on me." Delighted by Chandler's candor, Roberts gave the interview front page play and later credited Chandler's stance for strengthening Rickey's resolve.[6]

That same year Rickey set out to sign a black player. At some expense he sent scouts to cover the black leagues in search of "a good one"—a talented, college-educated, married player, one who might dispel popular myths of black stupidity and sexual promiscuity. While today such demands would seem incredibly patronizing, for his time Rickey's stand was bold and courageous. Indeed, he paid a price; he was bitterly denounced by officials, and even his own family begged him to desert his crusade.[7]

Rickey's eye focused on Jack Roosevelt Robinson, second baseman of the Kansas City Monarchs. Robinson signed a contract in October, 1945 to play for the Dodgers's Montreal farm club. The news electrified the sporting world. With Rickey as author of the script and the handsome, six-foot, 26-year-old Robinson as principal actor, an American morality play began. Arguments both pro and con swirled about Robinson and reverberated far beyond baseball. "I guess I'm just a guinea pig," said Robinson, amidst the stormy protests. Minor league President William Bramham accused Rickey of pandering to northern blacks; ex-player Rogers Hornsby opined that Negroes had no place in baseball; active player Bob Feller questioned ability; and Dodger captain Dixie Walker threatened to quit the team.[8] Even some black owners were alarmed that Robinson's signing would undermine the black majors. This fear proved to be valid, as black owners stood helpless against a tide of black enthusiasm for Robinson's cause. As black fans turned to the white majors, attendance at all black games tailed off. Recalling the seasons of 1946 and 1947 in the black leagues, Buck Leonard lamented, "We couldn't draw flies."[9] The collapse of the black majors left some 400 ball players jobless.

No black player shouldered so heavy a psychological burden as Robinson. By 1947 he had snagged the full glare of national publicity; should he flag or fail, the cause might be lost. Robinson, however, was used to adversity. The youngest of five children born to a poor share-cropping family in Cairo, Georgia, the child Robinson knew poverty. Fortunately, his family moved to California and Robinson's athletic ability opened doors. He lettered in four sports at UCLA and briefly played pro football before World War II intervened and he became an Army lieutenant. While in service, he denounced discriminatory policies; he was court-martialed for insubordination and honorably discharged. He joined the black majors in 1944. As second baseman for the Monarchs, his speed, hitting, and aggressive play attracted Rickey's scouts.[10]

Rickey worked to curb Robinson's temper. In counselling sessions, Rickey played the role of racist bigot, screaming insults and urging Robinson to react docilely, like "a white man's nigger." Rickey judged that meekness was essential and he also urged Robinson to marry—but Rickey stoutly defended his ball player. In a widely publicized speech at Wilberforce State University, Rickey exposed and discredited an owners' manifesto against blacks. Furthermore, to ease Robinson's ordeal, Rickey moved his training camp to Latin America, traded hostile teammates, and attacked the bigoted acts of rival teams.

Rickey's altruism was tinged with dollar signs—he declared, "It's right. It's profitable"—yet Robinson never wavered in his gratitude. Even in his disillusioned last years, he regarded Rickey as a father figure and a humanitarian.[11] In 1946 Robinson's courage was severely tested at Montreal. His manager was a Mississippian reputed to be prejudiced against blacks. Robinson's league-leading hitting and the glory of a Little World Series triumph were hard to downplay; the manager allowed that Robinson was "a gentleman." Still, Robinson paid a fierce price. Every game brought taunts and insults; under pressure, his hair grayed and he came close to a nervous breakdown. He prevailed, fortunately, and was rewarded with a $5,000 contract and promotion to the Dodgers. He was tested harder in 1947. To add to his troubles he was posted at first base, an unfamiliar position. The disheartened player started slowly; daily he endured insults from hostile teammates.

Opposing teams were even harder to bear. When the Phils came to town, unbelievable taunts were hurled, prompting teammate Ed Stanky to call the Phils "yellow-bellied cowards." When the Dodgers visited Philadelphia, owner Carpenter begged Rickey to bench Robinson. Fortunately, newspaper backing and Commissioner Chandler's stern warning cowed the Phils. The Phils's manager, Ben Chapman, almost lost his job over the incident, but Robinson saved him by posing in a conciliatory newspaper photo.

The Cards planned a strike at St. Louis, but Stan Woodward of the *New York Herald-Tribune* broke the story and aroused a tide of Robinson support. League president Frick belatedly joined the support, threatening suspensions and pledging to "go down the line with Robinson." Still the Cards harried Robinson all year and one Cardinal player spiked him. Robinson retaliated with batting and baserunning to pace the Dodgers to the flag and win Rookie of the Year honors. Such prowess converted his teammates and convinced others. By season's end he no longer stood alone—Veeck introduced Larry Doby as the first American League black. Doby played 29 games in 1947, batted .156, and sustained insults and spittle from tobacco-chewing infielders.[12]

One more season ended the cruel initiations; then blacks won grudging acceptance. Thus, in 1949 Rickey told Robinson, "You're on your own . . . You can be yourself now." Freed at last, Robinson lashed out at his detractors. He warned Chapman: "Look you SOB . . . You've been on me for two years. If you open your mouth one more time, I'm gonna . . . kick the ---- out of you." His outbursts and his demands for better treatment for blacks earned Robinson the label "a Hitler" and the reputation of a troublemaker. When Rickey departed, O'Malley urged Robinson to humble himself. One sportswriter advised Robinson to show gratitude if he expected to win the 1949 MVP Award. Robinson retorted, "If I have to thank *you* to win . . . I don't want the ----ing thing!"[13]

Robinson's 1949 batting feats left writers no choice but to name him MVP. From that year through the 1954 season, he consistently batted over .300; his .311 batting over a ten-year career helped the Dodgers capture six flags and a world title.

Robinson was definitely a baseball hero. Rewards came his way, including an annual salary of more than $40,000, along with endorsements and speaking invitations. His picture graced the cover of a 1950 *Life* magazine and a grade B movie recreated his achievement.[14] Most importantly, in 1962 he became the first black to be voted Hall of Fame membership.

Nevertheless, he grew increasingly despondent over the slow progress of blacks in baseball. His last Dodger days were sad ones. When his career wested in 1956, O'Malley sold him to the Giants "for the good of the team." In retaliation, Robinson announced his retirement in an exclusive magazine article. Although a Dodger spokesman sneered that the ball player would pocket the magazine money and sign with the Giants, Robinson retired from the game.

Jackie Robinson continued his struggle for black equality outside of the baseball world where his reputation offered him opportunities on one hand and exploitations on the other. Always the integrationist, he opposed the black separatists, arguing that equality must be won within the American system. Robinson's intellectual odyssey can be traced through six biographies, all which appeared during his lifetime. The first two were puerile works that dutifully praised white baseball for giving him his chance. The last four were more revealing. His bitter confrontations with prejudice and discrimination in the baseball world are sketched in each; but the final two documents offer, in addition, Robinson's mature reflections on his role as trailblazer for black equality, on his constant, though qualified admiration for Rickey, and on his own sad life. Robinson agonized when he looked back, asking: "What have I really done for myself and my people?" His honest answer was that he saw himself as a black man who "never had it made" in a white world.[15]

Robinson died on October 24, 1972. His was a hero's funeral; one editorial eulogized him as an authentic All-American "who made a memorable impact for good in his country and his time."[16]

In death he was extolled as the symbol of black equality in baseball. Inspired by his example, black players moved into lineups and performed so brilliantly that the expansion era stood out as the age of the black player, a label which included many Latin Americans of dark skins as well. Moreover, record-breaking feats by black players is a fact of the expansion era.

This was Robinson's legacy and his glory. Because of him, many black players echoed Willie Mays when he said, "Everytime I look at my pocketbook I see Jackie Robinson."[17]

3

Born Out of Time: Players of the Postwar Era

T
The Black Vanguard
o probe the experiences of black players who followed Robinson into the majors is to examine racist sentiments which required these men to "prove" themselves. That they did was evidenced by their growing numbers; 100 blacks played in the major leagues by 1960.[1] As pioneers they were blamed by some for having killed off the black majors, even though it was the white leagues that scooped up the best black players and gave scant compensation to the former owners in return. At least the passing of the black majors marked an end to American baseball's long "apartheid era." And though the records of most teams and the names of many players who starred in the black leagues are largely forgotten, a few of those principals are now enshrined in baseball's Hall of Fame.[2]

Throughout the 1950s black players still suffered in the majors. While their white teammates sometimes avoided their company and would seldom room with them, several prominent owners continued

to refuse to sign black players; among this group were Dan Topping, Walter Briggs, Philip Wrigley, Bob Carpenter, August Busch,
and Tom Yawkey. Yawkey was the last to yield, but Wrigley delayed
bringing in Ernie Banks, and George Weiss of the Yankees complained that wealthy seatholders might refuse to "sit with niggers."
Indeed, only the astounding success of his white teams saved Weiss's
reputation, and some felt his attitude kept the Yankees from bidding
on promising black players like Willie Mays.

Because of strong pressure from the outside, Weiss signed Vic
Power in 1952; he then dropped him, alleging that Power was
unsuitable.[3] In 1955 Weiss signed on outfielder Elston Howard, the
1954 MVP of the International League. When Weiss said that Howard had "manners," he implied that the new player was so determined to succeed that he would endure slights like segregated
housing and insulting remarks. Manager Stengel called Howard
"Eightball," and joked, "When I finally get a nigger, I get the only
one who can't run." Howard stoically survived and excelled, but
thanked his wife for her psychiatric services.[4]

Other American League owners also bided their time, waiting for
blacks to prove themselves; when they did act, the best black players
were already National Leaguers. However, in that league some
owners questioned the wisdom of playing too many black players lest
attendance be affected by a supposed "tipping point." After performing a statistical study, critic Aaron Rosenblatt reported that
black recruits had to be better than their white competitors. Rosenblatt also observed that blacks stood a better chance of entering the
majors as outfielders.[5]

Although blatant discrimination lessened, some managers still regarded blacks as naturally "lazy." On the other hand was Bill Veeck,
who believed that blacks were naturally more agile than whites.[6] For
whatever reasons, by 1960 black National Leaguers outperformed
the whites. Robinson set the standard by winning an MVP crown.
After Roy Campanella won his second MVP crown in 1953, the next
six went to blacks, including "Campy's" third and Ernie Banks's two
consecutive titles.

Black National Leaguers were also winning seasonal honors in
batting, homers, base stealing, and RBIs. In the 1950s Robinson and
Mays each won a batting championship and Hank Aaron won two.
Monte Irvin took RBI honors in 1951, and black players won an
additional four by 1960. Mays became the first black homer titleist in
1951, and Aaron and Banks accounted for three more during that

decade. The year 1951 also marked the beginning of black preeminence in base stealing. After Sam Jethroe won the title in 1955, seven of the next eight titles went to Mays or Bill Bruton. In the early 1960s Dodger speedster Maury Wills captured the first in his record-breaking string of stolen base honors. Among black pitchers of the 1950s Don Newcombe twice led the National League in winning percentage.

Over in the American League, where fewer blacks were signed, Larry Doby of the Indians won two homer titles and an RBI title, while Orestes Minoso, a dusky Latin American, won a base-stealing title.

It was becoming clear that black players would join the company of baseball's immortals. Pathfinder Robinson was fading in 1956 when Willie Mays was heralded as the first black superstar. Unlike Robinson, Mays reveled in the joys of baseball, playing with a boyish, aggressive style. One observer noticed that he brought "jazz" to the game by running, swinging, and fielding "black."

Snatched from the black majors for a paltry $5,000, outfielder Mays joined the 1951 Giants as a 20-year-old prodigy who "could do it all." "Nobody ever showed me," he told Durocher, but his painful debut nearly broke his spirit, as he managed only one homer in his first 22 at bats.[7] At times he wept in frustration and fear, but Durocher confidently stayed with him. Indeed, Mays recovered to bat .274, pole 20 homers, and spark a pennant drive. He missed two seasons for military service, but returned in 1954 to bat .345 with 41 homers and 110 RBIs. Such heroics helped the Giants land their first world title since the 1930s.

Seldom serious, Mays charmed writers, who preferred his cheerful, earthy repartee to Robinson's militant candor. "Unaffectedly accommodating," he was a popular favorite—but to many white fans he was still a black face.[8] Though Mays was overshadowed by the great trio of DiMaggio, Williams, and Musial, it was evident that he was marked for immortality along with the great Hank Aaron.

Like Mays, Aaron's full flowering awaited the expansion era. An outfielder judged the best of "my era" by Mantle, Aaron was purchased for a mere $1,000 from the black Indianapolis Clowns. Only twenty when he broke into the Braves's lineup in 1954, the shy, low-keyed outfielder was a brilliant fielder and versatile hitter. In time "Hammering Hank" would to break two "untouchable" hitting records.

No one else matched this prodigious pair, but others stood out. As the first black to play in the American League, Larry Doby posted a .283 average in 13 seasons as an outfielder. Also, outfielder Monte Irvin, despite joining the Giants at thirty, batted .293 over eight seasons, and was voted into the Hall of Fame.

During the 1950s the most honored black player was Campanella, whose prowess as a catcher was rivaled only by Berra. Plucked from the black majors, the 26-year-old Campanella lasted ten seasons. A gifted receiver and power hitter, he thrice won MVP honors, and upon retirement, he took his place in the Hall of Fame. Like Campy, Ernie Banks powered his way into the same company by many years of solid hitting. Arriving in 1952 as the Cubs's 22-year-old shortstop, Banks won a pair of homer and RBI titles.

If men like Banks had years on their side, Satchel Paige lived on borrowed time when called to Cleveland in 1948. Even so, the legendary, middle-aged pitcher showed white fans the twinklings of his glory. His six wins contributed to the 1948 Indian pennant drive and drew large crowds to see him pitch in three home games. Thereafter, he posted but one winning season, but his awesome past earned him a place at Cooperstown.

Only a handful of black pitchers won fame in the 1950s. Still, few pitchers matched Newcombe's 149 wins posted over ten years—his 27–7 record in 1956 won him both the Cy Young and MVP awards. Among other black pitchers, Sam "Toothpick" Jones pitched a no-hitter in 1955, and in 1959 he won 21 for the Cards. Also, Joe Black set a high standard for relievers in 1952, winning 15 and saving 15 for the Dodgers.

These stalwarts formed the black vanguard who cleared the remaining pockets of resistance and smoothed the way for a coming generation of black stars. The young players toppled records like sheaves in the early expansion years.

Mercenaries of the 1950s

In 1946 the majors were flooded with returning servicemen seeking to resume their interrupted playing careers. Because so many came with reformist notions about discipline, salaries, pensions, and job security, their old bosses trembled. High on the list of demands was that of a players' union; owners defused this appeal by granting reforms, including a pension plan tied to radio and television receipts, and a company union plan which allowed player representatives to meet with owners.

The farthest reaching of these concessions was the precedent

Black hitting stars, Willie Mays (*top left*), Ernie Banks (*top right*), and Roy Campanella (*lower right*) won National League MVP Awards in the 1950s. Outfielder Larry Doby (*lower left*) was the first black to play in the American League.

owners set by conceding a share in the coming television bonanza. Years later this would trigger a salary revolution, but the war veterans gained little at this time. By 1947 most of the prewar players were gone, beaten out by younger players. Because canny prophets like Rickey predicted this outcome and usurped the best young talent, many clubs soon faced an acute talent shortage. To catch up the clubs engaged in bidding wars and shelled out lavish bonuses to young prospects. Thus came the "bonus baby era"—so named by journalists who marveled at the $52,000 the 1941 Tigers paid to prospect Dick Wakefield. Although stifled by the war, bonus bidding flared anew in the 1950s when one hundred of these golden boys were signed, including 37 in 1955 alone. Owners, interested in stopping this spree, ruled that any prospect receiving over $4,000 in bonus money must be kept on the team's major league roster.

The remedy came too late to halt the impact on salaries. Not surprisingly, envious stars grumbled: Johnny Sain compared his $15,000 salary as the Braves's ace pitcher with the $75,000 bonus paid to benchwarmer Johnny Antonelli. Moreover, scouts complained that youngsters demanded big bonuses up front. Hence, while the trend lasted, clubs spent heavily: the Red Sox spent $476,000 over seven years with limited results. Also, bonuses were blamed for corrupting young players, some of whom quit rather than endure low paid lives in the minors.[9]

As the bonus trend triggered demands for better pay and playing conditions, players were branded spoiled mercenaries. Scorning the postwar crop, writer Bob Considine called them molly-coddled opportunists and Eddie Collins denounced them as money-hungry, homer-happy ordinaries. As a glaring example of this "gimme generation," critics cited Duke Snider's blatant admission that he played for money.[10]

These youths merely reflected the spirit of American affluence. By now half the players were college-educated. Many critics blamed increased education for instilling alien values like individualism, lessened dedication, and defiance in the players. Likewise, critics faulted postwar players for spending frivolously and for committing matrimony, as did eight of ten by 1956![11] Yet these athletes were wholly in tune with the times. The vast majority of the 1,260 players who reached the majors in the years 1947 to 1958 were whites, but one hundred were blacks and 78 were Hispanics. Compared with their brothers of the 1930s, this crop averaged twenty pounds heavier and two inches taller. Reflecting population shifts, more of this crew originated from the far west and south; and since only thirty of the entire lot played in their hometown, they were indeed "mercenaries."[12]

In the 1950s player salaries outdistanced those of skilled or college trained workers, ranging from $6,000 to $80,000; and a handful topped $50,000. Only the vaunted quartet of Musial, DiMaggio, Williams, and Mantle topped $100,000. Indeed, a 1957 survey pegged 75 percent of the salaries between $10,000 and $25,000—very good money for the times. Given time, college grads in professions or industry could earn as much; thus, some blamed the emerging talent scarcity on college-trained athletes' opting for job security.

Even though they were eagerly recruited, young prospects still faced a grinding and decimating trek to the majors. Making "the bigs" took talent, fierce determination, and, as always, dedication. Beyond that, energy-draining travel and night games added intensity to a pressurized life.[13] The mettle of the players was tested, and some, like Jimmy Piersall, broke under the strains. Making the majors signaled the end of a long ordeal that began when a player was scouted, signed, and assigned to a minor league team. At this time a six-year apprenticeship in the minors was the norm, and once a player was in the majors he could expect a stay of less than five years, as was the average. Hence, many failed to qualify for minimum pension benefits. A cut player faced the harsh choice of hanging on in the minors or quitting.

Still, being on top was no bed of roses. Fear of failure, of being replaced, platooned, fired, traded, injured, and discarded at 30 were familiar prospects. A player's joy and curse was to ply his trade in the full light of public exposure—his daily performance scrutinized, criticized, and published for all to see. There was the constant possibility of being booed and taunted by fans. Other external pressures included night ball, air travel, and the ever-present possibility that in the minors lurked some rookie who was better. Still other menacing outsiders included umpires whose decisions could hurt, writers whose words could help destroy, and rival teams whose deeds could thwart. Heavy external pressure came from the major league environment and its unique laws like the reserve clause.

As usual there were internal pressures generated by the team itself. A team member belonged to a total community that forced conforming standards. Exclusive cliques still added loneliness to the list of fears. Newcomers and marginal players suffered the most, at times over-conforming to gain acceptance. Indeed, few could escape team pressure to conform.

Once the long season had begun no other social group was so important to the player. From the team the player often acquired the nickname he wore for life. Beyond this, the group linked him with a roommate and imposed a unique and dynamic language. By now baseball jargon included such labels as a "flake" for a blithe-spirited, impulsive type; a "head in the locker" for a moody player; a "dead body" for a useless player; a "bad hose" for a sore-armed pitcher. A fast runner had good "wheels" and could "motor," but a "slow bat" was a baseball death sentence.

Also the "book" on a rival pitcher took note of his fast ball, noting if it was a "high hard one" or "hummer"; a "sneaker" was a decep-tive fast ball; a "sailer" was a lively one; a "scroogie" was a screwball. Terms like "long men," "short men," and "stoppers" denoted differ-ent types of relief pitchers. Similarly, batters fell into types, like "flit guns," or spray hitters; "banjo hitters" for lucky ones; along with "guess hitters" and "clutch hitters."[14]

For mutual survival players freely exchanged notes and gossip on the strengths and weaknesses of pitchers and batters. Officials mainly tried to ban such exchanges, but neither threats nor fines stopped the grapevine. Nor could officials halt the ancient practice of heckling rivals. At least the old-fashioned foul-mouthed bench jockeying style abated—except for hard cases like Johnny Logan of the Reds.[15]

Some critics deplored such mellowness and complained about the dull sameness of these players. Indeed, these were mostly clean-shaven, crew-cut white boys. As ever, most were right handers, though the platooning strategy placed a premium on left-handed batters and pitchers and on versatile switch-hitters. The taller, faster, stronger players of this era seemed tailored to the "big bang style."

However, there is no denying their colorlessness. "Where are the drunks of yesteryear?" mourned owner Veeck, who fondly recalled such bygone characters. Certainly there were a few; Giant "Dusty" Rhodes's boozing bouts were hushed, and when his batting skills faded, he was quickly shunted out.[16] Such high-handed repression suggested a tyrannical policy of decorum; sportswriters dutifully censored breaches so that the few published high jinks hardly brightened a dull landscape.

Pitcher Sal Maglie was criticized for wearing long sideburns, pitch-ing with a two days' growth of whiskers. Ted Williams was scolded for wearing his knickers too low and for answering boos and gibes with spittle and obscenities. Of course, brawling, aggressive players—Robinson, Early Wynn, Clint Courtney, Billy Martin, Johnny Logan, and Johnny Temple—were marked men. Mean Johnny Temple dared challenge officials and, on occasions, slugged writers, teammates, and rivals. He was once fined $1,000 for hitting a writer, and on another occasion he defiantly paid a $50 fine in pennies. Eccentric acts like Jimmy Piersall's running out a homer backwards, slinging bats, and going to the plate without a bat evoked jeers and boos. Scorned as a "flake" and a "nut," Piersall's acts were actual symptoms of an impending nervous breakdown. "They said I was crazy and I was," he later wrote.

So strong was pressure to conform that the players were scolded: slugger Ted Kluszewski for wearing short sleeves that revealed his massive biceps, Mickey Mantle for chewing bubble gum, Willie Mays for his jazzy outfield "basket catches." Small wonder that Veeck complained!

The increasing number of married players was blamed for crushing the blithe spirits. Rickey was one to welcome this trend, exulting in 1953 that there were only 32 bachelors in the majors.[17]

Sadly, ballplayers discovered that marital bliss was a mirage. Baseball wives chafed under the strains of long separations, sudden uprootings, house-hunting, and worries over their men's performances. Mrs. Allie Reynolds worried herself into a painful attack of shingles. Both players and wives worried over the activities of their absent partners.

Some foundering marriages contributed to team failure. Analyzing several cases in the 1950s, Al Stump cited Joe DiMaggio's 1946 slump as a result of his "quietly going crazy" over a divorce suit. Manager Jack Onslow's imprudent 1950 ban on wives at spring training hurt his club. The angry wives retaliated with a "Down With Onslow" movement that divided the team and accounted for the seventh place finish that cost Onslow his job. Similarly, in 1951 manager Sawyer banned 20 wives from the Phillies's training camp, citing them for distracting players with late bridge games and divisive cliques. Fighting back at "Stinker Sawyer," the wives helped bring about his 1952 ouster; some claim this dropped the Phillies out of contention.

This action also worked in reverse; by questioning a manager's decisions, wives sometimes undermined their husband's careers. Acting on wifely advice, Jack Harshman resisted the White Sox attempts to convert him to pitching, until their divorce changed his mind. Billy Martin's choice of baseball over marital togetherness triggered an agonizing separation, whereas the fear of divorce affected the play of both Jim Gilliam and Willie Mays.

As always, "baseball Annies" excited alarmists. While sympathetic sportswriters still hushed these affairs, some incidents came to light. In 1949, a Philly infielder was incapacitated for a year after being shot in a hotel room, allegedly by a love-crazed woman. In 1951 a Dodger pitcher, reportedly distraught over his ruined marriage, shot himself to death in the wake of a camp follower's paternity accusation. In 1953 a White Sox infielder suffered a fractured finger in a dancehall brawl over a woman. The injury only kept him out of three games, but gibes like "Wanna Dance?" resounded from bench jockeys for much longer.

At a time when any sexual relations outside of marriage were strongly condemned, the notion that players might indulge in deviant sex was unspeakable. One player was charged in 1958 with child molesting, was fined and suspended. Allowed to attempt a comeback, his baseball gum card cryptically read that he "got off to a late start."

Officials seemed paranoid about sexual misconduct. Devices for curbing sex adventuring included bed checks, curfews, and fines; rumor told that one training camp was mixing saltpeter with scrambled eggs. Nevertheless, sexual dalliance posed chronic problems. Reportedly, an inability to curb such adventuring prompted Joe McCarthy and Billy Southworth to resign their managerial posts. Manager Marty Marion caused a rift in 1955 by fining four of his players for their misbehavior. The episode led to his dismissal and his grim summary that "dames wrecked more teams than bad liquor, big bonuses, or all the sore arms."[18]

Postwar Heroes

Any distractions notwithstanding, postwar players performed mightily on the diamond, employing the big bang style with devastating effect. In 1950 National sluggers struck 66 grandslam homers, and major leaguers in 1956 smote 2,294 homers, each of these going for seasonal records.

The young, right-handed swinging Ralph Kiner joined the Pirates in 1946 and proceeded to homer at a remarkable rate. He led the league his rookie year, then repeated this for six straight years, setting a record. In 1947 he struck 51, and in 1949 his 54 threatened Ruth's seasonal mark. Although he lasted only 10 seasons and batted .279, his slugging won him a place in the Hall of Fame.

At a time when Ruth's lifetime total of 714 blows seemed untouch-able, Aaron hit thirteen in 1954 to begin the 21-year assault that toppled Ruth's record. That same year Aaron's teammate, Joe Ad-cock, drew more attention, smashing four homers and a double in a game at Ebbets Field. The following year Banks hit 44 homers and Dale Long, a journeyman first baseman with the Pirates, dazzled National League fans by homering in eight consecutive games. Such prodigious blasting had team public relations men measuring homer distances; "Red" Patterson of the Yankees claimed a 565′ shot for Mantle at Griffith Stadium.[19]

So much Thor worship prompted some to ask what happened to Mercury. American League base stealing now lagged so badly that Dom DiMaggio's 15 led in 1950, while the total 1957 Senator output was 13! If base stealing was a casualty of the homer mania, some likewise blamed the free-swinging style for increasing strike-outs, lowering run production, and increasing guess hitting. Slugger Ad-cock defended guess hitting, arguing that pitchers forced it upon batters by their varied deliveries; while slugger Jim Lemon laughed off his frequent strikeouts, saying, "I strike out to keep my job."

Even a homer-happy age had its offensive innovations. Switch-hitters like Mantle revived a tactic used successfully in the past. Batting right-handed off left-handed pitchers and left-handed off right-handers, Mantle became the deadliest switcher of all time. As offensive theory held that left-handed swingers had an advantage against right-handed pitchers and vice versa, managers platooned hitters accordingly. Mantle, delivering broadsides from either side of the plate, became an indispensable regular in an age of platoon-ing. Inspired by his example, the number of switchers increased from 11 in the 1950s to 35 in the 1960s.[20]

Now pinch-hitting was honed to a fine art. By the 1960s, pinch-hitters batted more than 4,000 times a season, making a dependable pinch-hitter a real treasure.[21] This vogue was initiated by postwar masters like Jim "Dusty" Rhodes, the star of the 1954 World Series, and big John Mize, whose 43 timely blows keyed five straight Yankee championships. Others included Mize's successor, John Blanchard, and Jerry Lynch of the Pirates, one of the most productive of all time.

But prince of pinch-hitters was a portly, unruffled catcher named Forrest "Smoky" Burgess, who entered the majors in 1949 and was kept for 18 seasons, mostly for his ability to hit in clutch situations. Before retiring in 1967 Burgess owned the all-time record, having

Baseball's legendary hitting triumvirate of the postwar era included Red Sox Ted Williams (*left*), Yankee Joe DiMaggio (*center*), and Cardinal Stan Musial (*right*).

delivered 145 pinch-hits in 547 tries. Unfortunately, his reign was brief; in 1961 his successor, young Manny Mota, collected his first hit but, ironically, his only one in 15 tries.

Still, the most celebrated heroes were versatile batters who played regularly and hit for average and distance. In the postwar era, both leagues glittered with such stars, 17 of whom made the Hall of Fame. Among them were Aaron, Mays, Mantle, Banks, Berra, Al Kaline, Eddie Mathews, and Clemente—all of whom spanned the 1950s and lasted well into the expansion era.

The great 1950s triumvirate of DiMaggio, Williams, and Musial set standards that lesser players spent their strength trying to match. Of this trio, none surpassed the great DiMaggio in all-round ability. The Yankee owned a lifetime average of .325 and 361 homers, compiled over an injury-plagued 13-year career. Twice he led the league in batting and twice in homers, achievements that far surpassed those of Williams and Musial. "The Dago," as his mates knew him, had an aura of leadership and mystery about him, qualities that inspired his mates and magnetized baseball fans. His 1949 signing of the first $100,000 contract in baseball history only increased his fame; DiMaggio inked two more before his retirement in 1951.

For DiMaggio to outshine the mighty Ted Williams was a triumph of class over crudeness. In sheer batting virtuosity, the left-handed swinging Williams was rivaled only by Cobb, Ruth, and Hornsby. Over a 19-year career that twice was interrupted by combat service as a fighter pilot, Williams posted a lifetime .344 average with 521 homers. Six times he led his league in hitting and four times he led in homers; twice he took the coveted Triple Crown and his .406 batting mark of 1941 was the last toppling of the .400 barrier by anyone. Incredibly, only once in his career did he bat below .300. Even so, he stood second on the all-time list in slugging percentage and bases on balls received.

This greatest all-round hitter of modern times was blessed with excellent eyesight and strong wrists. By dint of tireless, monastic practice he developed what many considered to be the most "rhythmic and coordinated" swing in the game. This deadly pull-hitter could defeat any enemy defense by hitting to all fields.

Yet this big, handsome outfielder was deficient as a fielder, and still worse, he carried the reputation of being a sore-headed prima donna, a "mixed-up adolescent." When booed or criticized, he sulked and swore, sometimes delivering obscene gestures. Once he hurled his bat at box seat patrons in Fenway Park and happened to strike owner Yawkey's 60-year-old housekeeper. An earlier spitting episode, described in detail by sportscaster Mel Allen, resulted in a $5,000 fine, the largest levied since Ruth's day. Stubbornly vindictive, Williams refused to tip his hat when applauded and he denied interviews to hostile scribes. Such petulance worsened a bad situation, prompting his teammates to fault him for lack of leadership and poor fielding. As center fielder Piersall complained, "I ought to get two salaries. I'm covering both fields."[22]

The peevish Williams paid dearly. After winning a second Triple Crown in 1947, he lost the MVP award to DiMaggio by a single vote when a Boston writer refused him as much as a third-place vote. After hitting .388 in 1957, he again lost to Mantle. Indeed, it was his fate that the tenor of the times ran against his personality. What his fans expected of him was expressed in an angry letter, denouncing him for refusing to wear a necktie and tip his hat, but also for not bunting, stealing, and hustling. "In short he'll continue to be what he's always been—the prize heel ever to wear a Boston uniform."[23]

Williams still commanded a salary of $125,000 a year and attained his goal of becoming baseball's all-time best hitter. Years later, he admitted his shortcomings, but then the old rebelliousness welled up and he added, "I would probably do them again if the conditions were the same." He left baseball in 1960 with head high and pride undiminished. Then 42, he batted .316 with 29 homers; his last homer came in his final at bat at Fenway. As the ball sailed over the barrier the fans gave "Teddy Ballgames" one last rousing ovation. For an instant he considered tipping his hat, but true to his code, he did not. As John Updike explained, "Gods do not answer letters."[24]

In 1960, as Williams joined DiMaggio in retirement, Stan Musial, the youngest of this great triumvirate, was still assaulting records in the National League. Stanley Frank Musial, a quiet, colorless athlete, was once a sore-armed pitcher whose hitting prowess gave him a second life. As a Cardinal fledgling in 1942, his .315 average won for him Rookie of the Year honors. He went on from there to earn seven batting titles, and in two years won both the batting title and the MVP award. Beginning in 1950, he won three consecutive batting titles, and in 1957 took his seventh and last with a .351 mark.

Although he pounded 475 homers, he never won a homer title. His string of batting titles over 22 seasons and his relentless consistency produced a new National League record of 3,630 hits. Musial delivered an incredible 1,815 hits at home and the same number on the road, compiling a lifetime .331 average. An awesome batting machine, the lean, left-handed hitter coiled with knees slightly bent and stared with cold eyes at the pitcher from a point just above the V of his right elbow. Always expecting a fastball, he relied on quick reflexes to adjust when crossed up. The tireless Musial maintained a regimen of running, weight lifting, and bat swinging. If this training could be imitated, Musial's icy ability to relax and concentrate could not:

> I don't consciously feel any thrill out of any good play or any winning hit. Now don't get me wrong. Sure I enjoy my hits . . . but what I mean is that I don't get that thrill that makes fellows howl with delight or dance for joy. . . . I can get into the spirit . . . but I don't feel it like they do.[25]

Had he played at Yankee Stadium, New York's publicity mills would have lionized him. Quietly playing 22 seasons in St. Louis kept him earthbound. Perhaps his most controversial moment came in 1946 when he pondered a $75,000 offer to jump to the Mexican League. That year he lamented over his meagre $13,500 salary and the prospect of shifting to first base. Then, when the owner anted up $5,000 more, he stayed and mastered the new position well enough to play a thousand games at that spot.

Musial saw action in only one World Series, but still cash and glory came his way. In 1948 he received a $31,000 salary; ten years later, after rapping his 3,000th hit, he became the first National Leaguer to receive $100,000. He played until 1963 and celebrated the birth of his first grandchild with a homer, then retired, saying that he had lost his ability "to pull the trigger on the fast ball." The departure of this star left an awesome gap; so beloved was he that on rare occasions when booed, defenders placed apologetic ads in local papers. His number 6 was retired with the ball player; his locker and uniform were dispatched to the Hall of Fame as a permanent exhibit.[26]

The great postwar triumvirate was pressed hard by young demigods. As DiMaggio played his last, the young Mickey Mantle was showing remarkable promise. Mantle, a speedy, hard-hitting youth, was summoned to the big team in the spring of 1951 and was converted to outfield play. He started the opening games, but after hitting safely only once in nineteen tries, he was sent down. For a time the crestfallen youth considered quitting, but his father harshly reminded him of his alternative—a lifetime in the local lead mines.

To the minors Mantle went and after a lusty performance, he rejoined the 1951 Yankees and finished the season with a .283 average. He injured a leg in the first game of the World Series; indeed, weak legs always plagued him. A poorly treated football injury had led to bone disease, so now that leg was daily taped and bandaged. Mantle never knew the feeling of playing healthy.

Nevertheless, the young outfielder was a fast runner who matured into an awesomely powerful switch-hitter. A consistent long ball and .300 hitter in the 1950s, he played his best in 1956 when he batted .353, poled 52 homers, and drove in 130 runs—good enough for a Triple Crown and the first of three MVP awards. This made him a $100,000 player, but because he lacked charisma, struck out often, and openly vented his frustrations, he was much booed by Yankee fans. Only in his sunset seasons did the crowds open their hearts to him.

Less fortunate than Mantle was Pete Reiser, who played out a brief and tragic career mostly with the Dodgers. This rookie phenomenon won the 1941 National League batting title with a .343 average, but injured himself running into the Ebbets Field wall. After military service and just as he had regained his full powers, a similar collision in 1947 left him partially paralyzed. He was never the same: a leg injury in 1948 slowed him, and after four seasons of battling, Reiser retired. A switch hitter with power and a fielder who threw well with either arm, Reiser was a speedy, daring base-runner who once stole home seven times in a season. Durocher called Reiser the best player he ever saw, a man who "had everything but luck."[27]

That so promising an athlete failed while so ugly a duckling as "Yogi" Berra succeeded underscored fickle baseball's fortunes. The Yanks paid $500 in 1942 for this unschooled, poor boy from St. Louis. Short and stocky, Berra hit hard, but fielded poorly. He learned to catch, and despite small fingers, Berra became a skilled and durable catcher. In 17 seasons he batted .285, smote 358 homers, and walked 704 times. His laughable malapropisms—such as "Dickey learned me how to catch"—cast him as a buffoon. He queried Bobby Brown, "I liked my comic book, how did yours come out?" when he saw Brown reading *Gray's Anatomy*. When asked what he liked most about school, he replied "closed" and "recess." Still, the ugly duckling became a swan who thrice won MVP awards and set World Series records for most games played (75) and most hits (71). Upon retiring, this Hall of Famer turned to coaching and managing.

Like Mantle and Berra, other poor white boys used postwar baseball as a road to cash and glory. Another escapee from the mines was Gil Hodges, the slick-fielding, hard-hitting Dodger first baseman. Hodges played 18 seasons, appeared in seven World Series, and left with a lifetime .273 average and 470 homers. He later managed the Miracle Mets. Joining others at Cooperstown were Hodge's teammate "Duke" Snider and the slugging Ed Mathews of the Braves, who used his 512 homers for credentials.

Another poor boy whose baseball play led to the Hall of Fame was Al Kaline. Signing a $35,000 bonus offer, this untried, 19-year-old Baltimorean joined the 1954 Tigers. The following season he won his only batting title, but consistent hitting over many years produced over 3,000 hits. Retiring in the 1970s, Kaline was a $100,000-a-year star who outlasted 12 managers.

Only recently did Hall of Fame recognition come to a most formidable hitter of this era. When summoned to military service, big John Mize was an established National League slugger and batting champ. Returning from war duty, the left-handed swinger had lost his speed, but none of his strength. A valuable Yankee cog, Mize's hitting helped the Yanks win five world titles. Upon retiring, Mize owned a .312 average and a formidable slugging percentage.

Although the 1950s emphasized the big bang, some players stung pitchers with short hits. Among the best of these batters was "Nellie"

Fox, the little second baseman who played for 14 years with the White Sox. An artist with the bat, the tobacco-chewing Fox was a formidable contact hitter who once went a record 98 games without striking out. A dangerous slap hitter, he led the league in singles for seven straight years; indeed, his total of 2,663 hits included 2,161 singles.

Sadly, the prevailing homer mania kept such hitters from stardom. Among the singles was a trio of two-time batting champs: Mickey Vernon, Richie Ashburn, and Ferris Fain. Vernon, who led American hitters in 1946 and 1953, was the best bunter in the league, but a poor subject for prying reporters. "I'm not much for interviews," he admitted. "I don't talk." By comparison, Ashburn was flashy and colorful. This two-time National League bat champion, whose lifetime .308 average included 2,580 hits and 234 stolen bases, drew $57,000 as his top salary. Ashburn's performance bettered that of the forgotten Ferris Fain of the A's, who won back-to-back bat titles in 1951 and 1952.

Another limbo dweller, Billy Goodman captured the 1950 batting title. Though averaging .300, an official once curtly dismissed him as a "rag bag player."[28]

Pitching Prowess Regained

Curiously, despite the homerics of the era, pitching performances steadily improved over prewar efforts. Since the 1920s, and especially in 1930 when National League averages rose to .300, pitchers had grown accustomed to being hammered. Indeed, as late as 1936, an ERA of four runs per game was respectable, while in 1936 American pitchers averaged more than five!

Thereafter, ERAs dropped, especially during World War II when pitchers lorded over *ersatz* wartime hitters. Expectations that postwar hitters would redress the balance were stillborn. True, they pounded plenteous homers, but fewer batters topped the .300 mark. In the years of 1920 to 1941, .342 was the lowest mark posted by a batting champ in either league; in the postwar era, lesser marks often won, and in 1960 no titleist topped .330.

Such figures suggest a pitching renaissance, though the trend was uneven—there were seasons when pitchers were shelled. Indeed, prior to 1960, nine seasons passed during which pitchers in either league allowed ERAs of 4.0 or better. Lowering ERAs by 1958 indicated that pitchers dominated.

Why the pitchers turned into tigers after so many years of being cuffed about is difficult to explain. Some fans blamed homer-happy managers of the 1950s, whose bomb 'em strategy resulted in more strike-outs. However, the pitchers were themselves improving. On the whole, they were bigger, better tutored, better trained, and better armed with a variety of deliveries. Moreover, clubs carried more pitchers, including corps of relief pitchers whose effective work steadily reduced the number of complete games pitched by starters. Here, again, figures tell the tale. American League starters in 1946 completed 561 games, and the Nationals, 493; in every season after 1954 fewer than 400 complete games were pitched in either league. Thus, by 1960 reliefers were used twice as much as in 1946.

Although reliefers were used throughout the century—including some who starred in the role—until the late 1940s they were a forlorn lot. They were often jeered in their bullpens, and sometimes were bombarded by missiles. Usually they were aging or sore-armed starters; and not seldom was a reliefer some "dumb guy who'd come in and throw hard." Even their heroics went unsung, since the custom of awarding statistical "saves" was not instituted until 1960. Still, official *Baseball Encyclopedia* statisticians have blissfully awarded retroactive saves to all reliefers, both quick and dead, and the "Fireman of the Year Award" was initiated to honor the best reliefer.[29]

The heroic reliefers were indebted to "percentage playing" managers who believed left-handed pitchers were more effective against left-handed batters, and vice versa. Conventional wisdom dictated the manager's choice of which reliefer to put into the game. They were now classified as long men, middle men, and short men, with the elite short men called upon for late game duty when a few outs were needed to save a game.

Helping to upgrade the role were charismatic short men whose dramatic entrances added to the tension of games. Early in the era, the best of the short men were Joe Page, Jim Konstanty, Hoyt Wilhelm, and Roy Face. In 1947 Yankee Page epitomized the role of the heroic fireman. Once a starter, this easy-going lefty now found relieving more exciting and less arduous. Often called for late-inning heroics, Page took ten pitches to warm up his fast ball. From 1947 to 1951, the handsome, swaggering Page appeared in 205 games and saved 73.

As Page faded, the spotlight fell on Casimir "Jim" Konstanty of the champion 1950 Phillies. This failed starter became a chief reliefer and in 1949 learned his new trade in 53 appearances. In the next season, Konstanty, relying mostly on his palm ball and slider, broke into 74 games, winning 16, saving 22, and pitching the Phils to the pennant. For this display he won the league's MVP award, a rare honor for any pitcher.[30]

Konstanty faded after one brilliant season, as did Dodger Joe Black, who won Rookie of the Year honors in 1952. However, as these meteors burned out, Hoyt Wilhelm became the brightest and most durable of reliefer stars. A wounded war veteran, Wilhelm was 28 when he joined the 1952 Giants. His knuckle ball was his dependable "out" pitch; the thrown ball floated to the plate with little rotation and moved erratically under the influence of climatic conditions. One observer said the pitch "swerved like a moth in a hallway, and plumped feebly into the catcher's glove." Wilhelm was himself baffled, as were his battered catchers who tried using bigger mitts to handle the pitch. For this reason, the pitcher was often traded, although he lasted 21 seasons. When he retired in 1972, his credentials included 1,070 games played, 1,018 relief appearances, 227 saves, and a 2.52 ERA.[30]

Wilhelm was in his second season when his great rival, Elroy Face, joined the Pirates. Short and slight, Face's strength came from years of carpentry work. Boldly confident, Face's varied "out" pitches included a good fastball and a superb "fork ball." The fork ball, like the knuckler, was a dancing, teasing pitch thrown by gripping the ball between the second and third fingers of his right hand. From 1956 until 1960, Face used this pitch with telling effect and led all reliefers in appearances, saving 26 games in 1958 and rescuing three games in the 1960 World Series. More than a savior, Face won a record 22 consecutive games over 1958–1959; his 18–1 mark in 1959 set a pitching percentage record. Had he not been beaten by a broken bat single, he might have tied Marquard's National League record of 19 consecutive wins set in 1912. The "Baron of the Bullpen" became the highest paid Pirate, proving his worth for 15 years by appearing in 777 games, saving 189, and winning 92.

Among other relief aces, Dick Hyde of the lowly Senators used his submarine ball to notch nineteen saves and ten wins in 1958, personally accounting for 29 of his team's 61 victories. Ryne Duren starred that year as a fireballing Yankee reliefer, while Larry Sherry surfaced as a future Dodger hero.

The tactical use of reliefers stirred the pitching renaissance that marked the early expansion era. An artful blending of better-trained starters and reliefers went far to redeem the old maxim that pitching was 80 percent of the game.

The renaissance owed much, however, to the new and varied deliveries that pitchers added to their time-honored fast ball and curve ball repertoire. The most popular and effective new delivery of this time was the slider. Actually the same as the old "nickel curve," the slider was well known but little used. A cross between the fast ball and the curve, the slider was thrown hard like a fast ball, but upon reaching the plate it took a short break and "slid" into the strike zone. Because the pitch resembled a fastball, it baffled batters like Irv Noren: "That devilish pitch is making it harder . . . for a man to get a base hit. Most of the time it appears . . . like a fast ball until about the time you are ready to swing . . . . Then it all but hits you on the fist."[31] More easily mastered than the curve, the slider now ranked second to the fastball as a pitcher's most dependable weapon.[32]

Meanwhile, bigger and stronger pitchers challenged the batters with better fastballs. A batter's best hope for hitting one of these 90 mile-per-hour missiles that reached the plate in just less than a second was his 200 mph swing. Speeds were then measured by electronic "pitchometers"; in 1946 Bob Feller's fastball could be timed at 98.6 mph. As better devices appeared, pitchers were expected to throw at a 90 mph norm.

Such precise measuring devices eventually gave pitching coaches a valuable tool, but for now, clubs were only beginning to use pitching coaches. In 1947 the Indians named veteran pitcher Mel Harder as one of the first. Others followed, including Jim Turner, Ted Lyons, Whit Wyatt, and John Sain. The coaches diagnosed pitching weaknesses, taught techniques, and often set the starting rotation and chose relievers.[33]

The teaching and training of pitchers was a primitive art in the early 1950s. Rickey still demanded that his pitchers throw curves, and others were equally dogmatic. Because pitcher Sain was a curve master, Coach Sain urged pitchers to rely on them. Also, the coaches' judgments of speeds were faulty and they didn't know what conditioning regimens to recommend or how to deal with sore arms. The usual remedy for a sore arm was to send the wretch to the bullpen or to the minors to "work it out." If the regimen failed, little was lost since younger arms waited in the wings.

Sore-armed pitchers usually received little sympathy and were often told "it's all in your head," with cowardice hinted at. Such intolerance stung Yankee prospect Mal Mallette, who heard the same even after a physician discovered his severely injured tendon.

What the pitchers' weary arms needed was rest and, thankfully, larger staffs and four-man rotations provided this. Cleveland manager Al Lopez efficiently deployed a superb corps of starters and reliefers. From 1952 to 1954, he rotated starters Bob Lemon, Early Wynn, and Mike Garcia, who turned in a total of 188 wins. To provide rest Lopez used Feller, Hal Newhouser, and Art Houtteman as spot starters; for relief help the bullpen offered Ray Narleski and Don Mossi.

Pitching coaches now decided that a pitcher's own judgment should be heeded when warming up for duty. At one extreme, Newcombe of the Dodgers might throw 150 warmup tosses and deliver only 110 in a game; at another, Page was often ready after throwing four tosses.

Some pitchers employed a "no-windup" delivery for better control. This revival of an ancient tactic was actually the stretch motion pitchers used with men on base. Manager Stengel thought that big, powerful men like Don Larsen and Bob Turley could benefit by using the no-windup at all times. It worked for a while, but batters adapted and the fad faded.[34]

In 1955 pitchers were granted their biggest break when the strike zone was officially enlarged. The zone was defined as the "space over home plate between a batter's armpits and the top of his knees when he assumes his natural stance." Pitchers complained of crouching batters, shrunken strike zones, and umpires who refused to call strikes on the "corners." With improved coaching, however, pitchers learned pinpoint control: by "throwing to spots," they "set batters up" for unexpected pitches. Additional help came from systematic studies of batter weaknesses and from informal gossip of the same circulated by the "grapevine."

In their duel with batters, pitchers still threw at the man at the plate. The number of hit batters was averaging over 200 a season, a menacing advance over prewar averages of 130. Throwing "beanballs" was a psychological weapon used against batters who dug in or crowded the plate. While batters accepted the tactic as part of the game, they reacted violently, of course, when pitchers tried to hit them—an outlawed action, but one which umpires could never be certain of. To add to the confusion, pitchers routinely threw at batters who homered off of them, or threw at the next batter after having yielded a homer, or threw at opposing pitchers for having done the same.

Once, after one of his men was hit, manager Mel Ott ordered his

In 1954 Cleveland's vaunted pitching trio of Bob Lemon (*left*), Mike Garcia (*center*), and Early Wynn (*right*) won 65 of the team's record-breaking 111 victories. The Giants, however, downed the Indians in four straight games in the World Series.

notoriously wild pitcher to retaliate. Knowing that failure meant a fine, the pitcher took aim and miraculously hit his man on the leg. "I got him!" he shouted, and the company broke into gales of laughter, even from the umpire. When hot-hitting Dino Restelli was beaned, however, it was no laughing matter. Struck on the shoulder by one of Ewell Blackwell's wicked deliveries, Restelli never regained his confidence.

Still, veteran hurlers like Maglie, Reynolds, or Wynn wasted little sympathy on batters. All three claimed the outside three inches of the plate as their turf—any encroaching batter was knocked down. Indeed, Wynn's catcher used a special sign for the knockdown pitch.[35]

The appearance of batting helmets after 1952 brought some relief to batters, but pitchers too were vulnerable. Being hit by a line drive was a constant fear, and whistling liners sometimes found their target. Kirby Higbe of the Dodgers had marks on most areas of his body as proof. Years after smashing a liner off the aluminum leg of

Two of the winningest postwar era pitchers were Robin Roberts (*left*) of the Phillies, who notched a lifetime total of 268 wins, and Early Wynn (*right*) of the Senators, Indians, and White Sox, who won an even 300.

war veteran Lou Brissie, Ted Williams still shuddered at the memory. The most tragic incident came in 1957 when Gil McDougald's liner ruined the career of Herb Score. McDougald's missile struck the talented pitcher on the right eye and he fell, bleeding from nose, mouth, and eye. His nose was fractured and his eye so distorted that it was feared he would lose his sight. After a slow recovery, Score attempted a comeback, but it was in vain.

The best pitchers mastered both their fears and the hitters. Among the redoubtable starters of the 1950s who entered the Hall of Fame were two left-handers: Warren Spahn, the winningest southpaw ever, and "Whitey" Ford, who owned the best winning percentage. Early Wynn, Bob Feller, Bob Lemon, and Robin Roberts are a few of the right-handers who were also enshrined.

Ironically, the incomparable Spahn was so relentlessly efficient as to be taken for granted. This slender lefty was 25 when he rejoined the Braves after the war and won his first big league game. The hard-throwing Spahn added the curve, slider, sinker, screwball, changeup, and a superb pickoff to his repetoire of pitches. In 1947 he won 21 games and posted a league-leading 2.33 ERA. The next year he pitched the Braves to the pennant, one of only three championship seasons in his long career. Still, "Chief Hawknose" was a consistent winner, a record-setting strike-out artist who fanned at least 100 batters a season for 17 straight years. He also topped the 20-victory mark thirteen times and his 363 wins included 63 shut-outs.

Spahn, an ageless marvel, was 39 when he pitched his first of two no-hitters. At 42-years old he won 23 games with a 2.60 ERA, but then age and bad knees caught up with him. He was released unconditionally in 1965; the announcement that he might be claimed for a token $1 waiver fee brought a response from a hopeful little league team.

Burly Early Wynn, a year older than Spahn, also joined the 300-win circle. Dubbed "Gus" by his mates, this intimidating right-hander pitched with icy concentration. As part of his pitching rhythm, he routinely threw at any batter who dared dig in. Two of Wynn's stable-mates also entered the Hall: Bob Feller and Bob Lemon. When Feller was called for military service in 1942, he was an established star with a string of strike-out records and three 20-win seasons. He returned in 1946 and his 26 victories in one year included a no-hitter and 348 strike-outs. Before retiring in 1956, he posted two more 20-victory seasons and twice led the league in strike-outs. He finished with 266 wins and 2,581 strike-outs. Bob Lemon, a 25-year-old third baseman in 1946, was another of the immortal right-handed pitchers. Because he threw a natural sinker ball he was converted to pitching. Though the immediate results were nominal, two years later he won twenty games; this would be the first of seven such seasons. Lemon won 207 games in a 13-year career.

Robin Roberts of the Phillies was more impressive than any of these pitchers. A bonus baby signed out of the University of Michigan, Roberts needed little more than his fastball, and so never developed a varied repetoire or used intimidating tactics. This rapid-working control pitcher challenged batters to hit his pitch. Big and strong, he thrived on work, averaging 300 innings a season and starting 609 games in his career. The clean-living, church-going Roberts slept 10 hours a night and lasted in baseball until he was 40. From 1950 to 1955, he won twenty or more games each season, and had he been with a winning team or heeded advice to arm himself with a slider he might have bettered his 268 career victories.

Ed "Whitey" Ford of the Yankees, another of this pride, outclassed the great trio of Raschi, Reynolds, and Lopat. This brash, cocky New Yorker joined the 1950 Yanks when he was 21 years old. He finished his career with 236 wins, 45 shut-outs, a 2.75 ERA, and a winning percentage of .690.

Louis "Bobo" Newsom and Jim Bunning, sadly overlooked by Hall of Fame electors, deserve reconsideration. Newsome, a barrel-chested right-hander, retired in 1953, having pitched since 1929. One of the most bartered players of all time, Newsome won 211 games. Another 200-game winner, strike-out king Jim Bunning won over one hundred games for the Tigers in the 1950s. When traded to the Phillies, he won 100 games in the National League and joined company with Cy Young.

Strangely enough, it was 1956 before officials honored great pitching. That year the new Cy Young Award went to Newcombe of the Dodgers as the best seasonal performer. The next four awarded went to Spahn, Bob Turley, Wynn, and Vern Law. Prior to 1967, only one award was given, but thereafter the best in each league was honored. Regrettably, the award came too late to honor Sain or Maglie, a pair of gifted right-handers who later became outstanding coaches.

The Darkness Before Dawn

It was the fate of most postwar players to miss out on the dawning affluent age. These old-timers came to know by bitter comparison just how dark it was before the dawn. Certainly this generation had problems: they naturally worried over salary cuts, trades, blacklisting, and peremptory dismissals. A 1979 *Sporting News* article reported that Joe Garagiola accepted $600 a month in 1946; his best salary of $14,000 was earned in 1951, his last year of play. The same article implied that Tony Kubek signed with the Yankees in 1956 for a $1,500 bonus, made only $7,000 as the 1957 Rookie of the Year, and narrowly escaped a pay cut in 1959. In nine seasons his highest reported annual salary was $36,000, and he remembers once being told that his World Series check counted as a raise.[36]

The threat of blacklisting remained. This surfaced in 1946 when the Mexican League jumpers were inveighed against. Though a lawsuit at a later time prohibited this action, writer Roger Kahn related that Carl Furillo was barred from a job in baseball for daring to sue owner O'Malley for back pay in 1960. Fortunately, players of this time enjoyed a pension plan, which provided a qualifying player with a regular income when he reached age 50. A few players in the

1960s drew small sum; Kirby Higbe was paid $210 a month and Hank Thompson received $225.

As always the players worried about their postplaying careers. Unlike some other professional athletes, many ball players didn't have college degrees and could not move easily into the business world. Nor did owners care what happened to pink-slipped players. In 1953 the Phillies became the first club to look after their alumni when owner Bob Carpenter gave each veteran a season's pass and a subscription to a newsletter. A news item in one of those letters told of retired Phillies working at sixty different jobs. Most owners knew nothing of the whereabouts of their retirees. This fact came to light when medical researchers, seeking a link between tobacco chewing and cancer, could obtain almost no data from club owners. The Cincinnati Reds were among the first to try to locate their alumni. Interestingly, the Metropolitan Life Insurance Company researchers discovered in a study that recent baseball retirees lived longer than those of past generations, and that for some strange reason third basemen lived longest of all players. More importantly, writer Roger Kahn's interviews with the Dodgers of the 1950s showed that in retirement these men lived out their years in quiet desperation.[37]

Most retirees did adjust, and some even prospered. Among others, Garagiola, Piersall, Rizzuto, and Ashburn found profitable careers as sportscasters, while Chuck Connors became an actor. For those seeking baseball careers, however, the opportunities were few. Some of the great Yankee and Dodger stars became managers and coaches; others, like Gil MacDougald, Enos Slaughter, and Ed Stanky, became college coaches. Most players fell into a variety of ordinary jobs; only a few—like Dr. Bobby Brown, the heart specialist, or Congressman Wilmer Mizell—gained fame in second careers.[38]

To invest one's youth in pursuit of a big league career that averaged four years in duration was an awesome commitment, and players were rightly paranoid about its sudden ending. Moving day, even for regulars, was never far off. Since 1900, no outfield combination had played together for more than six years and no infield quartet lasted more than five—the Pirate outfield of Clemente, Virdon, and Skinner lasted six years and the Dodger infield of Hodges, Robinson, Reese, and Cox lasted five. Four years was the longest stretch any eight-man lineup played together.

Players lived with the constant terrible knowledge that to fail was to be fired, and slumps, errors, injuries, and losses virtually guaranteed failure. Even the best players sometimes embarrassed themselves. Once, good-hitting George Kell went hitless in ten at bats in a 20-inning game; in a doubleheader Al Dark got one hit, fanned three times, made two errors, and was ejected by an umpire. Indeed, the peerless DiMaggio once caught a ball and thought he had made the third out. He raced to the clubhouse while the winning run scored.

Because even the best were booed, crowd fear was endemic. Browns owner Bill DeWitt employed a psychiatrist to help his players cope with such tensions. While poor attendance reduced the threat of agoraphobia, Dr. David Tracy's mass hypnosis failed to boost playing performances. He was ridiculed and soon dismissed.

Players sometimes needed professional help, some desperately, as dramatized by Piersall's nervous breakdown and Dodger pitcher Willie Ramsdell's suicide. Many suffered from alcoholism and marital troubles; and most needed legal and business advice, especially when bargaining for salaries. Still, owners insisted on isolating players. Agents were barred, and if some stars used them to set up investment ventures, they ran the risk of hiring a crook. Although Mickey Mantle was successfully swindled out of his first World Series check, the club assisted him in escaping a bad deal by which a crooked agent was promised half of his lifetime endorsement income.[39]

Such was the sad lot of postwar players, who were locked into a disadvantaged time frame. For being born too soon, they were fated to play out their careers under conditions soon to be swept aside by reformist winds. Thus, fate made them onlookers who could hardly be blamed for envying the fortune-favored new breed.

Postwar Potpourri

The Changing of the Guard

The owners who controlled the players of the postwar era continued to wield ultimate power over baseball. There were indeed times when a strong league president like Ban Johnson or a commissioner like Judge Landis ruled, but their powers were limited. Johnson's strength owed a debt to a united front of American League owners against the Nationals, but once the American League was airborne, the president's wings were clipped. The same happened with Landis after memories of the Black Sox scandal receded.

Most of the sixteen major league club owners of 1946 had battled through the depression years. Each owner ruled by his franchise rights to field a team in a well-defined territory, a park which might be owned or leased, and a number of players. The owners' control over players was the major source of their power.[1]

Seldom united, the owners were often disputatious and fiercely independent. Indeed, no typical owner nor club existed. Clubs differed by owner personalities and policies, geographical location, personnel, and a host of tangibles and intangibles, including ethereal traditions.

By 1946 fans and writers believed that owners were essential to baseball. This mystique was embellished by those owners who posed as civic-minded gentlemen-sportsmen. Cynics disputed this claim, holding that most owners were mercenary investors looking for glory and profits, a contention difficult to quell since the accused refused to divulge financial statements.

If, as in the opinion of a *Fortune* magazine writer, "Nobody ever bought . . . a club because it represented the soundest way of making money," then also few ever went bankrupt in baseball. Most benefited—some lived off their club earnings, some used baseball to boost business or political interests, and all gained prestige through their involvement.

Given the modest worth of baseball investments at this time, the payoff in prestige was inordinately large. In 1937, for example, the most expensive club cost about $600,000 a year to operate, while salaries for all the major league players totaled less than $500,000. Although a small scale industry, baseball was run like no other.[2] Owners were bound together in a common enterprise, and rituals, such as annual meetings, rules, and commissioner rulings, contributed to their organization. Some called this a monopoly, although it more aptly resembled an ineffective cartel. Instead of pulling together, each owner ran his club his own way; in a larger scheme, however, rivalries and divisive cliques did often form and subsequently clashed.

An anonymous opinion, "Baseball must be a great game because it survives the people who run it," could be applied to the owners of 1946. Their ranks were in fact thinning; within a decade old age and death cut down at least ten, including hoary old Connie Mack and Clark Griffith.

Once a formidable figure, by 1946 Mack was an anachronism. Heavily in debt by 1950, he saw his once powerful Philadelphia franchise tottering. He had outlived his legend and was left a tight-fisted, horse-playing curmudgeon. Forced to sell in 1953, he watched sorrowfully as his successor, Arnold Johnson, quickly moved the club to Kansas City. Within a year of the transfer, the nonagenarian was dead.[3]

Griffith's Washington Senator franchise, like Mack's, resembled a general store in a supermarket era. By 1950 his stadium was antiquated, lacking comforts and parking space. History was kinder to this "old fox"—who is credited with the preservation of baseball during World War II and with the opening of doors to Latin American players—yet soon after his death in 1955, his foster son Calvin jumped at the chance to move the club to Minnesota in the 1961 expansion.

The changing of the guard also saw the passing of the famous Comiskey family at Chicago. Mrs. Grace R. Comiskey, the second female owner in baseball history, labored from 1941 until her death in 1956 to keep the White Sox in the family. Dubious of her son's abilities, she passed her shares to her daughter, Dorothy Rigney, touching off a bitter legal battle which ended with the 1959 sale of the club to a syndicate headed by Bill Veeck.

Likewise, the death of Walter O. Briggs in 1952 ended another notable dynasty. Briggs's interest in the Tigers harked back to 1919; in 1935 he installed his son, W.O. "Spike" Briggs, Jr., as heir apparent. After the father's death, however, lawyers for his estate declared the Tigers an imprudent investment and barred young Briggs from using estate money to buy the club. After four years of wrangling, the team was sold for $5.5 million to a syndicate headed by radio-television executive John E. Fetzer, who gained full control by 1960.

Similarly, the executors of the Jacob Ruppert estate sold the Yankees in 1945 to Leland S. MacPhail, Del Webb, and Dan Topping, Jr. for the wartime bargain price of $2.8 million. The purchase was a vintage MacPhail coup. On leave from military duties, he heard of the opportunity and without funds, brashly signed a purchase agreement. MacPhail recruited wealthy sportsman Topping, who in turn brought in Webb with the lion's share of the cash. Webb later admitted that he joined into the deal to gain lucrative stadium contracts for his construction firm. MacPhail, however, was soon gone from the Yankees. Ever the stormy petrel, he fought with his co-owners and general manager Weiss, and sold out in 1947. Topping assumed control, and with Weiss as his advisor, the team became the league power and Topping ruled in league councils.[4]

Veteran owner Alva Bradley was meanwhile ousted from his Cleveland ownership. Learning that Bradley lacked full stock control, young Veeck teamed with two wealthy colleagues and bought majority control of the Indians for $1.2 million. Baseball itself would benefit from this deal because of Veeck's enthusiasm.

The Indian coup was the peripatetic Veeck's first of three ownership stints. By 1975 he was thrice harried out, but returned four times to the delight of players, fans, and writers, who admired his free-wheeling style. The son of a former Chicago Cub general manager, Veeck was born to the game. A World War II injury cost him a leg and continuing complications threatened his life, but baseball promotion provided his *élan vital*. A profitable minor league system led him to bid on the Phillies in 1943, but officials snubbed him and branded him a dangerous maverick. As a promoter he hatched promotional schemes that included an exploding scoreboard, baby-sitting facilities, and a variety of free "give aways" that might include "anything but free tickets." He angered mossback owners, but his enterprise charmed Cleveland fans, who came two million strong to the park.

Personal financial difficulties forced him to sell out in the following year. However, Veeck never disappeared from baseball because he always courted wealthy backers who admired his style and trusted his baseball sense. He bought the St. Louis Browns in 1951, for less than $1 million, but failed to save that dying franchise. By dint of promotional stunts—like playing a midget—he doubled the team's miserable attendance. When the rival Cardinals fell into wealthy hands, Veeck's battle to survive in St. Louis was sadly lost.[5]

Veeck sought in vain to move to a more lucrative site, but opposing owners forced him to stay in St. Louis. Drained by financial losses, he staggered through the 1953 season. Finally, he was allowed to sell to a Baltimore syndicate.

The indomitable Veeck resurfaced six years later as the purchaser of the White Sox. After a glorious pennant-winning debut, a final amputation of his leg amounted to a virtual death sentence and forced him to sell his interest to the brothers Arthur and John Allyn.[6]

Veeck survived and prospered over the next several years as a racetrack operator, though he longed to get back into baseball. He returned in 1979, but lasted only two years before soaring expenses drove him out.[5] Still, no owner was so beloved as Veeck. He wittily revealed in three autobiographical works what went on among owners. In two of these volumes, *A Hustler's Handbook* and *Veeck—As In Wreck,* he told how wealthy men bought clubs to become celebrities, to gain tax advantages, and to enhance their outside businesses. Manipulators like O'Malley, carpetbaggers, and commissioners felt his wit-lashing and fumed over his reform proposals.[6]

Veeck was the first to put the players' names on the backs of their uniforms; in 1976 he outfitted his White Sox with three different uniforms, including briefly used shorts for hot weather. He constantly nettled his colleagues with brash proposals like limiting the authority of umpires, shortening games with automatic intentional walks, suggesting interleague games, and, most shocking of all, urging the equal division of television receipts. None of these were adopted, but Veeck never stopped tinkering and thinking. He was a rare owner who loved the fans and mingled with them; his sideshows, meant to lure and entertain audiences, occasionally turned riotous. For his enterprise, he was accused of turning baseball into a popular entertainment. Veeck cheerfully pleaded guilty to this, yet he never slighted the game on the field.[7]

If only Veeck had been blessed with owner Tom Yawkey's wealth. Like Veeck, Yawkey was the son of a baseball executive, but the comparison ended there. Yawkey inherited a $20 million fortune from his adoptive father; in time this swelled to $200 million. Incredibly, after lavishing $10 million over 40 years on his Boston Red Sox, Yawkey never landed a world title.

Throughout his long tenure Yawkey embodied the myth of the gentleman-sportsman owner. Though some owners thought he was eccentric, Yawkey enjoyed the company of his players and was generous to all his employees, coddling them with high salaries. Out of this grew Boston's reputation as a haven for lazy players; but when players won bargaining rights, Yawkey begrudged their gains, complaining, ironically, of pampered players.

This "sportsman owner" never blamed himself for inspiring baseball's high salary trend or for continuing the racist policies. After opposing the first black, he remained stubbornly unrepentant. Yawkey's prejudice prevented Willie Mays from playing for Boston; as it was, his team was the last to field black players. Yawkey died in 1976 and left a legacy of grudging acceptance of black players in Boston. Still, his reputation as a gentleman-sportsman owner earned him a place in the Hall of Fame.[8]

Although Yawkey was the last of the species in the American League, its twin league also hosted some sportsman claimants who sought to influence the game. Yawkey's National League counterpart was Philip K. Wrigley of the Chicago Cubs. Wrigley also fell heir to an enormous fortune handed down by a baseball-hobbyist father. The elder Wrigley gained control of the Cubs in 1925 and willed the club to his 38-year-old son Philip in 1932 along with control of the family chewing gum empire.

Shy and aloof, owner Wrigley landed four pennants through

1945. He strove in those years to improve his team and the game at large. To strengthen his team, he expanded the farm system and financed scientific schemes for spotting promising recruits who would be nurtured in a developmental academy. He also hired, first, a psychologist for his own team, and then, a sorcerer to hex opposing teams! He sponsored staff studies on alternatives to the reserve clause and on the feasibility of night baseball.

However, only his farm system worked. The psychologist was shunned by sneering players and Wrigley escaped ridicule by prudently keeping the sorcerer caper quiet. Wrigley might have become a genuine reformer, but most of his studies never saw daylight. A tinkerer, he liked to scheme and plan, but feared implementation. His night baseball plan was creative, but when others beat him to it, Wrigley stubbornly forbade night ball at Wrigley Field. His players complained of playing half daylight and half night games, but Wrigley insisted that baseball was a day game and that nearby residents might be disturbed by the bustle of night traffic. At least Wrigley Field fans benefited from his concern. Many judged his as the neatest park in the land, boasting comfortable seats and loudspeakers that carried radio commentaries. Ivy grew on outfield walls, and the only advertising permitted was an unobtrusive pair of imps, totems of the gum firm.

A kind and concerned employer, Wrigley gave his fans their money's worth, and until the coming of baseball unionism, his Cubs were the best paid and treated of all players. Like the patriarchal Yawkey, however, Wrigley rewarded players on his own terms and became testy when confronted by unionists. Yet few knew this recluse. After 1945 he attended few games, shunned fellow owners, and avoided Cub stockholder meetings—though no threat was posed since he owned 80 percent of the club stock.

Comfort without glory was the lot of Cub fans. From 1946 through 1977, Wrigley's teams owned the worst record of any major league club. They finished in the second division in 26 of those seasons, and their rare challenges ended in ignominious collapse. The fault clearly lay with Wrigley; for demanding and rewarding obedience and loyalty, he attracted complacent and sycophantic players and officials. Still, a man who once promoted a loyal concessions manager to general manager could not expect any better.

Wrigley's ill-advised kindnesses to rival owners also hurt his team. When O'Malley sought to move his Dodgers into the Cub-owned minor league territory of Los Angeles, Wrigley eased his rival's path

Postwar baseball club owners: reclusive Philip Wrigley (*left*) of the Cubs and flamboyant Bill Veeck, Jr. (*right*) of the Indians, Browns, and White Sox.

by selling his holdings for one million dollars less than O'Malley offered. Earlier, Wrigley had approved Perini's Milwaukee move though it encroached on Cub territory.

Such generosity in the dog-in-the-manger world of owners was apt to be one-sided. As Wrigley allowed his farm system to founder and indulged in foolhardy schemes, like using rotating coaches as field managers, rivals snickered and kicked the hapless Cubs about. When the 82-year-old Wrigley died in April of 1977, the reins of the family business passed to his 47-year-old son, William Wrigley III. By then, Chicagoans could be forgiven for wishing away the honor of being served by a gentleman-sportsman.[9]

Cub fans were not the only ones so served. August Busch, Jr., more tough-minded than Wrigley, affected the sportsman-owner image with the St. Louis Cardinals. This wealthy brewer was cut in the mold of the magnate owners of the 1890s, but no 19th-century brewer-magnate matched his wealth. The scion of the Anheusers and Buschs who built the great beer empire, August Jr. succeeded his father as head of Anheuser-Busch in the late 1940s. Under his direction the company met such success that by 1979 annual sales totaled $3.3 billion and profits $144.2 million.

Busch applied his business magic to save a shaky franchise when he purchased the Cardinals in 1953. The steadily declining club fortunes had reached crisis proportions in 1952 when owner Fred Saigh was indicted and sentenced for income tax evasion. Busch saved the day by buying the team for $3.75 million. Although he posed as a public benefactor, Sportsman's Park became Busch Stadium and the Cards helped to promote his frothy product. Running the brewery took much of his time, but, still, the self-styled "Big Eagle" hovered over the team, fussing and meddling in its operations. The team was Busch's fancy toy to be shown off to friends, whom he invited to don uniforms and work out with the players. These charades continued until general manager Frank Lane dissuaded him, saying, "You're too smart a man to have people poking fun at you."[10]

Along with other mistakes, that *lese majesty* cost Lane his job. Patriarch Busch demanded obedience, loyalty, and praise. Given proper deference, he was generous to his baseball "family"; until the players won bargaining rights, Busch's payroll was among the highest. Moreover, the proud owner invested $5 million of company money toward the public financing of a capacious new park in downtown St. Louis—this also bore his name.

Busch's fear of the independence and affluence of players changed the owner from a mere conservative to a sour, testy reactionary who lashed out at "mercenary" players and complained that baseball no longer belonged to the owners. He petulantly hired and fired managers and general managers, and in one blundering fit of anger, triggered by Steve Carlton's salary holdout, he traded a future Hall of Famer for an average player. He would not relent, but continually railed at colleagues for not being tougher with the demands of players.

Of course, all his bluster could neither put baseball back where he wanted it, nor produce pennants from his tension-riddened team. In the late 1970s he relinquished the team to his son and secluded himself at his estate.

Luckily, old guarders like Busch had wealth to fall back upon. Horace Stoneham of the Giants was not so fortunate. Like the Griffiths, Stoneham was one of the last of another vanishing species—the independent clubowner who relied on baseball for his livelihood.

Born the son of Charles A. Stoneham, the New York gambler, bookie, and ticket scalper who purchased the Giants in 1919, the 32-year-old Horace inherited the club in 1936. He was a chubby man who looked like a soft touch, but who knew baseball. After winning back-to-back pennants in the 1930s, he waited fourteen years for another take. Then, in 1951, by dint of shrewd trades, and sound player development, he won the miracle pennant and repeated the performance in 1954.

Unfortunately, the ramshackle Polo Grounds and its deteriorating neighborhood no longer attracted crowds. Stoneham, facing certain bankruptcy, harkened to O'Malley's proposed west coast movement. Actually, Stoneham had no choice; New York writers knew this and poured most of their ire on O'Malley, while Stoneham prospered. The San Francisco move was a shot in the arm—his Giants averaged a million fans a year for ten seasons.

Despite the generous terms of his lease, Stoneham's Candlestick Park was a liability. The fans and players suffered, plagued by the cold, wind, and fog. Still worse, in 1968 Charles Finley moved his A's into an encroaching position at Oakland across the bay.

The beginning of the end was in sight for the financially strapped Stoneham. He was a player's owner—overly sentimental and generous to a fault—who overspent on salaries and benefits. When attendance tailed off, he cut back on player development, sold his athletes, and in 1976, sold his beloved club for $8 million. The purchasers, Bob Lurie of San Francisco and Arthur Herseth of Phoenix, Arizona, typified the new breed of wealthy, corporate owners. Having no previous connection with Lurie, meat-packer Herseth showed up with $4 million and bought in, saying: "I'm fifty-five years old and I figure it's time I had a little fun."[11]

Such men of wealth by then dominated the owner ranks. During the war years and for a decade thereafter, every National League club but the Cubs and Giants changed hands. First to go were the owners of the Braves and Phillies. In 1943 Boston contractor Lou Perini took over the Braves, and later used falling attendance as an excuse to move to Milwaukee. For this, Boston fans dubbed him "the Benedict Arnold of baseball." Perini, however, netted a profit of $600,000 in his first year at Milwaukee, and in 1962 sold out at a fat profit to a Chicago syndicate headed by Bill Bartholomay.

Meanwhile, the Phillies grew strong under stable new ownership. The bankrupt Jerry Nugent sold the club in 1943 to the National League for $500,000; the league then resold it to William Cox for $230,000. Before the year was out Cox was ousted for protesting decisions and for betting. This turbulent year ended with the purchase of the Phillies by Robert M. Carpenter.

A scion of the wealthy Dupont family, the low-keyed Carpenter hired an astute general manager and spent lavishly on bonus babies. Philadelphia fans responded by rallying to the Phillies. The Phillies prospered even when Carpenter routinely closed his office over the winter months.

In the wake of World War II, another National League team, the Pittsburgh Pirates, changed hands. Bill Benswanger sold the team in 1946 for $2.5 million to Ohio syndicate head John Galbreath. If this millionaire preferred building skyscrapers and raising horses to baseball, still his money made the team a contender.[12]

As the Pirates waxed strong, so did the Reds. Long under impersonal foundation control, club operations were handled by a succession of general managers, including Warren Giles and Gabe Paul. In 1960 Bill De Witt succeeded Paul and later bought the club from the foundation, but resold it for $7 million in 1966. The new buyer was a local syndicate, headed by newspaper publisher Francis Dale, which has continued to operate the Reds as a civic enterprise while delegating operations to general managers.

Thus, the dawning of the expansion era witnessed a changing owner guard, as the wealthy plutocrats moved in. Because many were neophytes, they looked to Walter O'Malley of the Dodgers for indoctrination and leadership. O'Malley's impact was so great that his place among the famed shaping trio of the new age seems assured.

GMs to the Fore

Businessmen-owners, entering the baseball landscape, brought formalized business practices to club operations. One such transferred custom introduced cadres of experts, hired to deal with the growing complexities of baseball promotion: legal problems, taxes, television contracts, public relations, promotional campaigns, insurance matters, and others. Not least among the experts' tasks was that of concealing the ignorance of their masters.

In the postwar era, the general manager (or "GM,") was the most visible specialist. Few owners ran their own shows; most employed general managers and endowed them with titles like President, Vice-President, and sometimes the formidable appellative of "General Manager and Executive Vice-President." The generic term "general manager" applied to any hireling charged mainly with the procurement, recruitment, and development of players.

The GM was no new presence. Billy Evans was among the first of this group to appear, having stepped into the Cleveland post in 1928 when bewildered owners sought an experienced baseball man. Others followed suit, and in 1940 most clubs had GMs.

By the 1950s these ubiquitous experts were vested with such authority that ancient Clark Griffith complained: "Baseball was healthier when we all owned our teams and had to depend on our ingenuity to make a living. When you talked trade in those days, you spoke with men who had authority. Now it has to go through channels." Stengel was in agreement; he aimed shots at anti-Yankee GMs like Frank Lane and Hank Greenberg: "The post of general manager is a latter day origination. . . . Not until the rich men got into the game as a hobby . . . was the post created."[13]

Of course, the archetypical GM was the legendary Rickey, who built the great Cardinal and Dodger dynasties and labored in his twilight years to vitalize the Pirates. Most GMs were now Rickey imitators, including veterans Eddie Collins of the Red Sox and the wondrously successful George Weiss of the Yanks.

Weiss built a farm system for the Yankees that was a model of profitable efficiency. His scouts signed hundreds of young players and Weiss cut the ordinaries, content with getting one prospect out of 25. The best of the lot stocked the Yankees for years, and by selling the surplus Weiss netted $2 million for his bosses. In addition, if a seasoned player was needed, Weiss used his surplus as bargaining chips.

Nobody outworked this humorless, introverted man who often labored every day of the week. The chief mission of the zealous Weiss was to field a strong and deep Yankee team, which he did by recruiting, farming, and supervising hordes of prospects.

The aging Weiss had many detractors and few friends. The New York press viewed him as cold and dictatorial, while Yankee players who talked salary with him perceived their natural enemy. Usually Weiss won these battles by bullying or by invoking the myth of the Yankee family. Although Weiss boosted the myth by loans and medical assistance grants, he tried to recoup by holding down salaries.

Weiss was well paid, being the first GM to earn over $100,000 a year, and he was honored by colleagues, who voted him more Executive of the Year awards than any other. But the man who had a hand in the signing of every Yankee player earned his pay. Indeed, he hired Stengel to pilot the Yankee champs of the 1950s.

Even this genius, however, was vulnerable. Weiss and Stengel were dumped after the 1960 World Series loss. This dose of Weiss's own medicine hurt. He cleared his desk, left without a word, and later suffered his first bout with ulcers. The malady disappeared when he became GM of the expansion Mets in 1961. By hiring Yankee discards Stengel and Berra, he scored an avenging coup when the Mets outdrew the fading Yankees. Weiss served for six seasons, laying the foundations for the Mets's 1969 victory. A year before his death in 1972, he joined Rickey in the Hall of Fame.

Thanks to Rickey and Weiss, the recognition of the GM as a vital cog was rampant. Owner Busch learned at this time that a brewery executive could not do the job. The GMs of the 1950s came from varied backgrounds, some from the player ranks or minor league posts, while a few, like Veeck or John Quinn, were born to the job. John Quinn learned from his father, a former owner of the Red Sox and, later, a GM for the Braves and Dodgers. Quinn succeeded his father as the Braves's GM and built three champion teams, scoring coups by signing Hank Aaron and pitcher John Antonelli. Quinn then moved on to the Phillies and served as GM until his 1972 retirement. During his tenure, the Phillies narrowly missed a pennant and of Quinn's 17 player trades, 13 were rated "pluses." When he died in 1976, his son became the third generation of Quinns to serve in this role.

Three of Rickey's protégés won "Executive of the Year" awards. One, Bill De Witt, in a long career as GM and sometime owner of various clubs, built champion teams. Another, Joe L. Brown, son of the movie comedian, apprenticed under Rickey during the woeful Pirate years, then presided over the team turned dynasty in the 1970s.

Rickey disciple Emil J. (Buzzy) Bavasi succeeded the master in 1950. As General Manager and Executive Vice-President of the Dodgers, Bavasi basked in the Brooklyn glory years, then rebuilt the team in Los Angeles. The tough-bargaining Bavasi prided himself on his ability to defeat player salary demands, but he met his own comeuppance in 1966 when Koufax and Drysdale staged a joint holdout. Bavasi also took credit for persuading the reluctant O'Malley to retain manager Walt Alston. However, when O'Malley's son came of age, Bavasi was dumped.[14]

Gabriel Paul, another effective GM, apprenticed under Warren Giles in the minors, then followed GM Giles to Cincinnati, and in 1950 succeeded to the post. With the Reds, Paul was handicapped by an austere budget, but this GM had the mind of a poker player and by dint of canny trades, built a firm contender. The poker model also applied to "Trader" Frank Lane, who preferred wild card games. Lane emerged as GM of the 1948 White Sox, the first of six posts in his mercurial career. Charged with rebuilding, he landed pitcher Billy Pierce and infielder Nelson Fox. Lane made 240 trades in seven years with the Sox, dealing so compulsively that his men feared to send out their laundry lest they be gone before pick up time!

Unfortunately, Lane blundered at St. Louis, giving up Bill Virdon for a nobody, and then assured his ouster by dealing away the popular Red Schoendienst. Hired by Cleveland in the late 1950s, Lane dealt Roger Maris for two journeymen, swapped managers with Detroit, and offered to trade his entire team for the Tiger team. All this was very heady, but when Lane traded heroes Rocky Colavito and Herb Score, he was hanged in effigy and sent packing.

By 1955 Lane had concocted over 200 trades, and before his career ended, he managed 500. While this frenzied wheeler-dealer popularized the trading mystique, he was never credited with a championship. Nevertheless, traders like Lane fortified the myth that GMs were more important than field managers. While Rickey and Weiss lent substance to the notion, Lane's flashy moves exaggerated the dealer function and downplayed the important task of player recruitment and development, a vital function in a time of increasing talent scarcity.[15]

The Landis Legacy

Since 1920 baseball owners had been burdened by an albatross of their own creation. This beast was the Commissioner, a supposed arbiter of power created for the sanctimonious purpose of persuading the public that there would be no more chicanery in baseball—like the Black Sox scandal. For taking on this magistrate, owners paid the price of abiding the stern Judge Landis, whose theatrical posturing and popular appeal lasted until his death.

Landis's Olympian reputation as the man who housecleaned the game eventually galled the owners. In suffering this Commissioner, the owners immediately learned the bitter lesson that if you empower a saint, you make yourselves sinners. Having grasped this point, the owners determined to bury the power with the man, and when the 78-year-old curmudgeon died in 1944, no succeeding Commissioner ever wielded such authority. Even in death, however, Landis had his way. As if following Nietzche's advice of "know when to die," Landis left the Commissionership as a legacy, and owners were compelled to continue the office. They did this, but future incumbents learned that survival depended on serving their owner-masters.[16]

The owners waited a decent interval after Judge Landis's death before naming a successor. At the December, 1944 meetings, owners unanimously pledged to retain the office with all its powers, but hedged by declaring that future Commissioners must be approved by a three-fourths majority of owner votes.

During the interregnum, the air crackled with names of possible successors. National League President Ford Frick was much talked about, along with highly touted outsiders like Jim Farley, Fred Vinson, and Senator A.B. Chandler. These outsiders were well-known Democratic politicians: Farley and Vinson had been Roosevelt allies, and "Happy" Chandler was the Senator whose 1942 cry of "Let's keep 'em playing" kept wartime baseball alive.

The warring owners divided into embattled cliques. Nobody expected a quick decision at the April, 1945 meeting called to screen the candidates, but MacPhail, caucusing behind the scenes, rounded up votes for Chandler; the electors fell in line as soon as the senator was nominated. The sudden announcement that Chandler would become the new Commissioner took the baseball world by surprise.

Albert Benjamin Chandler was also surprised. In his drawling, southern accent, the big, smiling senator exulted: "Ah love baseball. . . . I would rather be Commissioner of Baseball than President of the United States."[17] In sooth, Chandler had gone as far politically as a Kentucky politician could expect. The 47-year-old had served his state as Lt. Governor, Governor, and Senator. The role of Commissioner of Baseball now afforded him a national podium and a $50,000 salary that was five times that of his senatorial stipend.

In the honeymoon period that succeeded his election, writers welcomed his good-humored folksiness and predicted a "happy" era. They, in fact, were wrong. Before the year was out, Chandler's flamboyance alarmed the owners, who belatedly realized that this man had a mind and mouth of his own. Chandler lectured his bosses, saying, "You don't own the game. . . . The game belongs to the American people." He followed this with a promise that "the stands will go empty" if people think that owners put profits foremost.[18]

The words could have been ghostly Landis utterances, but the mouth and mannerisms were human and vulnerable. Functioning as the part-time Commissioner while closing out his senatorial duties, his few moves stirred controversy. Minor league officials rejected his baseball promotional scheme; major league owners carped at the small sum he got selling radio rights to the World Series and at his support of raises for umpires. The honeymoon first year ended with talk of his ouster.

Chandler, ignoring the storm signals, boldly tackled the issues challenging baseball. Most pressing were the racial question, the Mexican League threat, the specter of player unionism, and the press of television—and all seemed contingent upon the questionable power of the Commissioner to deal with issues. When Chandler backed Jackie Robinson, he angered some owners, but more blamed his blacklisting of Mexican League jumpers for inciting a lawsuit against the reserve clause. Moreover, his attempt to defuse the players' union by supporting a pension plan to be funded by radio and television money set a dangerous precedent. When he negotiated his first World Series television pact, he was lambasted for selling too cheaply.

A seer might have perceived that these heavy issues broadly outlined the unfolding course of baseball history. Chandler, however, pragmatic and fumbling, was no baseball statesman. His weakness was his need for public adulation, and his enemies cited his folksy cracker-barrel commentaries and his occasional folk-singing as evidence of an addled pate. Within a year of his election his critics included enough owners, sportswriters, players, fans, and umpires to truly bruise.

The critical tribe increased in 1947 when Chandler suspended manager Durocher for assaulting a fan, for consorting with gamblers, and for thinking "he was beyond the law . . . bigger than baseball itself." For this rhetorical and circumstantial judgment, writers blasted Chandler and martyred Durocher.

Even when Chandler acted judiciously within baseball law—as when he freed minor league players from improper contracts—he was undone. By 1950 he was mocked as "the Bluegrass Jack---," and a "posturing pol."

Thus, Chandler fell before his term expired. The blow came in 1951 when he naively requested a vote of confidence. Finding the opening that they had been seeking, the owners ousted him with a 9-7 vote. Disheartened, Chandler took the sop of a year's severance pay and retired.

Having abided by an autocratic saint and an unmanageable southern senator, baseball owners now determined to elect their kind of

After sacking Albert B. Chandler (*shown on left flanked by Senators Joe Kuhel and Joe Fitzgerald*), the owners settled on compliant Ford Frick (*right*), who served from 1951 to 1965.

Commissioner—a figurehead who would represent the game, while keeping his nose out of important decisions. Owners floated names of national heroes as possible successors, perhaps because Chandler's abrupt dismissal raised suspicions about their motives. A quixotic suggestion that Bill Veeck be chosen was brushed aside, while J. Edgar Hoover and Air Force General Emmett (Rosie) O'Donnel were touted. These suggestions were grandstand plays; Hoover was entrenched in his governmental empire and when approached, he chided the owners for firing Chandler. Meanwhile, President Truman pre-empted the owners' decision, scheduling O'Donnel for Korean War service.

From there the choices narrowed to baseball insiders and after several ballots, it was announced that National League President Ford C. Frick would serve. A compromise candidate, Frick was owner O'Malley's man; his nomination illustrated the kingmaker O'Malley's growing power among owners.[19]

Frick served for fourteen years as a Merovingian Commissioner. Had the entire country been searched, owners could hardly have picked a more reliable front man than this tall, ascetic-looking, 57-year-old. An Indiana farmboy turned sportswriter, his boosting, "gee whiz" style of baseball coverage pleased the owners. In 1934, when the National League needed a president to replace ex-sportswriter John Heydler, Frick came forward to serve faithfully and rattle no cages. He proved a dependable figurehead. During his 14 years of service, he acquiesced in the degradation of the post, admitting to being a follower rather than a Czar. Later, he argued in his self-effacing autobiography that it was the same with Landis and Chandler. Whatever the case was, as the owners' overseer, Frick limited his scope to administering rules and procedures laid down by his masters.[20]

Given an expanded staff as a trapping of royalty, Frick busied himself with routine details and avoided the fiery issues that enrounded him. When pressed to account for his indifference, he was wont to say that such issues were "league matters . . . not in the Commissioner's jurisdiction." Frick stood by as carpetbagging owners abandoned ancient franchises; as the first expansion weakened clubs; as Congressional subcommittees probed for anti-trust violations; as players formed a protective Association; as owners vied for bonus babies; as television became a reshaping force; and as the minor leagues sickened unto death.[21]

At a time when critical leadership was needed, Frick offered none. Owner Veeck thought he was a disaster. By standing silent during the bonus bidding craze, he let some $60 million be siphoned out of baseball that might have gone to the ailing minors if only Frick had urged an orderly free agent draft. During the anti-trust investigations, Frick appeared before the subcommittee to declare the uniqueness of baseball law and its continuing necessity.

Frick seldom bucked owners or supported players. Once he helped to unseat an owner, but only because that fellow was found guilty of income tax evasion. It was more typical for Frick to follow the owners. His anti-player stance was not lost on cynical players, who remembered his treatment of Roger Maris. When that jittery player broke Ruth's seasonal homer record, Frick insisted that the achievement must be listed separately because it took Maris 162 games instead of 154.

Thus, Frick's stance helped to inspire major league player unionism. While these players later gained a powerful advocate, the failing minor leagues and the fans did not. At least fans could vent their displeasure at the turnstiles, but not even falling attendance stirred Frick. Instead, at the 1961 meetings, with the fateful expansion decision underway, Frick complimented owners for concluding their business in seven minutes, saying, "This has been our finest meeting."[22]

Forever the trimmer, Frick asked the owners in his 1965 farewell speech to strengthen the Commissioner post and to allow successors to act on matters "construed to be detrimental to baseball," in order to insure "good, clean entertainment." His memoirs, published shortly before his death, still toadyed to officialdom. The book read like a ghosted version of his baseball life.[23]

Baseball's ancient marriage to newspapers was threatened in the postwar era by the challenge of television and by the rise of monopolistic newspaper syndicates. Whereas the television menace was more obvious, its damage to the profession of baseball writing was less than had been expected. While the threat posed by monopolistic newspaper syndicates proved its mettle in the increasing starvation of the independent American daily newspaper, this thunder might easily be viewed as a boon for sports in print.

When the circulation of big city newspapers declined in the 1960s and 1970s, some observers suggested a general decline in reading habits; however, magazine and book sales still thrived. When several papers adopted a much touted "new journalism" style, readers responded. Suburban newspapers increased in circulation and appealed to readers; their focus on national themes consequently stimulated the growth of major sports like baseball and its competitors. Thus, sports promoters were blessed as traditionally free newspaper coverage was augmented by radio and television.

The popularity of sports sections continued; hence of the shrinking veins of news that ran through ad-bloated papers, at least 15 percent dealt with sports. In response to reader surveys that showed sporting news ranking second only to front page stories, sportswriting staffs were increased—some big city sports editors commanded as many as forty writers.

The new wrinkle was the variety of sports covered. As rival sports gained popularity, fewer columns were devoted to baseball and the beat lost some of its appeal. Even baseball's bible, *The Sporting News*, opted for general sports coverage in the 1960s. Still, owing to its strategic summer position, baseball coverage was strong. Although pro golf, tennis, and other sports encroached, and the "shrinking of the seasons" soon had pro basketball and hockey competing in the spring and pro football challenging in August, baseball was still well served.

As baseball faced the challenge of rivals, so did baseball writers, who were routinely scooped on game scores and game highlights by more rapid radio and television reports. Also, the continental time lag prohibited eastern morning papers from carrying accounts of west coast night games. Writers coped by adopting new styles of coverage, generally offering "more analysis, more summary, more side issues." Baseball writing always had been a dynamic art. In the past, alternative styles had vied for popularity, so that veteran writers were used to switching styles.

In his revealing *Sports Page*, published in 1949, sports editor Stan Woodward of the *New York Herald Tribune* described the diverse styles of sportswriting. Woodward marked the 1920–1940 era as the low point in the profession's history, a time when writers deserved the epithet of toilers in a newspaper's "toy department." While colorful, much of the writing was sophomoric, overly romantic, and marred by mixed metaphors, cutesy phrases, and overblown rhetoric. As a newspaper sports editor, Woodward declared war on the romantics, banning their "unholy jargon," their "godding" of players, and their inappropriate idioms, such as "belting a home run." Indeed, to demonstrate the impossibility of that feat, Woodward once took off his belt and flailed away. Pioneering a new sporting journalism, Woodward aimed at making sports coverage newsworthy, critically informative, and respectable. Convinced that readers first turned to his sports section, he once urged a managing editor not to "bury a good story" by running it on page one!

Woodward criticized the three styles of sportswriting that characterized the 1920–1940 era: the "Gee Whiz" school of hero-worship led by Grantland Rice and his disciples; the belittling "Aw Nuts" school of Westbrook Pegler and his ilk; and the "On the Button" school, whose advocates turned in stereotyped game descriptions based on the who, what, when, where, and how formula.[24] Some writers cleverly combined the three styles and used a lively language with hyperbolic descriptions and jargon that tried the patience of copy-editors.

A fun-loving, boozing, prankish lot, oldtime writers used a stylized language, studded with puns and inside jokes. To print a phrase or break open an outlandish story was a much-prized coup, and to sneak an off-color double-entendre past a prudish copy-editor was a badge of fame. Thus, one half-century later, Fred Lieb recalled Charley Dryden's scatalogical coup of the 1910s. Writing of Cleveland pitcher Gene Krapp's labors, Dryden described how "Krapp squeezed his way out of a tight hole . . . [by inducing] Rollie Zeider to line to Bill Wambsganss for an inning-ending double play."[25]

Even if a prank had a deadly effect, the caper was still good for a laugh. Once, Tom O'Reilly of the *New York World Telegram* answered a late night phone call from a drunk who asked if a player ever hit a fair ball out of Yankee Stadium. O'Reilly answered no, but when the drunk asked him to settle a bet by telling this to a companion, O'Reilly told the companion, "Yeah, Gehrig did." Then the smirking O'Reilly hung up, but the next day a news item carried a story of a fatal shooting over a baseball argument at a Hoboken saloon.

Such antics belonged to a cliché-mongering, upbeat devotion to baseball that lingered long. Even as death and retirement thinned their ranks, enough old tortoises toiled into the expansion era, still writing, but befuddled by the new "chipmunk" writers and ever mourning the passing of the "golden age."

Dan Parker, one-time sports editor and columnist of the *New York Daily Mirror*, argued with Woodward, insisting that the 1920s was indeed the golden age. Parker preferred the old zesty style to the commercialized shoddiness of the 1950s. Joe Williams of the *New York World Telegram and the Sun* agreed, affecting a cynical "Aw Nuts" style, yet surrounding himself with romantic boosters like Dan Daniel, Harry Grayson, and Tom Meany.

In 1932 Williams made a huge contribution to the profession by hiring Willard Mullin as sports cartoonist. Over the next 35 years, Mullin drew 10,000 cartoons, including famed caricatures of the "Dodger Bums," cocky Yankees, blockheaded Giants, and the "St. Louis Swifties." Mullin was one of a kind, not only because few papers hired cartoonists for sports, but also because his sketches were truly appreciated by the fans. Upon retirement in the 1970s, Mullin was hailed the "Rembrandt of sports cartoonists" and was named "Sports Cartoonist of the Century" by the National Cartoonist Society. Several Mullin cartoons adorn the Hall of Fame.

A willingness to sugarcoat the game that fed them typified tortoises. As the 80-year-old Dan Daniel put it, "I was eager to run baseball up." So was the venerable voice of the Cardinals, J. Roy Stockton, although his attacks had helped to evict Veeck's Browns.[26]

As ever, New York was the mecca of baseball writers. Romantics like Frank Graham and Jimmy Cannon stroked their city readers with eloquence, while the neglected seamy side of baseball was revealed to fans by Harold Parrott, who served a stint as travel secretary of the Dodgers and wrote down what he saw. This ex-*Brooklyn Eagle* scribe later vented his cynicism in a muckraking book, *The Lords of Baseball.*

Milt Gross of the *New York Post* needed no such on-the-field experience to treat baseball realistically. He filled his syndicated columns with in-depth interviews in which he probed the feelings of ballplayers. Gross especially empathized with black and Latin American players. Always on the hunt for revealing stories, Gross's books and articles fed fans a realistic blend of information, insight, and opinion.

By the 1970s such giant tortoises of the New York school were gone, along with the writers from outside of the mecca. Bostonians Al Hirshberg, author of many notable baseball texts, and Harold Kaese of the *Globe;* Shirley Povich, the forty-year veteran of the *Washington Post;* Chicagoan Warren Brown, whose sharp coverage of the White Sox earned him the Spink Award; Les Biederman, who vividly reported 39 years of Pirates tales for the *Pittsburgh Press* and who sorrowfully watched the passing of the Negro major league— these writers and more delighted readers for decades with their sympathetic, intelligent, authoritative, and often witty reportage.

Yet the New York school had always predominated, and especially the *New York Times* staff of John Drebinger, James P. Dawson, and Art Daley. It was once said that Drebinger, a precise, upbeat reporter who preferred underdogs to the lordly Yanks, wrote "the purest and most intelligent baseball stories in the country. . . ." Still, more than Drebinger or the competent Dawson, Arthur Daley personified *Times* leadership. An eclectic sportswriter who penned the famed "Sports of the *Times*" column for 32 years, Daley preferred baseball for its characters, its humor and drama, and its universal appeal. This "Gee Whiz" stylist loved the players, especially "class" types like Ott, DiMaggio, and Williams. Though younger writers criticized his romantic pratings, Daley preferred to keep alive baseball's mythical past and saw no reason for muckraking, "not when there were plenty of nice, amusing guys around." Daley's simple eloquence won him a Pulitzer Prize in 1956.

Daley was king at the *Times* when Walter Wellesley Smith joined in 1971. Smith had been with the *Herald Tribune* and, buoyed by the fame of his widely syndicated column, had been proclaimed the "laureate" of sportswriters by intellectual fans. When the *Tribune* folded, he reluctantly joined his great rival.

Smith's roots were sunk deeply into the brisk, new epoch of baseball writing. Each game was different, he argued; all that was needed was the ability to keep one's tongue stuck in its natural habitat, "the left cheek." Always informative, Smith reported baseball with wit, candor, and intelligence. From his tough-minded tutor, Stan Woodward, Smith learned to stop "Godding up those players."

He brought to the *Times* a witty, salty, well-crafted style, one that Ernest Hemingway once described as "the most influential single force in American sportswriting." He was 67 when he joined the *Times*, but no contemporary was more adaptive or younger in spirit than the pink-cheeked, owl-eyed Smith. His language was as sharp as his wit; references to a "yammer of radio announcers," "a conceit of managers," "a dawdle of magnates," "a braille of umpires," or a "bibulation of sportswriters" were often found in his columns.

Smith admitted that as he grew older, he also grew more liberal and more convinced that baseball writing must reflect society's concerns. His crusades against racism, the reserve clause, arrogant owners, and the undermining force of television made Smith the dean of the new breed of baseball writers.[27] Smith's intellectual odyssey would have delighted his old tutor Woodward, who waged his own wars on romanticism, incompetence, pomposity, and hypocrisy as sports editor of the *Herald-Tribune*. His probing essays of the late 1940s and the 1950s printed in *Sports Illustrated* inspired many young writers of his ilk. As the force behind the new journalism, Woodward's books *Sports Page* (1948) and *Paper Tiger* (1964) continue to serve as penetrating descriptions of the sportswriter craft.

Nevertheless, enough romantics survived to make reformers despair of success. "Gee Whizzers" of the 1950s glorified players, inventing heroic nicknames like "Jolting Joe," "The Thumper," and "Stan the Man" for the great triumvirate. Lesser lights were glamorized by contrived names like "King Kong," "Harry the Cat," "Shotgun," "the Reading Rifle," and "Scooter."

Meanwhile, the "Aw Nuts" belittlers weighed in with names like "The Great Expectorator" and delighted in exposing the clay feet of diamond gods. "The Milwaukee Braves died with their boots" ran a devilish lead that was almost too subtle for a ham-handed copy-editor. There was no subtlety, however, in Dick Young's caustic comments like "Labine the new fireman, with gasoline" or "Shuba fields with his bat." Hardier than the fading "Gee Whiz" school, the "Aw Nuts" school drew strength from a growing climate of cynicism in American life.

Humorist Russell Baker blamed the new breed of college-educated writers for the passing of the romantic school, but Woodward welcomed the reformers and sped them along. He urged his staffers to familiarize themselves with law, politics, economics, family studies, and war, since these and other institutions affected sports. Moreover, Woodward hastened the day when baseball cov-

The *New York Times* sportswriting trio of the postwar era: John Drebinger (*top*) with Yankees DiMaggio, Page, and Shea, and Pulitzer prize-winners Art Daley (*bottom left*) and Walter "Red" Smith (*bottom right*).

erage became a team project with one writer doing the lead, another the background, and another providing local color and postgame interviews. This became the norm in the expansion era, as writers were obliged to travel across the country, covering as many as 200 games per season. In the early 1950s distances were shorter and traversed by trains; also, a writer covered one club which picked up his expenses. By decade's end, however, newspapers banned such cozy customs and ordered writers to refuse gifts. More objectivity and less sycophancy was certainly wanted, if for no better reason than to discount Weiss's cynical remark: "To hell with baseball writers. You can buy 'em with a steak."[28]

By the 1960s a new breed of writers had planted the critical, probing new journalism style into baseball. Many of these new-comers wanted meaningful careers, and some, like Gary Cartwright, found the new journalism no shield against baseball's recurrent ritu-alisms and inherent infantilism. Cartwright saw most writers as "old men regardless of age," who acquired permanent sixth grade men-talities: "No man should cover sports once he reaches thirty-five because he has seen all the games there are to see and talked to all the athletes he needs to talk to."[29]

From his west coast perch, sports columnist Wells Twombly agreed, noting that by the mid-1960s his "toy universe" had turned shabby. While he applauded the new realism, Twombly was repelled by the "smutty torrent of poor taste" which pocked player biogra-phies done by writers. If the new journalism meant snickering voy-eurism, Twombly opted for the old, discredited romanticism.

Other new-breed attributes also grated on old tortoises. Early in the expansion era, while working a Yankee game, Jimmy Cannon was disturbed by some chattering younger writers. Their sneering comments about the players enraged Cannon, who told them, "You sound like small, furry animals. . . . You sound like a God damn lot of chipmunks."

This label stuck, and in later years Cannon expanded his "chip-munk" characterization to embrace young writers who dress nattily, wear long hair, and primarily discuss what they have written. They seldom watch games, he charged, and usually prefer the controver-sial characters on a team's roster. As to their interviewing, Cannon faulted chipmunks for posing rude, insulting questions that might end the dialogue.

Still, Cannon admitted that the chipmunks were revolutionizing sportswriting. By an "indiscriminate use of personal reactions" and by delving into the social implications of sports, this new breed pro-mised to better the oldtimers. They were a dominant force of the expansion era, and their impact might have been greater had the big city newspapers not met their precipitous decline.[30]

The Marconi Constellation

One could blame the alarming newspaper decline on the rising "Marconi Constellation"—Marshall McLuhan's metaphor for the electronic media revolution that swept America. Radio and television quickly became sources of entertainment and information, with television by far the giant of the two. Still, radio had been the great force for popularizing baseball, gathering millions of fans by bringing the game into living rooms and automobiles. Fans were enchanted by the siren voices of radio sportscasters who entranced them with highly colorful descriptions of heroic deeds, actions seldom seen by fans who viewed the same games at the parks. The charismatic announcers of the 1940s—Red Barber, Mel Allen, Dizzy Dean, Harry Heilmann, Waite Hoyt, and By Saam, to name a few—were favorites of radio fans. Indeed, these men seemingly shaped the outcomes of the games. Their stirring descriptions of ball park action enticed listeners into believing in the enchanting dimension of baseball.

This imaginative trip was unforgettable for some early radio fans. Recalling his boyhood fascination with Tiger broadcasts, writer Bil Gilbert admitted that his image of baseball was set by "radio—mysterious, disembodied, vivid as a dream." Gilbert's siren was the rich baritone of sportscaster Harry Heilmann. Gilbert prayed for Heilmann's intervention on behalf of the Tigers. There were many enchanted radio fans like this, who were often disenchanted upon seeing a live game.

The 1950s club owners no longer saw radio baseball as an attendance threat; the money paid from local stations and national networks helped change their minds. In 1934 owners divided $100,000 paid by the Ford Motor Company for rights to air the World Series. A nice windfall at the time, it converted most owners into radio baseball advocates. Each owner was still insistent that he be allowed to negotiate his own local radio pact for broadcasting seasonal games; later owners applied this dog-in-the-manger policy to telecasts. Although the owners now permitted a national "Game of the Week," they steadfastly refused to surrender local radio and television rights. Even as national radio broadcasts scored high ratings among listeners while local radio revenues declined, owners clung to their local rights.

It didn't matter much in the end because, sadly, the radio age was short-lived. At least, in radio's brief span of popularity before the onslaught of television, radio sportscasters made their own place in baseball history. The most memorable of these announcers were Red Barber, Mel Allen, and Dizzy Dean.

Red Barber got his big break into the business when he signed to broadcast the games of the Cincinnati Reds. A diligent worker, Barber honed his southern drawl and delighted listeners with player interviews, becoming a local favorite. He gained national prominence when he was chosen to broadcast the 1935 World Series. However, Commissioner Landis laid down strict rules, ordering him to report the plays and the celebrities in attendance. He forbade critical remarks, a policy which owners soon imposed on all sportscasters.

Moving to Brooklyn in 1939, Barber became the darling of Dodger fans who loved his eloquent, wordy descriptions. His language was studded with southern phrases, and some—like "rhubarbs," "sitting in the catbird seat," "the pitcher deals," and "the bases are FOB" (full of Brooklyns)—gained national fame. Barber narrated that year the first televised college baseball game. The announcer used his usual radio style and the broadcast stirred little interest. Fewer than a thousand sets tuned in on this pioneer event.

Still, over the next six years Barber's radio reputation soared. MacPhail offered a three-year, $100,000 pact in 1946 to draw him to the Yankees, but Rickey topped this by $5,000 and kept the "Voice of the Dodgers." In 1954 Barber did join the Yanks. By then television was a growing force and radio men like Barber worked both media. To adapt to television, Barber learned to talk less, dress more stylishly, and devote more time to creating pre- and postgame shows.

Barber's salary now climbed to $50,000 a year, but continuing censorship grated on him. He was told to boost the club and to play down errors and bad weather. When he spoke out on the team's failings, he drew fire from players and owners. Still worse, commercial sponsors hired ex-players Phil Rizzuto and Joe Garagiola to work at his side. Barber judged that Rizzuto lacked finesse and Garagiola chattered incessantly, but when it came to a showdown, the eloquent Barber was the one to be fired. A 33-year career ended, and the sportscaster was left bewildered and angry.

The same cruel fate befell Mel Allen. Allen began his career at the University of Alabama where he narrated football games and taught speech classes. In 1936 he won an announcing job at CBS by demonstrating his resourceful ability to improvise.

Three years later he was broadcasting baseball games in New York. Like Barber, he loved the language and the sound of his own voice. As the "Voice of the Yankees," Allen gave his heart to the team. His dramatic, "Gee Whiz" style enchanted fans, who hung on his colorful comments like "nail biting time at Yankee Stadium" or "any man with a bat in his hand is dangerous." When the Yankees crashed homers, Allen sent spirits soaring with phrases like "There goes a Ballantine blast" or "Going, Going, GONE" or "How About That!"

Barber joined Allen and Jim Woods in 1954 to give the Yankees the most famous radio-television sportscasting crew in the land. The team was broken, however, when in 1956 Woods was sacked for Rizzuto; then, in 1964, just as the Yankee dynasty was sinking, Allen was ousted.

The Allen firing was cruelly delivered in the unexpected and ambiguous fashion of so many sackings in the radio-television field. Vicious rumors attributed the ouster to a range of maladies: senility, drunkenness, hypochondria, and homosexuality were a few. The embittered Allen faded into retirement, but resurfaced in 1978 with a television show called "This Week in Baseball." His old élan won over a new generation of fans. He and Barber were honored that same year with Frick Awards for broadcasting excellence. Sadly, others received the same cruel treatment. As ex-radio men tried to convert to television, some found holding their tongues easier than coping with inhibiting restrictions.

Radio baseball's last decade was the 1950s, the golden era of colorful announcing. It was a time when radio broadcasters rivaled scribes as troubadors; the innovative announcers re-created games via telegraph hookups and experimented with "dream games" that pitted all-time stars in fantasy games. Author Willie Morris fondly recalled how listening to these broadcasts "made pristine facts more actual than actuality."[31]

In later years, sportscasters recalled the 1950s as the Indian summer of creativity. Curt Gowdy, an Allen protégé, was the popular voice of the Red Sox; By Saam did his overblown best to tout the Phillies; Russ Hodges vented his joyous yawp over the Giants's playoff victory; Bob Prince cheered the hapless Pirates; and "Dizzy" Dean charmed listeners with his country boy style. Indeed, Dean was the antithesis of eloquence. Comical, colorful, and knowledgeable, he refused to "purty up" games; he once advised listeners to turn to another network for a better game. His producers were appalled, but the irrepressible Dean went on butchering the language, mispronouncing names, and criticizing poor play.

Dean, of course, spearheaded the trend of hiring ex-players as sportscasters. Product sponsors liked the idea, recalling the effectiveness of Heilmann, Hoyt, and Walter Johnson, but nobody could match Dean's independence and earthy candor. Dean's dismissal in 1965 ushered in an age of banality. Television ruled the air waves, but the radio game had not died.

The television takeover forced many radio announcers to convert. Some managed to keep a hand in each medium, so that by 1979, eighteen of the 26 major league clubs used the same crews to handle both media. The banal impact of the television era stemmed from the muzzling of announcers by owners and producers. What the bosses wanted and received was boosterism and low-keyed, entertaining chatter. It was a no-win situation for the sportscasters: if they conformed, they were puppets; if they did not, they were fired. Most adapted and became cheerleaders, surviving by dint of statistical chatter and endless interviews. Naturally, sportswriters flogged the sportscasters for giving in, and for talking too much, spewing statistics, missing key plays, and preening. It was a brutal revenge, wreaked on defenseless rivals who no longer threatened "liberated" sportswriters.

The television boom spread across America with awesome speed and completeness; set-watching became America's most popular leisure outlet of the 1950s and 1960s. Indeed, the later introduction of the color set did much to spark the national economy. From the beginning of the television era, producers regarded sports programs as a sure-fire way of attracting viewers. In 1941, when the medium was still young, a major league game was crudely televised for several hundred set owners in the New York City area. After the war, however, fans flocked to bars and taverns to watch televised ball games, wrestling matches, and prize fights. Such attractions spurred set sales, and in 1951 an estimated three million set owners and an equal number of barflies watched the Giants defeat the Dodgers in the climactic playoff game. Thus, televised sports was credited with the conversion of millions of Americans into rabid sports fans.

Network producers knew by the 1960s that there was gold to be made in televised sports. The millions spent by CBS for football programming was easily recouped by selling blocks of advertising time. The path led only upward from there for the marriage of television and sports; by 1970 each sports club annually received $1.5 million as its share of television profits.

Happily, major league baseball of 1946 was positioned to gain large profits from television. All that was called for was bold leadership, but, instead, owners responded with timidity and selfishness. By rejecting shared network contracts, baseball lost ground to their rivals; football and basketball profited by sharing network money, and built strong clubs while expanding their leagues.[32]

Understandably, owners worried over television's impact on live gates; the memory of lean attendance during depression and war years was a frightening bugaboo. Night baseball then proved a savior, providing the most lucrative format for televised games. However, when networks dangled offers, the owners resisted. Dazzled by soaring attendance through 1948, they wanted no disruption; moreover, many had belatedly accepted radio baseball and were now negotiating local radio deals.

In fact, early experiences with television-baseball stirred honest fears. After a record 1948 attendance, Cleveland's gate admittances slipped 67 percent by 1956, a calamity that officials blamed on their generous local television policy. As total major league attendance in 1953 sagged six million below that of 1948, more owners felt they had been bitten by television's sirens.

Such losses made a television-phobic of Rickey, who blamed the medium for killing attendance, decimating the minors, and creating a player talent shortage. Damning television for producing "major league fans out of minor league fans" and for turning big league baseball into a disastrous free show, Rickey urged owners to regulate all telecasting. This meant putting strict territorial limits on local telecasts and pooling all revenue for use in shoring up the minor leagues. His proposal, however, got nowhere. Congressional laws forbade limiting the range of baseball telecasts, and enough owners had been dazzled by local television profits to refuse membership in any pooled sharing system.[33]

Such unsportsmanlike behavior widened the ancient gap between rich and poor teams and mocked official claims of competitive balance. Had the owners emulated pro football, negotiating national network pacts and sharing the money, they might have met a better balance.

However, at this time only the revenue from All-Star games and World Series matches was shared. This income was not properly handled, as Chandler was faulted for selling television rights too cheaply—upon obtaining $6 million for six years of televised Series rights, owners and organized players squawked. Although players groused over small pensions, they still staked a claim on future shares of national television revenue. Truthfully, nobody knew what the games were worth. In 1956 Commissioner Frick sought $3 million per year for Series rights; until 1966 such revenue produced about $3.5 million a year, with the All-Star game paying $250,000.

Such windfalls were only the beginning. In 1947 the first Series telecast netted each club $15,000. Five years later the individual gain was $70,000, and by 1957 the dividend topped $100,000. Thereafter, shares skyrocketed; a whopping $687,000 was the take in 1969. Local television revenue offered the sixteen clubs a net total of $2.3 million in 1950, $6.2 million in 1956, $12.5 million in 1960, and $20.7 million in 1969.

Although the combination of national and local revenue looked impressive, organized players were understandably not in awe. Their pension fund tapped only the smaller national television source. Moreover, owners whittled away at player shares. The 1952 players received 90 percent of the total, but the 1969 percentage was cut to 32 percent, and by then some owners were seeking to eliminate any claim of players to a vested interest.

As a divisive influence, television pitted players against owners and rich clubs against poor, with more problems on the horizon. Such problems, however, were dimmed by ever-dazzling profits from televised baseball.

II *The Expansion Era*

Plastic Baseball

The Expanding Majors

As baseball owners fretted over the rival Continental League challenge, Walter O'Malley schemed to defuse the threat. Indeed, some such stroke was needed in 1959, lest the major league's dual system be broken.

In advancing the new league, Rickey argued that America—especially the populous areas like New York, Houston, Denver, Toronto, Minneapolis-St. Paul, Buffalo, Atlanta, and Dallas—needed more major league baseball. Better to plant and stock teams in such areas and match them against one another, he urged, than to add four new teams to the existing majors and pit them against established teams. Thus, the Continental League raised its standard, announcing in 1959 that each new owner had deposited $50,000 in earnest money and was pledged to spend up to $3 million over the cost of a playing site. Taking a year to organize their operations, the Continental League club owners planned to open in 1961.

This announcement distressed major league owners, who feared costly talent bidding wars and a loss of television contracts; a forfeit of fans also seemed likely, as their aging ballparks could not stand up to the newer Continental facilities. They dared not tamper with the new league, as advocate Senator Estes Kefauver served notice that he would carefully monitor the situation.[1]

O'Malley was the leading blamesake of this crisis. When he and Stoneham pulled out of New York, William Shea at first sought a replacement franchise, but then joined forces with Rickey. Working behind the scenes, O'Malley withheld major league recognition until the Continentals paid exorbitant indemnity costs for their territorial rights. Outmaneuvered by this, the Continental leaders opted to allow the established majors to absorb their most promising sites. Thus, in the style of a loveless shotgun marriage, the major leagues blundered into their expansion era.

The first phase of expansion called for the major leagues to agree on the choice of the new franchises. Upstaged earlier by the Nationals, who occupied San Francisco and Los Angeles, the Americans sought to be first to grab the most. For allowing the Nationals to plant a new team in New York, the Americans demanded representation in O'Malley's Los Angeles territory; at the same time, they freed owner Cal Griffith to move his Washington Senators to Bloomington, Minnesota. Griffith's move, however, forced the majors to plant an expansion team in Washington. Under these arrangements, the Americans expanded to ten teams in 1961, a year ahead of the Nationals.

Meanwhile, the Nationals moved to invade New York and Houston. Dubbed the "Mets" after a half-forgotten American Association team, the New York club played its maiden season in 1962 at the Polo Grounds, while awaiting the completion of Shea Stadium, a civic-built park at Flushing Meadows. Likewise, the "Colt-45s" spent their early years at a minor league park, while their future home, the domed, all-weather "Astrodome," was erected. When the team moved in, they were renamed the "Astros."

Along with a hefty initiation fee that only profited the established clubs, each newcomer was treated like a bastard child, given second-rate players via an expansion draft. This allowed each new team to rummage among the fifteen most expendable players from the 40-man roster of each established club. At the fixed rate of $75,000, this made for costly slim pickings, with the veteran teams pooling and dividing the monies. Future expansion moves followed this same windfall procedure.

The initiates accepted these patronizing impositions, but other tributes galled. Owner Gene Autry's new Los Angeles Angels opened play in a ramshackle minor league park. They soon fared worse, though, becoming O'Malley's tenants in his new Dodger Stadium. The latest Senators faced the horrendous task of rekindling interest among resentful Washingtonians. Although this expansion team played at the new D.C. Stadium, they were upstaged by the nearby Orioles. Thus, the bickering Senator owners faced financial losses. Indeed, the American League's 1961 expansion was ill-advised; only the carpetbagging Twins thrived, as American owners rightly felt worsted by their National rivals.

Certainly, the Nationals did better in their round. The Colt-45s hung tough at Houston, and prospered after 1965 as the rechristened Astros. The Mets confounded observers by their popularity in New York. The losers of 120 games in 1962, the "Amazing Mets" endeared fans by their well-known ineptitude. Later, after moving into Shea Stadium, they outdrew the fading Yankees.

With mixed success, baseball's 10-club format lasted through 1968. There were positive highlights, like the addition of the amazing Mets, Maris's record-topping 61 homers in 1961, the new ballpark boom, and increased television revenue. These glimmers were dimmed, however, by charges that some owners put tax breaks, television dollars, and entertainment ahead of baseball. The tremulous Frick voiced these complaints in his 1964 farewell address; at the same time the Commissioner, ever the trimmer, urged owners to add two more teams to each league. His advice offered no new ideas, as some carpetbagging owners already planned their jump to more fertile areas. These precipitous moves forced another round of expansion in 1969.

In one such move, the 1966 owners of the Braves quit Milwaukee to gain the greater advantage of a new, low-rent public stadium and generous television concessions at Atlanta. With little forethought, the National League owners allowed the shift, provoking a lawsuit from enraged Milwaukeeans. The move also angered Charles Finley, owner of the Kansas City A's, by dashing his plan to occupy Atlanta. Having alienated Kansas City fans, Finley now threatened to sue the American League if his colleagues refused him permission to move to Oakland where a new stadium beckoned. When given a green light, Finley left Kansas City amidst a chorus of protests that carried to the floor of the U.S. Senate.[2]

Both of these moves were blatant acts of second-degree carpetbaggery. Did such residence changes portend a promiscuous era wherein anyone might quit a town for a better deal elsewhere? If so, what were the legal rights of a jilted territory? This last question carried a whiff of possible anti-trust action and had fearful owners promising to plant new expansion teams at Milwaukee and Kansas City.

As outside pressures influenced expansion moves, so did the power struggle between the major leagues. Potentially profitable territories petitioned for big league memberships and so expansion became a game of beating the rival league to the draw. To strike first was the right tactic, and the Americans did. After allowing Finley to move to Oakland in October, 1967, the Americans unilaterally announced plans to plant new teams in Kansas City and Seattle, and to commence play in 1969 under a 12-club league, with a two-division format.

Stung by this coup, the Nationals initially threatened war, but cooler heads prevailed. After voting to expand to 12 clubs by 1971, O'Malley persuaded his colleagues to join the Americans and move their timetable to 1969. This allowed a new San Diego team to encroach on O'Malley's Los Angeles territory, along with a new entry from Montreal.

With both 1969 leagues fielding 12 teams and using a divisional format, baseball broke sharply with established tradition. Under the divisional system, each league divided its teams into two factions, with the winners of each engaging in postseason playoffs to determine the league champion. Added to a 162-game schedule, the playoffs, followed by the World Series, extended baseball's calendar late into October.

The new format worked surprisingly well, despite the forceps delivery. As in the first expansion, new entrants paid hefty initiation fees. This time each American newcomer deposited $5.25 million, while the National newcomer rendered $10 million. This was another windfall for established clubs, who also benefited from another expansion draft which stocked each newcomer with forty second-rate players at the price of $175,000 per man. The newcomers willingly paid, possibly because they were impressed by the game's dynamic popularity.[3]

Not all went smoothly. The National League San Diego Padres and the American Seattle Pilots were both shaky. Not until hamburger king Ray Kroc bought control in 1974 did the San Diego situation stabilize; by then, the Seattle disaster was history. That city's bankrupt team had been dumped on American owners before the 1969 season ended. Four days before the next season's opener, the league sold the team to Milwaukee interests. While this provided the promised Milwaukee franchise, a lawsuit started by jilted Seattle interests forced owners to promise that town a future replacement!

Faltering American league clubs, like Cleveland and Washington, now coveted an attractive site in Texas, located between Dallas and Fort Worth. By pleading poverty, owner Bob Short wrung permission to move his Senators in. The announcement raised protests from fans, including President Nixon, who expressed "grief," and congressmen, who threatened investigations. However, Short departed in 1971, and protesting Washington fans were quieted by a vague—and still unfulfilled—promise of another replacement.

A third expansion move occurred in 1976 when the American League unilaterally added franchises in Seattle and Toronto. This latest Seattle team, amply financed and reborn as the "Mariners," occupied the new, publicly financed, all-weather "Kingdome." The Toronto acquisition meanwhile stole a march on the Nationals, who had eyed the site. Although these new moves threw American League schedules off balance, any gamble paid off and, in fact, coincided with a wave of baseball prosperity. The dawn of the 1980s saw restive clubs in both leagues licking their chops over promising new sites, like Miami, Denver, and New Orleans.[4]

The Expanding Sports Bubble

In this era of global expansion, the sovereign rule of American baseball was threatened by organized baseball played in foreign lands (notably, in Japan). More menacing, however, was the home-bound competition from rival sports. Television, the catalyst behind this sporting bubble, played no favorites; having found gold in sports, the major networks panned sports to the tune of 1,100 hours per year by 1974, and close to 1,400 hours by 1980.

Baseball was one of a flock to benefit from television exposure. Along with baseball, rival team sports like football, basketball, and hockey and individual sports spectacles like tennis and golf stirred a sports-television mania that enraptured fans of both sexes and all ages, classes, and interests. In a short time, television sports presented a rich menu of sports and pseudo sports.

Half-angel, half-devil, television powered the boom, dispensing favors and exacting tolls. Among its blessings, the medium stimulated attendance at the major team sports. In 1964 baseball led rivals with 21.2 million admissions, followed by football with 6 million, basketball with 4.7, and hockey with 2.8. Ten years later baseball pulled in 30 million paying fans, basketball 10.9, football 10.2, and hockey 13.6. These were sturdy gains, yet such figures were dwarfed by attendance at horse races, auto races, and boxing matches.

By the 1970s the various team sports were crowding one another on the calendar. Expanding schedules caused an overlapping effect that destroyed the old rhythm of established sports seasons. Replacing the orderly succession of the 1950s was a bewildering "squeezing of seasons." Now football, basketball, and hockey schedules overlapped baseball's expanded 162-game schedule, leaving only June and July clear of competition. Although pro football posed the biggest threat, with its fall schedule overshadowing baseball's stretch drives and playoffs, it also suffered, as baseball teams had first priority to stadiums which were shared with fifteen pro football teams.

Professional basketball and hockey schedules also lengthened, encroaching on football and baseball. For some bewildered fans, an old cultural clock was destroyed; television producers, too, were vexed, while scholastic athletes, who once had participated in several sports, found themselves concentrating more on one.[5]

Still, pro football posed the strongest challenge. Buoyed by the game's popularity at the grassroots, pro football became the game's dominant form. The National Football League's popularity of the 1960s was such that a rival league, the American Football League, rose to challenge. The two leagues bid for college players and salaries soared, until the two rivals merged. The merger, completed in 1970, was a model of efficiency. Under the banner of the NFL, two conferences were formed, the American and the National, each housing Eastern, Central, and Western Divisions. Each team battled division rivals, and faced rivals from both conferences on a staggered basis. This format offered an exciting regular season, followed by a nail-biting "second season" of playoff competition fought between division winners and two "wild card" entries. Then, the two surviving conference champions met in January in the climactic Superbowl, a sports extravaganza that rivaled the World Series.

So attractive was this format that baseball officials imitated the plan. Pro football leaders, observing such emulation, proclaimed their sport the national game. In vouchsafing the claim, NFL Commissioner Pete Rozelle cited 1969 and 1972 Harris opinion polls showing that fans preferred football. Stung by the assault, Commissioner Kuhn defended baseball's ancient claim, finding succor in a

1977 poll showing baseball rebounding to the top. The two leaders wasted words on a dead issue; neither conceded the obvious, which was simply that Americans loved sports. Still football's surge was real, and by the 1970s its popularity was as solid as the $5 million a year which each NFL team received from network television pacts.

Almost as impressive as football's challenge was that of pro basketball. From eight clubs in the 1950s, the National Basketball Association had expanded to 23 clubs by 1980 and paid the highest average salaries of any team sport. Like football, the NBA was forced to fend off a rival major league, but the challenge sent salaries spiraling. The NBA lost ground after it merged with the rival American Basketball Association in 1976; thereafter, falling attendance and lowering television ratings took their toll on the sport. Causes cited for this reversal were high salaries, the lengthened season, high ticket costs, and competition from college games. One observer suggested that the players were too good and that the number of black players in the NBA might have exceeded a "tipping point."[6] Others thought that too many divisions and too many games had "over saturated" the market.

Stimulated by television, pro hockey also expanded. From six teams in the 1950s, the National Hockey League doubled in size in 1967 and grew to 21 teams in four divisions by 1980. Along with hockey's continental expansion came an expanded playing season that overlapped those of other team sports. Such overlapping reflected the growing competition for television money.

On some weekends baseball was jostled by professional golf and tennis. When telecasted tournaments cut into baseball's television ratings, the major league club owners felt competition of a different order. Nevertheless, baseball's live attendance figures rose steadily. While such summer rivals as these could be discounted as a parttime threat, soccer posed a distant yet sounder challenge. This, the world's most popular team sport, was a minor amateur sport in America when promoters pushed professional soccer in 1967 as a summer alternative to baseball; however, the timing was bad. Not only did Americans know little about the game, but promoters oversold the product by fielding two rival leagues. Although television networks put up $1 million for 21 soccer telecasts, ratings were bad and the pace of the games allowed no logical commercial interruptions. Even so, the venture scared five baseball owners into purchasing soccer franchises as a hedge against the sport's success.

Soccer's disastrous 1967 season dampened the immediate threat;

however, in 1975 the surviving North American Soccer League scored a publicity coup by luring the great Pelé, Brazil's soccer star, to its ranks. Furthermore, the NASL stimulated interest at the scholastic level; by 1977 soccer was a popular team sport in American schools. To meet such threats to baseball's youthful talent supply, Commissioner Kuhn circulated thousands of booklets entitled "Baseball: The Now Career."[7]

Professional soccer still faltered; unable to attract television sponsorship, the NASL lost $30 million in 1980. However, a modified, fast-scoring version of the sport did well as a winter spectacle; summer soccer still awaited the education of the American fans and the cultivation of native stars.

Baseball was becoming hard pressed by rivals in the competition for young talent. Faced with a dwindling talent flow, the majors adopted an annual free agent draft in 1965, whereby each club picked over the nation's prospects. The minor leagues were by then in such disarray that the majors converted most of the surviving camps into player development centers. Further relief for the shortage came from scouts who were combing Latin America for talents and from clubs resorting to college scholarships and instructional schools to nurture prospects.

On the other hand, talent scarcity was a boon to players. In tandem with increasing television money, the shortage increased salaries, as did a strong players' union which freed this generation of players from the reserve clause and gave them more power than any had known since 1875.[8]

Baseball's Plastic Style

The American arena of this era has been referred to as "plastic." Indeed, much use was made of synthetic materials in baseball, and the game was ruled by tractable, posturing men. However, "plastic" also conveys a sense of creativity, an ability to adapt to change. Thus, the plastic style of baseball's expansion era betrayed a gamut of meanings; "plastic" insured the game's survival and carried it to new peaks of popularity.[9]

Amidst all the mercenary carpetbagging and the blundering that blighted its expansion, major league baseball managed to plant thriving outposts in every section of the mainland, and even reached into Canada. Such outward growths fortified the game, while the new ballparks catered to the comfort-seeking crowds.

Ten new parks opened in the 1960s (seven in the National League alone), and each conformed to the outfield dimensions set by a 1958 edict. Some observers thought the new parks looked monotonously alike; their fan-shaped outfields resembled, thought Michael Oriard, "utilitarian machines for sports." Most were built in suburban areas near major highways and were surrounded by parking lots. Inside, the fans cheered from colorful, plastic seats that were so removed from the playing field that watching a live game seemed like viewing the same action on television.

All the parks ranged in cost from $14.5 to a hefty $31 million. These exorbitant prices forced all but Dodger Stadium to be publicly financed by city, county, state, or federal taxes; or, as in the case of St. Louis's Busch Stadium, the stadiums were backed by a semi-public authority. As public ventures, they were built either to lure ball clubs or to keep itchy ones from leaving town; voters were assured that their investments would produce capital gains. Unfortunately, that promised "multiplier effect" proved illusory. Not only did the new parks fail to recoup their costs, but they lost money through operating expenses, and they generally failed to upgrade neighborhoods or to increase business and job opportunities.

So strong was the mystique of hosting a ballclub that citizens voted tax monies for the building of stadiums and for expensive refurbishing projects. By 1979, therefore, another half-dozen parks were erected at costs that reached as high as $3,900 a seat. This latest building boom cost an estimated $7 billion;[10] against this pervasive trend, only four of the old parks remained in 1980: Tiger Stadium, Fenway, and Comiskey of the American League, and Wrigley Field of the National. Baseball had become a predominantly nocturnal spectacle, served to the customer in comfortable surroundings. Indeed, three parks were domed, air-conditioned structures; media analyst Marshall McLuhan likened the effect of the stadiums to being inside a pinball machine. However, this ultimate in ballpark comfort hit ground when confronted by the rising energy cost of the 1970s.

Nevertheless, owners pandered to the creature comforts of the patrons. Ticket prices were luringly lowered to undermine those of rival sports. Promotional gimmicks were widely employed, including the dispersal of free baseball artifacts to children and fetching trinkets to adults. Inside several of the parks, rows of lights set along the upper decks eliminated the ancient, vision-blocking light towers. At one time in the 1970s, ten parks boasted plastic artificial playing surfaces that could be sucked dry of water by pumping machines; thus, the problem of rained-out games was lessened.

Although each is at least sixty years old, these American League parks are still in service. Fenway Park (*left*) houses the Red Sox and Yankee Stadium (*right*) hosts the Yankees. (Notice the Polo Grounds, former home of the Giants, across the river from the Stadium.)

Two of the newer expansion era parks: Candlestick Park (*left*), home of the National League Giants, is much criticized for its cold, windy climate; whereas in the Houston Astrodome (*right*), home of the National League Astros, fans enjoy weather-proofed comfort.

Seated now in broad, plastic seats, fans enjoyed varieties of food and drink which were sold and served in sanitary plastic wrappings. Before the game and at break, they were lulled by music and on-field entertainments, including the antics of clowns garishly dressed as totemic animals. Electronic scoreboards flashed messages, led cheers, and boomed salutes at the exploits of local heroes. The television screen-like scoreboards displayed portraits of the players, disgorged statistical information, and sometimes offered replays of the game action. Indeed, some parks mounted television screens for the benefit of addicts.

Although the game on the field resembled baseball as it had always been played, rules were now changed to enhance scoring. The need for such tinkering soon reached crisis proportions because a 1963 decision to widen the strike zone had weakened the offenses. As pitchers dominated batters, scoring tailed off alarmingly, reaching a nadir in 1968 when batting averages sank to .236 and every fifth game pitched was a shut-out. Thoroughly alarmed by falling attendances, officials voted in 1969 to shrink the strike zone and lower pitching mounds.

This remedy worked for the National League, but American offenses still lagged. Therefore, in 1973 the Americans adopted the designated hitter rule, which allowed a regular hitter to bat for the pitcher. Although rejected by the Nationals, the "DH" rule was used by the Americans with successful results. Not only did batting averages rise, but the designated hitters became the highest-paid players by position.[11]

By creating a new specialist-hero, the DH rule boosted American League prestige. American turnstile totals had been low since 1953, but now the deficit was cut. New parks helped this upward trend, as did the 1977 American expansion coup. However, though American attendance now matched that of the Nationals, the rival league continued to lead in statistical wars and dominate All-Star game encounters. Hence, inter-league jealousies blocked profitable cooperation on such proposals as inter-league play and divisional realignments.[12]

Perhaps such proposals were best shelved, since enough changes had occurred to confuse even the most adaptable fans. The American League opened in 1961 with ten teams and a 162-game schedule; the Nationals followed with the same in 1962. The 1969 expansion offered a divisional playoff format, and the American League attempted an awkward mini-expansion in 1977.

These mind-boggling changes were joined by others which involved players and equipment. Many resented the new breed of highly paid, outspoken players. Products of television and devotees to militant unionism, this new breed drew salaries that averaged better than $100,000 by the late 1970s. Yet far from alienating most fans, baseball's attendance and television ratings climbed to unprecedented heights.

Indeed, this generation of players differed from all others in looks and free-spirited behavior. Ken "Hawk" Harrelson was a prototype of this plastic age player. An overrated slugger of modest attainments, the blithe-spirited Harrelson, along with a few others, introduced such player appearances as long hair, batting gloves, sweat bands, and lamp back smears under the eyes to reduce light glare. Harrelson was ridiculed for such foppishness but when released for insubordination, the free agent joined the Red Sox for a $75,000 bonus. This grand slam made him a hero among peers, who imitated his style.

Changes in equipment also cast the ball player in a different mold. At the dawn of the era players still wore the familiar flannels; now the lineup appeared in dashing new uniforms. Some tailored these uniforms to fit snugly, while owner Finley outfitted his A's in vivid white and green uniforms of imported materials. In 1971 the Pirates appeared in flashy uniforms of man-made, double-knit fabric that would accommodate gaudy designs. The sexy, skin-tight cut of the uniform offered a new look that caught on quickly, and soon the Pirates mixed solid colors with stripes, coming up with as many as nine different uniform styles and appropriately matching caps. Other teams were equally daring: the White Sox tried shorts and many ballplayers wore colored shoes, some with ripple soles or soccer cleats instead of traditional spikes. The new breed looked good—both on the field and on color television—as no earlier generation had appeared so richly clad.

That clothes made new men of the ball players was amply demonstrated by the catchers of the era. Not only were they better protected by fiber glass skullcaps, by masks of high-impact plastic, and by neck flaps which covered their throats, but lighter chest protectors preserved safety *and* increased mobility. By the late 1970s, most catchers wore shortened chest protectors because groins were protected by improved high-impact plastic cups attached to athletic supporters.

The evolution of the fielders' gloves in size and efficiency now allowed for one-handed catches. Attempts to lessen their size were half-hearted and the gloves grew larger; one San Francisco outfielder blamed a fielding error on winds that, he said, blew his glove shut as he waited for a fly ball! Gloves also came in bright, brash, colors; some catchers even experimented with "target mitts" that included a panel of fluorescent vinyl designed to aid a pitcher's concentration.

Bats also changed. Although major leaguers were barred from using the new metal bats because of presumed risks to life and limb, players found ways of modifying their light, whippy bats. Some used heavy clubs, while the Japanese-inspired cup-ended bats appealed to others. Among illegal modifications were new ways to "dope" bats; after inserting small rubber balls, cork, or mercury in the barrels, the dope was sealed inside with epoxy glues. Many on-deck hitters no longer ritually swung several bats. Instead, they swung one which was fitted with a heavy metal ring (doughnut), or they swung odd-looking winged bats. Such new rites joined ancient acts of bat coddling, with names like "soul pole" or "my business partner" now bestowed.

While the differences in bats were accepted with interest by players and fans, ball changes stirred real controversy. Over the years, critics often accused officials of introducing livelier balls, but the use of cowhide balls after 1973 convinced many observers that this was indeed true. Because manufacturers sent balls to Haiti to be hand sewn, batters and pitchers complained of tight-seamed, hyped up "voodoo balls." The changing market conditions forced baseball to take the new balls or nothing. Indeed, the Spalding Company in 1975 ceased to manufacture balls, leaving the Rawlings Company as chief supplier of the 300,000 annually consumed by the teams.[13]

With so many changes occurring swiftly in this plastic age, the shock of each surfacing innovation grew increasingly less. Umpires no longer wore drab blue, pitchers were clocked by radar guns, television tapes diagnosed performances, walkie-talkie radios were used to set defenses, pitching machines delivered every pitch but the spitter, and colorful, cap-shaped vehicles delivered relief pitchers to the mound. Small wonder then that future-shocked fans scarcely responded to the disturbing allegations that some players used drugs or pep pills to cope with the tensions of daily competition.[14]

Like the plastic men who ran the game and the plastic men who played, pliable baseball fans nodded at such changes. Evidence that the audience approved of the expansion game's style was seen in booming attendance and accelerated television ratings. Thus, "this supposedly stolid, permanent game" displayed remarkable resilience. Was it the game's genius, the *Time* writer asked, that "no other sport is so accurate a reflection of the supposedly stolid, permanent, and ultimately changeable country?"[15]

Profile: Walter O'Malley, Expansionist

Commissioner Landis posed as baseball's all-powerful arbiter; at his death, the club owners resolved to inter the myth with the man. Thus, when Landis passed away in 1944, the owners seized control of the game in a manner reminiscent of the robber baron owners of the 1890s. That these men wanted no more like Landis was evident in 1950 when they thrashed A.B. Chandler for declaring that he was no mere owners' commissioner. The next man to assume the official role was much better fit for their style: when Ford Frick became Commissioner, the owners at last had found a plastic man who would oblige their wishes while wallowing in his title.

That power fully reposed in the hands of owners was noticed by sportswriters, who prated about "The Lords of Baseball." Although intended as a derisive label, the term suited the new breed of owners, who bought clubs for various reasons; perhaps they sought the public light for themselves or publicity for their business interests. Personal glory now loomed large among the perquisites of ownership. Affluence was widespread, with so many Americans becoming millionaires that the achievement was robbed of its glory. However, if a millionaire happened to own a major league ball club, his celebrity status was assured. One critic cynically quipped: "When you buy a professional team, you put yourself on page one of the sporting pages whenever you want.... You become a big man overnight."[1]

The passing of old guard owners in the 1950s—men like Connie Mack, Sam Breadon, Alva Bradley, Bill Benswanger, and five others in 1959 alone—afforded openings for status-seeking nabobs. There was no shortage of bidders; newcomers vied for ownership whenever a franchise was put on the block and quoted sums for new franchises that jetted prices to dramatic highs. Each fresh wave of expansion found new bidders with fat purses willing to push those prices higher still.

Unlike Bill Veeck or Cal Griffith—who were born to ownership and knew the game well, but depended on baseball earnings for their livelihood—most of the new breed were wealthy men with lucrative outside interests. Some owned breweries, radio and television stations, newspapers, and pharmacies while others piloted insurance, construction, trucking, real estate, or investment firms. To at least eleven of the twenty club owners in 1969, baseball interests ranked second in their lives. Such men could be manipulated by a shrewd leader, but not by shrill activists like Charles Finley or Bob Short, whose shenanigans scandalized the rest of the group.

The new owners varied in personalities, commands of power, and degrees of commitment. They were individualistic, competitive, and mercenary—qualities sometimes gentled by altruism. Still, the new "Lords of Baseball" were an ungovernable lot. Most of them regarded the Commissioner as a mere hireling whose chief function was to support their interests. Like the old magnates, these Lords loved publicity and were especially enraptured by the narcissistic potential of television. Like their forebears, they battled among themselves, sometimes forming temporary power blocks, and pitted young Turks against old guardsmen in wrangles over player control, rule changes, television policy, league expansion, and other issues. Finally, like the magnates who ran against the temper of their times, the Lords bucked the reformist climate of the 1960s.

Indeed, they were much criticized and not only by the more liberal-minded. Television official Roone Arledge called them "a loose confederation of carney operators with a small sprinkling of enlightened statesmen thrown in." He favored licensing them; one sportswriter concurred, adding that each should be given a psychological test to weed out misfits. Few critics however, went so far as Marvin Miller, who branded them "unnecessary," adding that he found them peevish, overbearing, vindictive, gullible, vain, childish, and cruel.[2]

Still, there was no denying their powers. As big fish in a small pond, owners ruled over local television stations, commanded players and managers, and shaped the changing game; yet their stubborn independence diffused their powers and left them leaderless. Each jealously guarded his own franchise, running it as he pleased, negotiating television contracts, and retaining most home gate receipts. Vast differences among the clubs stirred jealousies, as the richest, located in the larger urban areas, drew more crowds, won more lucrative television contracts, and monopolized more pennants and profits.

Competitive equality was never a reality in major league baseball. Differences in wealth had always existed, proving that pennants and profits did not necessarily pass to the wealthiest. Had that been the case a competitive balance would have arrived with the new breed of wealthy owners. Indeed, something more was needed to tip the balance in favor of one certain direction. Call it ruthlessness or the hustling spirit, golden rewards were shed on the bold gambler who dared defy tradition and break new promotional ground. In this enterprise, none of the Lords of Baseball succeeded as brilliantly as Walter Francis O'Malley.

The contrast between the lordly O'Malley and his struggling hireling, Jackie Robinson, who "never had it made," is a lesson in the persistence of inequality in America. The son of the New York City Commissioner of Public Markets, from the day of his birth in 1897 O'Malley basked in wealth and privilege. As a student politician at the University of Pennsylvania, O'Malley honed the skills that would make him the most powerful of baseball men. Armed with degrees in law and engineering, O'Malley was a prosperous lawyer and investor when he replaced Wendell Willkie in 1941 as attorney for the Brooklyn Dodgers. As his passion for baseball grew, he maneuvered to unseat the dynamic Rickey as club president. Openly envious of his great rival, O'Malley fought Rickey, even opposing his Robinson venture, and eventually forced him to sell his quarter interest in the team for $1,050,000. When Rickey was gone, O'Malley still harbored a grudge and vindictively tried to discredit Rickey's contributions. He even forbade the mentioning of Rickey's name.

O'Malley determined to gain full control of the Dodgers and he did, purchasing the remaining 50 percent of the stock from the Ebbets estate for a mere $1 million. It was a bargain price for this powerful and profitable franchise; O'Malley recouped the entire million and more when he later sold Ebbets Field and the Montreal farm club for $8 million. Before long, word spread in owner circles of O'Malley's growing power. In 1950, when the owners voted to oust Chandler, the victim blamed O'Malley for charging the opposition.[3] Later, under the more docile Frick, O'Malley's name appeared on the powerful executive committee and other key baseball panels. As one of few owners willing to accept committee assignments, O'Malley legitimately expanded his powers.

By maintaining a low public profile and working behind the scenes, O'Malley became baseball's *éminence grise*. "He has a face that even Dale Carnegie would want to punch," was Veeck's description of the plump, cigar-smoking O'Malley, whose spectacles and Cheshire cat smile fenced in a cunning brain. Writer Roger Kahn shared Veeck's judgment, remembering the Depression days when O'Malley served subpoenas on bankrupt firms. As a young reporter, Kahn heard O'Malley deride sportswriters as "freeloaders" and ball players as "money hungry," yet writers knew O'Malley as a flatterer who convivially referred to himself as "Fatso."[4]

Howling Brooklyn fans damned O'Malley after the 1957 Dodger exodus. Brooklyn had been the most victorious and profitable of all National franchises. Even more lucrative than the Yankees, the Dodgers of the 1950s alone contributed 44 percent of the league's gross profits and annually drew over a million fans to antiquated Ebbets Field.

O'Malley, however, dreamed of bigger profits. Mindful of the demographics of Brooklyn and Ebbets Field, he pressured New York City politicians for land on which to build a new park with a better location. This smokescreen concealed a more ambitious scheme; having watched carpetbagging owners profit from moves to Milwaukee, Baltimore, and Kansas City, O'Malley hatched the biggest coup of all. Eying the lucrative Los Angeles territory—a sprawling, populous urban region that was growing into the richest market in America—O'Malley made his move.

In 1957 rumors of his intentions alarmed Brooklyn fans and prompted a Congressional subcommittee investigation into possible anti-trust violations. Summoned to tell the committee what he knew, National League President Warren Giles reported that the owners had okayed the O'Malley and Stoneham joint move. Giles declared that he himself was "not interested" in the decision to leave the east coast; such matters were outside the scope of his $50,000 job. How-

Horace Stoneham (*left*) and Walter O'Malley (*right*), owners of the Giants and Dodgers respectively, whose joint move to the west coast touched off major league baseball's expansion era.

ever, Giles did relate that Commissioner Frick had warned the owners by telegram that the proposed move might hurt the Pacific Coast League.

Frick's warning was ignored. What counted in the owners' decision was that O'Malley and Stoneham had purchased territorial rights to Los Angeles and San Francisco from fellow owners Philip Wrigley and Tom Yawkey. Moreover, O'Malley and Stoneham had promised to defray the increased transportation costs that their moves would impose on other clubs. The entire maneuver was a crafty bit of planning on O'Malley's part, and it won approval. Still, the Congressional committee was shocked to learn that such decisions were made solely by owners, with no input from the Commissioner.

O'Malley appeared before the committee and related that he had "euchered" himself into a position "where I had sold my ball park and I had to have a place . . . to play ball and the first group of people that . . . showed that they had a little old-fashioned American initiative . . . was the people from Los Angeles." He denied that he once sought public money to build a park in New York and retorted, "I don't want to be a tenant in a political ball park. I want to own my own ball park and run it the way I think it should be run." He had divested his holdings toward this end, and now planned to use the money to build a park in Los Angeles.[5]

Cleverly, O'Malley revived the American reverence for free enterprise to justify his movements; but, in fact, he had been offered 300 downtown acres by Los Angeles politicians. The condemned land was known as Chavez Ravine, although O'Malley insisted that it was really Goat Hill Ravine. Along with his land he received mineral rights and a promise of publicly financed access roads. Indeed, O'Malley had waged a sure bet; no pioneer going west had ever been so certain of lining his pockets when he got there. The public scolding he received for abandoning the loyal and profitable Brooklyn territory stung the hardest. O'Malley's mercenary move was called the "most distasteful" of all the franchise shifts. Taking refuge in silence, he did venture the cynical comment: "If I'm going to a carpetbagger, I might just as well carry the satchel."[6]

The west coast fans flocked to see the Giants and Dodgers. While both clubs profited, it soon became apparent that O'Malley had by far the richer territory. The Dodgers proceeded to break all major league attendance records, drawing over two million fans a season for a dozen years and luring more than three million in 1978 alone. Even during the first four seasons when the club played at the Los Angeles Coliseum, a converted football stadium, fans lined up to lease uncomfortable, backless seats, where from poor vantage points they watched games played under horrible field conditions. The field rewarded right-handed hitters with cheap homers, while robbing hard-hitting lefties. Still, the players adjusted and the fans kept coming. After a dismal finish in 1958, the team won the pennant in 1959. To cap off the season, 270,000 fans jammed the Coliseum for the three World Series games played at home. This turnout set a record that still stands.

In 1962 the Dodgers moved into their new, $20 million home, an edifice designed and owned by O'Malley. The owner, ignoring public gifts, boasted that Dodger Stadium was the only privately owned park. Dodger Stadium indeed epitomized the profits that a hustling owner could wring out of baseball. O'Malley fussed over his baby. He haunted the park, insisting on high standards of cleanliness. He set low ticket prices and kept them at the same rate until 1976, when the pressures of inflation forced him to raise them a dollar. Even this altruistic act had its mercenary seedling; O'Malley explained, "The future of all pro sports has to do with building a grass-roots following, starting with youngsters going to games with their parents."[7] By luring fans to the park for night games that started at the early hour of 7:30 and by limiting the number of free water fountains, O'Malley could count on profiting from the hungry and thirsty hordes at concession stands, where revenues far exceeded ticket income.

The television fans didn't escape O'Malley's attention either. Insistent that no viewer get a free showing of the Dodgers, he schemed to sell Dodger games on pay television. That idea is being adopted today by most owners, and its profit potential is formidable, but in the 1950s O'Malley was stayed by a California referendum which banned the paid televising of sports events. O'Malley retaliated by offering the fewest number of televised games of any club, yet he still obtained a profitable television contract.

O'Malley's Dodgers led all clubs in profits and stood second only to the Yankees in championships won. Their leader, the first Lord of Baseball, headed the Dodgers from 1950 through 1969, during which time he saw his teams win eight pennants and four world titles, and twice tie for league championships, only to lose in the playoffs. He announced his 1970 retirement as Dodger president at the peak of his glory, though by designating his son Peter for his position, O'Malley wielded power until his death in 1979. He also served until then as Dodger Board Chairman and remained a power in league councils and an unofficial counselor to the Commissioner.

Although his successful west coast coup sufficiently ranked O'Malley as a giant of this era, his powers reached far beyond his Los Angeles barony; they extended to the nerve centers of baseball. Kingmaker O'Malley was more influential than any of the three Commissioners he crowned. As head of the mighty owners' executive committee, he maneuvered behind the scenes to make and break commissioners. Thus, he fired Chandler, manipulated Frick, hired and fired William Eckert, and advised Bowie Kuhn on what to do and say. O'Malley pushed Kuhn into the post as his compromise candidate and saved him later from a headhunting cabal of owners. Understandably, Kuhn objected to newspaper stories which depicted him as O'Malley's man: "Those stories are actually a tribute to his [O'Malley's] stature. I respect it, but don't bow to it. We think alike."[8] However, after barring Charley Finley's 1976 multi-million dollar player auction, Kuhn admitted in sworn testimony that he had acted on O'Malley's advice.[9]

In the judgment of astute observers like Veeck and writer Leonard Koppett, O'Malley was baseball's "most influential individual," a smooth politician who shaped decisions on weighty matters like expansion, divisional playoffs, World Series night games, and labor contracts with the Players Association. In 1965 Arthur Daley wrote that O'Malley ruled baseball in all areas, save those dictated by television interests.[10]

With a curious blend of vanity and self-effacement, O'Malley disclaimed his powerful role. While admitting that he held key committee posts, he insisted that those offices were due to his dedicated availability. Other owners, he argued, had the same opportunities to serve, but chose not to in favor of outside business interests. When accused of gaining huge profits from baseball, he attested that he paid $850,000 a year in Los Angeles real estate taxes, a higher tax burden than all the other clubs combined. Charged with being all-powerful, he claimed that his policies did not always win: he had opposed the rookie free agent draft and his 1969 expansion proposal had failed, forcing him to accept the present system. O'Malley would only admit to being the compromising voice among owners.

O'Malley always looked after his Dodger fief. In 1961, when the Nationals allowed the Americans to put an expansion club in Los Angeles, O'Malley held the interloping owner hostage. As O'Malley's tenant at Dodger Stadium, Gene Autry paid a high rent and was zealously billed for half of all Stadium expenses, right down to the toilet paper. Meanwhile, O'Malley canceled his radio contract with one of Autry's stations and awarded the contract to a rival. Such ruthless treatment was O'Malley's way of handling a poacher—and it was effective. Badly beaten at the gate by O'Malley's glamorous Dodgers, and yet forced to pay immense costs, Autry surrendered and moved, leaving O'Malley in full charge of his turf.

O'Malley's other enemies also met their comeuppances. Critical sportswriters were starved for stories; this included Roger Kahn, who had known O'Malley for forty years. Tough-minded field managers like Leo Durocher and Chuck Dressen were sacked and replaced by sycophants like Walter Alston, who labored for 24 years under the pressure of one-year, renewable contracts. When Alston retired, Tom Lasorda, a longtime Dodger hireling who knew his place, took over. Lasorda wrote doggerel poetry in praise of "Dodger Blue" and O'Malley's manor.

Sportscaster Red Barber was dismissed for requesting a raise. At the time Barber earned $50,000, but O'Malley replaced him with Vince Scully, who took the job for $7,500. Likewise, business manager Harold Parrott was cut loose and general manager "Buzzy" Bavasi, a 30-year servant and the victor of many salary negotiation battles with players, was shunted off to San Diego. Such was

O'Malley's cunning that some suspected Bavasi's presence in San Diego as a way of dealing with a nearby rival.[11]

O'Malley, baseball's dominant profiteer, amassed a fortune unmatched by any owner in baseball history. His genius for minting dollars extended to designing and building a golf course and to starting a housing development on surplus acreage from his land grant. O'Malley even turned the salary revolution, so frightening to other owners, into profit. With a 1977 payroll of $2.5 million, O'Malley counted on return publicity to pay for this feat; the fans who turned out to watch his plutocratic players more than made this up. Though his reasoning in money matters seemed odd, O'Malley worked by his own logic. He once complained to fellow owners of losing $2 million over one season; his colleagues were shocked until they learned that he really meant his profits had fallen by that amount. Thus, a $3 million profit spelled a $2 million loss over the $5 million he had expected to make.

Sometimes O'Malley expansively pondered baseball's future and envisioned a global league that would include the most profitable cities of Japan and Latin America. At other times he opposed interleague play for the major leagues because "the economics are not there." While the magnate's money hunger paints him as a zealot, O'Malley was actually in tune with his time. For many Americans, money was the measure of success; judged by this yardstick, O'Malley stood tallest among owners. His 1977 franchise was valued at $50 million, an enormous sum by baseball standards, but modest enough when compared with other contemporary industries.

In 1978 the 75-year-old O'Malley received the first annual August A. Busch award for "meritorious service to baseball." The award was instituted by Busch, a wealthy owner who shared O'Malley's world view. O'Malley, however, didn't need a trophy to prove his importance. His place among baseball's symbolic leaders is secure because he epitomized the hustling spirit that transformed baseball in the expansion era. O'Malley surely was a towering figure, but whether posterity will recall him as hero, villain, or fool is debatable. Assessed by the values of profit, power, and growth, he was a giant. Seen as an evolutionary throwback to the robber baron owners of the 1890s, O'Malley might yet be judged the last of a doomed species, a baseball Brontosaurus.

Expansion Baseball: The National League

The Ten-Team League, 1962–1968

The campaign that ended with the humiliation of the Reds in the 1961 World Series was the last eight-club National League race. The following year the Nationals joined the Americans in expanding to ten teams; a player draft was held that winter to stock the new Houston and New York outposts. Because the draft stripped teams of able reserves, clubs who harbored productive farm systems, like the Giants and the Dodgers, were favored in the 1962 race.

Few observers picked Cincinnati, but Hutchinson's Reds battled hard, winning 98 games on stout pitching by Purkey and Jay and the inspired batting from Frank Robinson, who hit .342 with 39 homers and 136 RBIs. This bettered their 1961 winning gait, but the Dodgers and Giants each won 101 to force another playoff.

In reviving their dynastic claims, the Dodgers relied on pitching and record-breaking speed around the bases. Big Don Drysdale, now at the peak of his career, won 25 to lead all pitchers, while

Koufax, still trying for greatness, won fourteen games. Drysdale's teammate, outfielder Tommy Davis, led the league in batting and RBIs, so he and Drysdale each seemed the likely MVP candidate. At the same time Dodger shortstop Maury Wills electrified the baseball world by stealing 104 bases to break Cobb's seasonal record. Thus, the team's total of 198 steals doubled the output of any rival.

During most of the season, speed and pitching kept Alston's men out front, but the surging Giants caught them at the very end and deadlocked. Using battle-tested tactics like power hitting and pitching, the Giants outgunned all clubs in batting. A quartet of Giants—Orlando Cepeda, Felipe Alou, Willie Mays, and Harvey Kuenn—topped .300, and Mays's league-leading 49 homers produced 141 RBIs. The pitching foursome of Jack Sanford, Juan Marichal, Billy O'Dell, and Billy Pierce won 77, led by Sanford's 24 total. Still, the Giants needed a Dodger collapse, and the Dodgers obliged by losing 10 of their last 13, including the final four.

To decide the championship, the fourth playoff in league history followed. In appeared in all and because they lost two, writers had a field day dredging up memories and calling the Dodgers "chokers." The playoffs opened at the Giants's new Candlestick Park. The home team fell upon the ailing Koufax for three early runs and coasted to an 8–0 win behind Pierce's three-hitter. Action shifted to the new Dodger Stadium, where the Dodgers fell behind 5–0 and then rallied for seven in the sixth to eke out an 8–7 win. Ghostly 11-year-old memories swirled around the deciding game, as the Dodgers took a 4–2 lead into the ninth. To get the clinching outs, Alston called on reliefers, but they loaded the bases on a single and two walks. Then, an infield single, a sacrifice fly, two wild pitches, two walks, and an infield error produced four Giant runs. Thus, once again, the Dodgers beat themselves, as 45,000 Los Angeles fans watched in stunned disbelief.

Following this eerie repeat of the Giants's 1951 victory, the script once again called for a Giant loss to the Yanks in the World Series. The action unfolded with the well-balanced opponents exchanging victories—first the Yanks, then the Giants—and with bad weather delaying the final game for thirteen days. Then 44,000 fans saw the Yankees win game and title at Candlestick Park. The Giants came agonizingly close; with two on and two out, Willie McCovey's smash went right to the second baseman for the final out.

Ironically, the next season mirrored the 1951 aftermath. As they did in 1952, the 1963 Dodgers rebounded, winning 99 to finish six games ahead of the Cards. Moreover, Koufax at last fulfilled his promise. Having solved his control problems, he next fell victim to chronic elbow arthritis that pained his every outing. The strange circulatory ailment that numbed a finger of his pitching hand had sidelined him in 1962, but improved this year; he won 25 and led the league in winning percentage, strike-outs (306), and ERA (1.88). Combined with Ron Perranoski's great relief work, this pair carried a weakened pitching staff and overcame toothless batting. The Dodgers managed a weak .251 average, but Davis won another batting title while Wills batted .302 and led the league with 40 steals.

The ancient script again called for the Dodgers to lose to the Yankees, but the 1963 Dodgers did some rewriting. In the opener at Yankee Stadium, Koufax set a Series strike-out record by fanning 15 Yankees enroute to a 5–2 win. Next Podres, with help from Perranoski, won a 4–1 decision. Moving to Los Angeles, Drysdale blanked the Yankees 1–0, and the next day Koufax completed the sweep by outpitching Ford, 2–1. It was an awesome display of pitching prowess: Yankee batters were held to a .171 average. While the Dodgers batted only .214, consistent hitting by Davis, Frank Howard, and ex-Yankee Bill Skowron made the difference. The Yankees suffered their most humiliating Series defeat.

The incredible Koufax pitched another no-hitter in the succeeding season; he lowered his ERA to a stingy 1.74, averaged nine strike-outs a game, and blanked opponents seven times. Unfortunately, chronic arm pain limited his appearances, and when Podres failed to win a game, the pitching collapsed and the team fell to sixth.

Still, the 1964 race was so hotly contested that even the Dodgers finished only 13 games out. That year seven clubs stayed close, with only the Mets and Astros hopelessly out. Curiously, the Mets set attendance records, even as their bumbling play rivaled the Phillies in their worst years. The 1964 Phillies turned tartars. Only three years earlier they had lost 107 games, including 23 in a row, a feat which just missed tying the record losing streak of the 1899 Cleveland "Wanderers." This year, however, manager Gene Mauch had a sturdy pitching staff headed by Jim Bunning, an ex-Tiger ace. Off to an early lead, the Phillies entered the September stretch drive 7½ games ahead of the pack. It was a patchwork team, though, that was too dependent on the hitting of rookie Richie Allen, an erratic third baseman. With 12 games left, they led by 6½; then, horribly, they lost ten straight and ended in a tie for second with the Reds.

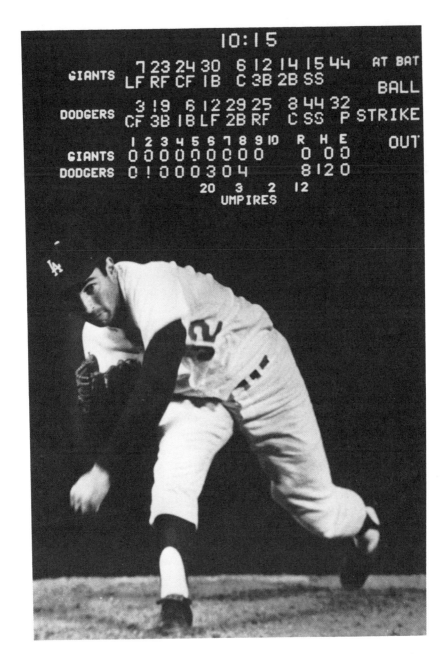

Brilliant pitching by lefty Sandy Koufax led the Dodgers to new heights in the 1960s. Koufax is shown here completing one of two no-hitters he hurled against the Giants.

As the Phillies fell, the Cardinals rushed to their first flag since 1946. Their only triumph over the years was a local one; in 1953 they drove out the Browns and claimed St. Louis as their fief. Thereafter, owner Busch's Cardinals lived on promises—that the club would revive, that a new park would replace their decrepit old one, and that a new hero would replace the retired Stan Musial.[1]

Even after a strong run in 1963, little was expected from the team, despite Busch's raging threats to shake up the club. In August he fired general manager "Bing" Devine and rumors had manager John Keane's head on the block; yet it was Devine and Keane who turned this team around. Devine piloted a legendary deal in June, obtaining outfielder Lou Brock from the Cubs in exchange for Ernie Broglio, a sore-armed pitcher. As Broglio faded, Brock leaped to stardom, batting .348 in 1964. Over the next 15 seasons, Brock became Musial's worthy successor, as he set base stealing records and topped the 3,000-hit mark.

The discredited Keane meanwhile assembled a fighting team. First baseman Bill White and third baseman Ken Boyer anchored a fair-fielding, heavy-hitting infield that included Julian Javier at second and Pirate castoff Dick Groat at short. Brock's arrival strengthened an outfield that included the able Curt Flood, who also batted .311. Talented Tim McCarver, the league's best catcher, hit .288. In addition, pitchers Ray Sadecki, Bob Gibson, and Curt Simmons were capable starters, and in another coup Devine acquired Barney Schultz for relief help.

Gibson joined the all-time great pitchers. Handsome and intelligent, Gibson fought off racial slurs and retaliated against fickle fans by stubbornly refusing to sign autographs. He argued that if a boy wanted an autograph, he should get his father's. Gibson used "powder river," his lively fastball, to win 19 in 1964. Before ending his career at 39, he won 251 games and held league records for strike-outs (3,117), most years with 200 or more strike-outs (9), and most consecutive games as a starting pitcher (303).[2]

In late August the Cardinals languished in fourth place, eleven games behind the Phillies. Then, unpredictably, the Phillies swooned and the Cards won 28 of their 39 outings. Schultz offered a big boost when he relieved in seven games and yielded no earned runs. Not until September 30, however, after sweeping three wins from the Phillies, did Keane's men take the lead. Even so, the Phillies and Reds challenged; however, the Reds fell to the Phillies, as the Cards beat the Mets. A mind-boggling three-way tie would have resulted if the Cards had lost that day.

Three stars who paced the Cardinals to two world championships during the 1960s: outfielder Curt Flood (*left*), ace pitcher Bob Gibson (*center*), and outfielder and base-stealing leader Lou Brock (*right*).

The Cards now faced the ever-victorious Yankees, whose star of empire was setting even as they came from behind to snatch a fifth straight flag. This was a strange confrontation between two unexpected winners whose managers had both been served with dismissal notices. One even more bizarre twist existed: the Yankees had already hired Keane as their 1965 manager! This apparent conflict of interest assuredly had no impact on the struggle. In the opener at St. Louis, Ray Sadecki, a 20–game winner, outpitched Ford with help from Schultz. Then Mel Stottlemyre outpitched Gibson, and at Yankee Stadium Jim Bouton beat Simmons 2–1 on a Mantle homer. The Cards took the next two games and returned home needing one win to clinch. Bouton now turned back the Cards to force a deciding game, which Gibson won 7–5 behind a ten-hit barrage. It was a glorious and unexpected victory; Busch was forced to eat crow because Keane, voted Manager of the Year, spurned an offer to return.

The winds of change that toppled the Yankee empire in 1965 transformed the baseball world. The pitiful weakness of the American League was exposed and the adoption of the free agent rookie draft upended the free enterprise scouting system. An alarming predominance of pitching, the opening of a new indoor stadium in

Houston, and the installation of "unknown soldier" William Eckert as Commissioner of Baseball were other major changes which occurred that year. The batting decline was the most menacing development. Although the Cardinals boasted the great Gibson, he could not carry a faltering team alone. In a year that produced only a dozen .300 hitters, fortune favored the fine-pitching Dodgers.

Alston's Dodgers batted only .245 and suffered the loss of Davis, who broke an ankle after playing only 17 games. Alston relied on speed and Wills's fine base stealing and .280 batting to compensate for weak hitting. Still, 49 victories by the great pitching duo of Koufax and Drysdale made the difference.

That year the close race took its toll on Koufax's arthritic arm. The Giants, a more balanced team, dogged closely and as the race grew feverish, these rivals staged a memorable brawl. On August 22, Giant pitching ace Juan Marichal was batting when Dodger catcher John Roseboro fired a ball past his ear. Infuriated, Marichal hit Roseboro's head with his bat, drawing an eight-day suspension and a $1,750 fine. This rash act probably cost the Giants the flag. The race was so close in early September that only half a game separated the Dodgers, Reds, and Giants, with the Braves, Pirates, and Phillies not far behind. With two weeks to go, the Giants won 14 straight to take the lead, but the Dodgers took 15 of 16—including six by Koufax and Drysdale, to land the pennant.

The Dodgers faced the Minnesota Twins in the World Series, a team that had risen from a sixth-place depth to succeed the fallen Yankees. Given little chance now, this hard-hitting team stunned the Dodgers by blasting Drysdale in the opener and downing Koufax the next day. When the action shifted to Los Angeles, 165,000 fans saw the Dodgers sweep three games, during which the Twins scored three runs while the Dodgers rolled up 20. In the last of these three games, the great Koufax put the Dodgers ahead with his four-hit shut-out. The Twins fought hard; they squared the Series in the sixth game at Minnesota. For the deciding game, Alston pondered whether to pitch Drysdale or Koufax. He chose Koufax, who responded with a three-hit shut-out that won the title.

In the following spring, Koufax and Drysdale staged a joint hold-out which aimed at forcing O'Malley to pay them what they deserved. When the two aces' terms were met, their combined salaries topped $200,000; this ignited a general salary revolt. Certainly O'Malley could afford to pay more, because his attendance totals had topped the two million mark for the seventh straight year.

Koufax earned his every penny that year. Pitching in great pain, which was relieved only by cortisone shots and postgame ice treatments, the lefty won 27 and again led all hurlers in victories and ERA. Drysdale slumped to 13–13 and the slack was taken up by Claude Osteen, rookie Don Sutton, and reliefer Phil Regan, who went 14–1 with 21 saves.

This year batting improved, as the team averaged .256 and powered 108 homers. Returning to limited duty, the ailing Davis batted .313 and was the only man to top .300. This was enough for a repeated league victory, but only after another close race. Again the Giants challenged, this time behind ace pitchers Marichal and Gaylord Perry, the league's winningest duo. However, after a brilliant 1965 season, Mays slumped to .288 and hit fewer homers. Even so, the Giants and the hard-hitting Pirates hung close, making the Dodger victory margin a thin game and a half.

The rising Baltimore Orioles dominated the American League. Managed by ex-Yankee Hank Bauer, the Orioles mounted a formidable attack, powered by ex-National League star Frank Robinson. Robinson won a Triple Crown, but even with Robinson and a corps of fine young pitchers, the Orioles looked like grist for the Dodgers.

An incredible display of pitching prowess followed that underscored baseball's imbalance problem. In a Series marred by record weak hitting, the Orioles batting .200 and the Dodgers .142, the Orioles swept the Dodgers. Ex-National Leaguer Moe Drabowsky relieved in the opener, blanking the Dodgers after they scored their only two runs of the Series. Then, in successive outings, Oriole youngsters Jim Palmer, Wally Bunker, and Dave McNally hurled shut-outs to close the Series and restore a measure of American League prestige.

Soon after this terrible defeat, the 31-year-old Koufax retired, acting on the medical advice that continued pitching would cripple his arthritic arm. This was a stunning loss because Koufax had won 165 in 12 seasons, with 97 victories coming in his last four years. His brilliant record included four no-hitters, 40 shut-outs and 2,396 strike-outs. Moreover, the finish of the great pitcher prefigured the fall of the entire Dodgers team; in 1967 they sank to eighth place.

It was a Giant opportunity, but with the slumping Mays joined now by pitchers Marichal and Perry, the club finished second behind the Cardinals. After their 1964 victory, the shaken Cardinals had lapsed into the second division. Owner Busch had further crippled morale by hiring tight-fisted general manager Bob Howsam. Salary squabbles now erupted over miserly offers of $1,500 raises to stars like Flood and Gibson. Howsam imposed childish disciplinary rules, like ordering bullpen pitchers to sit up straight, insisting that socks be worn the same way, and ordering baserunners to stay off the grass while dashing to first base!

Loud hosannas greeted the 1967 departure of this martinet, though Howsam had strengthened the team by acquiring veteran hitters Roger Maris and Orlando "Cha Cha" Cepeda. Maris was indeed no longer the homeric of 1961, but he added depth to the outfield. The real prize was Cepeda, who took over first base and became the team leader and the MVP winner. Shortstop Ed Bressoud added another new face, and manager Red Schoendienst completed the job of rebuilding his infield by converting outfielder Mike Shannon into a passable third baseman. Gibson, of course, dominated the mound staff, but Dick Hughes and young Steve Carlton also pitched well. Now ensconced in new Busch Memorial Stadium, fans turned out two million strong to see the 1967 team in action.

They watched the team grab an early lead and go on to earn 101 victories, leaving the second-place Giants 10½ games behind. Flood led the attack, batting .335; Cepeda hit .325 and piloted the league in RBIs, Brock slammed .299 and ran the league in stolen bases, and McCarver smacked .295. The young pitchers offset the loss of Gibson, who, after winning 13, suffered a broken leg when hit by a line drive off the bat of Roberto Clemente. With Gibson out, Hughes, Carlton, Ray Washburn, and Nelson Briles filled the slack and reliefer Joe Hoerner saved 15.

Matched against the miracle Red Sox—the winners of a close American League race—the Cardinals were gladdened by Gibson's return. In the Boston opener, Gibson scattered six hits enroute to a 2–1 victory. After the Red Sox squared the series on Jim Lonborg's shut-out, Briles won the third and Gibson blanked the Sox 6–0. Down three games to one, the Sox rebounded to win the next two. Now Gibson came back to beat Lonborg and win the decisive game 7–2; this was his third complete game of the Series. Furthermore, Brock's 12 hits led all batters.

Gibson's magnificent 1968 pitching helped to force a decision on the sagging hitting problem. He won 22 games that year, 13 by shut-outs, and his earned run average of 1.12 set a new league mark. He took both the Cy Young and MVP awards. Meanwhile, American League hurler Denny McLain won 31 games, a feat not seen since the 1930s. Such titanic pitching produced record low batting marks—a .243 average for National batters and a .230 mark for Americans. If 1968 was "the year of the pitcher," it was also the year of a frightening attendance decline. The thoroughly alarmed officials opted to help 1969 batters by lowering pitching mounds and narrowing strike zones.

Indeed the dull 1968 race affected attendance. That year the Cardinals broke fast, then dropped to fourth after losing 11 of 13 games in May. By Memorial Day they regrouped and launched a winning streak that ended the race. Winning 54 of their next 70, they led the Cubs by 14 and went on to win a "laugher" by nine games over the Giants. They did this on a .249 team batting average, highlighted by Flood's .301 and Brock's league-leading 62 base steals. Pitching told the tale: the starters allowed fewer than three runs a game and relief ace Hoerner saved 17.

The Cardinals were heavily favored to beat the Tigers in the Series and the first game was touted as a duel between pitching aces Gibson and McLain. Nevertheless, it was no contest, as Gibson fired a shut-out and fanned 17 Tigers, establishing a new Series record. After one Tiger victory, the Cards swept the next two matches by hefty scores, including Gibson's 10–1 laugher. Needing one, the Cards took a three-run lead in the fifth game, but the Tigers rallied to win. Action shifted back to St. Louis, where the Tigers won again. Still, the Cards had Gibson ready for the kill, and the great right-hander held the Tigers scoreless for six innings. The game was scoreless in the seventh when Gibson got two quick outs, but then a pair of singles and a misjudged fly ball by Flood allowed three runs. This was enough to give the Tigers the world title.

Baseball's 1969 Moonwalk

Baseball fans, having digested the sprightly Tiger victory, now pondered the tradition-shattering impact of the upcoming 1969 expansion plan. The new format of both major leagues fielding 12 teams and subdividing into two six-team divisions was hard to visualize for some fans. The winners of the divisions would engage in five-game postseason playoffs to determine the league champions. Equally disruptive was the staging of another talent-draining expansion draft in order to stock the National's new Montreal Expos and San Diego Padres and the American's new Seattle Pilots and Kansas City Royals. Still more confusion welled from the possibility of a players' strike in 1969. Marvin Miller, the zealous director of the Players Association, told players in February not to sign contracts until the pension plan was reformed. A strike was averted when Commissioner Bowie Kuhn, virginal in the office, persuaded owners to meet with Miller; this produced a three-year Basic Agreement that resolved the pension dispute and established the Association as a permanent bargaining agency. While this assured that there would be baseball as usual, the impact of such changes was bewildering to fans; they might as well have been asked to accept the idea of men walking on the moon.

Actually, merely surviving the turbulent 1960s in America inured one to the effects of drastic change. It was a time when leadership was sorely needed to dampen blazing external and internal problems. The American government's involvement with Cuba and with Vietnam forced our citizens to face menacing war threats that continued through the 1960s and beyond. Our fruitless involvement in the Vietnam conflict kindled widespread protests here at home against the government and the military. By 1973, the protests effectively ended the war and with it died the military draft, but a result of all the strife was an undermining of faith in the presidency, the Congress, the courts, and the military and industrial combines that supported the war. Like other institutions, baseball was dragged into the controversy; not only did players face being drafted, but some took anti-war stands that incensed the generally patriotic owners and officials.

In the late 1960s, protests spilled into other areas that affected the game and its principals. Colleges were hotbeds of social protests; students on many campuses held demonstrations against militarism, racism, sexism, and other hot issues. Because baseball now recruited many college players, it was inevitable that such ideas came along to the diamond. Black players took aim at racist policies in baseball. Although they still suffered discrimination, at least several worthy stars reaped more cash and glory. Doors were now opened to admit a few black umpires, along with coaches and a manager or two. Demands for social and sexual liberties were heard from other fronts, and some gained considerable headway in the 1960s. The women's search for equality won some employment opportunities; the battle fought here profoundly altered the relations between the sexes. The world of baseball certainly felt this stirring; confessionary books told of players who challenged sex taboos, of married players who adapted to equalitarian demands from wives, and of women who slowly gained success to jobs in baseball, with a few showing up as baseball writers and minor league umps.

The Greening of America, a popular book of the decade, predicted that a new social consciousness—based on new values of individualism, equality, love, and peace—would reign. By the early 1970s the steam was out of the protest movements, yet much that was positive survived. The struggles provided increased freedom and equality for deprived minorities, especially blacks and women. Moreover, many Americans had learned how to organize effectively—this included ballplayers and umpires.

The 1960s were indeed upsetting years for Americans. Buffeted by changes, bewildered by transience, novelty, and diversity, Americans appeared to be future-shocked.[3] Each passing year sent tremors through the society, but those of 1969 stood out vividly. The death of Eisenhower that year evoked memories—however mythic—of a stable American society of the 1950s, when baseball still fielded two eight-team major leagues. In sharp contrast, President Lyndon B. Johnson's Vietnam policies had divided the nation, as did baseball owners with their ten-team major leagues. Then, in the summer of 1969, Richard Nixon led a captivated nation to applaud the successful moonwalk by American astronauts.

That moonwalk was only a promise when fans tried to "dope out" the upcoming 1969 divisional races. The six contenders in the National League's Eastern division included St. Louis, Pittsburgh, Chicago, Philadelphia, the new Montreal Expos, and the lowly New York Mets. Any thought that the latter might contend this year seemed as remote as the idea of walking on the moon. The West carried San Francisco, Los Angeles, Houston, Atlanta, Cincinnati, and the new San Diego Padres. Although 162 games were still scheduled, the balance now tipped because each team played more games within its division.

Experts took note of the Cardinals and pronounced the eastern circuit the stronger. Indeed, these two-time winners appeared invincible, having acquired outfielder Vada Pinson, first baseman Joe Torre, and reliefer Dave Giusti in trades. With Pinson joining Brock and Flood, the Cardinal outfield appeared to stand second to none. Moreover, with Torre replacing the aging Cepeda at first, the infield ranked with the best. The redoubtable Giusti backed a pitching staff of proven superiority.

The Cardinal starters won 62 games, but the quartet also lost 41 times while the vaunted batting attack fizzled. The team finished a distant fourth in the East. Internal and external pressures told the tale of failure. Internally, Busch's wild raging damaged morale. Incensed by high salary demands, he summoned reporters to a team meeting in March and proceeded to denounce his men as ingrates and unionists who would either shape up or be shipped out. Flood thought this tirade destroyed morale; however, Busch did not relent; when the team flagged, he ordered manager Schoendienst to play rookies.[4]

Meanwhile, outside pressure came from the amazing New York Mets. In preseason forecasts, odds-makers had rated this team 100–1 to lose. Upon their debut in 1962, the Mets had lost 120 games; since then, their record stood at 394 wins and 737 losses. In keeping with tradition, the Mets unfolded their latest season by dropping their home opener.

By now, however, a charismatic aura enrounded this sorry team. Hordes of fans had been aroused during their brief history. The Mets were the Darlings of Gotham, but how long could this last? Weiss and Stengel were gone by now and the fad needed feeding. The 1968 Mets finished an unfortunate ninth, and hopes for 1969 were dimmed when manager Gil Hodges suffered a heart attack. Spring training, however, found Hodges at his post, drilling the team in fundamentals and striving to stop them from losing "by doing dumb things." Early results looked good and one rival allowed that the Mets looked like "pros."[5] Perhaps they did, but this was a nondescript mixture of promising youngsters and aging vets. The youthful pitching staff was headed by Jerry Koosman and Tom Seaver, and catcher Jerry Grote had made the 1968 All-Star team. Otherwise, pickings were slim; of the five outfielders, only Cleon Jones had hit decently. A lackluster infield consisting of bonus baby Ed Kranepool at first, Ken Boswell at second, Bud Harrelson at short, and Ed Charles at third had Hodges subbing Al Weiss and Wayne Garrett. Donn Clendenon, a veteran first baseman, was welcomed from Montreal.

True to form, the Mets lost seven of their first ten games. Then they rallied, balanced their record in May, and won 11 straight in June to stand behind the rampaging Cubs. These Cubs finally looked like winners. After twenty years of futile tinkering—including a disastrous co-manager experiment—owner Philip Wrigley had Leo Durocher managing the team. Durocher, leading the team to the second-place spot in 1968, now looked like a winner. For most of the season his Cubs held a big lead, but his tactics and those of Wrigley Field's "bleacher bums" infuriated rivals. Thus, every time the Cubs ventured into enemy parks, they encountered vengeful opponents.

Sturdy pitching by lefty Jerry Koosman (*left*) and by Tom Seaver (*right*) as well as steady defensive play by shortstop Bud Harrelson (*center*) enabled the "Miracle" Mets to become the first expansion team to win a World Series. This victory happened in 1969.

They came to Shea in July for a three-game series. Met fans jammed the park for each game, and one stay-at-home television fan reportedly struck and killed his wife for switching channels. The Mets took the first two games, but errors cost them the third. Durocher sneered, "Those were the real Mets." Indeed, the team foundered and fell 9½ back.[6]

Then the Mets rallied and doggedly closed the gap. In September, when the Cubs returned to Shea, they held a scant 2½ game lead, which pitchers Koosman and Seaver trimmed to half a game with consecutive victories. More than 50,000 fans stormed the stadium each day, and just before the second game, a fan dropped a black cat in front of the Cub dugout. Perhaps this act helped, but destiny hung like a bright star over this Met team. Down by 9½ in mid-August, they won 38 of their last 49 games, while the shattered Cubs won only 19. The Met charge made a shambles of the race, as the team's 100 wins pushed them ahead by eight games.

This "The Impossible Dream" was blown into the sports story of the year—baseball's equivalent of the moonwalk. It far overshadowed the league's Western division race, where the Braves, Giants, Reds, and Dodgers fought a furious, season-long struggle. Winning 17 of their last 20, the Atlanta Braves clinched the title and ended with 93 wins, three better than the Giants.

The new league format now called for a five-game playoff series to decide the league championship. The Braves showed the better offense, with a .258 team batting average and 141 homers. Hank Aaron's .300 average and 44 homers led the attack, while Rico Carty batted .342 with 16 homers. The Braves also received strong pitching from knuckle-baller Phil Niekro, winner of 23, and bullpen ace Cecil Upshaw, savior of 27 matches. Although the Mets won seven more games, their hitting paled. Pitcher Seaver of the Mets led the league with 25 wins and Koosman added 17.[7]

The starstruck Mets swept the first playoff series. Relief pitcher Ron Taylor starred in the first two games, played at Atlanta Stadium. Down 5–4 late in the first game, the Mets rallied for five in the eighth, with Taylor coming on to save the game. In the second game, the Mets soared to an early 8–0 lead, but the Braves routed Koosman. Again, Taylor stopped the threat and, with help from Tug McGraw, preserved an 11–6 win. Moving to Shea, the Mets clinched the pennant with a 7–4 victory behind the pitching of Gary Gentry and Nolan Ryan.

The Baltimore Orioles won three consecutive American League pennants in 1969 through 1971 behind pitching aces Mike Cuellar (*left*) and Jim Palmer (*right*).

Now the Mets went to Baltimore to face the indomitable Orioles in the World Series. Winners of 109 games and easy playoff victors, the Orioles heavily outgunned Met hitters and boasted baseball's most balanced pitching staff in Mike Cuellar, Dave McNally, and Jim Palmer. With pardonable pride, a Baltimore paper proclaimed: "Met Miracle Story Nearing End."[8] The outcome of the first game supported this prophesy, as Cuellar outpitched Seaver and toyed with Met batters, winning 4–1. The Mets squared matters when Koosman pitched a two-hitter and took a close 2–1 victory. Moving to Shea, 56,000 Metomaniacal fans saw Gentry and Ryan shut down the Orioles 5–0. Up by a game, Hodges sent Seaver against Cuellar; Seaver won this time, hurling ten stout innings, in a game highlighted by two acrobatic, "game saving" catches by right-fielder Ron Swoboda. Needing one to clinch, Koosman again faced McNally. This time the desperate Orioles took an early three-run lead, but in the sixth Jones proved by a smudge of shoe polish on the ball that he had been hit. He was awarded first base and then carried home by Clendenon's homer. Then, weak-hitting Al Weiss, whose .455 batting led all Series hitters, unexpectedly homered in the seventh to tie the game. Two Met doubles and two Oriole errors in the eighth settled the issue.

The last out triggered a riot, as the fans burst onto the field, some tearing up clods of soil for fetishes. Tons of shredded paper snowed from Manhattan office windows, bus drivers disdained fares, and a newspaper headline read, "A Grateful City Goes Wild." Metomania quickly swept the nation, creating a legend of the team whose improbable success fulfilled Everyman's fantasies.

However, most great American success stories end with payoffs, and this one had the eyeballs of Met players turning into dollar signs. Each Met player received a record-high Series check of $18,338. This was followed by an unprecedented number of endorsement offers, television appearances, magazine features, and the usual souvenirs; within six months a dozen books exploited the event. Later when Hodges won the Manager of the Year award and Seaver netted the Cy Young trophy, the stakes were raised.

The cash, of course, tarnished the glory of the miracle. A spate of obscene phone calls followed Seaver's announcement of his "availability" for commercial offers. Eventually jealousy and backbiting destroyed team unity. Thus, recalling the Greek tragedies, the miracle ended with a whimpering collapse in 1970.

The Big Red Machine and the Bucs, 1970–1978

Although a new decade blew in with 1970, it must not be supposed that some heavenly trumpet sounded the end to the storm of the 1960s. Protests continued in full fury, extending beyond the end of the Vietnam War in 1973 to the Watergate affair that forced President Nixon's resignation. When the storms subsided, the cynical, soul-sick people turned inward, taking refuge in individualism and conservatism.[9]

Commitment to individualism now allowed a wider ranger of accepted lifestyles, though this was counteracted by a stronger tendency for Americans to reaffirm their faith in the capitalistic system. Thus, the decade's dawning saw a return to dynastic monopolies in baseball. Instead of the competitive balance predicted by supporters of the new division system, two powerful National League minidynasties dominated. The Eastern Pirates were winners of five races from 1970–1975, before yielding to the Phillies in the next three. In the West, Cincinnati's "Big Red Machine" took five of seven races from 1970–1976, before the Dodgers won the next two. In playoff duels, six of the nine league pennants were won by the western powers.

The Mets, Cubs, and Pirates battled in the East, with the Mets touted as likely winners of the 1970 race. However, they sank to third and the Cubs performed their usual collapse. Manager Danny Murtaugh led his Pirates into the breach and to the top for the first

The Orioles's matchless Robinson boys: third baseman Brooks (*left*) set an all-time fielding record at his position, and outfielder Frank (*right*) won MVP awards in each league, was awarded a Triple Crown, and later became the first black manager in the majors.

time in a decade. Only Mazeroski and Clemente remained from the 1960 champs; if the fading Mazeroski showed his age, the 36-year-old Clemente was at his dazzling best, leading the team with a .352 average. An established superstar, this handsome Puerto Rican was both the team leader and the hero of Hispanic–Americans. Sharply critical of discrimination, he battled to improve the lot of Hispanics. For this and for his alleged moodiness, Clemente was criticized by conservative writers, but his all-round play propelled him to diamond immortality and his active concern for the downtrodden placed him amongst world heroes.

Leading the Pirates to victory in 1970, Clemente anchored an outfield of Matty Alou, Willie Stargell!, and Al Oliver. Stargell and Oliver supplied the offensive power, Alou the short hits, and Clemente did it all. With a sound inner defense and reliable bench strength, Murtaugh platooned effectively, using young Dave Cash and Fred Patek to spell Mazeroski and Gene Alley, while Bob Robertson and Richie Hebner were fixtures at first and third. Catcher Manny Sanguillen doubled as a reliable .325 hitter. Pitching, how-

Slugging outfielder Willie "Pops" Stargell (*left*) was the heart and muscle of the Pirate teams for twenty seasons. Manny Sanguillen (*right*), a good catcher with the Pirates, was eventually traded for manager Chuck Tanner.

ever, posed a problem. Shaky starters Dock Ellis, Luke Walker, and Bruce Del Canton needed constant help from fireman Dave Giusti, whose 9–3 record included 26 saves. Therefore, the Pirates relied on a .270 team batting average for their 89 victories, five better than the runner-up Cubs. Stargell and Clemente set batting records enroute, Stargell tying a major league record with five extra base hits in a game and Clemente setting a new one with ten hits in two games.

As the Pirates broadsided to victory in the East, manager "Sparky" Anderson led his "Big Red Machine" to an easy win in the West. The Pirates blessed their new Three Rivers Stadium with a division title; the Reds similarly baptized their new Riverfront Stadium. Again mirroring their rivals, the Reds relied on batting and defense to shore up weak pitching. At .270, these rivals tied in batting, but the Reds led the league in homers, with 191. Moreover, three Reds—first baseman Tony Perez and outfielders Pete Rose and Bob Tolan—topped .300 and catcher Johnny Bench, hitting .293, led the league in homers (45) and RBIs (148), and took MVP honors. However, Anderson's starting pitchers were flogged so often that he earned the nickname of "Captain Hook" for yanking them for reliefers Wayne Granger, Clay Carroll, and Don Gullett, a threesome who combined to save 57 games.

The real Red hero, however, was a stocky, muscular, pixie-faced scrapper named Pete Rose. This 29-year-old switch hitter was an established star who won consecutive batting titles in 1968 and 1969. Dubbed "Charlie Hustle," his aggressive play stirred memories of Cobb. The relentlessly consistent Rose later set a league record for most hits and threatened Cobb's all-time mark.

With the league's best offense, Anderson's Reds rolled over Western opponents, winning 102 and finishing 14½ games up on the Dodgers. Enroute to a playoff sweep, the Reds beat the Pirates by oddly symmetrical scores of 3–0, 3–1, and 3–2. Rose led a tenth-inning uprising in the opener at Pittsburgh, as Gary Nolan pitched a shut-out. The next day Tolan homered and scored all three runs, and Jim Merritt and Gullett staved off the Pirates. Returning home, the Reds used homers by Perez and Bench to clinch.

Now the Orioles invaded, imbued with terrible resolve to avenge their 1969 World Series humiliation. Adapting quickly to Riverfront's artificial turf, the Orioles scored two single-run victories. In the third game, three Oriole homers powered a 9–2 win. Down by three, the Reds rallied for a 6–5 victory, but another nine-run Oriole assault gave the American dynasts the world title.

Forecasts of a rematch in 1971 were proven only partly true when the Reds failed. Although Rose batted .304 and young Gullett pitched well, team batting fell by 29 points and the relief corps failed to bail out the battered starters. Hence, the Reds sagged to fourth place and the San Francisco Giants rushed to the fore. Manager Charlie Fox drove these perennial bridesmaids to victory by one game over the Dodgers. The win gave a needed financial boost to owner Stoneham, whose stadium attendance had eroded under competition from the rising A's quartered across the bay. The Giants's boost came via an 11-game lead compiled in June, but was then squandered by losing 18 of 24 in September. The team barely outlasted the Dodgers. Indeed, the Giants had sturdy pitchers in veterans Perry and Marichal, but the team's .247 batting was solely brightened by Bobby Bonds's .288 average, which included 33 homers and 102 RBIs. Sadly, as weak as the hitting was the leaky infield that led the league in errors.

Meanwhile, the Mets had gotten off to their best start, while Red Schoendienst drove the revived Cardinals into the fray. In July the Mets faltered and the Pirates surged to the top. Except for Dave Cash at second, manager Murtaugh fielded the same lineup. The rebounding hitters were led by Clemente and Sanguillen, while Stargell's 48 homers led the league. Overall, the Pirates batted .274, but pitching made the Buccaneer difference, as Ellis won 19, young Steve Blass took 15, and Giusti saved 30 games. Still, help was needed and it came; Nelson Briles, a Cardinal castoff who now pitched for the Pirates, won eight matches and, ironically, provided padding for the Pirates's winning margin over the Cards.

So far the league's postseason playoffs had seen sweeps by the winners, but this time was different. Losing the opener to the Giants in San Francisco, the Pirates returned with a 9–4 victory, Robertson driving in five runs on three homers and a double. Back home, the Pirates clinched with two straight victories, the first by 2–1 on homers by Robertson and Hebner; the clincher was a 9–5 slugging festival, decided by a pair of three-run homers by Hebner and Oliver. The Giants purposely walked Stargell to pitch to Oliver, who in turn broke a 5–5 tie with his blast.

Installed as underdogs, the Pirates faced the Orioles in the first nocturnal World Series. The Orioles had finished with a magnificent 14-game winning streak, including a playoff sweep, and so were touted as victors. Opening at home, the Orioles took the first two by scores of 5–3 and 11–3, and experts muttered mismatch. Murtaugh defiantly snarled, "You haven't seen the real Pirates yet." When action shifted to the synthetic turf of Three Rivers Stadium, his prophesy unfolded.

In the third game, Blass pitched a three-hitter, winning 5–1. Then Kison and Giusti combined for a 4–3 win, as the Pirates overcame a 3–0 deficit, battering Oriole pitching for 14 hits. Fifty-one thousand Pittsburgh fans next saw their team move ahead on Briles's two-hit shut-out. At home again, the cornered Orioles used three of their elite starters in a last stand that produced a 10-inning 3–2 victory. Only the decider was left—"a four pack thriller," as measured by tobacco-chewing Murtaugh. Blass and Cuellar now locked in a tight duel that saw Clemente club the first Pirate hit, a solo homer, in the fourth inning. Jose Pagan doubled home a run in the eighth, making it 2–0. The Orioles fighting back touched Blass for a run, but the Pirates held tight winning the game 2–1 and the title.

As the Pirate locker room resounded with joy, President Nixon phoned congratulations to Murtaugh and the heroic Clemente complained to reporters of likely financial discrimination for the team's black and Hispanic stars. Meanwhile, Pittsburgh fans staged the "Big Buc Binge." Early reports counted 40,000 rioting fans downtown— some danced nude, some broke windows and burned cars, some made love in public, some injured friends and foes, and some 98 were definitely incarcerated. Mayor Pete Flaherty, trying to avoid any suits, refused to term it a riot, but the 100,000 revelers reminded observers of the active protestors of the 1960s. Whatever the case, Pirate fans would wait eight long seasons for a similar excuse to explode.[10]

Baseball's second general strike staged in the following spring caused a far greater stir than the "Buc Binge." Before the players were finally granted increased pension funding, the 1972 strike wiped out spring training and some of the seasonal games. Hence, no team played its full 162-game schedule. Fortunately, decisive victories by the Reds and Bucs stilled the sour grape talk of tainted winners.

Pittsburghers mourned that winter the ailing Murtaugh's retirement. His was a tough act to follow, but Bill Virdon took over and drove the Pirates to a third straight Eastern title. With the exceptions of sending newcomers Gene Clines and Vic Davalillo to the outfield and moving Stargell to first base, Virdon fielded the same team. Again, Pirate hitters led the league; Clemente, Oliver, Clines, Hebner, and Davalillo all topped .300. In addition, improved pitching ranked Pirate flingers second in ERA. Blass, the leader, won 19, while relievers Giusti and Ramon Hernandez together saved 36 games. Such talent and statistics made for an easy gait and an 11-game finish over the Durocher-less Cubs. The Cards once again suffered their owner's pique, as Busch denounced the strike settlement and hung tough on salary demands. In a petulant mood, he dealt star pitcher Steve Carlton to the Phils, thereby losing a 27-game winner. Likewise, the Cards watched as Clemente's heroics sparked the Pirates. Indeed, on September 30, Clemente slapped his 3,000th career hit to join the elite circle.

The Pirates romped, but so did the Big Red Machine with a boost from "Spec" Richardson, the blundering GM of the Astros. Richardson dealt five players to the Reds, including infielder Joe Morgan and pitcher Jack Billingham, in exchange for Lee May, Tommy Helms, and a utility player. Anything the ex-Reds did for Houston was overmatched by Morgan alone, as the little second sacker soon copped two MVP awards. Billingham joined a battered pitching staff which completed only 25 games! As Anderson daily hooked starters, reliever Carroll notched a league-leading 37 saves. The team was saved by its running attack, its league-leading fielding, and its hitting. Only Rose topped .300, but Bench again led the league in homers and RBIs, taking another MVP award. By winning 63 games in the second half of the season, the Reds outlegged the Astros by 10½ games.

The playoff of the mini-dynasties lasted five games before the Reds landed the pennant. After dividing two games in Pittsburgh, the Pirates pushed ahead. The Reds, facing extinction, captured the fourth, but in the decisive game the Pirates carried a 3–2 lead into the last of the ninth. After a Bench homer to tie and a pair of singles, Virdon summoned reliefer Bob Moose, whose wild pitch sent the winning run across. Following this maddening loss, a worse disaster struck the Pittsburgh club; Roberto Clemente lost his life while on a postseason mercy mission. The Buccaneers would not recover from such a blow for several years.

Meanwhile, the Reds carried the standard into the 1972 World Series. They faced the Oakland A's, whose controversial owner decked his team in green and white uniforms, long hair, and mustaches. Still, the A's were proven winners. In 1972 they stood on the threshold of winning three straight world titles. This remarkable feat was doubly difficult under the present divisional format. Moreover, the A's faced the Reds without their leading slugger, Reggie Jackson.

The garish A's squared off at Cincinnati against the close-cropped, traditionally uniformed Reds and took the first two games. Playing at home, they lost the third, but gained the fourth. Needing one more, the A's finally pulled through in the seventh game. As victors, the "hippie" team from the west coast set a new trend in fashion.

"You Gotta Believe"

Although conservatives fumed over the spread of modish hairstyles, they grew apopletic when the American League adopted the "designated hitter" rule in 1973. National officials haughtily rejected the idea of permitting a designated batter to hit in place of the normally weak-hitting pitcher. Although this was a limited victory for traditionalists, there was nothing traditional about the outcome of the 1973 league races. The Dodgers's new "Mod Squad" of young infielders and veteran outfielders threw an initial scare into the Red dynasts. However, forced to overcome an 11-game deficit, the Reds battled to a 3½ game win over the rising Dodgers.

The Big Red Machine used familiar battle tactics to gain their victory. Once again, they led in stolen bases and they supported the running attack with a .254 team average and 137 homers. Again,

Rose alone topped .300; his league-leading .338 won him MVP honors. Once more shaky starting pitchers plagued, forcing the bullpen corps to save 43 games.

Meanwhile, the Mets shocked experts by winning a close Eastern race with a paltry 82–79 mark, the lowest winning percentage in baseball history. So weak was the division that all six teams combined for a losing 470 500 record. The Pirate collapse was the Mets's opportunity; after the Clemente tragedy, pitcher Steve Blass suffered unaccountable control problems that limited him to three wins and soon ended his promising career. While Blass suffered, so did the team. Virdon was hastily sacked and the ailing Murtaugh recalled, but the Irish talisman managed only a second-place finish.

In that strangest of races, all six teams surged and fell back. The Cubs led by eight in June, but faded in July, leaving the field to the Cards, Pirates, and Expos. The Cards led briefly, until Gibson suffered a knee injury that eventually ended his career. Then, the lowly Mets, trailing 11½ games on August 5, made a move. In the place of deceased manager Hodges, ex-Yankee Yogi Berra wrought his own miracle.

Berra counted heavily on his pitchers to compensate for weak-hitting. Despite a sore arm, Seaver led the league in wins, strike-outs, and ERA—a Cy Young award effort. Koosman, on the other hand, had an off year and newcomer George Stone's fine 12–3 performance was offset by Jon Matlack's failings. Reliefer Tug McGraw appeared when help was truly needed, saving 25 games. At .246, the Mets's hitting was the worst in the East; their 85 homer total was pitiful. While singles hitter Felix Millan led the team in batting, Rusty Staub batted .279, poled 15 homers, and drove in 76 runs. Catcher Grote, Cleon Jones, and veteran Willie Mays, playing his twilight season, also supplied needed hits in the stretch drive.

Luck rode with this ragbag team in 1973. From early August to month's end, they won 34 and lost 19 to topple the Bucs. In a key September series, they took four of five games from the Pirates, two of which were heaven-sent victories. In one of these, the Mets scored five in the ninth to overcome a 4–1 deficit; in the other, a long Pirate hit bounced off the wall into an outfielder's glove, who then pegged a Pirate runner out at the plate.

The triumph was a shabby show, but, owing to the idiosyncracy of the division format, the Mets had a shot at the pennant. Inspired by McGraw's "You Gotta Believe" battle cry, the team thrashed the powerful Reds in the playoffs. After Seaver lost the opener at Cincinnati 2–1, Matlack evened the match with a 5–0 shut-out. Next, the Mets won the third 9–2 at Shea on Koosman's steady pitching and two homers by Staub. After the desperate Reds squared the match, Seaver took the finale 7–2 behind a 13-hit attack.

Only the A's barred the way to an awesome miracle. A Mets win in the World Series would mark the first time that so lowly a team scaled the heights. Purists were horrified at the prospect, but the Mets very nearly did it. They led after five games, but the A's took the last two for a second consecutive world title. Sadly, this Met mirage signalled the club's decline, as penurious policies so weakened the team that fans turned to the reviving Yankees for solace.[11]

"Dodger Blue" and the Phillies Too

Record-breaking performances rather than miracles marked the 1974 campaign. At the season's opening, durable Hank Aaron of the Braves needed two homers to break Ruth's record total of 714. With the eyes of the nation watching, the 40-year-old slugger bashed number 715 in an early season game at Atlanta. By season's end, the aging star raised his total to 733, at which point his churlish employers dealt him to Milwaukee of the American League. The aging homeric was upstaged by Cardinal outfielder Lou Brock, whose 118 stolen bases set a new seasonal record and enabled the 38-year-old speedster to close in on Cobb's lifetime total of 892 steals. Brock failed to receive the MVP award and Aaron was barely considered.

True to form, critics worried more about the chance that the newly introduced cowhide baseballs would inflate batting and slugging. Their fears were groundless; National averages totaled a mediocre .255, though batting carried the Pirates and Dodgers to divisional victories. By derailing the Big Red Machine in the West, the Dodgers signalled the revival of the league's most winning dynasty. As the Dodger "Summer Boys" ruled in the 1950s and the Koufax-Drysdale duo dominated the 1960s, now the "Mod Squad" arose. This was a balanced team with fine pitching and sturdy hitting. Pitcher Andy Messersmith led the league with 20 wins, and Tommy John and Don Sutton gave stout support. Reliefer Mike Marshall emerged from bullpens 106 times, winning 15 and saving 21

Opposite: In the 1970s and beyond, Dodger success in the National League's western division was indebted to this most durable of infield combinations in baseball history: shortstop Bill Russell (*top left*), first baseman Steve Garvey (*top right*), second baseman Davey Lopes (*bottom left*), and third baseman Ron Cey (*bottom right*).

matches to earn the Cy Young award. First baseman Steve Garvey hit .312 with 21 homers and 111 RBIs, and earned MVP honors. Along with Garvey, the infield of Dave Lopes at second, Ron Cey at third, and ex-outfielder Bill Russell at short became the most durable combination in history. The Dodgers had two talented catchers, Joe Ferguson and Steve Yeager, and a reliable picket line in Willie Crawford, slugger Jim Wynn, and Bill Buckner. Dodger pitching made the difference against the Reds. As usual, the Reds lacked reliable starters, but they won 98 games to close within four of the Dodgers.

The Eastern race was tighter. For half the season the Cards led the foundering Pirates, who stood 14 games below .500 in mid-July. Then, a brawl with the Reds seemed to awaken the Bucs. Rallying strongly, they finished with 88 wins, but their spirits were boosted by another brawl involving a rival. A donnybrook erupted late in September between the Cards and the hapless Cubs, and ended with Bill Madlock of the Cubs getting the winning hit; later, Madlock keyed another Cub victory. Since the Cards lost to the Pirates by a mere 1½ games, their disturbance of Cub hibernation seemed decisive.

In the playoffs, however, the Pirates fell to the Dodgers. The Dodgers took the first two at home. In the opener, Sutton hurled a four-hit shut-out, and Messersmith took the second behind a 12-hit attack. Moving to Pittsburgh, the Pirates won one, but were buried 12–1 the next time out.

This year fans caught the full impact of expansion when baseball featured the first west coast World Series matchup. Finley's bickering A's came to Dodger Stadium and seemed misplaced in O'Malley's slick park and outmatched by the disciplined Dodgers. Once unleashed, however, the A's won easily. After splitting two games in Los Angeles, the A's swept the Dodgers at home. It was a time when good pitching yielded to superb pitching.[12] That winter, however, a breached contract withdrew Finley's best pitcher; a similar suit filed by a disgruntled Dodger would soon free all players from the trammels of the reserve clause.

This historic emancipation was a year away. Meanwhile, the National League's 1975 and 1976 campaigns were dominated by the relentless Red Machine. In 1975 Anderson's minions won 108 games, 20 more than the groveling Dodgers in second place. The Reds batted .271 and led the league in fielding and stolen bases. Four Reds—Morgan, Rose, Ken Griffey, and George Foster—topped .300, but little Morgan's .327, in addition to 17 homers and

94 RBIs, won him MVP honors. Johnny Bench, batting .283 with 38 homers and 110 RBIs, was the league's finest catcher. Even the pitching improved, as Gullett, Billingham, Gary Nolan, and Fred Norman combined for 57, and relievers Rawly Eastwick and Will McEnaney saved 37 contests.

The Pirates had beaten the Phillies by 6½ games to win the East. Clemente's successor had finally emerged; young Dave Parker led the team with a .308 average, 25 homers, and 101 RBIs. Still, the Reds easily dispatched the Bucs in the playoffs. In the opener at Cincinnati, Gullett pitched and batted the Reds to an 8–3 win. Then, Norman and Eastwick held off the Pirates, as Perez homered and singled in a 6–1 win. The tournament ended in Pittsburgh with a 5–3 Red victory, Rose's two-run homer spoiling a 14-strike-out effort by Pirate rookie John Candelaria.

The Boston Red Sox, conquerors of the A's, now stepped forward to meet the Reds in the World Series. Although heavily favored, the Reds were chronic Series losers. Since Boston hadn't won a Series in 50 years, vindication was an added fuel. The zealous contenders fought one of the most thrilling battles in history.

It began in Boston, with veteran Luis Tiant pitching the Sox to an easy 6–0 win; Tiant celebrated afterwards with a fat Cuban cigar. The next day Boston nearly repeated, but lost in the ninth on clutch hits by Concepcion and Griffey. Moving to Cincinnati, the Reds won a 6–5 game marred by an ump's refusal to call obvious interference on a Red batter. The Sox rebounded to win behind Tiant, but lost the next outing when Perez and Morgan powered a 6–2 Red win.

The Reds were in need of only one win, and Boston fans waited three stressful days for the rain to abate. When the action resumed, a capacity Fenway crowd and 62 million television viewers saw an epic battle. With both teams squandering 3-run leads, the game was tied 6–6 when a 12th-inning Boston homer landed the game. The finale was equally dramatic: the Sox led 3–0 for five innings, but the Reds tied in the seventh and then won in the ninth on Morgan's run-scoring bloop hit.

Tempered in that struggle, the Reds romped over the West in 1976, finishing ten up on the Dodgers. Morgan again led the attack and took another MVP award, making his the fifth such award handed to a Red in this decade.

The seeds of disunion sprouted during this centennial campaign. Late in 1975, an arbitration panel undermined the reserve clause by upholding a player's right to finish the option year of his contract

Chief members of Cincinnati's "Big Red Machine" of the 1970s: second baseman Joe Morgan (*top left*), shortstop Dave Concepcion (*top right*), catcher Johnny Bench (*bottom left*) and the ubiquitous Pete Rose (*bottom right*), who played as either infielder or outfielder.

and then sell himself. When upheld in the courts, the angry owners locked their teams out of spring training camps in an attempt to force the players to limit their new freedom. The crisis ended on a compromise, but veteran players were still freed to resell themselves. This decision soon destroyed the Reds's vaunted unity. Gullett was branded disloyal for spurning a club offer and opting for the fall re-entry draft. Then, when Tony Perez was coldly disposed of, other veteran Reds no longer responded to "family loyalty" invocations.

Indeed, Gullett and Perez were key cogs in the Red Machine's 1976 victory. Moreover, both played active roles in defeating the reborn Phils in the divisional playoffs. After cellar finishes in 1972 and 1973, general manager Paul Owens's trading landed key men like outfielders Bob Tolan, Jay Johnstone, and Garry Maddox, pitchers Jim Lonborg, Tug McGraw, and Gene Garber, and second baseman Dave Cash. Blended with home-grown products like Greg Luzinski, slugger Mike Schmidt, and shortstop Larry Bowa, the team won the East, goaded by Bowa's feisty admonition: "You either bust --- or go half----ed."[13]

The Phils seized the lead in May and compiled a huge 15½-game lead in August. Then they sagged, losing eight straight as the charging Pirates won ten consecutive matches. More losses whittled the lead to 4½ by September 8, but then they rallied, finishing nine up on the Pirates.

Still, the Olympian Reds led the league in all offensive categories: batting (.280), stolen bases (210), fielding, hits, doubles, triples, homers, RBIs, extra base hits, and attendance—2.6 million fans passed through their turnstiles. The fact that their pitchers were mortal hardly assuaged the Phils's fears when the Reds came to town.

The Phillies's errors in the playoff opener handed the Reds a 6–3 victory, and the next day the Reds won again. Then, at Cincinnati, ninth-inning homers by Foster and Bench overcame a 6–4 Phillie lead to complete the sweep.

In the World Series, the Yanks took an even harder fall. Back on top of the American League after a 12-year hiatus, the Yanks fought for five games before wresting the league title from the stubborn Kansas City Royals. It was a tired team that manager Martin took to Cincinnati. Seizing the advantage, the Reds won the opener 6–1 behind Gullett, then, in bitter cold weather, they snatched the second 4–3, aided by a ninth-inning Yankee error. Up by two, the Reds stormed into newly renovated Yankee Stadium and swept the Series with 6–2 and 7–2 victories. Thus, the Reds earned the distinction of being the only National team in half a century to win consecutive world titles.

In the afterglow of victory, Anderson likened his Reds to the 1927 Yanks, but that fatuous claim was punctured by the loss of Gullett and Perez. Just these two absences crippled the Reds, and neither the acquisition of Tom Seaver midway through the 1977 campaign nor Foster's all-round mighty batting could compensate. Amidst nagging slumps and gripes about stingy owners, the team collapsed, prompting manager Anderson's sanctimonious observation: "When money becomes the only goal, we are in a very sick society."[14]

A fighting Dodger team rushed into the gap. Striking hard and early, they won 17 of their first 20 games and opened a chasm which the Reds never bridged. The Dodgers fielded a superbly balanced team. Leading the offense was Garvey, the cleancut darling of California conservatives, who batted .297 with 33 homers and 115 RBIs. Also fueling the offense was the new outfield of Reggie Smith, Dusty Baker, Lee Lacy, and Rick Monday, while timely pinch hits came from aging vets Manny Mota and Vic Davalillo. Supporting the hitters was a starting quartet of pitchers Tommy John, Sutton, Burt Hooton, and Doug Rau, backed by a versatile bullpen.

This year veteran Alston was replaced by freshman manager Tom Lasorda; "It's like inheriting the Hope Diamond," was Lasorda's joyous reaction. Well-groomed for the job, cheerleader Lasorda kindled a fraternity house spirit among his charges. While some critics properly recoiled at such sophomoric Lasordisms as "Cut me and I bleed Dodger Blue," or after death, "I'll meet the great Dodger in the Sky," he led the Dodgers to consecutive flags.

By winning 98, the 1977 Dodgers lapped the Reds by 10 games and prepared to meet the Phils, who were Eastern champs for a second straight year. This year the Phils won 100 and eyed their first league title since 1950. After splitting a pair at Dodger Stadium, the Phils took a 5–3 lead into the ninth in the third game. Quickly, reliever Garber gained two outs, but, then, pinch hitters Mota and Davalillo delivered hits that triggered a winning Dodger rally. The next time out the Phils met a feeble failure before 65,000 sullen, rain-drenched fans.

The Yankees meanwhile, fortified with hirelings like Gullett and Reggie Jackson, narrowly won a second American pennant. In opening Series matches at Yankee Stadium, the Yanks and Dodgers exchanged victories. Next, the Yanks won two at Dodger Stadium.

Cornered now, the Dodgers exploded for 13 hits and a 10–4 triumph, but back at home the Yankees, with Jackson homering three times, captured the Series. Thus, the modern Dodgers came to know the miseries of their older brothers.

Lasorda's positive approach was sorely tested in the gruelling Western war of 1978. The Reds and Giants led for most of the season, but Lasorda jollied the team, reminding them that as family, they were loved by the Dodger sky god. Such rhetoric was needed to quell team tensions, including a clubhouse brawl between Garvey and Sutton. Lasorda carefully dampened the flames and then goaded Lopes and Smith into leadership roles. By September the team righted itself, taking a slim lead and guarding it.

On another front, the Reds collapsed in the stretch, nullifying storied performances by Foster and Rose. Foster again led the league in RBIs, but Rose excited the nation, first with his 3,000th career hit and then by hitting safely in 44 consecutive games to tie Keeler's old National League record. Though poor pitching did in the Reds, general manager Dick Wagner later sacked Anderson and refused to meet Rose's salary demands. Rose, in turn, signed with the Phils, while at home fans hung Wagner in effigy.[15]

The 1978 Phils went through a harrowing race, catching the Cubs in mid-season and building a hefty August lead, then faltering badly before eking out a two-game win over the onrushing Pirates. It was the third straight Eastern title for the Phils, but their experience was of no help in the playoffs. Opening at home, they lost two games by decisive scores and set out for Los Angeles with hometown boos ringing in their ears. At Dodger Stadium they stayed execution for one day, then piddled away the decisive game on two ninth-inning errors. Losing a third pennant so ignominiously, most Phils probably shared Tug McGraw's agonized words: "It's the worst feeling in the world."

The Dodgers now faced their Yankee jinx in the Series. This season the heaven-blessed Yanks had survived two playoff struggles before winning the American flag; a Series triumph would rank them amongst legendary comeback victors.

To fire his men, Lasorda mounted a crusade. Two days before the Series opener, coach Jim Gilliam, one of the popular "Summer Boys," passed away. His memory now became Lasorda's magical symbol. The crusade was dedicated to Gilliam; players wore mourning bands emblazoned with his number 19 and listened to words of scorn directed at Yankee mercenaries. Thus, Lasorda made ready.

The strategy worked at home, the Yanks dropping two games, but Yankee magic prevailed in New York. Aided by inspired fielding and a controversial umpire's call, the Yanks quickly squared the Series. Then, in the fifth game the Yanks lashed a record 16 singles to crush the Dodgers 12–2. Next, the Yanks stormed Dodger Stadium and completed a four-game sweep. Dodger magic was a total failure: their rivals became the first team ever to score a four-game Series sweep after losing the first two games.[16]

This Dodger humiliation inspired the down-trodden for 1979. Having lost ace pitcher John in the re-entry draft, the team was ripe for plucking and, except for the talented Rick Sutcliffe, their pitching collapsed. The Dodgers led in homers, but, except for Garvey, batting fell off. Pummeled by early losses, they fell to fifth and stayed low, until a late season revival lifted them to third place. Indeed, it was a doleful, discordant year, which not only saw the death of O'Malley, but also sustained the loss of 486,000 fans.

While gloom soured Los Angeles, sunny optimism invaded Houston, where attendance increased by 774,000 and the Astros seized the Western heights, holding that ground all summer. Offsetting a frail offense was the brilliant pitching of fireballing James Rodney Richard and knuckle-balling Joe Niekro. Formidable in size and speed, Richard fanned over 300 batters, won 18 games, and led the league in ERA. Even more effective was the slow-balling Niekro, whose 21 victories tied for the league lead. Overall, Astro pitchers posted the second-best ERA in the league. Their impotent offense, on the other hand, poled only 49 homers and batted a weak .256; yet seldom did a team go so far with so little. They built an early lead, but played only .500 ball after July. Nevertheless, they remained in contention until beaten by Dodger spoilers in a late season game.

Picking up on the Astros's loss, the revived Reds snatched their sixth Western title of the decade. Unfortunately, the Reds of 1979 were a wheezing version of the Big Red Machine. Missing were helmsman Anderson and the team's hustling superstar, Pete Rose. The fans, responding to the loss of Rose, stayed away 175,000 strong. Still, manager John McNamara used a balanced attack to dog the Astros. Young Ray Knight replaced Rose at third and batted .318, but Rose bettered him at Philadelphia. The big offensive gun in 1979 was Foster, who hit .302 and led the club in homers and RBIs. Behind him, Bench batted .276 and Concepcion hit .281 and fielded brilliantly at short. However, veterans Geronimo and Morgan slumped badly. Also, the pitching was shaky; veteran Seaver led the staff with 16 wins, while Mike La Coss and Bill Bonham combined for 23. When arm trouble sidelined Bonham, McNamara relied on bullpen help, and Tom Hume and Doug Bair answered with 21 wins and 33 saves. Such scrambling produced 90 wins—enough to eke a 1½ game win over the Astros.

That year Eastern powers dominated the Westerns, where only the Reds and Astros owned winning records, and hopes ran high for breaking the West's five-year pennant monopoly. The three-time champion Phils were favored at the start of the Eastern campaign. With Rose in the lineup, this solid team lacked only pitching. Installed at first base, Rose's easy mastering of an unfamiliar position and his solid .331 hitting inspired the team. Also, Schmidt regained his power, pounding 45 homers and driving in 114 runs. The team's .266 batting, however, was deceptive. For all his power, Schmidt hit .253, a point above the much booed Luzinski. Among other disappointments, slick-fielding Bowa hit only .241, and highly touted Manny Trillo was slowed by injuries. Worse still, the pitching staff lived up to gloomy forecasts. Battered for more than four runs a game, the staff was in the league cellar. Carlton held up, winning 18 and fanning 213; otherwise, manager Ozark combed through 15 assorted flingers in a hopeless quest.

The Phils broke fast, carrying a three-game lead into mid-May; then, after two encounters with the Expos, they fell and stayed down. The expansion Expos, still looking for a winning season, now seized the heights and held most of the way, pulling strength from the league's best pitching. Their offensive attack was sparked by third baseman Larry Parrish, who batted .307 with 30 homers; supporting Parrish were Gary Carter, Ellis Valentine, Andre Dawson, and veteran Tony Perez. Still they were pressed hard by the Cards and the Pirates.

With a lusty .278 team average, the Cards fielded a quartet of top hitters, including first baseman Keith Hernandez, whose .344 led the league and produced 105 RBIs. Shortstop Gary Templeton hit .314, veteran Lou Brock completed his career at .304, and outfielder George Hendrick smacked .300. Sadly, lacking power and consistent pitching, the team was conquered by the rampaging Pirates.

Blessed with the best-balanced team in the East, manager Chuck Tanner pulled all stops to drive his Pirates past the Expos to a hairline victory. Not until the last day did they seize the flag; the victory then established the Pirates as the winningest National

League team of the decade. Except for the 1973 Met triumph, only the Pirates won Eastern titles from 1970 to 1975. The Phillies had captured three, but 1979 belonged to the Pirates. Six divisional titles in a decade was dynastic, but the Pirates were notorious playoff flops, winning only the 1971 league pennant.

The versatile 1979 Pirates ranked near the top in pitching, batting, homers, and stolen bases, and led all rivals with 775 runs scored. Their pitching ranked high, but its strength was concentrated in a bullpen which saved 52 games. Heading the crew was skeletal Kent Tekulve, who pitched 134 innings and appeared in 94 games, winning 10 and saving 31. For all his heroics, though, this submarine-baller was surpassed by Cub reliefer Bruce Sutter, who won the Cy Young Award.

Offensively, no team matched the versatile Pirates. Their leader, Dave Parker, batted .310 and conducted the team in RBIs, runs, and doubles; first baseman Willie "Pops" Stargell led in homers with 32. Additional support came via early season trades that landed short-stop Tim Foli and third baseman Bill Madlock. These were decisive acquisitions; ex-batting titleist Madlock drove in 85 runs with a .298 average, while Foli anchored the infield and matched Madlock's average. Not to be outdone, second-baseman Phil Garner hit .293 for a career high, and speedy Omar Moreno's 77 base thefts led the league.

Starting slowly, the Pirates pressured the Expos who did not yield until the last day. Injuries beset Pirate pitchers in the stretch drive, but Kison won four and Jim Rooker, hapless for most of the season, won a pair of key games. The race ended when the Pirates, up by a game, downed the Cubs on a three-run homer by Stargell, while the Expos lost to the Phillies. The Pirates swept the Reds in the playoffs. Stargell carried the tired pitchers, smashing two homers, batting .455, and forcing six runs in the three games. The final victory came before a raucously singing home crowd, who shouted the lyrics to the rock song, "We Are Family."

The Pirates staged a doughty comeback against the Orioles in the World Series. Down three games to one, they took three straight, scoring the final two wins in Baltimore. Once again Stargell led: his three homers were the only his team struck, his seven RBIs led all, and his 12 hits included seven extra base knocks. Big "Pops" was at his best in the decisive game, racking a pair of doubles and a homer. Therefore, the leader added the World Series MVP award to his playoff trophy and later shared seasonal MVP honors.

After nearly a century of National League campaigning, the Phillies won a World Series in 1980, powered by third baseman Mike Schmidt (*left*), switch-hitter Pete Rose (*center*), and pitching ace, "Lefty" Steve Carlton (*right*).

Still, the Series victory was a team effort. Incredibly, seven Pirates batted .300 or better, as the team averaged .323. Garner's 12 hits tied Stargell's count and his .500 average led all. After a slow start, Moreno connected for 11 hits, one more than Parker and Foli. Finally, reliefer Tekulve saved three games.

An exuberant, united team chorused "We Are Family" before leaving for winter haunts. Its youth stirred dynastic fears. Indeed, the oldest member, 39-year-old "Pops" Stargell, insisted that he, too, was "young at heart."[17]

Expansion Baseball: The American League

The Pandora's Box of Expansion

Upon the outset of their new expansionist course, American owners might have profited from reading the ancient legend of Pandora's box. Granted, more clubs meant more profits, but would fans accept the new format? Wouldn't the quality of play suffer if the already scarce playing talent were stretched to stock new clubs? The players seethed at their exclusion from the decision-making process and complained of being required to play eight more games per season at the same pay rate.

The most paralyzing problem of the moment, however, was the Yankee tyranny. The strong Yanks thrived under the 10-club format. From 1961 to 1964 the Yanks won four pennants, extending their latest skein to five in a row. In 1962, when dogged by the Minnesota Twins and the Los Angeles Angels (teams with strange sounding names), stout pitching by Ford, Terry, and rookie Jim Bouton carried the day, with the aid of lusty batting from Mantle,

Berra, Skowron, and Howard. Mantle won MVP honors for a third time.

That autumn another pack of strangers hosted the Yanks in the World Series; the San Francisco Giants were the winners of the National's first expansion season. In the Series of 1962, the Giants battled until the last out. These antagonists swapped victories from the start; then an estimated forty million television viewers settled back to watch the finale. They witnessed Yankee pitcher Ralph Terry carry a 1–0 lead into the last of the ninth. The first Giant batter reached base, but Terry fanned the next two. Next up, Mays doubled to right, but fast fielding by Maris prevented a score and suddenly the game ended, as McCovey lined to Richardson. The Yanks took the title, but this hard-fought, luck-assisted win would be their last such title for fifteen seasons.

Nevertheless, the Yankee tyranny endured two more years. In 1963, with Ford's 24 victories leading a superb pitching staff, the Yankees won by ten games over Lopez's White Sox. Then the Dodgers came to town. Matched against Ford in the Series opener, the great Koufax fanned 14 Yankees and triumphed 5–2. This was the start of a great humiliation, as Dodger pitchers limited the Yanks to just two more runs and closed the Series in four games. The sweep went far toward settling old scores.

The humiliation of 1963 actually ended the Yankee tyranny, but the team notched one last victory. This gallant effort came in 1964, despite wrenching upheavals within the Yankee organization: popular manager Houk became the unpopular GM because of his stingy salary policies, and the selection of Berra as playing manager confused the players. Wrongly labeled a buffoon, Berra was crippled by early misfortunes, and his head was rumored on the block in early July. Far more shocking, however, was the August news of the team's sale to the Columbia Broadcasting System. The news triggered a fresh blast of Yankee hatred, along with the usual threats of Congressional investigations.

Sirens like these concealed the real reason for the team's slow start—six key men were injured. As late as September, the Yanks trailed the leaders by six games, but, then, as the contending Orioles and White Sox divided six games, the Yanks gained ground on steady pitching from rookie Mel Stottlemyre. Soon afterwards, the Yanks mounted a nine-game winning streak, seized the lead, and hung on tight to win by one game over luckless Lopez and his White Sox.

Meanwhile, manager John Keane led his Cards to a narrow National League victory. Like Berra, Keane had been maligned and, ironically, was courted and chosen by the Yanks to be their manager for 1965. Thus, it was a great embarrassment when Berra and Keane met in the World Series. While both performed well, Keane rallied the Cards to victory in a tightly fought, seven-game Series.

Sic Semper Tyrannis

The 1965 flag belonged to the Yanks—on paper. The team looked sound and manager Keane was a proven winner. With the backing of the CBS empire, all signs pointed to more glory. Still, like the wonderful one-hoss shay, the Yanks suddenly collapsed. They fell to eighth in early June, and this year no last-ditch heroics saved the day.

The 1966 season was worse. In May the Yanks stood dead last and only managed an eventual crawl to eighth. This made them the laughing stock of the league and the butt of gallows jokes. But their rivals soon learned that a sick Yankee team meant epidemic for all. For too long rivals counted on the Yankees to boost their home attendance; now, when these Yankees no longer drew, American attendance fell five million behind the Nationals.

Naturally, pundits came forward with reasons for the Yankee collapse. One writer blamed the management for failing to buy bonus babies, for weakening the farm system, for dismissing Stengel and Weiss, and for angering radio and television fans by sacking Mel Allen and Red Barber.[1] Another critic blamed the changing baseball scene, citing trends—such as the scarcity of talent, the new free agent draft rule, the fresh breed of wealthy owners who no longer needed money from player sales, and canny general managers who outsmarted their Yankee counterparts—as slippages found first in this once-great dynasty.[2]

Those closest to the Yankees noted how injuries savaged stars like Ford, Mantle, and Maris. These stars had seen their bright years; much harder to explain was the collapse of younger men like Bouton, Joe Pepitone, and Clete Boyer. So many failures destroyed the team's spirit. The Yankees had always rallied about some natural leader, like DiMaggio, or followed a charismatic manager, like McCarthy, Stengel, or Houk. But now the heroes were passing and there were no strong successors.

As the Yanks lay bleeding, others climbed over them. The obvious successor was Lopez and his White Sox, but their strength was spent.

Instead, a new power emerged from the north. Once called the Senators, the Minnesota Twins were piloted by Sam Mele, who employed ex-Yankee pitching coach John Sain. Under Sain, pitchers Jim Kaat, Jim "Mudcat" Grant, and Jim Perry blossomed. Another defrocked Yankee, Billy Martin, coached the infield, shaping a good defensive unit. The 1965 Twins took the pennant by seven games over the White Sox. The team's modest .254 batting average led the league, and Tony Oliva's .321 won him a second straight batting title. For owner Cal Griffith, scion of the late Clark Griffith, the victory ended a drought of over thirty years.

That October the Twins faced Dodger pitching aces Koufax and Drysdale in the World Series. The Minnesotans were picked to lose and they did, but before falling they fought the Dodgers to a standstill. Their fall in the last game marked the American League's third straight Series setback. In the following season, a warlord from the south wrested the pennant. Like the Twins, the Baltimore Orioles were transplants who relied on Yankee discards. From 1959 to 1965, general manager Lee MacPhail—a former Yankee administrator and the son of a former Yankee owner—acquired pitchers Dave McNally, Darold Knowles, Jim Palmer, and Wally Bunker, catcher Andy Etchebarren, and infielders John "Boog" Powell, Dave Johnson, and Mark Belanger. MacPhail was succeeded by Harry Dalton in 1965; Dalton's final goal was to build a good farm system, but he immediately drafted relievers Moe Drabowski and Gene Brabender, and then performed an incredible trade by dealing pitcher Milt Pappas to the Reds for big Frank Robinson.

The manager of the Orioles was ex-Yankee Hank Bauer. Rookie manager Bauer came close to beating his old team in 1964, but his 1965 team skipped to third. In the following year with Robinson batting at an early .471 clip, the Orioles won 16 of their first 20 games. At the season's halfway point they suddenly caught fire to sweep five from the Twins and lead by seven. Although the Twins rallied, the Orioles never gave ground. The hitters backed their young pitchers with a league-leading .258 average; Robinson's .316 batting, 49 homers, and 122 RBIs won a Triple Crown and MVP Award, making him the first to win MVP Awards in each league.

Still, nobody expected the Birds to fly against the World Champion Dodgers in the Series. Surprisingly, Bauer's young pitching corps outclassed the great Dodger duo. In the opener at Dodger Stadium, the home team drove McNally from the mound with two runs in the first three innings. Bauer then summoned reliefer Moe

Drabowsky, who stopped the Dodgers with eleven strike-outs, en-route to a 5–2 win. When Palmer, Bunker, and McNally hurled consecutive shut-outs to complete a four-game sweep, the decisive victory restored some faded American glory.

However, any dynastic dreams the Orioles had were rudely dashed when a rash of arm injuries struck the pitchers and the batters slumped. As the 1967 team faded to sixth, four rivals battled through the final days. Among the favored contenders were the White Sox and the Twins, the latter spurred by the batting of Harmon Killebrew and newcomer Rod Carew. The Tigers also pressed hard, relying on good pitching by Denny McLain and Mickey Lolich. Even the dormant Red Sox arose.

Moribund since the early 1950s when so many Yankee defeats broke their spirit, the Red Sox were derided as a country club team whose players genteelly went through the motions. A Boston team had not contended for a decade, and as recently as 1966 two managers were sacked for losing. Thus, this year owner Tom Yawkey handed promising rookie manager Dick Williams a one-year contract. A tough disciplinarian, Williams's strict rules ordered bed checks, morning practices, and stiff fines for overweight players. This sent a parade of complainers into Yawkey's office, but the draconian policies turned the team around. Skinned of excess poundage, first baseman George Scott batted .303 with 82 RBIs; outfielder Carl Yastrzemski won a Triple Crown with his .326 average, 44 homers, and 121 RBIs. The Sox now led the league in batting and homers.

Still, the climb to the top was tortuous. As the last big league club to field black players, Boston's blacks encountered blatant discrimination. A confident Reggie Smith might have compensated for the tragic loss of slugger Tony Conigliaro, downed by a pitched ball; however, merciless booing in 1967 destroyed the black fielder's confidence. Still, Williams held the team together, and with Yastrzemski delivering a barrage of September hits, the Sox won by a single game. The race, decided on the last day, had the Red Sox beating the Twins and the Tigers dividing a doubleheader. The Red Sox edged the Twins and the Tigers by one game, while the White Sox were bettered by three.

A strange replay of Boston's 1946 Series experience followed. Again the Sox faced the Cardinals, again the Series went seven games, and again the Sox lost the final game. The winning Cardinals relied on Gibson's pitching wins and Brock's hitting. For nearly at-

Triple Crown batting by Carl Yastrzemski (*top left*) and solid hitting by Tony Conigliaro (*top right*) led the Red Sox to a pennant in 1967, but they lost the Series to the Cards. However, strong pitching by Denny McLain (*bottom left*) and Mickey Lolich (*bottom right*) enabled the Tigers to square accounts in 1968.

taining the "impossible dream," Williams was named Manager of the Year.

The 1968 season was the last played under the time-honored single division format. Henceforth, teams would contend within two six-team divisions, with the winners meeting in a postseason playoff to decide the league pennant. This was a tradition-breaking move prompted in part by the profit motive. It would take time for fans to adjust psychologically to new teams with strange totems and changed rivalries and to the new-fangled playoff matches.

At least the 1968 season promised a wide open race. Since the fall of the Yankees, each campaign had produced a new titleist. There was no team hungrier than the Detroit Tigers, pennantless since 1945. Losers by a single game in 1967, they returned with a terrible resolve. The Tigers had a brilliant right-handed pitcher named Denny McLain. In 1968 McLain won 31 and lost six, with a 1.96 ERA. By breaking the 30-win barrier, a feat not attained since the 1930s, McLain joined the exalted company of Dizzy Dean and Lefty Grove. With lefty Mickey Lolich adding 17 victories and Sain coaching the pitching staff, manager Mayo Smith had a formidable pitching staff. Though the team's .235 batting was wretched, the league's best mark was the Twins's .240 effort. (Incredibly, Yastrzemski was the league's only .300 hitter, and he battled to the crown with a record low .301.) Therefore, in a year of pitching predominance, the Tigers prospered; their league-leading 185 homers supplied the needed punch. They won 103 games, exceeding the Orioles by 12.

Smith's players met the World Champion Cards in the World Series. Paired against McLain in the opener at St. Louis, Gibson took charge, fanning 17 Tigers for a new record and guiding the Cards to a 4–0 win. Lolich evened the Series with an 8–1 win, but the Cardinals took the next two. Needing only one, the Cards poised for the kill, but Lolich kept Tiger hopes flickering with a 5–3 win. McLain followed with his only victory, an easy 13–1 triumph, which set up a decisive match between Gibson and Lolich. It was a tight pitcher's duel, marred by a Cardinal error that allowed two Tigers to score in the seventh. Lolich hung tight to win his third game of the Series, and the Tigers were champions. Thus ended the last Series waged under the old format; this Tiger victory reminded the cocky Nationals that in Series duels the Americans still held the edge.

Nevertheless, there was no denying that American League power and prestige was at its nadir. To stand so far behind the Nationals in attendance and performance standards was humiliating for the circuit that once had revitalized American baseball. After all, it was Ban Johnson's "great American League" that restored the World Series, pioneered the "big bang" offensive, and housed the great Yankee juggernauts. Those, however, were old glories; since the 1950s the Nationals had set the records and outclassed their rivals. Topped in attendance, in new park construction, in All-Star games, and in choice expansion sites, the Americans nursed an unhealthy, but legitimate inferiority complex.

The Nationals occupied Montreal and San Diego in the 1969 expansion, while the Americans assumed a financially unsound Seattle entry and were forced, under threat of a lawsuit, to put a new team in Kansas City as a replacement for the A's. Ironically, the new Kansas City Royals grew vigorously and became the most competitive of all expansion teams. The Seattle failure surfaced as the immediate problem. By the spring of 1970, the Seattle Pilots were sold and moved to Milwaukee. Entering Milwaukee, a town abandoned by the Nationals in 1966, was for the Americans a bitter pill; moreover, the Americans seemed to be pulling National League chestnuts out of the fire. The humiliation still had its bright side, as, under vigorous ownership, the new Milwaukee Brewers prospered.

Winged Victory—The Oriole Dynasty

For all its labor pains, the year 1969 was a time of reborn hopes for American Leaguers. The old Yankee bugaboo was exorcised, lowered pitching mounds promised to end the hitting famine, and the Tigers looked like repeaters. Indeed, Tiger hurlers McLain and Lolich adapted readily to the pitching restrictions. That year McLain won 24 and Lolich 19 as the Tigers took 90 games, but the soaring Orioles won 109 games to capture the Eastern title.

The new Oriole manager, feisty Earl Weaver, had never played in the majors. Years of playing and managing in the minors had taught him strategy and tactics. He was knowledgeable, but he was also decisive, tough-minded, and sarcastic—qualities required to bring new life to the Orioles. Summoned to Baltimore midway through the 1968 season, Weaver drove the Birds to a distant second, despite the team's .225 batting.

Pitching was the Orioles's forte, and Weaver determined to keep it strong. The manager chose George Bamberger to be his pitching coach; the veteran minor leaguer offered an immediate contribution by rehabilitating sore-armed Jim Palmer. Bamberger also changed ex-Astro-hurler Mike Cuellar from an ordinary to a great pitcher.

Oriole batting increased, thanks to lowered pitching mounds; veteran sluggers John "Boog" Powell and Frank Robinson both topped .300 and accounted for more than 60 homers and over 200 RBIs. Overall, the team jacked its hitting to .265 and raised homer production to 175. This impressive reversal was accomplished with few changes. The infield of Powell, Johnson, Belanger, and Brooks Robinson was set, as was the outfield of Paul Blair, Frank Robinson, and Don Buford. Etchebarren and Elrod Hendricks took care of catching duties.

Oriole pitchers also adapted to the new pitching rules. Cuellar pitched effectively from the start, while "Dave McLucky" McNally won 15 games before losing. By mid-season, Palmer shook off his back injuries, and returned to starting duty, reaping 16 victories. When this trio won 18 of 19 games in August, the Eastern race was over. Clinching early, the birds ended the season on an 11-game winning skein.

Meanwhile in the west, a rookie manager worked to rejuvenate the twins: Billy Martin had been hired by Griffith to enliven a sorry team that drew 350,000 fewer paid customers in 1968 than in the previous season. The owner knew that he had spoiled his own players with too many fringe benefits, and now he turned testy. In this volatile ex-Yankee, Griffith had a man who used hot words and hard fists when needed. As a minor league apprentice, Martin was often ejected from games; being more emotional than Weaver but just as inspiring, he spurred the Twins to 97 wins and whipped the rising A's by nine games.

This year the Twins led the league in batting with .268, and young Rod Carew won the first of a string of batting titles with a .332 mark. Under Martin the moody Carew became a hustling leader and a base-stealer who accomplished a record-tying seven steals of home. Meanwhile, first baseman Rich Reese hit .322 and Oliva batted .309, with 24 homers and 101 RBIs. Killebrew also rebounded from a .210 season to hit .276; his league-leading 49 homers and 149 RBIs earned him the MVP award.

The league's first playoff series pitted Weaver and Martin in the first round of their long and intense rivalry. Weaver won this one, his Orioles sweeping the Twins. Still, the first two games were close, as Baltimore won 4–3 and 1–0 squeakers at home. After that the Orioles thrashed the Twins 11–2 at Bloomington. This sweep extended the Oriole streak to 14 and established the Birds as heavy favorites to crush the Mets in the Series. Consequently, when Oriole batter Buford homered on Seaver's second pitch in the Baltimore opener, the Orioles were on their way. However, the debacle came as the Mets swept to victory, locking the snakebit Birds into baseball folklore as the Goliaths slain by the Davidic Mets.[3]

Weaver set out to expunge the blotch. In 1970—with the exception of young Merv Rettenmund, who batted .322 as a reserve outfielder—Weaver sent the same crew of hardened regulars against his Eastern opponents. Again they won big, nearly duplicating the 1969 conquest. This time Frank Robinson and Powell combined for 50 homers and 192 RBIs to power the attack. Among the pitchers, Cuellar and McNally tied for league leadership, each with 24 wins; Palmer adding 20, the Oriole bullpen ruled the league. The strong Birds won 108; clinching on September 17, they led the reviving Yanks by 15 games.

The Twins won again in the West; this time the team was Martinless, the manager having been fired for criticizing the owner. Under Bill Rigney they won 98, despite the loss of Carew for most of the season. Carew had been batting .366; outfielders Oliva and Cesar Tovar now brought up the slack. Both topped .300, Oliva alone pounding 23 homers and driving in 107 runs. With Killebrew's 41 homers and 113 RBIs, the Twins romped home 12 games ahead of the A's.

The Orioles again swept the Twins in a playoff rematch. Pitcher Cuellar's grand slam homer in the opener at Bloomington paced a 10–6 victory, while Frank Robinson and Dave Johnson homered in an 11–3 win the next day. Finally, Palmer closed the playoffs, outpitching Kaat 6–1.

The Orioles romped over the Big Red Machine in the Series, and thereby established dynastic credentials. They did this by assaulting the Red pitching for 50 hits, and none batted more timely, nor fielded more brilliantly than third baseman Brooks Robinson. This fielding genius repeatedly choked Red threats with sparkling plays. In the Series opener at Cincinnati, his glove held off the Reds, while his team scrambled to overcome a three-run deficit. He homered in the seventh for the winning run, heralding a 4–3 victory. The Reds jumped to a 4–0 lead the next time out, but the Orioles rallied for five in the fifth and hung on to win 6–5. Back at home, McNally limited the Reds to three runs and smashed a grand slam homer, but three fielding gems by Robinson saved the 9–3 victory. The Reds stayed alive momentarily with a 6–5 victory; but Cuellar, after yielding three runs, pitched steadily behind a 15-hit assault that clinched the title.

Sadly, the 1970 Oriole victory had a bittersweet aftertaste. Poor home attendance dogged the team, who went on to land three more division titles over the next four years. Also, Weaver was miffed when not named the 1970 Manager of the Year. Upon missing again the next season, he groused, "Maybe some of them voters will get to see a major league game other than on television."[4] This disappointment came after he had driven his aging team to a third straight Eastern title and a third pennant. That year Brooks Robinson turned 34 and Frank Robinson showed his 35 years. Nagged by back trouble, big Frank made his last Oriole stint a memorable one. On the night of June 26, with his back aching more than usual, he hit consecutive grand-slam homers against the Senators. This was his swan song as an Oriole; that winter he became a Dodger, but not before he, Powell, and Rettenmund had sparked a league-leading .261 team batting effort for the 1971 Birds.

It was a year when the superb pitching staff boasted four 20-game winners in Cuellar, Palmer, McNally, and Pat Dobson. By now, Palmer was the leader, and the handsome Californian was the league's best for the rest of the decade. Meanwhile, this foursome's 81–31 performance buried the Tigers by 11 games.

Finley's Bay City Beauties

A new power in the west now challenged the Orioles in the playoffs. The colorful Oakland Athletics had risen; their owner, Charles Oscar Finley, was the most controversial club president of the era. Indeed, any search for a counterpart to this half-genius, half-buffoon must look back to the 1880s at Chris von der Ahe, "the boss president" of the old Browns. Successful businessman Finley bought the Kansas City A's in 1961. Those pitifuls were then going nowhere, but Finley drove them to fame. For six years he labored, firing and hiring a procession of managers, scouts, and general managers, until he alone made the decisions. He patiently nursed promising youngsters like Bert Campaneris, Jim Hunter, Dave Duncan, Joe Rudi, and Sal Bando. His team's biggest boost came in 1965 when their lowly position gave Finley first pick in the new rookie draft. Finley grabbed perceptively, choosing in the first year outfielder Rick Monday, third baseman Bando, catcher Gene Tenace, and, as a brilliant afterthought, reliefer Rollie Fingers. In the next year's draft he picked Reggie Jackson.

Although Finley paid big bonuses for these future stars, he was far less generous to local fans. Convinced that Kansas City politicos, fans, and writers were ingrates, he maneuvered a move to Oakland in 1968. There he zealously promoted the team; using gimmicks, like hiring Joe DiMaggio as batting coach, he vied for local support. Still attendance flagged, even as the A's scored their first winning season in 17 years. The undaunted Finley outfitted his A's in gaudy gold, green, and white garb, hired colorful announcers, paraded his celebrated mule, and proposed orange-colored balls and multi-colored bases. Naturally, the A's were ridiculed, but they played so well that by 1971 the guys in the multi-colored softball uniforms began a five-year tyranny in the West.

The 1971 season was Finley's fourth in Oakland; so far he had employed as many different managers. This year's skipper, the hard-driving Dick Williams, had been fired from the Red Sox for being too tough. At Oakland Williams suffered Finley's meddling, but won the respect of his players. In the opinion of Reggie Jackon, Williams was a flashy "hot dog," but he was also smart and inspiring. In three seasons his A's took three divisional titles, and when he resigned in 1973, Jackson exploded: "Finley . . . ----ed us out of the best manager in baseball."

Such candor came easily from outfielder Reginald Martinez Jackson. Six feet tall and a muscular 200 pounds, his strength made him a feared left-handed slugger, but also a victim of frequent muscle pulls. The explosive comments of this college-educated extrovert resounded like his homers; this combination marked him as the most colorful and controversial player of the era. Proud and fiercely independent, Jackson was a spirited battler against racial discrimination. Though he was a black man, he could identify with whites, blacks, Hispanics, and Indians.

His personality clashed with Finley's. For a time the two nurtured an odd love-hate relationship, but, inevitably, Jackson lashed out at Finley's pomposity and stinginess. The long feud ended when Jackson was sold in 1975; Finley was indeed the final loser of the deal.

In 1971 the 25-year-old slugger sought recognition that only victory could bring. He adored powering the offense: "God, do I love to hit that little round SOB out of the park and make 'em say 'WOW.' "[5] That year his .277 average and 32 homers led the team. With Monday and Joe Rudi beside Jackson, the A's had a stellar outfield. In the infield ranged hard-hitting third baseman Bando and slick-fielding shortstop Campaneris, with Dick Green at second and Mike Epstein at first. Duncan and Tenace handled the catching while the veteran Tommy Davis batted .324 and served as a utility outfielder.

Pitching was the team's forte. In 1968 Finley chose coveted left-hander Vida Blue in the rookie draft; after only a brief seasoning, the fast-balling Blue was ready. The 21-year-old was a sensation in 1971, winning the Cy Young Award on his 24–8 win, 1.82 ERA performance. As Blue blossomed, so did youngsters Jim Hunter, winning 21, and Rollie Fingers, saving 17. This trio helped the A's to 101 victories, 15 games better than the surprising Royals.

Williams took Manager of the Year honors, but Weaver's Orioles blitzed the young A's in the playoffs. McNally and Ed Watt out-pitched Blue in the Baltimore opener, 5–3. Cuellar held the A's to one run in the second game, as four Oriole homers, two by Powell, accounted for a 5–1 win. Finally, Palmer clinched at Oakland with a 5–3 win.

The sweep gave the Orioles a 14-game winning streak; facing the Pirates in the Series, they were favored to gain the trophy. Playing at home, the birds took the first two games by 5–3 and 11–3 scores, rallying behind McNally and Palmer. At this point an easy victory seemed likely, but the Pirates swept the next three in Pittsburgh. Returning home, the desperate Orioles won the sixth game, but lost the finale. Another bitter defeat, Weaver would not compete again in the Series until 1979. With Frank Robinson absent and other veterans aging, the weakened Orioles lost their grip in 1972. The players' strike was partly to blame for this. All clubs played attenuated schedules, and critics warned that the skewed format might change the outcomes of the races. Their predictions were partly validated when the American League East showed effects of the strike.

In that race, the Tigers and Red Sox fought to a standstill, with the outcome determined by the quirky schedule. Despite weakened batting, Martin's Tigers led most of the way. In late September, however, the Red Sox took the charge; the last day of the season found the Tigers in Boston, striving to win a double-header. They proceeded to take the Eastern title, but the victory was earned only by winning an extra game. The Tigers closed with 86–70; the Red Sox stood at 85–70.

Tainted or not, it was Martin's second victory, and pitching had made the difference. Lolich won 22, Joe Coleman 19, and Woody Fryman 10; the staff toiled without McLain, who had been dealt to the Senators in return for infielders Ed Brinkman and Aurelio Rodriguez. Otherwise, Al Kaline's .313 hitting atoned for the team's lowly .237 average.

The A's meanwhile had coasted to victory in the West, beating the White Sox by 5½ games. Finley deserved mixed credit for the win. On the one hand, he acquired powerful lefty Ken Holtzman from the Cubs; on the other, his stinginess ruined Blue's season. For his 1971 heroics, Blue was paid a paltry $13,000, which Finley reputedly offered to augment with a car and a few thousand extra if he would change his first name to "True." The insulted Blue refused the bonus and demanded $90,000 wages; now Finley recoiled. After a bitter hold-out, Blue signed for less, but his absence diminished his effectiveness to six wins and stirred anti-Finley sentiments among other players.

Nevertheless, Finley wheedled his men into wearing long hair, sideburns, and mustaches in 1972. By paying $300 per face, Finley hoped to evoke a Gay Nineties motif, but, instead, his A's were seen as oddities and Finley's popularity stayed low—even when the long-haired style spread to other teams. However, with good pitching—including Hunter's 21 and Holtzman's 19 wins and 42 saves by relievers—and a league-leading 134 homers, the A's atoned for a lowly .240 team batting average.

Now they battled the Tigers for the championship. The A's took the first two, then struggled through three more games before winning. Opening at home, the A's took an 11-inning decision on Fingers's relief work. Next, John "Blue Moon" Odom pitched a three-hitter and won 5–0. Moving to Detroit, the A's first fell victim to Coleman's shut-out pitching and then blew a ninth-inning lead, walking home the winning run. In the tightly played finale, however, Tenace's only playoff hit scored the winning run for the jittery A's.

Because Jackson was injured in the playoffs, Cincinnati's powerful machine was favored over the emasculated A's. Forecasters, however, failed to reckon with unheralded Gene Tenace, whose Jacksonian exploits made the difference. In the Series opener at Cincinnati, catcher Tenace homered twice to account for the A's 3–2 victory. The next day Jim "Catfish" Hunter pitched brilliantly, but

Opposite: Superb pitching from lefty Ken Holtzman (*top left*), reliefer Rollie Fingers (*top right*), lefty Vida Blue (*bottom left*), and Jim "Catfish" Hunter (*bottom right*) enabled the Oakland A's to capture three straight world titles from 1972 to 1974.

needed a stellar ninth-inning catch and relief help from Fingers to triumph 2–1. The A's dropped the third game back at home, but the next time out, the doughty Tenace homered and scored two runs. Tottering on the brink, the Reds won the fifth game 5–4; then they tied matters at Cincinnati with a crushing 8–1 victory. In the final game, Williams used his four best pitchers to fend off the Reds, while Tenace drove in a pair of runs on a single and double to pace the 3–2 win. Thus, the despised "hippies" now reigned as World Champions.

Purists were soon outraged by the league's unilateral adoption of the designated hitter rule, which aimed at upping anemic batting averages. Bluntly rejected by the Nationals, the ploy raised American averages to .259 in 1973 and yielded a new class of heroes. Indeed, the fans liked it, but the rule also extended the careers of aging warhorses, like Orlando Cepeda, Jim Ray Hart, Tony Oliva, and Tommy Davis.

In 1973 "DHers" played significant roles in the divisional races. At Baltimore Tommy Davis batted .306 with 89 RBIs, boosting the Orioles to the Eastern title. Weaver also received .300 level performances from young outfielders Rich Coggins and Al Bumbry. Another newcomer, Bobby Grich, took second base and rookie Doyle Alexander pitched effectively. Meanwhile, the veteran Palmer won 22 games and another Cy Young Award. Buoyed by a .266 team batting average, the birds won 97 to outlast the runner-up Red Sox by eight.

Meanwhile, Williams had a tough time winning the West for a third straight year. Troubles flared, as Finley depressed salaries and berated fans for poor attendance. A mild heart attack in August briefly removed him from the scene. Spurred by "DHer" Deron Johnson's slugging and young Bill North's batting and base stealing, the A's fought off three challengers in June. By July the team took the lead and held it, finishing six ahead of the rising Royals. Johnson's efforts produced 81 RBIs, but Jackson was the hammer. His .293 average was his best, and his 32 homers and 117 RBIs guided the league. In total, the A's batted .260, stole 147 bases, and enjoyed the 20-win performances of both Hunter and Holtzman. Reliefer "the Vulture" Fingers saved 22, with a 1.92 ERA.

The autumnal playoff between the rival dynasties went five games. In the first at Baltimore, Palmer pitched a shut-out and the Birds flattened Blue enroute to a 6–0 win. The A's retaliated behind Hunter and Holtzman and grabbed the next two. The Orioles also fought back, only to fall in the final game, as Hunter allowed no Oriole to reach the third base while he pitched a 3–0 masterpiece.

Now the A's contested the ugly duckling Mets, whose 82–79 seasonal record was the poorest of any World Series qualifier. For once the A's were favored, but the feisty Mets nearly worked another miracle. In the Oakland opener, Holtzman pitched and batted the A's to a 2–1 win. Next, a record four-hour, extra-inning struggle went to the Mets, who scored four in the 12th to triumph 10–7. In an ugly postscript to this loss, Finley tried to replace infielder Mike Andrews for committing two errors. When the story broke, Finley was roasted by the press, scorned by his players, and fined by Commissioner Kuhn.

The A's moved into Shea Stadium for the Series and took a close 3–2 decision. The Mets, however, won the next two on the pitching of Matlack and Koosman. After the third loss, a shakened Finley, assisted by his cardiologist, left the Stadium amidst derisive jeers. Back at home, the beleaguered A's took charge, winning the sixth game on Hunter's pitching and Jackson's three hits. Then, the A's won the Series finale 5–2, but for all Holtzman's pitching and batting heroics, it took homers by Jackson and Companeris, plus relief help, to quell the Mets.

Finley faced more stormy criticism in the bitter aftermath of this latest victory. When interviewed after the final game, Williams announced his resignation, stating that he planned to manage the Yankees. He admitted to Jackson that Finley was trouble: "You'll see why I have to leave the man even if I didn't want to leave the team." For the moment Finley acquiesced, but he later invoked his contractual authority over Williams. When the manager refused to return, Finley recalled one of his earlier victims, Al Dark.

After a checkered managerial career, Dark now claimed that his baseball troubles and personal problems had been solved by a religious rebirth. He told reporters: "I've tried to think of how Jesus Christ would handle ballplayers."[6] Still, cynical players remembered that he once labeled black and Hispanic players as "dumb." In Jackson's opinion, Dark was a toadying hypocrite, who cowered before these words from Finley: "I'm in it to win, and if you don't get your ----ing --- in gear, you're gonna be gone."[7]

While the players disliked Dark's submissiveness, they despised Finley's bullying. Far from mellowing, Finley still berated his fans and his players. He blamed fans for poor attendance and threatened to move. When his lease blunted that threat, he raised ticket prices and refused to supply stamps for answering fan mail. He also refused raises for his players, but now his stinginess ran afoul of the new arbitration rule. To his horror, four men—including MVP Jackson—used the arbitration route to pry raises.[8]

It was an angry, bickering team that Dark led to a Western victory in 1974. When not sniping at Finley or complaining of Dark's ineffectiveness, they battled each other in clubhouse brawls. Still, they won the pennant decisively, beating Billy Martin's Rangers by six games. Their winning attack was paced by Hunter, who won 25 on a 2.49 ERA and earned the Cy Young Award. A poor team offensive average was offset by Rudi's .293 average and homers from Jackson and Bando. Again, fleet Bill North headed the running attack, leading all with 54 steals. Indeed, Finley was so impressed by the running attack that he hired Herb Washington, a world-class sprinter with no baseball experience, as a designated runner. The limited success of this bold move was drowned by ridicule.

Aside from the success of the contentious A's, the year 1974 was studded with other memorable events. Cowhide balls now replaced horsehide balls, Aaron broke Ruth's record, Kaline notched his 3,000th hit, Carew earned a third consecutive batting title, and Frank Robinson stepped on field as the first black manager in major league history. On the lighter side, Willie Horton's pop fly at Fenway killed a flying pigeon, whose carcass fell with frightening effect at the feet of the Red Sox catcher.[9]

In the American League East, the Orioles fell eight games behind on August 29 and a win by either the Yankees or the Red Sox seemed likely. Consequently, the Sox collapsed, losing 21 of their last 33, while the Birds won 27 of 33. During a ten-game winning streak, Oriole pitchers hurled five shut-outs, and by mid-September, the Yankees were dumped in a three-game Oriole sweep. At season's end, the Orioles won two 17-inning games to better the Yanks by two. Observers were hard put to explain how the Orioles did it. The team batted a mediocre .256, with no outstanding performances. Among the pitchers, Palmer slumped to seven wins, but Cuellar won 22, and McNally and Grimsley picked up the slack.

Chosen to lose to the A's in the playoffs, the Birds did so, but in highly eccentric fashion. The Orioles homered thrice in the opener, to win behind Cuellar, 6–3. Next, they were blanked twice, first by Holtzman, then by Blue, whose 1–0 win hinged on Bando's homer. The A's now closed it out with a 2–1 victory, but they gained only

Oakland manager Al Dark (*left*) talks with his slugging outfielder Reggie Jackson (*right*).

one hit off Cuellar, a double by Jackson, which combined with walks to make the sorry difference.

This victory matched the divided A's against the united Dodgers in the Series. The day before the opener, two Oakland pitchers brawled in the clubhouse, and Hunter charged Finley with breach of contract. In addition, Jackson was put on probation by Commissioner Kuhn for threatening a reporter. Meanwhile, the familial Dodgers sang their trite motto, "You Gotta Believe," in the background.

Nevertheless, when the first all-California Series opened before a celebrity-studded Los Angeles crowd, the A's won 3–2, scoring on a Jackson homer and a double batted by pitcher Holtzman. Stout relief work was needed to stave off the Dodgers who smote 11 hits and left 12 men on bases. The next game belonged to the Dodgers by a repeat score, as Dodger reliefer Mike Marshall picked off Finley's designated runner to snuff a ninth-inning rally. The jeers raised by his designated runner's failure were still ringing when Finley blundered again, vainly inviting former President Nixon to toss out the first ball. Still, the A's won the game 3–2, thanks to two Dodger errors. The next day Holtzman pitched and homered the A's to a 5–2 victory, though he needed his usual relief help. The Series ended a day later when the A's scored another 3–2 win, riding on relief pitching by Odom and Fingers. At the last out, Dark exulted, "Glory to God"—he might instead have praised the bullpen corps, whose saving grace assisted every victory scored by the A's in their three consecutive Series triumphs.

Time, however, was running out on the A's and their impulsive owner. At the A's victory celebration Finley put Jackson up to the prank of dumping champagne on Commissioner Kuhn's pate; "He was angry as hell, but he wouldn't show it," Jackson said, noting that Finley praised him, saying, "Job well done, champ."[10] All too soon Finley would learn that twisting Kuhn's tail was dangerous. In the meantime other events worked against Finley; over the winter the arbitration panel freed his ace pitcher Hunter to sell his services on the open market. The incensed Finley went to court and lost; he received no compensation from Hunter's departure. To top off the loss of Hunter, an arm injury to rookie pitcher Mike Norris placed most of the 1975 pitching burden on Blue and Holtzman. The duo responded magnificently, combining for 40 wins, while Fingers saved 24. After an early slump, the A's took the lead in July and hung on to win a fifth straight Western title. Theirs was a hollow victory, gotten in a sorry division where only three teams played winning ball. To his credit, Finley made the trades that revamped the team, gaining the prized second baseman, Phil Garner. The A's batted below the league average, but they compensated offensively with home runs and stolen bases.

The league's power balance was now shifting to the East. Newcomers Lee May and Ken Singleton revived the Baltimore batting attack, while Mike Torrez won 20 as a starting pitcher. As Cuellar faded, Palmer rebounded to win 23 to net another Cy Young Award. Nevertheless, the birds were beaten by the powerful Red Sox.

Two precocious young outfielders, Fred Lynn and Jim Rice, keyed the Boston attack. Each topped .300; Rice added 22 homers and 102 RBIs, while Lynn batted a mighty .331, with 21 homers and 105 RBIs—taking both Rookie of the Year and MVP awards. With catcher Carlton Fisk batting .331 in limited duty, the team's .275 batting carried an adequate pitching staff of Rick Wise, Luis Tiant, Bill Lee, Reggie Cleveland, Roger Moret, and reliefer Dick Drago. With a veteran infield of Yastrzemski at first, Denny Doyle at second, Rick Burleson at short, and Rico Petrocelli at third, manager Darrell Johnson kept his team out front by 4½ games.

Indeed, the Red Sox accomplished much more, sweeping the battle-tested A's in the playoffs. In the opener at Fenway, that "grimy, red brick . . . Old North Church of professional sports," Luis Tiant pitched a three-hitter and won 7–1. On the added strength of Yastrzemski's hitting, the Sox took the next two games to land the pennant.[11]

Now they battled the Big Red Machine through seven games—including two extra-inning contests—before falling. Boston's venerable owner Yawkey, who had endured similar near misses in 1946 and 1967, suffered his last heartbreak. To worsen his failing health his last baseball memories would be haunted by the Yankee bugbear, now loosed again after twelve years.

The Return of the Yankees

For the lordly Yankees, the period of 1965–1975 was agonizingly bleak. Ironically, just as CBS purchased the team and alarmists warned of the league becoming a Yankee fief, they collapsed and stayed down. The failure was an embarrassment to the giant firm, whose officials pondered the question of what to do with this expensive property which accounted for only 2 percent of its annual sales. Their apparent answer, to name Mike Burke as team president, offered no remedy. Although Burke oozed with personal charm and courted writers, he was ineffective in baseball. He flashed across the sports stage like a comet and even aspired to the Commissioner's post, but a string of poor seasons undid his dreams.[12]

By 1970 the task of rebuilding rested upon Lee MacPhail, and rumors swirled that CBS would sell the club to outside interests. Desperate to keep the Yankees, city officials agreed to refurbish the stadium if the team would agree to a 30-year lease. Negotiated by Burke, that deal cost the city far more than its budgeted estimate. It was Burke's last contribution; in 1972 he was offered the choice of either buying the team himself or finding a suitable purchaser. In a quandary, Burke sought advice from Gabe Paul, president of the Indians, who introduced him to George S. Steinbrenner III. Early in the following year, the announcement was made that Steinbrenner and Burke had purchased the team for $10 million. At a price $3 million less than CBS had paid in 1965, the purchase was a bargain—but not for Burke. Following a brutally short power struggle, Burke, MacPhail, and Houk were cast adrift and Steinbrenner took control, naming Paul as his general manager. From then on Steinbrenner worked to consolidate his position, controlling the majority of stock by 1978.

Power and prestige seemed obsessions of this portly, close-cropped millionaire. The young Steinbrenner had early plunged into real estate, acquired a pro basketball team and financed theatre ventures. Armed with a personal fortune of $100 million, Steinbrenner eyed the Yankees as his ticket to fame. Decisive and hypercritical, he fired or drove out at least a dozen underlings. Steinbrenner sought to restore Yankee glory. He tirelessly hectored his underlings, throwing harsh criticisms at President Paul, who was often chafed. Paul finally resigned in 1978 and his successor, Al Rosen, followed the same thorny route, as did field managers Billy Martin and Bob Lemon. Naturally, the players were wary of Steinbrenner, but some sensed his need to hobnob with them.

Like Finley, this aspiring leader of owners was shunned. Steinbrenner's most awkward problem stemmed from the political indiscretion of contributing illegally to Nixon's re-election fund. Under investigation, Steinbrenner seemingly tried to shift the blame, but was indicted on several counts. In the end, he escaped more serious punishment by pleading guilty to the charge of obstructing a Federal investigation, was fined $15,000, and was put on probation. After his 1974 conviction, Kuhn declared him "incompetent" to head the Yankees and suspended him for two years. The owner defied the edict and finagled an early amnesty.[13]

That Steinbrenner's prestige soared while under this cloud is an object lesson in public relations. For all his excesses, he ingratiated himself to fickle fans, who were won over by his 1973 promise to land a pennant within five years. When he delivered, few questioned his methods. Furthermore, his colleagues knew that a deteriorating Yankee team spelled losses for all. Indeed, the shabby appearance of Yankee Stadium symbolized fallen American League prestige. Steinbrenner's nicely timed arrival coincided with the city's stadium refurbishing project. After two years of playing at Shea Stadium as tenants of the Mets, the Yankees confidently entered their revamped stadium.

The team and its manager wore fresh faces. Steinbrenner hired Martin in 1975 to manage the team, while President Paul busily traded for new talent. To the 1973 nucleus of outfielder Roy White, third baseman Graig Nettles, catcher Thurman Munson, and reliefer "Sparky" Lyle, Paul's trades added first baseman Chris Chambliss, outfielder Lou Pinella, and pitcher Dick Tidrow. Steinbrenner won the auction for Catfish Hunter, and Paul engineered two key trades on the eve of the 1976 season. For outfielder Bobby Bonds he landed speedy center fielder Mickey Rivers and pitcher Ed Figueroa from the Angels. Next, Paul dealt pitcher "Doc" Medich to the Pirates for second baseman Willie Randolph, solving a glaring infield problem.

When they packed the "new" Stadium on opening day of 1976, fans saw a dozen new faces in the lineup. These strangers defeated the Twins 11–4 and began a march that brought them an easy victory in the East. For a time the Orioles hung close, but by August the Yanks built a big lead and coasted home, 10½ games ahead of the Birds. The glorious victory reminded some of the 1923 season when the Stadium first opened and the team responded as champions. This year over two million fans sat in new plastic seats and ogled the $3 million scoreboard. Still, the team was the greatest delight to watch. Rivers and Randolph hyped the running game, Munson batted .302 and took MVP honors, Nettles piloted the league in homers, and New York's Puerto Rican community cheered Figueroa on to a 19-game winning total.

At the same time, the rising Kansas City mini-dynasty succeeded the A's in the west. Finley named Chuck Tanner as his new manager; Dark reportedly had damaged Finley's reputation in a public statement and was fired for team treason. Also, fearing the probable loss of stars to the new re-entry draft, Finley sold Jackson and Holtzman to the Orioles, and was about to peddle others when Kuhn abruptly canceled the sales. The incensed Finley replied with a $3.5 million lawsuit, which he lost, along with the Western title.

Some Finley-haters from Kansas City recognized divine retribution in the dethroning of the A's by their new team. Now under an imaginative owner, Ewing Kauffman, the Kansas City Royals occupied a new stadium; directed by manager Whitey Herzog and blessed with good pitching, an able defense, and solid hitting, the 1976 Royals scaled the heights.

With only five games left to play and the Royals up by 3½ games, the A's mounted a gallant last stand. Tanner kept his talent-shorn club in contention that year by unleashing the most devastating running attack in league history. The team rampaged for 341 stolen bases, only seven short of the all-time record. Playing at home against the Royals, the A's took the first two games of a five-game series. Fans at the brawling opener witnessed a Royal player beat a fan with an umbrella. The third game went to the jittery Royals, won by the shut-out pitching of Yankee castoff Larry Gura. With tears of joy, the Royals celebrated their victory; no one was more jubilant than Amos Otis, whom Tanner once denounced as a coward, but whose homer and double decided the game.

Now the two reborn teams met to settle the league championship. This first test of strength went five games and ended at Yankee Stadium, with the Yanks taking the rubber match, 7–6. In the exciting climax, the Royals had men on base in the ninth and threatened to break the 6–6 tie. With two out already by Jim Wohlford hit into the hole over second, where Yankee shortstop Fred Stanley grabbed the grounder and gained a controversial out. The Yankees came to bat, and a moment later Chambliss ended the contest with a homer. When the blow was struck, thousands stormed past police pickets and prevented a terrified Chambliss from scoring. The riot lasted an hour, after which Chambliss emerged from the clubhouse and planted both feet on home plate to insure the victory.[14]

This was the Yankee zenith; the team met a humiliating defeat at the hands of the Reds in the World Series. Watching his club fail to win a single game was crushing for Steinbrenner, who returned a vow of vengeance. Indeed, the re-entry draft in the fall afforded a quick and efficient means. When bidding for available stars, Steinbrenner made the most of his cash and his appealing location. Still, the price was high. For a $5 million, multi-year contract, he snared Gullett, the Red's pitcher who tormented the Yanks in the recent Series; for a five-year contract worth $3.5 million, Steinbrenner obtained Reggie Jackson; he also purchased shortstop Bucky Dent and pitcher Mike Torrez. Such lavishness appalled fellow owners and critics, who dubbed the Yankees "the best team that money could buy."

Although Jackson was the key acquisition, Martin argued hotly against this controversial player. Events soon proved his foresight correct. From the start, the cocky Jackson grated on Martin and widened the rift between the manager and Steinbrenner.[15]

The 1977 expansion draft, which saw the league unilaterally expand to 14 clubs, cut into the Yankee bench strength. The new skewed schedule was troublesome enough for Martin, but other events added woes. Pressed hard by the Red Sox, who were fortified by the free agent draft, and by the Orioles, who relied on homegrown talent, Martin's moves were sharply criticized by Steinbrenner. That year the Yanks twice fell five games behind the slugging Red Sox, who blasted 210 homers during the season. Still, they rebounded each time, bolstered by the pitching of Torrez, Gullett, Ron Guidry, and Lyle's Cy Young award-winning relief work.

At the start of the season's final week, it was a three-team race. Holding a slim lead and needing a win to clinch, the Yanks eventually backed into the pennant; they were assisted by the Orioles, who forfeited one game and then eliminated the Red Sox with a key victory. In the Western race, the Royals briefly endured a four-way contest, but after mid-August they played .700 ball and won easily. The vastly improved Royal team boasted six men with 15 or more homers, two fine starting pitchers in Paul Splittorff and Dennis Leonard, and an able relief crew.

By winning two of the first three playoff games, the Royals threatened to snare the pennant and with that, Martin's job. Steinbrenner's meddling threats even grated on the players; one told the owner to either fire Martin or shut up and let him manage. In the shadow of defeat, Martin boldly set his terms—a long term contract if I win and "If I get fired, I'll beat him [Steinbrenner]."

When playoff action shifted to Kansas City, the latter course seemed likely. Still, Martin refused to let his men pack their luggage, and the team responded with a 6–4 win. The match was tied, but late in the final game the Yanks fell behind. Then, a "scared to death" Paul Blair blooped a single, igniting a three-run rally that brought victory to the Yanks, 5–3. Upon the final out, a television camera caught little Fred Patek weeping in the Royal dugout.

The Yankees and Dodgers now met in the World Series for the ninth time; this time, however, the Yanks were cast as brawling misfits and their fans, as noisy boors. In the home opener, Gullett held the Dodgers for nine innings; whereupon Lyle replaced for the next three, until Blair singled in the winning runs in a 12-inning duel. The next day Martin unwisely chose the fading Hunter, who was shelled in a 6–1 loss. Play shifted to Los Angeles and the Jackson-Martin feud saw an untimely flare. Catcher Munson also jibed at Jackson; but when playing time came, the Yanks downed the

The reincarnated Yankees won world championships in 1977 and 1978 behind the slugging of "Mr. October" Reggie Jackson (*top left*), the pitching of lefty Ron Guidry (*top right*), the all-round play of third baseman Graig Nettles (*bottom left*), and the catching and leadership of Thurman Munson (*bottom right*).

Dodgers 5–3. The next day Jackson homered in support of Guidry, pushing his team up three games to one. Backs against the wall, the Dodgers rallied and sent the Series back to New York. There, 56,000 fans widely cheered a pregame announcement that Martin's contract was renewed, but before the game ended Jackson's name resounded louder. The 8–4 Yankee victory had been powered by Jackson's three consecutive homers. After each blow, thunderous roars of "Reggie! Reggie!" rang out—later a candy bar was named for Jackson.

Not surprisingly, Jackson's inflated ego added to Martin's woes. In the unbelievable campaign of 1978, Martin's troubles came to a head when, on top of Jackson-Steinbrenner annoyances, team injuries plagued the manager. Also, the Red Sox had demolished opponents this season with sheer power. A 93-hit barrage captured their first seven games and, by mid-July manager Don Zimmer's Sox led the Yanks by 13 games.

To fight this threat, Martin imposed strict discipline, backed by penalties. However, when Jackson was fined and suspended for a tactical violation, Steinbrenner backed Jackson. The furious Martin blurted to a reporter, "The two of them deserve each other. One's a born liar, the other's convicted."[16] This outburst cost Martin his job, but at Old Timer's Day on July 29 Yankee fans roared Martin's name for 15 minutes, as the sacked manager took his place among Yankee heroes of the 1950s. Then, in a bizarre development Steinbrenner announced that Martin would return the following season.

For now, Bob Lemon skippered the team. Paunchy and avuncular-looking behind spectacles, the 57-year-old Hall of Famer calmed tempers with a low-keyed approach. Mercifully, a long newspaper strike silenced muckraking baseball writers. Injured players returned and the team grew hot, mounting the greatest stretch drive since 1914. Leading the pitchers was lefty Ron Guidry, whose slider and fastball accounted for 25 wins and only three losses. When help was needed, big Bruce "Goose" Gossage, another expensive free agent emerged from the bull-pen to save game after game.

Holding second place on August 21, the Yanks trailed by 8½ games. Five days later they closed to 6½, and Nettles, whose six homers powered the surge, told his mates, "We can still catch them." He was right, as the famous Boston massacre demonstrated. At Fenway, the Yanks ruthlessly bludgeoned the Sox in four games, by scores of 15–3, 13–2, 7–0, and 7–4. It was too much excitement for one shell-shocked fan, who screamed at manager Zimmer: "You've really done it—my heart's been broken for good."[17]

As the onrushing Yanks grabbed the lead, the Sox recovered and battled back to tie. A sudden-death playoff was scheduled to settle the issue and, like the only other ever played, action would commence at Fenway Park. On October 2 Guidry took the mound against Boston ace Mike Torrez. It looked like Boston's day, after a Yastrzemski homer and a Rice single gave the Sox a 2–0 lead. In the seventh, however, the Yanks rallied for four; a big blow came from light-hitting Bucky Dent, whose homer barely cleared the left-field wall. A Jackson homer upped the Yankee lead to 5–2 in the eighth, but the Sox rallied back for two, making it 5–4. With two out in the last of the ninth, the Sox had the tying run at third when Yastrzemski popped to Nettles. The victory awarded the Eastern title to the Yanks; it offered only endless nightmares for the Boston co-owner, who admitted a month later: "I sit and stare, but I haven't come up with an answer yet."

Accordingly, the Yanks embarked for Kansas City, where the winning Royals waited to contest the league title. The Royals were edged in two past encounters, but Yankee momentum crushed them now. After losing the opener 7–1, the Royals took the second. Next, the teams were off to Yankee Stadium where the home team nailed down the title on 6–5 and 2–1 wins. In the first contest, Hunter pitched doggedly, though he was battered for three solo homers by George Brett. Then Munson's tremendous 430-foot swat into the center-field bullpen won it for the Yanks: "Nobody hits a ball like that," marveled Jackson. Finally, in the clincher, Guidry pitched as Nettles and White homered for the necessary runs.

The stage was set for the tenth Yankee-Dodger World Series. Inspired by Lasorda's maudlin exhortations, the hosting Dodgers blasted the Yankees 11–5 and followed with a 4–3 win the next night. Series history gave no hope for a Yankee comeback; however, the text was re-written by the 1978 Yankees. Playing at home, they took the third match behind Guidry, who was supported by four brilliant plays from third baseman Nettles. Next, the Yankees snatched a ten-inning, 4–3 victory, and were assisted by a controversial decision. Trying for a double play, Dodger shortstop Russell's throw to first bounced off Jackson's knee, enabling him to take sec-

Opposite: Veteran outfielder Carl Yastrzemski notched over 3,000 hits in more than twenty seasons with the Boston Red Sox, but his team never won a world championship during that span.

ond. The Dodgers screamed interference, but the decision stood and the Yankees rallied. Then, in the last of the tenth, they won on a walk and two singles.

With the Series tied, Lemon called on Jim Beattie, who pitched the Yanks to a 12–2 victory behind an 18-hit tattoo sparked by Dent and the unheralded Brian Doyle. The Series returned to Los Angeles, where fans briefly reveled in an early Dodger lead; however, Dent and Doyle ignited a three-run rally in the second, and Jackson's long homer in the seventh clinched the Series for the Yankees.

This was a triple miracle for the Yankees. Having rallied from afar to overtake the Red Sox, they snatched a playoff game and then, down by two, they swept past the Dodgers: such was the stuff of legends.

Nevertheless, the storied victory presaged no new pinstripe tyranny. In 1979 the team faltered. Hunter never regained winning form and retired from the mound at season's end. Nagging injuries befell pitchers Guidry, Beattie, and Figueroa. Worse still, the vaunted bullpen was crippled when Gossage, injured in a clubhouse ruckus, was sidelined for 83 days. Steinbrenner's latest plunge into the re-entry mart landed pitchers Tommy John and Luis Tiant. Ex-Dodger John won a superb 21, while crafty old Tiant lapped 13. Guidry recovered and gained 18, while young Ron Davis pitched well in relief.

Injuries also scythed the regular lineup, felling Nettles, Jackson, and Munson. Then, in August Munson died in the flaming wreckage of his jet plane. His loss negated Steinbrenner's remedies, such as dropping Lemon and returning Martin. This time there was no flareup of the Martin-Jackson vendetta; Jackson's .297 was his best effort, although his homer and RBI production fell. Still, if the Yanks finished with eight consecutive wins, it was too late and, sadly, Martin was not there to build on that record in 1980—Steinbrenner had sacked him again.[18]

As the Yankees floundered, the Red Sox and Brewers rushed forward. Outhitting all others, Sox batters pummeled pitchers all season long. For a time Lynn and Rice dueled for Triple Crown honors, but in the end they divided awards. Each had hit 39 homers, Lynn led the league in batting, and Rice led in RBIs. Thus, the Sox also guided the league in homers, with 194. However, because the pitchers allowed a generous 4.03 ERA, the Sox finished third—ahead of the Yanks, but 11½ games off the pace.

Similarly, Brewer pitchers yielded four runs per game, a deficit which the hitters partially offset with .280 batting and 164 homers. Paul Molitor, Sixto Lezcano, Cecil Cooper, and Charlie Moore all topped .300, while outfielder Gorman Thomas led the league with 45 homers. This helped the Brewers to 95 wins, but the Orioles were still eight games up.

For the Birds to win so decisively after losing key men in the re-entry draft belied alarmist claims that the draft favored the rich. Indeed, the Orioles had matchless assets in general manager Hank Peters and manager Earl Weaver. Through judicious trades and player development, Peters supplied enough talent to replace the prodigals. In a shrewd 1976 deal with the Yankees, for example, Peters snared pitchers Scott McGregor and Tippy Martinez and catcher Rick Dempsey—all stars with the 1979 Birds. For such efforts, Peters won Executive of the Year honors.

The real soul of the Orioles was firebrand Earl Weaver. Since taking control in 1969, his team was baseball's winningest. Despite heavy losses in recent re-entry drafts, he consistently rebuilt his teams and kept them strong. "What we have is a certain chemistry," said pitcher McGregor, and outfielder Ken Singleton explained, "We are good players who play together." Despite the club's modest salary policy, this was true. With only Palmer among the plutocrats, the Orioles were the best-balanced team in the league.

Ironically, Palmer added little to the 1979 effort. Harried by nagging injuries, he earned only ten games. Still the staff was the league's best. With 23 wins, Mike Flanagan led the circuit and took the Cy Young award; McGregor took 13, Steve Stone 11, and workhorse Martinez 15, while Don Stanhouse led the relief crew. The offensive crew offered plenteous homers to offset mediocre batting. Singleton and first baseman Eddie Murray each batted .295, and combined for 60 homers and 200 RBIs. Furthermore, Weaver owned the best defense in the league.

Only in April did the Birds falter, losing eight of their first eleven. Rallying swiftly, they won nine straight, and by mid-May, they perched on the heights. Except for one day in June, they stayed there all season, delighting home fans, who numbered 600,000 more than the year before. The crowds watched an exciting, unyielding team that won 32 games by a single run and was seldom beaten in extra-inning games. With more wins than any team in the majors this year, they coasted to an easy victory.

While the Orioles showed how to win with home-grown talent, the California Angels bought their victory. Owner Autry had struggled

In the early 1980s the Milwaukee Brewers became a power in the American League's eastern division on offensive strength supplied by outfielder Gorman Thomas (*top left*), shortstop Robin Yount (*top right*), and outfielder Paul Molitor (*bottom*), shown below sliding safely into home.

over the years to land a pennant, but calamities cursed his teams. During the decade, three auto accidents killed two players and paralyzed another; a promising pitcher died of a cerebral hemorrhage; a high-priced outfielder was shot to death; and injuries felled others. Here was Autry's cup of woe: with star players available for big money, over the years he spent $15 million in long-term contracts for accident and injury-prone stars.[19]

Still, Autry dreamed of happy trails to come, and his friend Richard Nixon told him, "Never give up!" Thus, his latest spending spree gave manager Jim Fregosi a bevy of stars. For $4 million the Angels acquired the great Carew for five years. With Carew at first, Grich at second, the aging Campaneris at short, and Carney Lansford at third, the infield was strong offensively. In the outfield, team captain Don Baylor, Joe Rudi, and Dan Ford supplied power. The pitching staff was headed by Nolan Ryan, the fastest hurler in the game, while catcher Brian Downing showed flashes of greatness. Of this talented array, eight men held multi-year contracts, each worth a million or more.

In 1979 these plutocrats toppled the thrice-champion Kansas City Royals, whose consistent playoff losses seemingly sapped morale. Except for Brett, who batted .330 with 23 homers, the Royal attack fizzled. They played losing ball for half of the season, and when Herzog inserted rookies to shake up the team, dissension mounted. Stormed at from all sides, Herzog's days were numbered. Not even a magical late-season drive saved him. After losing by three games to the Angels, he was gone.

The Angel injury jinx, in fact, made the race close. Still, Autry's men mounted their strongest offense in years, averaging 5.4 runs per game on a .282 team batting average and 164 homers. Following a brilliant first-half lead, injuries to Carew, Campaneris, Rudi, and rookie Willie Mays Aikens had them playing losing ball the rest of the way. Still, this was a fighting team that forty times rallied from behind to win. The indomitable Baylor took over as DH when injuries kept him from outfield duty. Overall, he batted .296 with 36 homers, and led the league in RBIs and runs scored. For Baylor, an ex-Oriole turned affluent Angel, this was vindication. When handed the MVP award he declared: "I really wanted the award . . . which just adds to attention for the club and attention for me."[20]

Limping home with 88 victories, the Angels won on one of the worst winning percentages ever. The injury jinx struck even as they toasted their victory with champagne and high spirits: pitcher Jim

Barr broke a finger banging his hand against a toilet seat. This ludicrous injury foreshadowed their fate as they crossed bats with the Orioles. The Orioles swept the first two games, played at Baltimore. Back at home, the Angels rallied to take the third, but Oriole lefty McGregor pitched a six-hit shut-out to land the pennant. The Angels were consoled in their defeat by a 750,000 attendance increase.

Weaver now prepared his Orioles to battle the Pirates in the World Series. Recalling his 1971 humiliation, he wanted revenge, but knew it would not be easy. Pitching and defense might give the Orioles an edge, but the Pirates excelled in hitting and base running. Moreover, because of the alternate year rule, Weaver could not use designated hitters.

From the start, freakish weather—including snow, rain, and unseasonably cold air—marred the Series. Luckily, Oriole ace Flanagan was from New Hampshire; he sneered at freezing night temperatures and guarded an early lead to win the opener. The next night rain marred a duel between Palmer and Bert Blyleven, but after a long delay, the Pirates won 3–2. More cold weather greeted the contestants at Pittsburgh. The Birds fell behind in game three, but after another rain delay, they rallied for seven runs to win 8–4. Then, in bitterly cold weather, the teams struggled for nearly four hours before Weaver's pinch-hitters blasted a 9–6 victory.

Up three games to one, the Orioles drew confidence from the knowledge that only thrice before did a team recover from such a deficit. Nor did the loss of the last game at Pittsburgh alarm, for now the home advantage was Baltimore's. At home balmy weather smiled, but the Pirates took the sixth game, and in the seventh they battered five Oriole relievers and snared the world title. The Pirate victory added another sparkling chapter to Series history; as the Yanks of 1978 authored a legend, the Pirates closed out the decade with another.[21]

Profile: Marvin Miller, Emancipator

Thehe expansion era owners should have heeded Francis Bacon's warning "that cunning men pass for wise." Having learned nothing from the century-old record of player resentment at being ill-paid or being bought, sold, and reserved, this generation of owners repeated those follies. This time, however, it was the owners, and not the players, who suffered the consequences.

What the poor benighted owners failed to grasp was that they were cast in the role of tyrants at a time when maximum personal freedom was in the ascendancy. They continued to exploit players, ignoring past warnings or present storm signals hoisted by organized groups of players. Players of this age (like those in the past) banded together against their masters, but this time the results were different. Players now succeeded in reducing the owners to the status of ordinary employers in a democracy; for owners, this humble pie was a just dessert after so much power-gorging. Moreover, the man who guided the successful players' struggle against these oppressors felt the glory of these times.

The player grievances of this era were essentially those same cries that stirred the great 1890 revolt and subsequent unionizing efforts. The players' demands, spelled out in 1910 by writer Hugh Fullerton, included salary and reserve clause reforms; they called for more money, protection against salary cuts, rights to collective bargaining, and recourse to arbitration when differences existed. Players requested that long-term contracts replace the reserve clause; they also sought the right to quit a team for another.[1]

In 1946 these rights were sought by war veterans returning to baseball; the players were backed by federal laws that supported some of their demands. Owners were then forced to concede a "Diamond G.I. Bill of Rights," which allowed for severance pay, credit for years spent in military service, a minimum salary, a limit to salary cuts, injury pay, and payment for spring training expenses. At first glance this docket seemed like a generous and patriotic concession; in fact, it was a desperate attempt to dampen player militance. Protests were widespread and bilateral, ranging from owner Connie Mack's complaints of back talk to serious talk among poorly paid players, with some of the latter seeking legal representation in salary negotiations. While such player demands reflected the rising cost of living, they also corresponded with rising attendance and higher prices for talent.[2] Moreover, veteran players were incensed by the high bonuses that owners were paying for untried rookies.[3]

Two incidents in 1946 frightened the club owners: the Mexican League affair and the strike threat by Pittsburgh players. The Mexican League was a grandiose scheme by wealthy Mexican promoters who sought to build a major league of their own, though stocking it with American stars. For a time, dazzling salary offers tempted players to jump; the few who did were blacklisted for violating the reserve clause. When the Mexican bubble burst, the blacklisted players sued for reinstatement; Danny Gardella's suit reached the U.S. Circuit Court of Appeals and seemed to be headed for the Supreme Court. Frightened by this threat to the reserve clause, the owners backed off, settled out of court, and grudgingly allowed the prodigals to return.[4]

The Pittsburgh strike threat was inspired by Boston attorney Robert Murphy's attempt to unionize the players. Heartened by the latest surge of unionism among American workers, the disgruntled players listened to Murphy, formed chapters, and elected representatives in the newly formed American Baseball Guild. In August a Pittsburgh strike vote concerning low pay and collective bargaining lost by a few votes, but scared owners into conceding the "Diamond G.I. Bill" and several other reforms: more meal money, $25 weekly "Murphy Money" for spring training expenses, a guaranteed World

Series pool of at least $250,000, and a pension. Of course, the pension plan was most significant. In granting pensions to five-year men, the owners pledged to fund 80 percent of its costs by linking payments to radio and television income. This was a portentous concession; not only were owners committed to fund the pension, but a precedent was set when players shared in media revenue. Since television money soon became baseball's gold mine, player shares became a major issue of the expansion era.[5]

The short-sighted owners prided themselves for killing off the Guild. By refusing to discuss reserve clause reform or the portioning of a traded player's sale price, their powers seemed intact. Union sentiment was indeed strong, but this wave was broken by a company union concession, allowing fruitless discussion of issues between owners and elected player representatives. When the owners tried to abolish the pension system in 1953, however, the sixteen player representatives met in Atlanta and hired Attorney J. Norman Lewis of New York to represent their cause. Angered by owner harassment of representatives and refusal to negotiate, militant players demanded pension reforms and more money.[6]

The Major League Players Association was born out of this crisis. While Lewis insisted it was a professional association, the owners trembled upon seeing their hirelings organizing under outside leadership. In vain they demanded that the players fire Lewis; when Commissioner Frick joined the chorus, the Association threatened court action if the pension plan was canceled. With press support behind the players, the owners accepted the Association and agreed to keep the pension plan.

The Association languished after this skirmish; Lewis was dropped, and late in the 1950s Judge Robert Cannon of Milwaukee filled the empty seat. Cannon catered to the owners throughout a tenure that lasted until 1966. His employment of personal diplomacy and gentlemanly manners in dealing with owners was outmaneuvered; thus, he did little for the players, but freed owners from the specters of strikes and collective bargaining. Indeed, Cannon stood still as owners rejected all proposals to modify the reserve clause and to formalize collective bargaining. Association President Bob Feller admitted that before employing Cannon the state of collective bargaining was "pathetic," and under Cannon it remained so.[7]

Still, events undermined the antediluvian stance of the owners. The 1960s' new spirit of militance spread unionist sentiments among even white collar workers, a group traditionally opposed to unions.

Thus, many organized masses—professors, teachers, hospital workers, Wall Street brokers, and government employees—were converting their impotent professional associations into bargaining agencies. The workers in the world of sports were also swept into the movement.

Crucial to the cause of baseball unionism were the players of these times. Better-educated than their ancestors, they were more critical of needless disciplinary codes and more union-minded. Old-time writers and officials carped at their money hunger, their self-indulgence, and their lack of commitment, citing with contempt an article written by one player, entitled "I Play for Money—Not Fun."

However, this player's attitude was in tune with the times. Like most Americans, security-minded players wanted pensions; these better-educated players also saw in baseball a limited career that must pay sufficiently to justify one's total commitment. Moreover, some athletes demanded rights of free expression; blacks and Latin Americans bristled at discriminatory slights; and many players questioned training rules and decorum recipes.[8]

It was not surprising, then, when midway through the 1960s the players united in an unprecedented display of union solidarity. The stage was now set for the emergence of a leader who would accomplish their emancipation. Association President Robin Roberts notified owners in 1964 that his group intended to replace Cannon with a full-time, paid Executive Director. Roberts had obtained a list of names of qualified men, and among those names was that of Marvin Miller, a labor economist for the United Steel Workers of America. Miller's qualifications were excellent; he was nominated and, after touring the spring training camps in 1966, was approved by a player vote of 489–136. Approval from Commissioner William Eckert and a committee of owners came grudgingly; National League President Warren Giles and others, in fact, tried to discredit him as a labor goon. These men were indeed right to worry because Miller turned out to be a bitter draught for owners to swallow and a stick in their craws for the rest of the era.[9]

Far from a labor goon, the 48-year-old Miller was a genius in labor relations. A hostile reporter admitted as much, while still depicting the slight, handsome Miller as "insipid-looking," with "waxed mustache and racetrack clothes."[10] Miller's wife, a professor of psychology, knew him as a perfectionist, a man committed to the cause of equal justice. Miller saw himself as a mild-mannered workaholic, whose choice of profession naturally involved him in controversy.

Marvin Miller, the players' "Commissioner," fields questions from the media about the impending 1981 players' strike.

The son of a struggling clothing salesman in Brooklyn, Miller was a gifted student who graduated from high school at age 15 and worked his way through New York University, leaving with a degree in economics. He landed a job with the federal civil service, but later found his niche serving with the National War Labor Board in World War II. Assigned to train labor mediators, he learned the importance of studying both sides in a labor dispute. After the war, Philip Murray, president of the United Steelworkers, hired him as a research director. Miller rose rapidly in U.S.W. councils, becoming assistant to President David McDonald, and gained a reputation as a superb strategist while serving on Presidential Commissions. His employers understandably regretted losing such a man to baseball; U.S.W. President I. W. Abel asked him to reconsider, but Miller chose to take up the players' cause.

Once in office, Miller determined to overhaul the Players Association, planning to reshape the structure from a passive instrument into an effective power tool. His predecessor had been ignorant of the Taft-Hartley labor laws, which required the filing of reports on salaries, hours, pensions, and working conditions to the National Labor Relations Board. When Cannon blandly told Miller to sign the owners' moral turpitude clause, Miller struck it out, asking, "Judge, have you ever heard of the Constitution of the United States?"[11] In transforming the Association from a "semi-paternalistic" organization into a bona fide labor organization, Miller used federal laws to force owners to negotiate formal contracts. This key reform aborted the practice of drawing ambiguous agreements that often ended in broken promises.[12]

Miller's initial encounters with commissioners and league presidents convinced him that they were owners' men—hence, his enemies. To battle the owners and their henchmen, Miller set out to weld the 500 players into a solid defensive bloc. He pursued the task tirelessly, meeting endlessly with players and their representatives and teaching his goals and methods. On one such mission, manager Leo Durocher allowed a coach to disrupt a gathering by hitting fungoes into the group; the incident evoked the full fury of Miller's rhetoric. His eloquent attacks on the establishment established him as the formidable debater on behalf of their cause. Most importantly, his zeal and courage won the solid support of the players.

Miller was indeed generously supported. His first two-year contract accorded him a $50,000 annual salary, plus $100,000 to establish an office. When the owners refused to divert some television pension money for this, the players raised their annual dues to $350, and Miller, invoking a checkoff law, forced owners to become dues collectors. The players struck a bargain upon hiring Miller; he won not only sweeping reforms at the bargaining table, but also the continuing support of his clients. In 1974, the emissary exulted that all 600 players were Association members, making theirs the strongest sports association in America.[13]

Miller's growing reputation as the player's emancipator gained luster with each of the four basic agreements he and his legal advisor, Dick Moss, negotiated. Against this duo the owners pitted their own hired negotiator, John J. Gaherin. Gaherin was quickly placed on the defensive by Miller's tactics; outgunned by his opponent's strong legal position and wily rhetoric, the freshman was overmatched.

The term "Basic Agreement" was applied to each formal contact hammered out between the owners and the Association. The first, negotiated in 1967, spelled out working conditions and increased owner contributions to the pension fund to $4.1 million a year. After a bitter fight, the minimum salary—pegged at $7,000 for a decade—was upped to $10,000 and daily expense allowances were increased.

The owners also promised a complete review of the reserve clause. This first agreement was a good beginning; its chief gain was that owners were now forced to bargain collectively and to ink concessions in a formal contract.

When this agreement expired in 1969, Miller and the players fumed over the owners' stalling tactics. Moreover, the club heads reneged on the promised reserve-clause study and refused to budge on matters like raising the minimum salary or conceding the vested rights of players to television revenue. Also, Miller worried that inflation would erode the pension plan and, further, that 59 percent of the players failed to qualify for pensions. For these reasons, the Association threatened to strike in 1969 and players were advised not to "report to spring training sites until the negotiations are satisfactorily concluded."[14]

The strike threat forced reluctant owners back to the bargaining table, but the second basic agreement was not ratified until May of 1970. This pact covered a three-year period and, in return for extended peace, owners had to recognize the Players Association as the official bargaining agency in all matters, except individual salaries. The players scored a major gain by winning the right to be represented by agents during salary negotiations. Here, a quietus was finally placed on the ancient custom of owners and GMs cowing players into accepting a lower salary. Hard-bargaining agents, usually taking ten percent fees, soon became familiar figures in salary sessions. Although agents pushed salaries upward, Miller recognized them as parasites who preyed on gullible players. Another important concession of the contract allowed outside arbitrators to settle certain disputes between players and owners. A signal victory for players, arbitration became the weapon players used to score some of their greatest contractual successes.[15]

This agreement also boosted salary minimums to $13,500, increased fringe benefits, and placed limits on salary cuts and restricting requirements on winter ball playing. Owners stubbornly refused to discuss shortening the playing season or scuttling the reserve clause. A legal challenge to the clause, instituted by player Curt Flood (protesting his 1969 sale by the Cardinals), failed in the U.S. Supreme Court in 1972 and, indeed, left little hope of support from that front. Warned by Miller that the suit might end his career, Flood still chose to sue. Miller convinced ex-Supreme Court Justice Arthur Goldberg to plead the case without fee. To strengthen his case, Flood sat out the 1970 season to the detriment of his career. Although he lost the decision, Flood's attempt suggested to players that ultimately a challenge to the one-year retention clause must be successful.[16]

Meanwhile, the second basic agreement expired. Negotiations for the third began early in 1972, and owners again dragged their feet. This time players sought a four-year agreement that called for a 25 percent increase in pension benefits and an appropriate rise in medical benefits. However, the owners chose to "stand firm" against the players, and the Association retaliated by voting 663–10 to strike. In March of 1972, battle lines for baseball's second strike were drawn and players quit the spring camps. The strike lasted until mid-April and touched off volleys of rhetoric; even President Nixon expressed his hope for a speedy settlement. The walkout ended with a compromise that funneled an additional $500,000 into the pension program. While both sides claimed victory, the shortened season cost owners an estimated $5 million in lost receipts. Although the players lost a portion of their salaries, the owners' hopes of breaking the Association had failed, as the players stood solidly behind Miller.[17]

The third basic agreement, ratified early in 1973, seemed inocuous enough on paper. The Association won a $16,500 salary minimum, a guaranteed $20,000 minimum for each player on the winning World Series team, and increased pension and health benefits. However, Miller's efforts at reserve clause reform, such as barring its use as a bludgeon in salary negotiations, had failed awkwardly. Instead, the owners stonewalled, promising only to study the matter and to publish their findings in 1976. However, this group agreed to extend the arbitration principle, allowing players with two years or more service to seek binding arbitration in salary disputes.[18] This might have looked like a small chunk of the loaf Miller was after, but the morsel contained enough yeast to swell up in the owners' faces.

The players were certainly not reluctant to use this weapon. In the following year, twenty-nine players took salary complaints to arbitration. Independent arbitrators were hired to adjudicate such appeals, but they were required to choose either a player's final demand or the owner's last best offer: no splitting of differences was permitted. Thirteen of the players won, and the sum was enough to burn skinflint owners like Charles Finley and Cal Griffith. Although Griffith groused, "I'll find a way to get it back," no one was daunted. Forty players went the same route in 1975 and four arbiters met to decide the cases. By then, it was apparent that the fear of losing such cases was forcing owners to pay higher salaries. Indeed, arbitration was proving its worth as a weapon.[19]

The full destructive force of this weapon now struck the owners. Late in 1974, an inkling of what was to follow surfaced when Jim "Catfish" Hunter, star pitcher of Finley's A's, won an important arbitration victory. That year Hunter's $100,000 annual contract had stipulated that half his salary must be paid as deferred income. Finley, disliking the added tax burden, demanded that Hunter take full payment. Hunter refused and the contract period expired with its original terms unmet. Hunter's country lawyer, J. Carleton Cherry of Ahoskie, North Carolina, now asked for arbitration. At the hearing Hunter accused Finley of contract violation and asked to become a free agent. The arbitration panel of Gaherin, Miller, and Peter Seitz, a professional arbiter, voted 2–1 in favor of Hunter. Therefore, without compensation for Finley, Hunter was freed to sell himself to any team. He chose the Yankees, who gave him a five-year pact worth $3.75 million in salary, deferred payments, and other emoluments. As a finishing touch, the panel's decision was upheld by a California Superior Court.[20]

Although the Hunter case seemed a freakish accident, it handed players an opportunity to outflank the reverse clause. The astute Miller had already spotted the opening. On the tail of the Hunter case, he filed a grievance procedure against the option clause in player contracts. Miller sought to know the entire meaning of the one-year option-to-renew clause in most player contracts. Did it amount to a perpetual "roll over" contract, binding a player to a club as long as the owner wanted him? Or, did it limit owners to one year's option on a man's service? Miller enlisted two players to test this question. His plan called for two players to refuse to sign contracts and then to play out the option year unsigned. The question then would be: are they now free agents? However, the test failed when both signed new contracts.[21]

The decisive test of the option clause was at hand. In 1975 two pitchers—Andy Messersmith of the Dodgers and Dave McNally of the Expos—who had played out the season without signing contracts appealed to the Association for an arbitration hearing on their status.[22] Miller filed, and once again he, Gaherin, and Seitz served on the arbitration panel. The central figure of the trio was Seitz, an elderly lawyer and professional labor-management arbiter who, as the impartial member of the panel, would cast the deciding vote. When voting time came, Seitz submitted a 67-page opinion which cast his lot with Miller. The arbitrator was peremptorily fired by the owners, who issued a statement charging him with inability "to understand the basic structure of organized baseball." Seitz replied to the charge: "I am not an Abraham Lincoln freeing slaves. I am just interpreting the renewal clause as a lawyer and arbitrator."[23]

This "Seitz decision" was later upheld against owner suits at both the federal district court and circuit court levels. Each time judges invoked the Supreme Court dictum of fifteen years standing that denied the courts power to overrule an arbitrator's decision in labor cases. Thus, the decision stood rocklike, while its destructive impact on the reserve clause shocked owners. Fighting back, the owners tried to close ranks, thinking that if no bids appeared, Messersmith would be forced back to the Dodgers. When two finally broke away and submitted bids, the conspiracy crumbled. Hence, Messersmith signed a three-year pact with the Braves at a salary well above the Dodger offer. Since McNally chose to retire from baseball, Messersmith became the symbolic victor over the hated reserve clause. Certainly his victory was portentous since most player contracts carried the same option clause.

The owners refused to take this all-out emancipation lying down; their chosen battlefield was the scene of the upcoming negotiations for a fourth basic agreement. The third agreement would expire at the end of 1975 and the players would be without a contract. At the owners' request, negotiations for a new pact were delayed, pending court tests of the arbitrators' decision on the Seitz decision. The owners also refused to open spring training camps, arguing that no agreement existed. Throughout the lock-out (an owners' strike against the players) the two camps sniped at each other. This lasted until March 17, when Commissioner Kuhn ordered the camps opened. However, continuing hostilities marred the celebrations planned for 1976. In addition to the nation's bicentennial celebrations, baseball owners had planned special observances commemorating the National League's 100th birthday. There was irony in this: player servitude actually began with the 1876 founding of the National League, but the players were freed one century later.

Miller meanwhile faced a dilemma as he negotiated the fourth basic agreement. Should he demand a literal interpretation of the Seitz ruling or should he compromise, allowing owners to keep players for a certain number of years in obligated service? Although some players demanded a strict interpretation and threatened to sue if their rights were violated, the majority favored a compromise. The owners demanded eight years of controlled service before allowing a player to opt for the new "re-entry draft"; Miller held out for six and triumphed. The six-year rule became the centerpiece of the fourth basic agreement, along with the new re-entry draft. The owner's compensation for the loss of a player to re-entry was a draft choice from the club who signed the player. A draft choice, however, afforded only an untried prospect, so the owners soon demanded a proven player. Miller stubbornly refused, and this hot issue became the focal point of renewed hostilities in 1980 and 1981.

Commissioner Kuhn threatened in 1976 to use his powers against the re-entry draft concept, but Miller publicly warned that if he tried to stop the draft, the Association would take him to court. Thus, the fourth basic agreement was ratified in August; retroactive to the first of the year, it carried through to the end of 1979. This historic document ended a century of owner control over player mobility, and, truly, it turned the baseball world upside down.

Miller was the hero of the hour. In the short span of thirteen years, he had become the single most powerful person in baseball. By masterly use of labor laws and by charismatic leadership, he forged the Association into a powerful veto group. His victories at bargaining tables won concessions that in the past came only when some interloping league battled the established majors, and then were snatched away when the interloper collapsed. Because of his efforts the 1979 minimum salary climbed to $21,000 a year, although average salaries by then neared $100,000 and one player earned a million dollars. Moreover, the baseball pension plan, engineered by Miller, was now the best in pro sports. Still, Miller's greatest contribution to the players' cause was the formal labor contract, arrived at by collective bargaining.

However, "nothing wrought by man was ever wholly good." This truism indeed applied to Miller's reforms. The Association ignored the struggling minor league players and gave little support to organized umpires during their 1979 salary dispute. Kuhn, the voice of the owners, blamed the Miller reforms for encouraging complacency, envy, and discord among players and for weakening the powers of field managers. Kuhn also parroted the owners' lament that high salaries threatened to bankrupt clubs, offset competitive balance, and saddle fans with higher ticket costs.[24]

In an eloquent rebuttal to Kuhn, Miller stated that television money covered salary and pension increases; thus, "Not one dollar comes out of gate receipts." Miller continued to explain: "Not once in eleven years of negotiations has a single club ever claimed financial hardship. If it did, law requires that it would have to open its books to validate the claim and if we saw the claim was true, we could bargain on a realistic basis as we do in industry. Clubs won't do this, preferring to claim poverty only in the press."[25] Miller employed historical statistics to negate Kuhn's charge that the re-entry draft destroyed competitive balance, demonstrating that four teams had taken 58 pennants in the years 1921 to 1964—65.9 percent of all the championships. Was this competitive balance? What the record showed, he argued, was that the reserve clause merely fattened owner profits and held down salaries.

Indeed, the owners had not faced such an eloquent adversary since John Ward led the players' strike of 1890. Owner Ray Kroc grudgingly admitted: "Miller knows . . . that the latest figures show our attendance is up, our total revenue is up. . . . He also is armed with something even more important—He knows that there never has been a team in baseball that has gone bankrupt. And until some clubs go bankrupt . . . there is nothing to prove we can't stand the gaff."

As the 1970s ended, Miller faced the grim task of defending his successes against avenging owners. In 1980 both sides summoned strength to do battle over a new basic agreement. Ray Grebey, Gaherin's successor, proved to be a tough hired gun who would fight hard on the issue of compensation for players lost in the re-entry draft. As the front of battle lowered, an evaluation of the causes showed Miller's to be the conservative one. After all, major league baseball had begun as a player's movement. That baseball again could be run by players was Miller's vision; the basis for his contention was that owners are "unnecessary."[26]

Miller foresaw, on the eve of the 1980s, a day when major league baseball would by governed by a council representing all the game's constituencies. Meanwhile, as advocate and chosen spokesman of the game's most salient constituency, Miller stood tall as the players' commissioner.

A New Breed of Ballplayers

Marvin Miller, the players' "Commissioner," watched over a class of players whose likes had never been seen before. This group was a breed apart: bigger, younger, more numerous, and better-educated. Their various personalities mirrored America's rampant individualism and its godsplenty of lifestyles and attitudes.

There were more of them because sixteen new teams had joined the majors since 1961; the ex-college students in the ranks accounted for a somewhat greater sophistication. They were comparatively young because they spent less time in the minors. Under enlightened policies, the clubs saw to it that their members were coached and doctored. While some critics felt this group was coddled—a point borne out by plush clubhouses with candy racks and bounteous buffets—the fact was that more than thirty players played past the age of forty. That they were taller reflected a general population trend; scouts favored physical size in prospects, although only after more basic attributes such as outstanding eyesight and hand-eye coordination, demonstrated speed, and arm strength.[1]

Moreover, this blessed group enjoyed the luxury of a seller's market for their talents, and, in fact, this talent scarcity factory helped to undermine some of the ancient draconian disciplinary codes. Even so, veteran managers were shocked by the cool sophistication of this cohort; some managers found them too polite and lamented the passing of hard-nosed ump baiters and bench jockeys, while others resented this breed's tendency to question established ways of batting, fielding, pitching, training, and conditioning.[2]

However, critics deplored the mercenary spirit of this breed. Truthfully, big league players always were mercenaries, but now the term was directed at high salaried players. This was indeed the highest paid cohort ever. Naturally the old-timers envied them, and wry quips from the players—like pitcher Tug McGraw's explanation of how he spent all his money—only fueled jealousy. McGraw had boasted: "Ninety percent I'll spend on good times, women, and Irish whiskey. The other 10 percent I'll probably waste."[3]

Sportswriters now haunted locker-rooms where many wisecracks were heard. Further, television made onstage celebrities of the players, and fans fed from a smorgasbord of revelations about them. While some players resented the spotlight, there was no denying that increased public exposure meant more cash and glory. Media men were continually concocting new lists of star performers; the rosters included all-time contact hitters, clutch teams, and even mean teams.[4]

Meanwhile, a "jock liberation" movement sought to raise the consciousnesses of professional athletes. This movement strengthened the Players Association and stirred cynical reactions to owner appeals for team loyalty and familism. Some players openly mocked owners and officials: pitcher "Spaceman" Bill Lee sardonically paid a fine imposed by Commissioner Kuhn for his alleged use of marijuana, then filed a grievance petition.

Other liberated players criticized their bosses in interviews and ghosted books. Kuhn's attempt to suppress pitcher Jim Bouton's revealing book led to an amusing sequel at Kuhn's expense. Reggie Jackson's autobiography lambasted Finley's "Jehovah Complex" in earthy language. Likewise, Joe Pepitone, Bo Belinsky, and Denny McLain boasted of flouting rules in authorized biographies. "I've done it my way," cried McLain,[5] but no player exceeded pitcher Mike Marshall's stalwart determination to control his own life. A certified expert in sports exercise, Marshall diagrammed the procedure for his arm operation and designed his own rehabilitation program.

On and off the playing field, the individualism of the new breed illuminated diverse character types. Present were old-fashioned hustlers like Pete Rose and Jake Gibbs; intellectuals like Jim Brosnan, Steve Stone, a published poet, and surgeon George Medich; wastrels like Pepitone and McLain; self-professed screwballs like McGraw and Lee; moody recalcitrants like Alex Johnson and Dick Allen; and woeful fumblers like Dick "Strangeglove" Stuart and Leon "Daddy Wags" Wagner. (Indeed, one observer compared Wagner with Pete Gray, suggesting that both Leon's arms worked like Gray's stump.)

These characters lent diversity to the ballplaying community. The players' language was more openly obscene; most spoke two languages—English and profanity. In their printable lexicon were terms like "downtown" and "taters" for homers; "hotdogs" for showoffs; "stonefingers" for inept fielders; and "wings," "hoses," and "canons" for pitching arms. As in past generations, the cheeks of many bulged with tobacco cuds, some opting for chewing to avoid the hazards of smoking. Chewer Clint Hurdle of the Royals was rebuked for spotting the astroturf with indelible blotches. After swallowing his "cud" while leaping for a ball, pitcher Ron Guidry removed himself from a game, saying, "I didn't want to be the first to throw up on national television."[6]

The Demigods of Televised Sports

Watching sports on television had become the favorite pastime of Americans by the 1960s, and pro athletes soon adapted to their role of entertainers. Of course, an unprecedented amount of cash and glory flowed into pro sports. Baseball was slow to grasp this profit potential, so rivals like football and boxing showed the way. The clever promoters of these sports provided viewers with celebrity gods to either worship or damn.

During the 1960s and after, the athlete who best profiled the new superhero was a handsome, powerfully built black boxer named Muhammad Ali. Ali charmed and infuriated fans by his behavior in and out of the ring. Nevertheless, he was the biggest celebrity in sports through the 1970s; his televised bouts brought him riches and made him the most recognized athlete of his time.

If Ali epitomized the superhero in boxing, Joe Namath did the same for football. The deification of Namath was a bold experiment on the part of promoter Sonny Werblin of the New York Jets. Werblin gambled that television revenue wrought by Namath's popularity would repay the $100,000 annual salary he paid this rookie quarterback. The money was indeed easily recouped. The "Namath effect" brought vast sums of television money into pro football, enriching owners and players there and spawning similar heroes in other sports. Television money swelled club incomes, ignited a salary revolution that benefited players, and turned more players into celebrities.

But where were the Alis and Namaths of baseball? In Bill Veeck's judgment there was no censensus celebrity among ballplayers of the 1960s. He urged owners to either conjure up colorful characters or risk losing ground to more enterprising rival sports. When asking "Where are the drunks of yesteryear?" Veeck called for charismatic characters to replace the dull, conforming "Herbert Hoover" types.

Roger Maris might have become a national celebrity in 1961 when the Yankee outfielder broke Ruth's seasonal homer record. Certainly fans were receptive, but the introverted Maris spurned publicity, avoiding reporters and television interviewers. Maris opted to remain the private family man he always had been. For rejecting the role of a star, booing fans turned his last years with the Yankees into a long nightmare. Officials also belittled his achievement, and to this day Maris is not enshrined in the Hall of Fame.[7]

Likewise, hostility to mavericks was evidenced by the officials' disapproval of Jim Brosnan's candid autobiographies. Published on the eve of the expansion era, Brosnan's two books disrobed the lives of players, demythologizing their romantic images. Brosnan's diary style of writing was refreshing to fans used to reading ghosted, bowdlerized works written in a trite, childish tone. These books were bracing; they offered witty, intelligent revelations about ordinary men with human appetites and emotions.

According to Brosnan, players of the late 1950s were incredibly repressed. Brosnan told how they were bullied in salary negotiations by the GMs and forced to settle for less. Minor leaguers suffered more, sometimes invited to big league training camps solely to prevent other clubs from claiming them. Furthermore, Brosnan depicted life in the "bigs" as rather drab. Most players viewed baseball as a challenging, unromantic job. Often lonely, they missed their wives, cussed a lot, and dwelt much on the joys of sex. Nor did clamoring fans and fawning writers necessarily lend glamor. After all, fans booed as well as cheered, and the trauma of boos lingered for days. Instead of being "copy" for romantic writers, many players preferred to be treated just as human beings.

Readers learned from Brosnan how some black and Hispanic players remained marginal men in baseball, much derided as "bucks" and "bean bandits." Yet nearly all players were derogated: eager hustlers were "hot dogs"; oddballs were "flakes"; sycophants were "bo-bos"; second stringers were "rinky dinks"; and among bullpen denizens, "long relievers" were inferior to "short men." A sharp-eyed "short man," Brosnan drew vivid sketches of bullpen life where occupants killed time by sneaking smokes, ogling female fans, sending out for food on the sly, and sometimes engaging in tobacco-spitting contests.

Such revelations annoyed officials, who turned censorious over Brosnan's characterization of manager Solly Hemus. Brosnan judged Hemus as woefully ignorant, yet canny enough to cover his deficiencies by baiting umps and raucously cheering his men. Still worse, the manager sometimes screamed racist epithets which Brosnan deplored.[8]

Paupers and Plutocrats
Pockets that bulged with coins marked this new breed. Players retiring in the early 1960s were too late to benefit from the coming salary revolution. While data on baseball salaries is suspect, evidence shows that postwar baseball salaries compared with those of skilled workers. Of course, attempts to compare postwar salaries with those of the expansion era are blurred by continuing inflation.

Inflation's impact in the realm of baseball can best be seen by comparing Babe Ruth's 1925 salary of $60,000 with a similar sum in 1950. In 1925 the federal income tax nibbled only 15 percent of the sum, allowing Ruth to keep $51,000 hard dollars. For a 1950 star to enjoy comparable purchasing power with Ruth's salary, his wages would have to border $300,000 to offset the assaults of inflation and taxes.[9]

Given the inflation factor, the few big salaries of the 1950s pale in comparison with Ruth's. Of those few salaried elite, DiMaggio, Williams, and Musial annually earned $100,000 or more. DiMaggio, the first to scale this height, opted for a straight $100,000 instead of an attendance bonus offer that would have earned $118,000.

After DiMaggio's retirement in 1951, Williams was the highest paid player. In 1950 he reportedly made $100,000, and late in the decade his $125,000 was unmatched by any American Leaguer until Carl Yastrzemski earned as much in 1969. In 1958 Musial became the first National Leaguer to earn $100,000. No other player in the postwar era scaled this height, although rumors had Hank Greenberg grossing $100,000 in 1947 and Ralph Kiner playing under a two-year, $130,000 contract in 1950–1951. On the other hand, minimum-salaried toilers received $5,000 in 1946, $6,000 in 1954, and $7,000 in 1957.

Still, ballplayers of the 1950s earned more than other pro athletes. Reportedly, baseball's total 1950 income was $40 million; $4 million of this was radio and television revenue. Twenty-two percent of the total income went for salaries, compared to 1925's 37 percent.[10] Of course there were disparities: the 1946 Detroit payroll of $550,000 was said to be the highest in history; three clubs in 1951 had payrolls of $600,000; and by 1960, $700,000 was the high. However, most club payrolls in 1951 averaged between $300,000 and $600,000, with teams like the Reds and the Braves getting by on payrolls of less than $300,000.

Similarly, payrolls were rarely equally divided among a team's 25 players. Median figures tell the tale: the 1951 median salary in the majors was $11,000, and in 1953 the American League's median salary had jumped another thousand. The 1952 Indians and Yankees had the highest salary medians at $16,000 and $14,000, while that year the Browns, A's, and White Sox had medians of $10,000 or less. Moreover, median salaries of the lowly teams failed to rise in the 1950s and as late as 1958, the Senators's median was $8,750. Even high-rolling teams like the Yankees and Indians cut salaries: after the Yankee defeat in 1954, their median dropped to $13,000, but rebounded to $16,000 in 1955; following a win in 1954, the Indians paid a $20,000 median in 1955, which fell to $18,000 in 1956.

The National League salaries lagged. The highest paid teams for the 1952 and 1953 seasons were the Giants, Dodgers, and Cubs. Following their 1951 victory, the Giants had a median of $15,000, while only two other National teams had medians above $10,000. Four National clubs in 1954 had medians of $13,000; the 1955 Giants led all with a $16,000 median. The lowest medians of the period belonged to the Pirates, Braves, and Reds.

From 1950 to 1963 the average major league salary rose from $12,000 to $16,000, with total club payrolls climbing from $6,920,000 to $8,225,000. Although player salaries were often augmented by endorsements and off-the-field earnings, average salaries of this period paled when compared to the salary revolution of the 1970s.[11]

The impact of the rising salary trend is seen better when fitted to a personal case. In 1970 outfielder Curt Flood testified to receiving less than the minimum he was paid as a Cincinnati rookie in 1956. Traded to the Cardinals in 1958, he said he played for $5,000. The following year he was paid $12,000, then $12,500 in 1960; as an established star in 1964 he pulled in $20,000. The stirrings of the salary revolution shot his salary to $90,000 by 1969. Flood's career ended just as he was making big money.

Those who retired in the early 1960s fared worse. As late as 1957, only forty players earned as much as $25,000 and only ten made $50,000. Of course, this was good money for the times. Some of the higher-paid players were members of the great Dodger teams; these included Robinson at $42,000, Furillo at $36,000, Newcombe at $30,000, and Campanella at $32,000.

Some Dodger players of those days were outwitted by GM Buzzy Bavasi, who revealed that O'Malley paid Robinson $1,000 more than any other player. Some athletes—Furillo, for example—were tough bargainers, but Reese and Erskine were more easily subdued. Skeptical of some players' spending habits, Bavasi reportedly chided Campanella for buying a $36,000 house and a $37,000 boat on a $32,000 salary. However, modest Joe Black accepted $12,000 after winning Rookie of the Year honors in 1952, stating: "I'm not worth that much."[12]

Other GMs used similar tactics. George Weiss told reporters he prayed for a star like DiMaggio whom he could pay $100,000; this mendacious bargainer counted World Series earnings as raises. Superstars were not excluded. Musial remembered owner Breadon's screaming tantrum at his request for $35,000 in 1947. It mattered little to Breadon that Musial led the league in hitting the year before, so Musial settled for $31,000.

Most players were forced to bargain alone, and GMs sweet-talked many into accepting less. As ever, a player's pay was based on his most recent performance. In an off year, a man's best hope was to avoid a cut, and his only defense was a rule preventing his boss from cutting his salary more than 25 percent.

After playing under this system, early postwar players could hardly be blamed for envying the new breed. It was their sad lot to be born out of time: too early to enjoy the salary revolution. Of course, players on championship teams received additional compensation from World Series play. In 1946 a player on the winning team got $3,750. Thereafter, winning shares increased to $6,700 in 1948, $8,300 in 1953, $11,100 in 1954, and reached a high of $11,200 in 1959.[13]

In the late 1960s club owners felt the tremors of the coming salary revolution that swept aside the old standards. Bear in mind that salary figures are estimates and that with actual figures unobtainable, these figures vary widely. The average player salary of $14,800 in 1964 rose to about $21,000 in 1967 and held there for three years. It surged to an estimated $34,000 in 1972, to $52,000 by 1976, and leaped to $75,000 in 1977.[14] A combination of factors forced this upward spiral. These were inflated dollars and living costs were sky-high, but television revenue also increased and the Association demanded its share of the national television income. Nevertheless, the $100,000 mark remained an awesome barrier. Since Musial retired in 1963, only Mantle and Mays commanded such figures—at least until 1966.

That year the great Dodger pitching duo of Koufax and Drysdale staged a joint hold-out to reach the $100,000 mark. In 1965 each received $70,000, but in 1966 they demanded a combined sum of $250,000 and each pledged to sign only if the other was satisfied. Both could rely on Hollywood film contracts for income while not playing. Moreover, Koufax insisted that the Dodgers bargain with his lawyer, J. William Hayes. Mindful of the precedent, O'Malley resisted for 32 days, railing bitterly that yielding would "lead to practices not possible to tolerate." Hayes was just as tough; at one point he warned Bavasi that if the club invoked the reserve clause, he would sue in federal court. Finally, the two signed for a combined total of $220,000, of which Koufax got $130,000. For his part, Hayes accepted a modest fee from Koufax and billed Drysdale a dollar. Henceforth, other players sought out agents to serve as bargainers. Press opinion at the time generally favored the players. James Reston of the *New York Times* viewed their victory as retribution against owners, who had used legal blackmail for too long.[15]

Miller took over the Association's reins that same year. He quickly persuaded his clients to reveal their salaries, each player writing his salary on a slip of paper and dropping it in a box to be picked up by their representative. Compiling data on 466 salaries, he discovered that 25 received $7,000 a year or less, including Mike Marshall who said he got $5,800. With these facts behind him Miller negotiated a $10,000 minimum salary for 1967.

Miller's first year coincided with an upward salary trend, sparked by the champion Cardinals's 1968 payroll of nearly $1 million. In 1969, Gibson's price exceeded $100,000 and the lowest of any Cardinal starter was $37,500.[16] In 1966 only Koufax, Mantle, and Mays earned $100,000, but in 1969 nine players were paid this sum. Naturally, some owners cried wolf. At Kansas City Ewing Kauffman opened his ledger to prove that he lost over a million that season. In 1971 Peter O'Malley of the Dodgers lamented that the new trend would force roster cuts and salary ceilings. The players, however, were unimpressed. The Orioles's 1971 payroll topped the million mark and Brooks Robinson joined the $100,000 club, but the ball player quipped, "There is much more to be made in baseball."[17]

This was true enough, and rising salaries became an irresistible contagion. The victorious Mets of 1969 were paid a total of $650,000. Flushed by success, the players demanded more money, boosting the 1970 payroll to $950,000. Still they were not satisfied; Ron Swoboda, who reluctantly signed for $42,000, angrily told a reporter, "I feel that I let my family down." Indeed, so much bickering led to a ban on salary debates in the clubhouse.[18]

Owner Busch learned the hard way that owner complaints only fired higher demands. Enraged over 1969 salary demands, he summoned his players to a meeting and with the press in attendance, scored player greed and invoked old shibboleths of the right of owners to profits. Busch's speech evoked little sympathy and he was widely criticized as cheap. Poor Busch resembled Canute trying to rule the sea, for the 1970s saw salaries cresting at heights undreamed of. The 1972 average salary was estimated at $34,000; in 1973 this dropped to $32,000 but jumped to $49,000 in 1974. In 1975 some estimates placed the average at $50,000; in 1976, $52,000; and in 1977 the newly established re-entry draft boosted the average to $75,000. Thereafter it winged to an estimated $90,000 in 1978 and reached the $100,000 mark in 1979. The speed whereby average salaries *increased* was dizzying.[19]

We must remember that salary estimates vary widely and that such figures are skewed by hefty salaries paid to some 100 stars among the 600 major leaguers. Many players complained of rising living costs. To average Americans such complaints would seem ludicrous. In 1973 pitcher Ray Sadecki earned $40,000 and was hard pressed to maintain two homes. Likewise, journeyman Bernie Allen claimed that his 1970 salary of $10,000 was inadequate to support his family. Of course, the usual disparities operated within the overall average range. The Yankees's average was estimated at a record $189,000, followed by the Phillies at $159,000. On the other hand, clubs like the A's, White Sox, Cubs, Astros, and Twins were well below the $100,000 mark.[20]

Of course, higher payrolls were linked with high attendance, lucrative local television pacts, and wealthy owners willing to spend money. Some clubs had all three going for them, while some had none. A 1978 salary study showed seven strong clubs—the Phillies, Yankees, Reds, Pirates, Dodgers, Angels, and Royals—paying the highest salaries. Among these elitists, salaries averaged from $96,000 to $140,000. Beneath them were 14 clubs with averages ranging from $54,000 to $88,000. At the ladder's bottom were five proletarian clubs—the Tigers, A's, Mariners, Twins, and Blue Jays—which all suffered low attendance and, except for the Tigers, received the lowest income from local television.

Among the dregs, Oakland occupied baseball's Siberia. Following a victorious honeymoon stint, lagging attendance prompted owner Finley's abortive attempt to move the franchise. Forced to stay, Finley fielded a relatively inexperienced team; of these none received $100,000 in 1978, sixteen earned less than $50,000, and six starters received the $21,000 minimum.

However, in the wonderworld of celebrity baseball, attention focused on plutocrats. In 1972 their ranks included 23 players who earned $100,000 or more. Aaron reportedly earned the most, followed by Yastrzemski, Mays, Gibson, and Clemente, each topping the $150,000 mark. A year later 30 players broke the $100,000 barrier, with Dick Allen's $225,000 branding the new high. Miller coolly replied to alarmists that only 17 percent of baseball's gross income went for salaries; this was less than the 22 percent figure of 1950 and far below pro basketball's estimated 1973 figure of 45 percent.[21]

The Greenbacking of the Game

In the late 1970s salaries of superstars shot so high that reporters likened affluent players to highly paid television entertainers. Evidence of the public adulation showed in soaring attendance at games and ever higher television ratings. Miller pushed the trend by winning salary arbitration rights, which several players exercised successfully in 1974; but still, this was only a glimmer of what was to come. Within two years, the Seitz decision effectively freed players from reserve trammels and brought on the annual re-entry draft marketplace.

The re-entry drafts launched a supernova salary explosion. After the frenzied bidding of the first draft, the 24 players had won a total of $25 million in contracts. Eight emerged with contracts worth $1.5 million or more, and the leading plutocrat, Reggie Jackson, signed a five-year Yankee pact worth $2.93 million. At $580,000 a year, Jack-

Among the highly paid stars of the 1970s were hitters (*top left to right*) Dave Kingman of the Mets, Dave Parker of the Pirates, and Rod Carew of the Angels, and pitching stars (*bottom left to right*) Jim Hunter of the Yankees, Nolan Ryan of the Astros, and Vida Blue of the Giants. Hunter and Blue shown here in the Oakland A's uniform.

son led all, followed by Mike Schmidt, who used the threat of entering the next draft to pry a multi-year pact from the Phillies, worth $566,666 per year.

Such gains enabled baseball stars to match or better the top salaries of other sports. Starting players then averaged $95,000, with the ten best paid averaging $250,000.[22]

The new player plutocrats stirred hostile criticism and rancorous envy. Met pitcher Seaver brooded over having earlier accepted a two-year pact at $225,000. Seeing a less talented hurler like Garland go the re-entry route and snag a 10-year, $2.3 million pact from the Indians seemed incredible to Seaver. Garland, just as stunned on his side, told his agent: "You gotta be kidding. Quick gimme a pen before they change their mind." Seaver asked president Grant to renegotiate his pact, but Grant refused. A war of words opened between the two that reached such a shrill pitch that Grant dealt Seaver away.[23]

Elsewhere, stars hungrily eyed the 1977 draft; when it arrived, the results were equally dramatic. Fourteen stars won hefty, long-term contracts, including Richie Zisk's Ranger contract worth $2.8 million over 10 years. Once again, fans read of newly minted player millionaires and responded enthusiastically, sending attendance and television ratings upward. Indeed, salary statistics rivaled those of performance in the popular judgment of ballplayers. This new dimension of hero-worship was obviously a boost for baseball; if the owners and Commissioner Kuhn were slow to grasp this point, Miller was not: "An athlete or entertainer draws people who buy his product; that determines . . . what return he gets."[24]

Even as officials forecast doom from high salaries, owner bidding set new records in 1978. Topping all plutocrats, star outfielder Dave Parker signed a five-year contract worth $900,000 a season; this zenith was tailed by outfielder Jim Rice's seven-year pact with the Red Sox, averaging $770,000 a year. It is noteworthy that this pair was paid by their original clubs, but among those who entered the draft, Vida Blue and Pete Rose snagged multi-year contracts worth $850,000 and $700,000 a season. Moreover, rather than lose Rod Carew in the next draft, the Twins traded that superstar to the Angels, who paid him $800,000 a season. As the dust settled from the latest salary explosion, the year 1979 saw top baseball stars earning more than their counterparts in football, basketball, tennis, and golf. By then, the average salary was $121,000 in baseball and the median stood at $85,000. Top payrolls for the year reached $4 million, with poorer clubs like the Twins laying out $1.9 million.[25] The trend peak was not at that point; in the fourth draft, held late in 1979, pitcher Nolan Ryan snared the first million dollar annual salary. Dubbed "the express" for his fast ball and his penchant for tossing no-hitters, Ryan spurned a four-year offer of $3.56 million and elected to pitch for the Astros for one million dollars.[26]

In a land where the pursuit of wealth motivates many, fan worship of the plutocrats was hardly surprising. This baffled owners and disproved Kuhn's complaint that the salary revolution was destroying the game by bankrupting teams, alienating fans, pampering players, and upsetting the competitive balance. Miller parried these thrusts, arguing that not only did salaries account for less than 20 percent of a team's income, but that television revenue added considerably to such income.

Far from alienating fans, the revolution worked like an aphrodisiac in stimulating their love of baseball. Not only did each salary surge push attendance up, but an opinion poll showed that most fans approved of the trend. The poll did show that fans generally believed owner claims that salaries increased ticket costs, but, at the same time, fans thought owners exploited players. In the main, fans accepted re-entry and conceded a player's right to play for the team that bid highest for his services.[27] Harder to quell were the owner charges that high salaries pampered players and destroyed their desire to win. One noted sports psychologist agreed, claiming that insecurity fanned competitive spirits. Still, sparkling performances by plutocrats gainsaid the charge, including Hunter's three good pitching years, Jackson's two brilliant Series performances, Rose's sprightly performance with the 1979 Phillies, and the outstanding play of Parker and Rice. It is true that some faltered, but injuries played a part in the failure of pitchers Garland and Gullett. Indeed, the jury was still out on the question of "money spoiled" players.

The charge that mercenary players destroyed competitive balance was a favorite of Kuhn's. Its absurdity was easily exposed, yet the myth that money can buy pennants was hard to down. As the greatest of dynasties, the Yankees enjoyed a competitive edge in bidding for draftees. After landing two world titles, however, "the best team that money could buy" collapsed in 1979. Into the breach rushed the Orioles and Angels, the former a modestly salaried team with a record of losing stars via re-entry, and the latter a highly salaried team and a big plunger in draftee bidding. The 1979 Orioles won the pennant, leaving this issue up for debate.

Still, there was a menacing side to the salary revolution. The freedom of movement won by the players threatened to end the practice of trading. Also there was a problem in disciplining men who owned long-term, no-cut contracts and earned far more than their managers or coaches. Equally menacing was the jealousy and envy that swept player ranks. Most threatening of all was the deep-seated hostility between owners and players; stung by defeats, the owners hired in 1980 a tough new negotiator and mounted a determined counterattack.

Certainly the owners rued the day they conceded to use of bargaining agents. Bob Woolf was among the first of this breed, hired in 1966 to represent Earl Wilson of the Tigers. Woolf was accepted by dint of legal tactics; in 1968 he won a hefty Red Sox contract for Ken Harrelson after that player had been cut loose by Finley.

Still, as late as 1970, owners resisted the use of agents. That year Miller won the right for players to be represented, and he hailed this liberty as a major reform. Then came a sober second thought. He soon came to oppose agents for attaching themselves to players, taking a percentage of negotiated salaries, imposing burdensome demands on owners, and attempting to re-negotiate contracts. Charging 10 percent of their clients' earnings, the worst of the lot secured powers of attorney from players, collected player checks, and proved to be as exploitive as the worst of owners.

Among the best was Bob Woolf. As a lawyer, Woolf tried to professionalize the role; he headed a Committee on Sports Law under the American Bar Association that sought to regulate agents by licensing, supervising, and bonding them. Following his own guidelines, he refused player demands to re-negotiate existing contracts, insisting on the sanctity of contracts. Woolf was trusted by a host of pro athletes, and in a dozen years he negotiated hundreds of contracts. In each case he fixed his fee in advance; sometimes he took nothing, never did he take as much as 10 percent of a player's pay.

However, where carcasses lay, vultures gather; some agents had especially sharp talons and big gullets. Miller vainly urged maximum agent fees of 4 percent.

Amidst the hostility and rancor stirred by the salary revolution, Miller took pride in obtaining fringe benefits that gave players lifetime security. A major blessing was the pension plan that now made a player's career the focal point of his economic life. In 1972, after working four years, a player would be assured of a series of monthly checks starting at age 50. In no other industry was such a lasting benefit possible after so brief a working stint. Thus, a four-year player could collect the minimum payment of $174 a month; if he waited until age 65, he could collect the minimum of $618 a month. Long-term veterans who waited until age 65 to draw on this fund could collect the maximum monthly payment of $1,945. Moreover, other programs included widows' benefits, life insurance, and a medical and dental program.[28]

This surfeit of cash and glory cast players of the expansion era as a breed apart from their forebearers. In a sport as tradition bound as major league baseball, this distinction was profoundly disturbing to the owners, who sought to redress the situation and to cripple the Association. Thus, it appeared there would be a bitter struggle in the 1980s, with dramatic portents.

Baseball Black and Beautiful

Color the new breed black, because black players led the offensive onslaught in this record-breaking era. Despite their minority presence in the years 1947 to 1970 black players captured 17 batting titles, 10 homer crowns, 19 MVP awards, a Triple Crown, a new stolen base record, and a score of 20-victory pitching seasons. At times—as in 1969, when thirteen of eighteen .300 hitters were black, or in 1970, when twenty played in the All-Star Game—the blacks were the majority.

The black tide crested in 1974 at 26 percent of the active major leaguers; thereafter the numbers lessened, allaying racist fears of an impending black peril. Nevertheless, blacks continued their awesome offensive, adding seven more batting titles, twelve homer titles, and usually leading in RBIs, runs scored, and total hits.[29]

Among baseball's superstars, blacks shone brightly; Hank Aaron and Willie Mays towered over all others in this era. They started the great triumvirate of the early expansion era, and if white Pete Rose owned the third spot, he was hard pressed by Rod Carew, a black Panamanian. Aaron's lofty credentials include a .307 lifetime average, a National League record total of games played, and, above all, a record-shattering 755 homers. Such feats lend poetic justice to the alphabetical coincidence which finds him listed first of all big leaguers in the *Macmillan Baseball Encyclopedia*. However, Mays batted .302 with 660 homers and compiled a brilliant fielding record.

This pair retired in the 1970s and watched Rose and Carew battle for the mythical third position. Both challengers were affluent new breed players. Carew, the younger of the two by four years, held seven batting titles at the close of the 1979 season, including a .388 effort—the highest mark since the war. While only Cobb held more bat titles, Carew was slighted for being a singles hitter and a superb bunter at a time when sluggers were prized. Hence, not until 1977 did he win an MVP award; thereafter, cash and glory rained upon him.

Carew's bid for immortality was matched by the fiery Pete Rose. An intensely competitive switch-hitter, Rose broke Cobb's record of most seasons with 200 or more hits by posting his tenth in 1979. He notched that mark a year after he joined the 3,000-hit club and captured headlines by hitting in 44 consecutive games to tie the National League record. Moreover, Rose broke Wagner's ancient record for most lifetime singles; this self-styled "Charlie Hustle" also owned six National League batting titles. In 1981 Rose broke Aaron's total hit record and threatened Cobb's all-time hit record.

Voted the Player of the Seventies by *The Sporting News*, Rose joined the Olympian trio, but Carew stood very near the throne. Despite nagging injuries, Carew recorded his twelfth consecutive .300 season by 1981 and his lifetime .334 batting average topped all contemporaries.

As this venerable foursome compared favorably with any past quartet, so did the exploits of other new breed stars. Thus, Maris's 61 homers in 1961 erased Ruth's seasonal mark. Heroes Mays and Mike Schmidt struck four homers in single games to join a lengthening list of such prodigies. Indeed, by 1979 seven expansion era sluggers ranked among the ten most productive long ball hitters of all time. The ever popular big bang style had sluggers still unleashing formidable homer barrages. Since 1961 three teams managed four consecutive homers in single games and five homers in a single inning were twice smashed off shell-shocked pitchers.

Of course, these free-swingers also struck out at a record-breaking clip. This dubious achievement happened so often that fans yawned when reading of sluggers fanning a hundred times per season. In 1970 Bobby Bonds fanned 189 times to break his year-old record of 187. By 1979 all-time whiffing records were owned by Mickey Mantle and Willie Stargell. On the other hand, Nelson Fox finished his 18-year career having averaged but one strike-out for every 43 at bats. Consistent hitting enabled Aaron, Mays, Rose, Clemente, Kaline, Brock, and Yastrzemski to join the 3,000 hit club, swelling its ranks to fifteen members. Frank Robinson and Yastrzemski joined the more exclusive Triple Crown club, while Manny Mota rang up a record total of pinch-hits.

Speedsters of the era stole bases in record style. In the 1960s, Maury Wills broke Cobb's seasonal mark with 104 swipes; in 1974 Lou Brock stole 118 and later broke Cobb's lifetime record.

The glory of the era, however, was its brilliant pitching. Pitching virtuosos now bettered the 2.00 ERA mark eleven times, headed by Bob Gibson's National League record of 1.12, set in 1968. Three pitchers of this period—Koufax, Seaver, and Palmer—won three Cy Young Awards apiece. The pitching prodigies freely blew down old marks. Denny McLain won 31 games in a season; Carlton and Seaver shared a new strike-out mark, fanning 19 in a game; Jim Barr retired 41 consecutive batters over the course of two games; Jim Bunning and Gaylord Perry each won at least a hundred games in both leagues; and Ron Guidry posted a 25–3 seasonal mark.

Perhaps most impressive was the pitchers' eclipse of most of the old-time strike-out artists, leaving only Walter Johnson and Cy Young among the top thirteen. Among the new claimants, Nolan Ryan and Koufax averaged better than one whiff an inning, while Gibson, Seaver, and Sam McDowell edged that mark. The fire-balling Ryan broke Koufax's seasonal mark of 383 strike-outs and also matched Koufax's four no-hitters. However, no-hitters were becoming commonplace, as flingers notched 70 in the years 1961 to 1979.[30]

Any quick student could cite fielding records and other measured performances to demonstrate the brilliance of this breed. Indeed, this was a statistically-obsessed era, when figure filberts cooked and served all kinds of performances. Such lists certified that some of the best and brightest of the new breed were black players.

Although Mays was a 10-year veteran when the expansion era opened, he was named Player of the Sixties by *The Sporting News*. At Candlestick Park, no Giant hit so timely, nor solved the park's tricky wind currents as well as Mays. Although he was team captain and a celebrated $100,000-a-year star, local fans preferred Cepeda or McCovey to the "Say, Hey Kid." Moreover, even the declining Mantle captured more headlines and endorsement offers. While racism explained some of this, reporters found the flashy Mays "poor copy" and militant blacks thought him an "Uncle Tom."

In 1970 the 39-year-old Mays punched his 3,000th hit, but when a commemorative ceremony was staged in his honor, only a batch of free tickets could fill the park. Two years later the aging Mays was sold to the Mets, where he responded to a royal welcoming with a flurry of key hits. Then he faded fast, lingered long enough to appear in the 1973 World Series, and retired. In 1979 he entered the Hall of Fame.[31]

Mays's passing turned the spotlight on to "Hammering Hank" Aaron of the Braves. A major leaguer since 1954, Aaron was over-shadowed by Mantle and Mays; for all his homerics, this low-keyed player waited until his 14th season to become a $100,000 man. When his mounting homer total and his 3,000th hit in 1970 spot-lighted the 36-year-old outfielder, he belatedly received a three-year contract worth $600,000, making him, briefly, the highest paid player. Publicists found him to be a modest, incredibly self-disciplined player, with formidable reserves of stamina and durability. Seldom injured, the compactly built, right-handed swinger had been clubbing homers for twenty seasons when he closed in on Ruth's lifetime homer mark. Yet seldom did he win annual homer titles; his list of coups counted only four homer titles, two batting championships, and one MVP award.

Playing with a lackluster team that flattened after winning two pennants in the late 1950s, the colorless Aaron blended in well. Although dedicated to the black liberation movement, the soft-spoken Aaron was no zealot; as a black playing in Atlanta, he prudently kept a low profile and rarely lashed out at goading fans.

Such was the man who accomplished the most dazzling feat of the era. For a time it seemed that the 39-year-old veteran must break Ruth's mark in 1973, but he fell a homer short of tying the mark. Aaron dodged interviews and offered no public comment about the popular song "Bad Henry" with its raucous lyric of "Move over, Babe," because Aaron's coming, "and he's swinging, man . . . he'll break that 714." Nor did he react to Commissioner Kuhn's sanctimonious warning of hefty fines for any pitcher "grooving" a pitch.

Over the winter, Aaron's feat fed the hot stove league. At least fame brought his first lucrative endorsement contract, a 10-year, $1 million pact from the Magnavox television company. Still there were bad moments, as when some pointed out that Ruth hit harder, batted fewer times, and enjoyed a fine pitching career. In addition, Atlanta Stadium was described as a "launching pad" which yielded cheap homers—yet speculators estimated that it would be worth $25,000 to the fan who caught the ball that broke the record.

When the 1974 season began, the man called "Supe" by his mates took charge. In the season's opener at Cincinnati, Aaron homered in his first at bat to tie the record. Needing only one to break it, the drama shifted to Atlanta, where on the night of April 8, 1974, before 53,755 fans and a national television audience, Aaron blasted a solo homer into the left field bullpen. The record fell at precisely 9:07 P. M.; as the ball sailed toward the stands, Atlanta relief pitcher Tom House leaped up to glove it in front of a fan's groping fishnet.

Was it a coincidence that the year Aaron broke Ruth's record, four biographies on Ruth's life appeared and only one was seen on Aaron? By rekindling Ruth's mystique, the books belittled Aaron's feat by pointing out that Aaron's homer rate and batting average

Braves outfielder Hank Aaron became one of baseball's immortals on the evening of
April 8, 1974 when he hit his 715th homer at Atlanta Stadium, breaking Ruth's
lifetime mark.

were lower and that Aaron took far more games to smite his total. Forced to battle a ghost, Aaron replied that he never intended to destroy Ruth's image, but he hoped fans might remember Hank Aaron.[32]

Big Frank Robinson was the first player to win MVP awards in both leagues. Though a star with the Reds, Robinson's bosses resented his outspoken, aggressive style. Indeed, his brutal baserunning later won him an unofficial place on baseball's all-time mean team. Finally, a speedy departure from the team followed an off-the-field run-in with the law, though the club president assured Reds fans that Robinson was an "old thirty years."[33]

It was Robinson's delight to cram that judgment down Red throats with a Triple Crown performance at Baltimore. Still, the outfielder gained little of the extra cash and glory that Yastrzemski reaped for accomplishing the same feat a year later. Robinson stoically bore the slight and set out to become the first black manager in the majors. Over the years 1966 to 1971, he spent winters playing and managing in the Puerto Rican League, "passing tests" and "paying dues" towards his goal.[34] Such experience put him at the head of the list of possible black managers, and in 1974 he became playing manager of the Indians. Although the press hailed the move and President Ford and Commissioner Kuhn added praise, it was no altruistic move.

The task of reviving the moribund Indians required a Moses. Over two seasons, his best effort was an 81–78 record; thus, Robinson also became the first black manager to be fired. Still, he was the pioneer and in his wake came Larry Doby, whose managerial stint was even briefer. Robinson took a coaching job and later managed again.

Meanwhile, other black players piled up honors. Black stars won 16 MVP awards during the expansion era, ten of which went to National Leaguers, including consecutive awards to Joe Morgan. Also, black players took 26 batting titles, with Latin American blacks heading the list, Carew taking seven, Clemente four, and Oliva three. In this era, too, a dozen sluggers joined the list of players with 200 or more lifetime homers, and three ranked among the four most prodigious sluggers of all time. Also, three black pitchers joined the elite list of hurlers with 200 or more victories.[35]

Chicago infielder Ernie Banks won a spot in the Hall of Fame in 1977. Although his peak years were the late 1950s, the durable Banks lasted until 1971 and ended a 19-year career with a .274 average, 512 homers, and over 1,600 RBIs. As the genial "Mr. Cub,"

Banks loved his baseball life too much to complain of racial slights. "Mr. Sunshine" greeted each game with a cry of "Great Day for Baseball! Let's Play Two." He tossed off racial problems with quips like, "the only race . . . is the one to beat the throw."[36] When Banks retired, his teammate Bill Williams moved to the fore. From 1963 to 1970, the durable "mechanical man" played in 1,117 consecutive games, forging a league record. He peaked in 1972, winning the batting title, poling 42 homers and managing 129 RBIs. However, the MVP award went to Johnny Bench, who had batted forty points below Williams. The disappointed Williams was partly assuaged by winning the *Sporting News* Player of the Year award and a $125,000 contract.

Slights like Williams's came all too frequently. Black stars excelled in this era, but received far less glory than whites. They did draw high pay, but covert discrimination still existed. Their dominance still could not be gainsaid; from 1960 to 1979, black hitters won 15 National and 12 American League batting titles. In those years, black superstars included Willie McCovey, Bobby Bonds, Joe Morgan, Maury Wills, and Lou Brock. McCovey was a giant of a man, whose slashing drives terrorized infielders. In 1969 "Stretch" led the league for the second straight year in homers and RBIs, while his clutch-hitting advanced runners 61 percent of the time. McCovey was rewarded with the MVP title and a $100,000 contract. Although forty years old in 1979, the popular McCovey played on, despite arthritic pains. By then he had pounded over 500 homers.

The next black MVP winner after McCovey was little Joe Morgan of the Reds, who took two straight in the 1975 and 1976 seasons. Only the second player to win back-to-back honors, the 5'7" tall Morgan used a blend of batting, fielding, and base-running. He hit .327 in 1975, stole 68 bases, and singled home the final run in a victorious Series effort. He hit .320 the following year, with 27 homers, 111 RBIs, and 60 base thefts.

Unlike McCovey and Morgan, who starred as rookies, Giant outfielder Bobby Bonds was obliged to wait for Mays's decline. Still, he was the only rookie in this century to smash a grand slam homer in his first major league at bat. Later, as a high salaried star, he became a much traded itinerant. Although frequent strike-outs marred his reputation, he set records by combining base stealing and power hitting.

When it came to larceny on the bases, however, Maury Wills and Lou Brock yielded to none. While restoring this ancient tactic to center stage, Wills stole 104 bases in 1962, breaking Cobb's seasonal mark. Although critics pointed out he used 162 games to turn the trick, Wills was pegged out only 18 times, and rang up 586 steals over 14 seasons.

Ironically, as Wills held his 1962 MVP trophy, his successor was already at hand. As a rookie Cub outfielder, Louis Clark Brock stole only 16 bases and followed with an undistinguished sophomore season. When dealt to the Cardinals in 1964, however, Brock made the deal look like one of the most one-sided in history. With the 1964 Cards, Brock batted .315, stole 43 bases, and led the team to its first world title since 1946. His Olympian career ended in 1979 with Brock established as a member of the 3,000 hit club and as baseball's leading base stealer.

Pitchers employed anti-theft measures to cope with Brock, while catchers perfected fast, low throws. Ex-math teacher Brock, in turn, studied films of pitchers and timed their moves. Thus, he learned that if a pitcher took more than a second and a half to deliver his pitch, the base was his. He knew how many seconds it took him to run from one base to another. To get an extra "jump," Brock used a set of "keys." When leading off first, he eyed the heel of a right-handed pitcher; when the pitcher shifted his weight to his right knee, he was committed to throwing the ball. Lefties had the advantage of seeing Brock clearly at first base, but Brock also learned their quirks.

Another essential key called for a patient batter to follow Brock in the batting order, especially one who would take pitches and bluff bunts. Both Brock and the batter benefited, the latter from shifting defenses which opened gaping holes in the infield. Brock stole at least 50 bases over a dozen seasons, and in 1974 the man called "Super thief" stole a record 118. Incredibly, he was passed over for MVP honors, prompting him to accuse the voters of racism at worst and invincible ignorance at best.

Late in his career, Brock closed in on Cobb's record total of 892 steals. Upon breaking the record at San Diego in 1977, the game was halted and Brock was awarded the base as a keepsake. This awesome achievement took Brock 700 fewer games than Cobb; for good measure, in 1979 he also broke Billy Hamilton's 19th-century mark of 937 steals. This was Brock's swan song; the 40-year-old star capped the year by batting .304 and joining the 3,000 hit club. It's sad to say that he never won an MVP award. His enshrinement in the Hall of

Fame is a certainty and, indeed, he will stand very near the thrones of the demigods.[37]

As the 1970s closed, other base runners, such as Willie Wilson and Rickey Henderson, carried on the larcenous tradition. Still, most of the cash and glory went to the heavy hitters, whose ranks now included dominant black sluggers George Foster, Dave Parker, Jim Rice, and the aging Willie Stargell. Stargell tied in 1979 for seasonal MVP honors and won both the playoff and World Series MVP awards. Along with his career total of over 400 homers, big "Pops" owned the league strike-out record.

At the same time, a flock of younger behemoths assaulted pitchers. The bevy included Dave Parker, who owned a pair of batting titles along with a reputation as a slugger and strong-armed outfielder. For sheer homeric power, however, no one outdid George Foster, Cincinnati's "Destroyer." In 1977 he smote 52 homers to become only the fourth National Leaguer to top the 50-mark; in both 1976 and 1977, this Bible-toting, right-handed hitter led the league in RBIs. In the following year, Jim Rice of the Red Sox won MVP honors in the American League by leading in homers and RBIs.

Don Newcombe won the first Cy Young award in 1956. To this day no black pitcher has achieved the 300-game winners circle, and only three rank with the 60-odd winners of 200 or more games. Of that trio, Gibson posted 251 wins and set a new strike-out record for National League hurlers. As the 1970s waned, Ferguson Jenkins, a 6'5" black Canadian, passed Gibson's victory total and had an outside chance of winning 300 games. Dubbed "the Dominican Dandy," Juan Marichal was a right-handed marvel with a bewildering assortment of deliveries which won him 243 games over his 16-year career. Because his best efforts were topped by Koufax, Marichal never won a Cy Young award.

Batters of the late 1970s were somewhat intimidated by the fastballs of Vida Blue and James Rodney Richard. The phenomenal left-handed Blue pitched a no-hitter in his first full season (1971) and completed the year with a 24–8 record, 301 strike-outs, and a 1.82 ERA. Until then, no black pitcher had ever won both the American League's MVP and Cy Young awards. Jaded by owner Finley's salary stinginess, Blue staged a hold-out; when the pitcher finally signed for $63,000, he returned to have a bad year. He rebounded, however, with 20 victories in 1973 and 22 in 1975. Finally,

Astro pitching star J.R. Richard (*left*) was thought to be malingering before he was felled by a stroke in 1980; and Dick Allen (*right*) was roundly booed by Philadelphia fans, who were resentful of his lifestyle.

after more bitter wranglings, Blue was traded to the Giants in 1978. With the Giants he won 32 games in two seasons, raising his victory total to 156. By then his "ultimate fastball" was gone, and advancing age curtailed his tomorrows.

J.R. Richard served time in the minors to correct his wildness before joining the major leagues. Despite scant offensive support from his Astro mates, Richard won 74 games over four seasons. Richard's towering 6'8" height made his fastball and his vicious, dipping slider more frightening. Fanning over 300 batters in 1978, Richard put the Astros in contention. In 1980 a near-fatal stroke struck him down; there had been warning signs, such as ineffectiveness and listlessness which some sportswriters interpreted as laziness. Richard's collapse while working out proved his problem was physiological.[38]

Several journalistic exposés drawn up in the protest years of the late 1960s reported blacks receiving less in the way of bonuses and endorsements, and suffering varied racial slights.[39] Gibson received hate mail telling him to go back to Africa; Aaron's mail was wisely screened by the club secretary. For marrying a white woman, Carew received a deluge of threats. Policemen brutally beat Rico Carty, calling him a "cop-killing nigger"; and mugger victim Willie Horton was also roughed by policemen.[40]

An angry loner, good-hitting Dick Allen was branded a trouble-maker and was booed out of Philadelphia by jeering fans. The moody Alex Johnson exhibited sullen defiance that saw him fined 29 times in 1971, and then suspended by the Angels. Finally, Flood, for challenging the reserve clause, became anathema to owners.[41]

Thanks to the Players Association, individuals could fight back. A landmark arbitration decision held that Johnson's behavior was mitigated by emotional disturbances; he was awarded his salary. In cases such as Cleon Jones's sexual adventuring or Len Randle's suspension for punching his manager, the Association's threats of counteraction forced fair treatment.[42]

Inspired by black protest movements, black players reported in books and interviews that "all is not well in the locker room." Thus, Gibson angrily declaimed that "America's All-American boy isn't black—He's crewcut and he's blond and they expect you to live with that."[43] Similarly, Aaron accused owners of treating blacks as "trained monkeys" to be "shafted." In his sardonic book, Dock Ellis branded Pirate officials as "cheapskates" and bigots; Flood attacked Busch on similar grounds, comparing the shipping of players "from one franchise to another" with slaveowners' shifting "men from one plantation to another."[44] Although such protests did force some reforms, when the steam blew out of the national protest movements, blacks in baseball continued to face covert forms of discrimination. Blacks now received better salaries, publicity, and endorsements; however, in 1979 there was only one black umpire among the major league staff of sixty, few black coaches, and very few blacks in administrative posts.[45]

Ironically, just as black players harvested fair shares of cash and glory, their numbers declined. From one of every four players in 1970, their presence sank to one in five by 1979, with the same trend noticeable in the minors. No easy answers can explain the shift, although better opportunities in the labor force and declining baseball programs in schools and colleges are certainly worth noting. Thus, the 1970s closed on a note of deja vu: was it possible that major league baseball was again becoming a white man's game?

"I am the best in baseball"

One black player dared to proclaim himself the game's leading celebrity. Reggie Jackson, the self-styled "chocolate hot dog," voiced

Baseball's leading celebrity of the 1970s
was hard-hitting Reggie Jackson, shown
here in a Yankee uniform.

his claim in no uncertain terms: "My name is Reggie Jackson and I
am the best in baseball. This may sound conceited, but I want to be
honest about how I feel. . . . No one does as many things as well as I
do."[46]

Here was that appealing celebrity so long sought by baseball lovers
to match the likes of Namath and Ali. While many hated him and
more loved him, everybody recognized this electrifying left-handed
slugger who wore number 44.

Jackson fanned often at the plate and his batting average was
tolerable; yet seasonally he blasted 30 homers and knocked in 100
runs, all in the best big bang style. Others batted as productively, but
none matched his dramatic clutch-hitting, nor nursed the colossal
ego that made him the most publicized and controversial player of
the era. The 23-year-old slugger smashed 47 homers in 1969 and
immediately held out for more money. Although Finley paid him
only $45,000 Jackson's flair won him a flurry of lucrative endorse-
ment offers. Therefore, Oakland fans booed him for holding out.
Jackson called them "bush" and Finley "cheap"; such utterances
made "good copy" and his six contentious years with the A's produced a waterfall of flippant, cutting barbs.[47]

One had to be good to be allowed such cracks, and Jackson's
Oakland years were seasons of glory. In 1973, after leading the
league in homers, runs, and RBIs, Jackson's clutch-hitting in the
Series carried the day, making him the unanimous choice for both

the MVP award and *Sport* magazine's auto award for the best Series performance. Naturally he sought a hefty raise; when Finley balked, Jackson's agent used the salaries of ten previous MVP winners to convince the arbitration panel to boost his client's pay to $135,000. Finley probably never knew how much his cheap opposition boosted Jackson's stock. If heroes needed villains, this owner was the perfect foil. Jackson's 1974 slugging put him on the cover of *Time* magazine and the story inside called him the "muscle and soul of the A's dynasty." *Sports Illustrated* depicted the goateed, bespectacled slugger in all his coiled power as baseball's "Superduperstar."

If Finley's actions came close to breaking Jackson's "spirit," the player's talent prevailed. By the end of 1974, he could no longer be counted among the mortals; Jackson golfed with President Ford, took that worthy for ten dollars, and told delighted reporters that he thought Nixon "a crooked cat."[48] Finally Jackson's taunts and escalating demands forced Finley to trade him. Wisely, the owner saw that Jackson could opt for the re-entry draft and leave Finley with nothing. As it turned out, the draft glamorized Jackson; from its start, he was the most courted prize, and after frenzied bidding, he signed a five-year Yankee pact for $2.9 million. Upon his arrival in New York, he brashly advised Yankee fans: "I'm the straw that stirs the drink." He even predicted that a candy bar would be named for him.

Thus, the swaggering, garishly clothed Jackson came to Gotham. Not surprisingly, fellow Yankees were unimpressed. Jackson answered his critics with clutch hitting in the 1977 World Series that burnished his "Mr. October" legend. Thanks to Jackson's .450 batting, the Yankees regained the heights; in the final game, as he watched his third homer sail, Yankee fans deliriously screamed, "Reggie! Reggie! Reggie!"[49]

That winter the "Reggie" candybar appeared; some said it tasted like a "hot dog," and other claimed that "Butterfingers" would be a better name. On opening day, however, when Jackson homered in his first at bat, fans flung a shower of "Reggie" bars onto the Stadium turf. Now began the nightmarish 1978 season, when tensions between Martin and Jackson erupted and led to Martin's ouster and the merciless booing of Jackson. Later in the season, "Mr. October" redeemed himself by canny baserunning and dramatic slugging in the World Series.

Now Jackson bestrode the baseball world as a colossus, though it was no easy task for a black man to be cast as the game's leading celebrity. Certainly he suffered in the role and admitted that his cocky, arrogant posturing was a defense mechanism. At times he spoke humbly, pointing out that in ten years of play, fans must expect a good player to be called out 5,000 times. In moments of glory he stated that he preferred to be treated as a man, rather than as a black man. He argued that while he supported the black equality case, he knew that he had to live amongst 180 million white Americans. Meanwhile, baseball was good to him: on top of a $300,000 annual salary, he earned $900,000 from endorsements and investments. Thus, Reggie Jackson bid fair to rank with Jack Johnson, Joe Louis, Jackie Robinson, and Ali in the annals of black sporting heroes.

The Conquistadores

As black players joined the majors, so did dusky Latin American players. Before 1947 the same color bar that prohibited blacks allowed only the lighter-skinned Hispanics. However, when given the chance to prove themselves, dark-skinned Hispanics took the majors by storm; in fact, by the end of the 1970s, they comprised 10 percent of the major league ranks and 40 percent of the minor league prospects.

At first, most Hispanic players were Cuban, but the new wave saw talented youths entering from Puerto Rico and such nations as the Dominican Republic, Panama, Venezuela, and Mexico. These lands housed many hungry players who could be had so cheaply that major league scouts now regarded the Latin countries as the major talent frontier.

Mostly poor boys, Hispanic prospects learned the game well by playing year round. Once scouted and signed for small bonuses, they came to America seeking gold and glory. Some found this dream, but only after confronting tough cultural shocks, caused by language differences, strange foods, and social isolation. Of many shocks, the worst may have been the confrontation with America's racial caste system. For these outsiders, it was an excruciating psychological experience to engage in a highly competitive sport in a land where one was judged inferior because of his skin color and was downgraded for Hispanic origins. Caught between cultures, no one was needed to tell these Hispanic players that they were marginal men.

Off-season home visits offered some solace, but after 1959, the year that Fidel Castro stepped into power, this comfort was denied the Cubans. Since Castro now banned major league scouts, denounc-

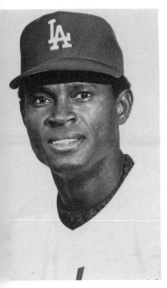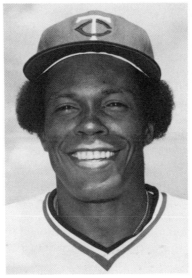

Latin American virtuosos include Manny Mota (*left*), who set a pinch-hitting record, Rod Carew (*center*), a winner of seven American League batting titles, and Luis Tiant (*right*), star pitcher of the 1975 pennant-winning Red Sox.

ing them as capitalistic exploiters, the American majors were excluded from this rich talent supply and the number of Cuban expatriates shrank until only four remained in 1978. In casting about for alternative supply sources, American scouts faced similar rejections from Mexico.

After the Mexican League fiasco, Mexican baseball no longer recruited major leaguers and very few stars from the aloof Mexican leagues ventured into American baseball. Nevertheless, Mexican star Bobby Avila became the first Latin American to win a major league batting title. Signed by the Indians in 1947 for a $7,500 bonus, this solid-hitting second baseman was hampered by language barriers, forced to abandon his refreshing siestas, and much kidded by teammates. Avila was sustained by a burning desire to save enough money to retire and live the life of a honcho grande, and, although troubled by ulcers, he succeeded. Lasting eleven years in the majors, his .281 career average was highlighted by a 1954 league-leading .341 effort. For that he became a Mexican hero and was honored with a silver trophy, but the Mexican ambassador recoiled in horror at the thought of awarding the trophy at the park: "No, No! At the embassy in the afternoon we will have a party and give him the trophy. Not at the ball park. By all the gods, not at the ball park. That would be too Cuban!"[50]

The exploits of many Cubans earned the respect of American fans. Minnesota outfielder Tony Oliva won back-to-back American batting titles in the 1960s, while Saturnino Orestes "Minnie" Minoso produced eight .300 batting seasons. Meanwhile, Tony Taylor and Orlando Cepeda became stars in the National League. Taylor suffered chronic homesickness before finding a home in Philadelphia, where fans voted him their MVP and the club retained him as a coach; likewise, Cepeda survived strange words and foods to become a hard-hitting Cardinal first baseman and an MVP winner.

Most Cuban stars, however, felt they received less than fair shares of cash and glory. Oakland shortstop and captain Dagobert "Bert" Campaneris was routinely ill-paid, as was first baseman Tony Perez of the Reds. Unfortunately, at this time Cuban Minnie Rojas was left paralyzed and destitute following an accident.

Three Cubans stood out among the great pitchers of this era. Camilio Pascual ended a 15-year career with 170 wins and the brilliant Mike Cuellar retired with 185. Still, the most talented and popular was Luis Tiant. The son of a famed Cuban pitcher, Tiant entered American exile in 1959 and waited until 1976 to see his parents again. The burly, mustachioed, cigar-smoking right hander won 21 contests as a 29-year-old rookie in 1968. Slowed by arm trouble, Tiant reentered the game as the charismatic "Looey," the beloved of Red Sox fans and blessed them with eighty-one victories over the years 1973 to 1976. Denied a long-term contract there, Tiant moved to the Yankees to serve as both pitcher and designated "specialist" in Latin-American relations. All that time, few clubs employed Spanish-speaking coaches, although a few managers, including Martin, Lasorda, and Weaver, spoke adequate Spanish.[51]

In the 1970s some clubs offered English instruction to Hispanic players, and during this period an official committee also began helping Latins with contract and injury problems. Social life, however, was sometimes difficult due to linguistic and cultural differences.

Writer Mike Granberg heard a number of harassment complaints as he interviewed Hispanic players in 1979. Some players claimed they were underpaid compared with Americans. First baseman Willie Montanez complained: "We're still viewed as foreigners. In that sense we struggle. When it comes down to American and Latin fighting for the same spot, American always wins. . . . Latin gotta be twice as good. Else he don't get past April."

For the 104 Hispanic players of 1979 who were aliens this was sometimes, but understandably, true. Quotas imposed by the U.S. Department of Immigration limited the number of foreign players on a team. As was the case with similar restrictions in other industries, this was done to protect the interests of players with American citizenship. In baseball any change in the number of foreign players under contract by a team had to be cleared with the Immigration Department. This ruling, of course, did not apply to Puerto Ricans, but it would have made it difficult for anyone wishing to field an all-Latin lineup.[52]

Such a mythical team could have been formidable. Its one weakness would be found in the catching position, because in this era only Manny Sanguillen stood out. Players at other posts were excellent; in addition to those already mentioned, the team's inner defense would include shortstops Luis Aparicio and Dave Concepcion. Concepcion batted .270 in the 1970s, fielded superbly, and played on five National League All-Star teams. Aparicio, who retired in the 1960s, played 2,518 games at short, stole 506 bases, and led American League base-stealers seven times.

This team would be well supplied with outfielders. Brothers Felipe, Matty, and Jesus Alou would supply an entire outfield. Each initially signed with the Giants, who expended only $2,500 in bonuses to sign the trio, then paid them only $600 in monthly salaries as minor leaguers. This was a monumental bargain for the Giants, which they failed to exploit: although each brother played six years with the team, only in 1963 did they play together. By 1969 the Giants had traded away the Alous, who went on to compile fine records. In seventeen seasons Felipe batted .286; in fifteen seasons Matty averaged .307 and won the 1966 National League batting crown; and Jesus batted .279 in thirteen seasons.

Meanwhile, a Dominican outfielder Rico Carty, rebounding from two years of inactivity because of tuberculosis, captured the 1970 batting crown as a member of the Braves. Dodger outfielder Manny Mota performed dexterously as a pinch-hitter; he rapped his 145th in 1979 to set a new pinch-hitting record.

While stars like these promise a formidable lineup for the all-Hispanic dream team, the addition of the magnificent trio of Juan Marichal, Roberto Clemente, and Rod Carew lends Olympian strength.

Surely destined for the Hall of Fame, pitcher Juan Marichal, a smiling, boyish-looking Dominican, used baseball to escape a life of poverty. It is reported that Marichal, a son of a widowed peasant, was once jailed by a relative of Dictator Trujillo for losing a game. Joining the Giants in 1960, the 23-year-old rookie used a unique high-kicking motion to power his fast ball and thereafter mastered half a dozen different deliveries. As the Giants ace, in one four-year stretch he pitched at least 269 innings a year, winning 93 games and losing only 35. His best year was 1966: he won 25 and posted a 2.23 ERA.

Unfortunately, not once in these four seasons did Marichal win a Cy Young award! Sadly for him, his glory years coincided with Olympian seasons posted by Koufax, Gibson, and Seaver. Marichal won 243 games in 16 seasons with an ERA of 2.89. Easily the best Hispanic hurler, Marichal ranks with the all-time greats.

Roberto Clemente, the great Puerto Rican outfielder, gained immortality. Before his career ended in a tragic accident in 1972, Clemente delivered 3,000 hits and won four National League batting titles. Owner of a lifetime .317 batting average, Clemente also won 12 Golden Glove awards as the best defensive right fielder of this era.

The young Clemente was romantically reported to have learned baseball by hitting a homemade rag ball with a guava branch and fielding with a glove fashioned from a coffee sack. Local fans marveled at the batting exploits of the boy they called "el negrito." He appeared as a Dodger prospect in 1954, but that team let him go and Rickey claimed him for the Pirates. With the Pirates in 1955 Clemente came alive; he singled in his first at bat and the following year this right-handed batter with a smooth, slashing swing topped .300. By 1960 he was a local favorite, acclaimed by Pirate fans, who screamed "Arriba!" when he came to the plate.

He helped the Pirates to the world title that year. Although he won three batting titles over the next five years, his only MVP award was taken in 1966, which was not one of his league-leading years. In 1967, however, he won a fourth batting title. His popularity was widespread; he once was mugged and kidnapped in San Diego, but his capturers, upon learning his identity, returned everything unharmed. He became one of the most admired of all active players, and his work to better the health and recreational opportunities for Puerto Rican youths earned much respect.

When Clemente died he was speedily voted into the Hall of Fame, his number 21 was retired, and "The Ballad of Roberto Clemente" became a best seller. One of the few worthwhile baseball films, "Roberto Clemente—a Touch of Royalty," honored the man and his efforts. Unfortunately, a memorial album intended to benefit charity proved to be a $250,000 swindle.[53]

Panamanian Rod Carew also received belated recognition. In 1967 the skinny, 170-pound second baseman joined the Twins for a paltry $5,000 bonus. It was a cheap price for a Rookie of the Year who batted .297. Two years later Carew won the first of seven batting titles. His achievements brought little recognition, though he received plenty of hate mail and some death threats for marrying a white woman.

After taking a fourth consecutive batting title in 1975, owner Griffith refused Carew's request for a $140,000 salary, arguing that he hit too many singles—a claim belied by his .619 slugging average. Carew's protest was defeated when taken to arbitration.

In 1977 Carew beat such a fierce tattoo on enemy pitchers that he forced recognition. For most of the season this intense, left-handed hitter, who used four different stances against varying pitching situations, batted over .400. In the end he batted .388, missing the magical .400 mark by only eight hits. This earned him the league's MVP award and an additional $100,000 bonus from Griffith, who stated that Carew's presence lured an extra 400,000 paying fans that year. Later, the owner even stated that Carew was underpaid; but in a 1978 banquet speech Griffith spoke degradingly against blacks. He soon apologized, but Carew announced his intention of playing out his option and following the re-entry draft. A pre-draft deal with the Angels gained Carew a multi-year contract, establishing him as one of the best paid players in baseball.

At the close of the 1970s, some steps were taken to honor the great Hispanic players. Officials at Yankee Stadium—now part of a major enclave of Hispanic residents—staged the first Latin American night in baseball history. The ceremony honored retired players and brought back former greats like Avila, Hector Lopez, Chico Carrasquel, Aparicio, Minoso, Vic Power, Luis Arroyo, Sandy Amoros, and Willie Miranda.

And the Great Majority?

More so than any past era, this was a time of pitching tyranny. The desperate plight of batters since 1963 became apparent as runs scored per game dropped from an average of 8 to 7 by 1968, with overall batting averages falling to a feeble .236. There were several causes for this downward trend: a 1962 ruling widened and raised strike zones, better gloves appeared, more sophisticated defenses were working, and relief pitchers were being used more effectively.[54] Pitchers, moreover, tormented batters with varied deliveries; fastballs were augmented by changeups, sliders, curves, fork balls, screwballs, and knucklers. Fastballs had to be lively and moving, and pitchers used offspeed and breaking pitches to "set up" batters for strike-outs, which came now at an unprecedented rate. Knuckle-balling specialists like Wilhelm, Wilbur Wood, and the Niekro brothers still baffled batters with their slow, flitting deliveries.

Despite all these weapons, pitchers still dabbled in the black art of illegal pitches, including spitters, greaseballs, emery balls, and cut balls. A rash of incidents in the late 1960s brought tougher rules, warnings, and ejections, all of which availed little. At least twenty suspects were targeted by cameras in the 1970s and some were subjected to body searches. Many thought the prize villain was Gaylord Perry, a masterful workhorse who won Cy Young awards in both leagues. Perry enjoyed his notoriety, even writing a book entitled *Me and the Spitter*. Perry was 43 years old and a 300-game winner before he was caught and fined for doctoring a ball. Greaseball advocates reportedly smeared pine tar, petroleum jelly, or even vaginal cream on their bodies and uniforms. Cutball suspects like Tommy John, Whitey Ford, Mike Marshall, and Don Sutton reportedly hid sharp objects to be used for defacing balls.[55]

Hurlers dominated batters. A third of the pitchers were lefties; including Warren Spahn, who finished in the 1960s with 363 wins, the most victories ever gained by a southpaw. Other big-winning lefties were Koufax, Steve Carlton, Ford, John, Mickey Lolich, and Jim Kaat. Among the right-handed masters, Early Wynn ended his long career by notching his 300th win, while Robin Roberts finished near that goal. Those records were hard pressed in the 1970s by Perry, Jim Palmer, Tom Seaver, Jim Hunter, Phil Niekro, Milt Pappas, and Don Sutton. The redoubtable Perry notched his 300th win in 1982.

This era saw some of the greatest starting pitchers. The 1960s Dodger duo of Koufax and Drysdale accounted for 209 wins in five seasons. However, Sutton, John, and Burt Hooton were effective successors; indeed, with little fanfare Sutton won more games and struck out more batters than either Koufax or Drysdale.

The greatest starting staff of the era was the Oriole trio of Dave McNally, Jim Palmer, and Mike Cuellar. From 1969 through 1971, they won 188 games and held batters to a 2.89 ERA. This was the finest pitching achievement since the war and the best of that triumvirate was Palmer, a tall, handsome Californian. As the best pitcher of the 1970s, he won 20 or more games seven times, and thrice won Cy Young awards.

Yet the pitching tyranny was indebted more to the bullpen deniz-

No hurler from the expansion era matched Warren Spahn's 363 wins, but Gaylord Perry (*left*) and Early Wynn (*right*) joined the select circle of pitchers with 300 or more lifetime victories.

ens. The "bullpen revolution," begun in the 1950s, came to full fruit now as relievers finished at least 75 percent of all games. The fact that American League starters finished more games than the Nationals was due in large part to the DH rule. As the newest pitching heroes, short relievers wallowed in cash and glory. Among the most effective and best paid were Sparky Lyle, Goose Gossage, Mike Marshall, Rollie Fingers, and Jim Kern. These rally busters counted coups by "saves" and since 1960 the Fireman of the Year award went to the best.

To help beleaguered batters, the officials lowered pitching mounds to 10 inches in 1969 and narrowed and lowered the strike zone. However, pitchers adapted so quickly that a 1978 proposal sought to extend the pitching distance from the hallowed 60'6" standard set back in 1893.[56]

Of course, some hitters needed no legislated advantage. Among them the very best hitter was hustling Pete Rose, but Al Kaline and Carl Yastrzemski also joined the exclusive 3,000 hit club. Durable outfielders of equal size and build, they matched closely in batting average and homer production. Moreover, both lasted over twenty years with their clubs, Kaline with the Tigers and Yastrzemski with the Red Sox.

Kaline was first on the scene as a 19-year-old youth in 1953; he was not yet 21 when he won the 1955 batting title with a .340 mark and 200 hits. Although he never again scaled such heights, he batted above .300 in nine of his 22 seasons and played in 2,834 games. An overall average of .297 with 399 homers and 3,007 hits won entrance for him into the Hall of Fame. A quiet leader who inspired others by hard work and baseball savvy, Kaline charmed a generation of Tiger fans. This wasn't the case with Carl Michael Yastrzemski of the Red Sox. Like Kaline, he was hard-working and incredibly durable, missing only a month's playing time in nineteen seasons. Still, "Yaz's" personality hurt his image. To fans and the local press, he was a mixed blessing. A $100,000 bonus baby, in 1961 he was too soon touted as Ted Williams's successor. Two years later he won the first of his three batting titles, and his Triple Crown performance of 1967 brought him MVP honors.

Yaz won a third bat title the following year with a .301 average; this season only two batters had reached .300. Thereafter, he managed only two .300 seasons, although he narrowly missed winning the 1970 batting crown. Later, as the team's senior citizen, he starred in the losing campaign of 1975, and when faced with the opportunity to win the 1977 sudden-death playoff, Yaz unfortunately popped out to end the game.

During his long career, the Sox lost at four championship opportunities, and so this highly paid superstar became the journalistic scapegoat. It was his heaviest burden: "It's eating my guts out. But I'll tell you something. Yaz is gonna be on a world champion before he retires from this club." Fate, however, ruled otherwise. In 1979, the year he rapped his 3,000th hit and his 400th homer, the Sox finished a sorry third.

This Boston team included one half-forgotten star who was one of only 16 men ever to win more than one batting title. Versatile infielder Pete Runnels was traded to the Sox in 1958 by the Senators.

With the Senators he once batted .300; he reeled off five such seasons in a row for the Sox. During the skein, he twice won batting crowns, reaching a .320 average in 1960 and a .326 in 1962.

In 1975 Boston fans saw handsome, hard-hitting Fred Lynn burst on the scene and lead the team to a pennant. Rookie outfielder Lynn batted .331 with 21 homers and 105 RBIs to win both Rookie of the Year and MVP awards. He took the 1979 batting title on a .333 average, but after the 1980 season, Lynn joined the affluent Angels as a million-dollar player. Western coast action saw Dodger first baseman Steve Garvey exceeding Lynn's performances. Since 1973, this hustling, right-handed hitter had topped .300 six times, averaged better than 20 homers and 100 RBIs each season, won an MVP award, and was a perennial all-star.

Few players of the era matched Lynn or Garvey at solid hitting, but for sheer slugging ability, Harmon Killebrew and Frank Howard stood clear and strong. Killebrew poled 573 homers over 22 seasons; his batting average was a mere .256, but the right-handed "Killer" was a devasting long ball threat. Eight times he smote more than 40 homers a season; six times he reigned as the American League's homer king. Because he toiled with the lowly Senators and Twins, however, he missed much of the glory. Still, he won an MVP award and demonstrated unusual versatility by making All-Star teams as outfielder, first baseman, and third baseman.

Ranking as one of the top sluggers of the era, the "Killer" overshadowed Frank "Hondo" Howard. This was no mean feat, as the muscular, bespectacled Howard stood 6'7" and posed a terrifying apparition to pitchers and third basemen. When prospect Howard signed for a $108,000 bonus, awed Dodger scouts predicted the coming of the next Ruth. This was exaggerated, but Howard played 16 seasons and struck 382 homers. Thrice he hit 40 or more and twice led the American League, and his $140,000 salary in 1971 ranked with the leading plutocrats.

Howard was not the only touted slugger of the period. Roger Maris broke Ruth's seasonal record in 1961, but managed only 103 slams over the next five seasons.

As these sluggers faded, third baseman Mike Schmidt of the Phillies and outfielder Dave Kingman vied for honors. At the close of the 1970s, this pair engaged in a fierce slugging duel. Schmidt led, taking three straight National League homer titles through 1976 and joining the select circle of those who hit four in a single game. A superior third baseman, Schmidt's shortcomings included a mediocre batting average and frequent strike-outs. Kingman, unfortunately, had no redeeming fielding reputation to counter the same defects. Still, his slugging was prized, and the moody outfielder concentrated on his sole saleable skill. For continually demanding higher pay, he was often traded; he burst forth with the 1978 Cubs, leading the league with 48 homers, driving in 115 runs, and posting his highest batting average.

At a time when consistent hitters were rare, stars like Boog Powell, Joe Torre, and Rusty Staub shone brightly. A beefy, 6'4" right-handed hitter, Powell smote 330 homers in 15 seasons as an Oriole and won an American League MVP award. National League third baseman Joe Torre won an MVP award in 1971 on a league-leading .363 average, 230 hits, and 137 RBIs. Over a 17-year career, this big catcher-infielder averaged .297 and stroked over 2,300 hits. Daniel "Rusty" Staub, on the other hand, failed to win an MVP award, but the powerful red-headed outfielder ranked with the best. Staub exercised tortuously, ate health foods, and drank only purified water; whether this helped or not, Staub played his 17th season in 1979. Summoned prematurely to the majors, the raw rookie came alive after three lackluster seasons with the Astros. He was traded to Montreal in 1969 and delighted Expo fans dubbed him "Le Grand Orange." One decade later Staub ranked with the five top players in total hits and RBIs. By then, this much-traded player was a full-time designated hitter and was among the best of that strange new breed.

Among the relatively few infield stars, third baseman Brooks Robinson was the defensive stalwart of the winning Orioles. He won MVP honors in 1964 for consistent hitting, fielding, and RBI production. Over 23 seasons this balding infielder batted only .269, yet attained nearly 3,000 hits. Still, fielding was his forte, and his .971 lifetime mark was the best of any American League third-base sacker.

Although Robinson had no peer, George Brett of the Royals and Yankee Graig Nettles were worthy successors. Brett, a perennial .300 hitter, won the 1976 bat title, but his .951 fielding was far below Nettles's .965 effort. Youth was on the side of the curly-haired Brett, whose heroics at the turn of the 1980s made him a million-dollar-a-year superstar. Meanwhile, Larry Bowa of the Phillies rewrote National League fielding records at shortstop. By 1978 the little veteran had handled 6,000 chances with only 115 errors, a record for shortstops who played over 1,000 games. This brash "little pissant" im-

Great white players of the expansion era: sluggers Harmon Killebrew (*top left*) of the Twins and Mike Schmidt (*bottom right*) of the Phillies, and versatile hitters George Brett (*top right*) of the Royals and Dan "Rusty" Staub of the Expos (*bottom left*).

pressed observers with his quick hands, strong throwing arm, and wide-range coverage.

Finally, three players starred at the all-important catching post. Johnny Bench of the Reds lorded in this position over his two great rivals, Thurman Munson of the Yankees and Carlton Fisk of the Red Sox. Only twenty when he became the Reds's regular receiver in 1968, Bench was the first catcher ever to be named Rookie of the Year. Although a solid hitter with power, he was also a fielding genius. Blessed with big hands—one of which could hold six baseballs—Bench easily adapted to the new, one-handed catching style using the now popular double-hinged glove. Moreover, he maintained a fielding percentage of .990, by far the best of the era. A cerebral catcher, good at spotting and exploiting batter weaknesses, Bench combined defensive skill and power hitting to earn MVP honors in 1970 and 1972.[57]

Bench was already a star when Munson appeared with the Yankees in 1970 as Rookie of the Year. Dubbed "Squatty" for his stocky build, this intense, moody player batted nearly .300 and fielded above .980 over the next nine seasons. A six-time all-star, he won MVP honors in 1976, but the clutch-hitting Yankee captain died tragically in 1979.

Munson's passing ended his duel with Carlton Fisk over catcher's bragging rights. Like Bench, Fisk stood tall and powerful, and like his two rivals, he won Rookie of the Year honors. Since 1972 he had rivaled Munson, then in 1975 he forged ahead. The next year Munson sparked the Yankees to victory and Fisk, refusing to play when hurt, was criticized for failing to emulate his gritty opponent. When their dual ended, Munson led in batting, but Fisk dominated in fielding and slugging.[58]

These men indeed found cash and glory; this was more than could be said of the majority of ordinaries whose baseball lives were daily survival struggles. Seldom studied or interviewed, they lived "on the jagged edge of insecurity," ever fearful of pink slips to be found in their mail.

Among the ordinaries was "Dirty Al" Gallagher of the Giants, who earned his nickname by diving for grounders at third base. Modestly, he dreamed of becoming a regular and qualifying for pension rights. His below-average salary of $25,000 in 1972 afforded a modest lifestyle, but his precarious position made him naturally paranoid and he feared to assert himself, lest he be branded a showoff, flake, or troublemaker.[59]

At least the ordinaries suffered none of the illusions of those stars who fell from glory. One of this tribe was Ron Blomberg, a celebrated Yankee rookie, whose bright promise was tarnished by injuries, poor fielding, and an inability to hit left-handed pitching. Catcher-first baseman Earl Williams hit 33 homers as a 1971 Brave and was named Rookie of the Year, but because of mediocre batting in 1978, he was cut loose. His resolute mother took out ads in *The Sporting News* and the *New York Times,* boldly headlined "EMPLOY-MENT WANTED BY BASEBALL PLAYER," detailing his eight years of service, his batting record, and his good health and attitude. Her footnote added that he had no police record. The last line, "HAVE BAT-WILL TRAVEL-WILL HUSTLE," screamed with sincerity, but there still were no takers.[60]

Living the Dream

Life in the majors was not all "peaches and cream." Careers were frequently short and many failures were inevitable. Moreover, during the baseball season life was rather hectic, with few days off and constant travel demands. Booing fans and carping sportswriters could cut through the most stalwart of defenses; therefore, it was not too surprising that some veteran players at times laughed at the supposed glamour in baseball. Still, just as often the opposite was true; many players felt that major league baseball was the best of all possible worlds. Some even marveled at the fact that they could get paid for something they would do for "fun."

Sometimes a team forged a surprisingly close group, but just as often cliques developed. Of course, it was never realistic to expect 25 competitive ballplayers to merge their personalities into a unified "team spirit." Friendships were frequently strong and long-lasting. However, among some players the fears of failure and of isolation produced serious problems. Most players accepted roommates as a necessary and welcome routine, but some demanded private hotel rooms. Travel secretaries indeed had difficulty at times matching personalities. This attempt was a far cry from olden times, when simple alphabetical listings sufficed.[1]

One writer stated that teams now resembled college fraternities. Like fraternity brothers, players spent about four to five years with a team, and few starting lineups played together for more than four years.[2] Moreover, like the greek societies, teams fielded practical jokers whose creative crudities evoked belly laughs. One player was jokingly ridiculed for his grossly sloppy tobacco-chewing; his bachelor status was blamed on the fact that "he even chews on dates."[3] Like other Americans—indeed like humans around the world— baseballers sometimes stooped to racial and ethnic gibes; the self-confident players, however, knew how to field or even to get ahead of these. Reggie Jackson boasted of his "chocolate" complexion; Joe DiMaggio once shocked a rookie by saying, "When you eat with the Dago, the Dago buys"; and Ted Kluszewski dubbed his muscular fist "my Polish joke stopper."

Although raucous jesting evoked many laughs, tensions among close-living men sometimes flared into conflicts. Writers of the time noted spats over salaries and playing time. Stars sometimes caused conflicts; Yastrzemski, for example, was accused by his mates of masterminding the ousters of men he disliked. Garvey was labeled "Goody Two Shoes." No team of the 1970s matched the 1974 A's or the 1978 Yanks for airing their inner turmoils publicly. Fist fights erupted among the Oakland players, who also denounced the owner and manager.[4] Open conflicts between Yankees Jackson, Martin, and Steinbrenner overshadowed other troubles. Nevertheless, these embattled teams won world titles.

The new divisional system further increased competitive tensions. Even a close-knit "family" team like the 1979 Pirates admitted that pressure to win the division was exhausting. "You think of the race all the time," one player complained, "even when making love."[5] Still, playing for a losing team like the 1979 A's was no less taxing. The A's players sustained a soul-destroying round of extended losing streaks, sparse home crowds, and low pay. For pitcher Matt Keough, who lost 16 consecutive games, the season was one long nightmare. Perhaps the most depressing position was to play for a team that fell short of expectations. The 1971 Angels, a highly touted, expensive "dream team," collapsed amidst salary squabbles, clubhouse brawls, a spate of disciplinary problems, and a few simple turns of fate.[6]

The Fear Factor in Baseball

Many players were bothered by fears. Fear of failure was the most frequent, but there was a range of concerns that bothered players: concern over injury, of psychic damage, of losing one's position, of being upstaged by rival players, of demanding owners and managers, of hostile fans and reporters, of marriage or family problems, of drug use consequences, of excessive weight, and of what to do when one's career was over.

At least two players committed suicide during this era. Perhaps the most gruesome case was that of the promising All-American college pitcher who failed to make the majors. Unable to cope with failure, he stood on the diamond of his former university, laid his All-American certificate on the ground, and shot himself.[7] A young Pirate prospect died as a result of an outfield collision; while others died in off-the-field accidents, including three plane crash and several auto accident victims.[8] Off-season sports participation also took its toll. So many players were injured playing basketball that some clubs banned the activity. However, players still managed to cripple themselves by skiing, biking, and hunting accidents—even by working at household chores.

Another problem was found at the dinner table; given hefty meal allowances and served lavish postgame buffets, players often overindulged. Among the legendary eaters of this era, Ron Blomberg was known to snack on hamburgers, steak sandwiches, and hot dogs, washed down with a pitcher of iced tea; two hours later he would attack a full-course dinner. He once won a bet by finishing a six-pound steak dinner in an hour. Incredibly, Blomberg was not fat, but so many Cardinals were that the club canceled postgame buffets. Some players resorted to crash diets to control weight and took reducing pills, sometimes with harmful consequences. Dietitians vainly tried to persuade players that red meat was not an effective energy source.[9]

Even greater dangers resided in drinking cups. As always, the player ranks included a few alcoholics whose problems won little sympathy. Even when they were effective on the field, alcoholics were likely to be traded, and not until the 1970s were these men given sympathetic treatment.[10] While booze was an ancient problem, the newer drug dilemma was present as an echo from the 1960s. By the 1970s baseball officials had attacked the common practice of taking amphetamines to get "up" for games, alerting their players to harmful effects. Amphetamines were revealed as habit-forming and dangerous to the heart, while pain killers and muscle relaxants were reported as harmful to the body. However, drug usage showed little sign of abating, as players, like other Americans, defied warnings.

The chance of injury was a daily companion. In the early 1950s, a young pitching prospect sustained a knuckle fracture on his pitching hand; without consulting his club's physician, he submitted to a finger amputation and ended his career.[11] That players had cause for concern was shown in studies which ranked baseball players behind their football brothers as the most injury-prone of athletes. Batters faced pitched balls that arrived at 90-mile-per-hour speeds and pitchers ducked batted balls that flew even faster. Pitchers, of course, were paranoid about arm and shoulder injuries that hard throwing inflicted on limbs ill-designed for such exertion. Catchers faced the same fear, along with broken fingers from handling pitches, possible cracked wrists from swinging bats, stunning blows from foul tips, and bruising collisions from hard-sliding runners.

Indeed, there were no safety zones on the diamonds. Infielders sustained cuts and bruises from sliding runners and broken fingers from "bad hop" balls. Outfielders sometimes ran into fences and could be subject to leg injuries, and runners were sometimes injured running the bases. Batters at least were protected by heavy plastic helmets. Some observers suspected that protective head gear emboldened light-hitting Ron Hunt to be hit a record 32 times in 1971. Sadly, four years earlier loose headgear had ended the career of slugger Tony Conigliaro. When a fastball bore in on him, Conigliaro jerked his head back, lost his helmet, and the ball struck the left side of his face with gruesome results. His left eye appeared crushed, and for a day it was doubted that he would recover; when he did, chronic vision problems doomed his hopes of coming back.[12]

Despite Conigliaro's tragedy, pitchers continued to brush batters back. Batters accepted the practice, grudgingly, as part of the game; they, in turn, terrorized pitchers by aiming shots up the middle. When a vicious liner tore off the tip of his ear, veteran Don Drysdale decided to quit. Jon Matlack vividly described being hit by a liner: "I got my bare hand up. It hit my fingertips. When it hit me, it was like a flashbulb going off in my face." Upon recovering from a hairline skull fracture, it took several outings before he regained his concentration.[13]

Arm miseries actually troubled pitchers more. Such ailments affected all within that rank, especially youngsters who often overtaxed themselves trying to impress: Jim Wright's arm gave out just as he was called to the Phillies. Arm trouble sometimes came on gradually, though relentlessly, as in the case of Koufax's painful arthritis that required cortisone shots and ice-packs. For veteran Tommy John, however, calamity struck on a single pitch: "It felt as if my forearm, wrist and hand had left my elbow." A ruptured ligament with nerve damage sidelined John for a year; then an unprecedented transplant operation enabled him to come back as a "bionic" marvel.[14]

In this era the active pitchers suffered heart attacks. Pitching in the minors, Joe Hoerner delivered an overhand curve and fell clutching his heart. He was rushed to a hospital and given last rites, but he pulled through, and a year later he was pitching again. Because certain doctors theorized that his overhand motion might have reduced the oxygen supply to his heart, Hoerner converted to side-armed pitching. Meanwhile, John Hiller of the Tigers resumed his effective relief pitching after missing the 1971 season because of a heart attack.

Catchers were ever more vulnerable to injury. "You got to be a dog to be a catcher," groused manager Joe Schultz. Pounded by runners and battered by foul tips, catchers often lost ten pounds in a game. Hard work eroded their batting and running, and they were prone to arm trouble. Also, fans learned of frequent testicular injuries to catchers, who were protected by only metal or plastic cups embedded in athletic supporters. Such injuries had been bowdlerized as "groin" injuries until 1975 when a writer boldly reported that Carlton Fisk's testicles were hit five times in a single month, resulting in chronic swelling and understandable problems.[15]

Infielders and outfielders were vulnerable, too. Roy MacMillan retired after playing over 2,000 games as shortstop, having suffered several broken bones. Macmillan left the game too soon to benefit from a 1978 rule that penalized runners for intentionally slamming into infielders. Of course, "intent" was hard to prove, so umpires seldom enforced the rule. Outfielders gained some protection against crashing into fences when clubs installed warning tracks, padded barriers, and light wire fences. Still, injuries came with depressing regularity, and players often "played hurt" to escape being accused of "dogging it" or being told "It's in your head." Stars like Koufax, Mantle, and Ken Singleton soaked arms, taped tortured legs, and concealed sore limbs. The spartan code of strength evaporated in the 1970s; more players admitted to injuries, refused to play hurt, demanded specialized treatments, and utilized their newly won rights to a guaranteed year's pay if disabled. Indeed, this new breed sought and won rights to full recovery without prejudice. In winning this concession, the Association brandished evidence which showed 127 disabled players in July of 1979, a figure three times higher than the entire year of 1970.[16]

Meanwhile, injured players benefited from the sports medicine breakthroughs of skilled orthopedic surgeons like Dr. Robert Kerlan and Dr. Frank Jobe, who performed surgical miracles on injured limbs. So successful were their techniques that teams took to hiring orthopedic surgeons. Proof of their skills showed in thin surgical scars on player arms and knees, indicating triumphs over maladies that once would have crippled. Hence, players returned to duty after ligament transplants, disc removals, tendon repairs, and even torn rotary cuff repairs.

The medical revolution included improved training and conditioning regimens, including year-round weight lifting and exercise programs, in addition to improved diets. These changes may explain why 31 players in 1979 stayed in the game after turning 40 years of age; however, the talent scarcity, platooning, and designated hitters also figure into this change. Whatever the cause, statistics suggesting that the ages 26 to 30 were a player's best years were nicely defied by sturdy oldsters like Rose, Stargell, Perry, and Kaat.

Although medical gains helped to control fears caused by career-ending injuries, players tended to discount advice from team doctors who might feel pressured to get injured stars back in lineups. Players now sought second opinions from objective specialists. Carlton Fisk, after playing while injured in 1978, finally refused to go onto the field until convinced he was healed. Others, like Bob Robertson, filed damage suits against clubs for aggravated injuries; in 1977 the Michigan Bureau of Workmen's Compensation awarded damages to Tiger pitchers Les Cain and Denny McLain.

As fear of bodily injury lessened, attention focused on the emotional problems of players. Players were used to repressing their problems; however, a growing tolerance towards mental health problems brought a change in attitude, especially when studies surfaced which purported to show that as many as 25 percent of all Americans suffered emotional problems. This evidence was a boon to players. Help might have come earlier had players not rejected psychological services provided by owners like Wrigley and Veeck. Many players of the 1950s saw little value in psychology, except perhaps when used as a weapon against opponents.[17] Thanks to

Jimmy Piersall, an unashamed victim of emotional stress, players once derided as "nuts" now received professional treatment. Alex Johnson won an arbitration decision on these grounds, and Marvin Miller hailed the verdict as a boon to all "uptight" players.[18]

Still, the fear specter was hard to exorcise. Perhaps the fear of success ended the career of Steve Blass, a star Pirate pitcher. After a great year in 1971 and a good one in 1972, Blass suddenly lost his touch. There was no storied comeback for him, but at least he received professional treatment and suffered no loss of pay or ruthless rejection.

Blass's case showed the limits of therapy, as did the story of Roger Moret. This Puerto Rican pitcher with a history of emotional problems suffered a catatonic fit; the Rangers paid his salary and medical expenses, and Moret attempted a comeback in 1980.

Under tension, the players reacted in wildly differing ways. Reliefer Moe Drabowsky used the bullpen phone to dial numbers all over the world. This admitted "phone freak" justified his behavior as a "defense mechanism against the pressure." Like countless others, outfielder Jackie Jensen was afraid of flying, a malady which probably helped drive him into early retirement. Jealousy among the players was a constant source of tension. George Brett narrowly edged his black teammate, Hal McRae, in the 1976 race for the league batting title. When Brett won by a single point on the last day, McRae emotionally accused the opposing team's manager of racism, claiming that he had ordered his outfielder to let a Brett blow fall for a single. That same year the National League batting race ended on the season's last day. The winner, Bill Madlock of the Cubs, went four for four in his final outing, while loser Ken Griffey of the Reds sat out his game in hopes of protecting his lead.

Under such circumstances, competitive jealousy was understandable; but the green-eyed monster worked in other ways. Met pranksters stirred trouble by awarding a monthly "snake award" for poor play. When Steve Garvey won the 1974 MVP award, his joy soured as his wife complained, "I changed my schedule for him, he didn't change his for me."[19]

The Biggest Headache

Mrs. Garvey's outburst underscored a major tension source. As citizens who followed the national trends, 75 percent of the players were married and, like most marrieds, they came to know the difficulties of living happily ever after. Players wanted wives to be supportive, inspiring, and comforting, and some, like pitcher Tom Seaver, found such mates. More in tune with the times, however, were the organized wives of the Atlanta players, who denounced the traditional homebound roles as dehumanizing.[20]

Like many Americans, some players found themselves mismated; their subsequent divorces mocked the myth of rosy baseball marriages. According to one writer, that myth derived from corny sports movies, whose plots had dedicated players replacing doting "moms" with "best girls." If such marriages ever existed, they now were rare. To keep the marital peace, some players defied rules and took wives along on road trips. Faced with a fine, Pirate Jerry Reuss threatened to take the matter to arbitration. At this point club officials backed down, but understandably refused to pay the wife's expenses. Nevertheless, clubs of 1979 generally opposed wifely escorts on road trips. That the limits to permissiveness might be breached was suggested by a much publicized wife-swapping incident. In a bizarre "life swap," pitchers Fritz Peterson and Mike Kekich changed mates, with the provision that if the arrangement didn't work out for both, each would return to his original wife. The deal, however, collapsed when Peterson married Kekich's wife, while Peterson's wife left Kekich. The affair shocked baseball officials, but one player observed sympathetically, "We're a crazy bunch of guys; every man to his own."[21]

Other incidents enlivened the old notion that sexual intercourse drained one's strength. This old myth seemed silly in light of the national obsession with the joys of sex. Although old Casey Stengel believed that bedding was less debilitating than chasing, other managers clung to the notion that indulgence sapped strength. That idea was disputed by some authorities. Dr. Warren R. Guild of the Harvard Medical School stated that "physical intercourse does not in any way sap one's strength or make one weak"; while philosopher Paul Weiss argued that neither doctors nor trainers knew enough about sex, diets, or exercise to issue dogmas.[22] Nevertheless, owner Cal Griffith blamed a player's slump on honeymoon exertions, grousing that the player should have waited until his career was established. Griffith's stand resembled Durocher's, who once replied to two elderly ladies' question of how a player was doing after his recent marriage: "I'll tell ya, ladies. Your boy Howard was a nice kid who didn't even know what it was for. Now that he's married, Howard's drilling for oil. . . . He's so weak he couldn't hit me with a paddle if I ran across home plate."[23]

Such beliefs by now seemed quaint. Perhaps the new breed of players had heard how the old Dodgers once tried to weaken an opposing pitcher by plying him with sex and booze. The victim pitched a shut-out, which sent the instigators back to the hired sex partner for an explanation. She claimed: "He drank two quarts of liquor and I guarantee he didn't sleep a wink all night."[24]

Players of the expansion era were besieged by sex offers. Even minor leaguers were propositioned by "baseball Annies." By the 1970s the "Groupies," "Bimbos," "Annies," and "Shirleys" seemed to have undergone a veritable population explosion. While visiting the 1975 White Sox training camp, Jim Brosnan observed "groupies" in waiting and wondered if they also underwent spring training. Brosnan grouped the players in waiting into categories of celibates, sometimers, and "shack up artists" who regarded sex as natural, nice, and necessary. Among the latter, one declared: "I read where a half hour of sex is worth an hour of jogging. I'm getting two hours of running every night." Still, the "sex is good" ethos had its tyrannical demands. Sex recipe books stirred anxieties by prescribing supposedly skilled techniques and quality orgasms. Apparently, female groupies thought players guaranteed athletic sex; however, one disappointed sex student demurred: "he-man athletes . . . are not necessarily any more sexually powerful than sedentary men."[25]

The majority of the groupies, however, thought otherwise. In a study conducted by Herb Michelson, fifteen women remarked that they viewed athletes as super-studs. Otherwise, groupies had little in common; they were sex-starved wives, celebrity-worshipping innocents, and sex thrill-seekers. Several were nymphomaniacs, including "Maggie," who one night serviced a score of athletes, and other mattress-backed heroines, like the legendary "Shirleys" of Chicago, Detroit, and New York. Access to the groupies came easily—sometimes by open invitation, sometimes more subtlely as part of ballpark "camera days." To avail was to run risks, though teammates and writers maintained a code of silence, the latter crew covering up troubles with evasive phrases like "personal problems." Indeed groupies did sometimes undermine morale, worry wives, and foment racial hostility. More than one paternity suit wrecked marriages; one player was obliged to make public apology after being caught *in flagrante delicto* in a parked van; and a busload of Yankees was rebuked for affixing their names to a young lady's buttocks.[26]

Naturally, players resented the candid books that told of such shenanigans. Brosnan's books of the early 1960s scared, but gave no details; these morsels were soon supplied by pitcher Jim Bouton. In two diary-style books, Bouton told of bumbling players and managers, mendacious owners, infantilizing rules, racial discord, and sexual adventuring. Reading Bouton was to learn about "beaver shooting"—a form of peeping tomism aimed at glimpsing the private parts of some comely female. The game was played everywhere—in hotels by peering through open windows, chinning from transoms, or drilling peep holes in doors. The open grandstands of the minors afforded vantage points, especially when the national anthem compelled fans to stand up. Binoculars were used in bullpens to "scope" quarry. Fortunately for the cause of modesty, the popularity of slacks afforded the quarry a protective adaptation. Offended by Bouton's first book, Commissioner Kuhn called the player into his office for a confrontation. Bouton was joined by Marvin Miller, who coolly parried Kuhn's charges. Later, when titillated writers cast Kuhn as Mrs. Grundy, Bouton churned out a sequel.[27]

Bouton's tour de force inspired others to write. Playing on the "disreputable" player theme, a spate of revealing books told of baseball drunks, swingers, screwballs, and intellectuals. Among the volumes, pitcher Bo Belinsky's ghosted autobiography told of his life as a baseball Casanova, recounting in vivid Anglo-Saxonisms how he bedded starlets, waitresses, and groupies. Belinsky argued that he did openly what others did furtively; he defended his wenching as being less harmful to club morale than card playing for high stakes. Moreover, Belinsky preferred groupies to the cliquish baseball wives, who were "spoiled bitches . . . sitting around . . . gossiping . . . drinking coffee all morning."[28]

The baseball establishments took offense. For telling tales, some player-writers were shunned by teammates and blasted by conservative journalists. Moreover, angry husbands and lovers retaliated, as Reggie Jackson discovered at a cost of $1,200, while Lyman Bostock paid with his life. Also, some wives demonstrated that sex adventuring was a two-way street. Indeed, some worried husbands chose to quit baseball. When a philandering club owner propositioned a pitcher's wife, the latter publicized the story and her husband won his release.[29]

Women, booze, and drugs were risky home remedies for coping with tensions; an alternative was to turn to psychiatrists. Increasingly players turned to psychotherapy, including Reggie Jackson, who sought help in coping, and pitcher Rudy May, who sought confidence when pitching with men on base. Some clubs used group therapy sessions to air grievances, share emotional problems, and discuss cracks in team morale. The 1965 Mets used such sessions in hopes of escaping the league cellar, while the Cardinals used them to build team spirit. Successes were debatable, but such efforts at least treated players as mature adults.

Like many other Americans, some players no longer trusted modern science to resolve all their tensions. As always some resorted to magic, religion, and popular fads. Professional witches were sometimes hired to cast spells on rival teams or to harness luck, and voodoo practices reportedly were introduced by several Hispanic players. Anthropologist George Gmelch, a former minor league player, respected such efforts. He explained that when chance, accident, and emotions can shape events, people turn to magical techniques. Certainly, ballgames qualified as uncertain events—especially batting episodes, when even the best only hit 30 percent of the time. Understandably, batters used magical devices in hopes of getting hits; among these accessories were fetishes, including coins, crucifixes, odd stones, necklaces, and clothes. In one odd clothing fetish, a player during a hot streak would not change his underwear. Other techniques included eating certain foods, closing one's eyes during the playing of the National Anthem, tapping home plate in a prescribed manner, touching one's genitals, or straightening one's cap. To bring *mana* to bear, some players sanded, rubbed, and heated bats, others compulsively avoided crossed bats. One magical taboo forbade any talk of a no-hitter in the offing, while others banned stepping on foul lines and wearing unlucky uniform numbers. Fetishes were not lightly considered, as desecrators painfully learned.[30]

Persisting magical rites in baseball mirrored anti-scientific attitudes in the culture at large. Like many Americans, some players turned to astrologists or soothsayers; when the biorhythm craze swept America, players numbered among the two million aficionados who plotted the high and low points of their physical, emotional, and mental cycles. However, biorhythms and baseball parted company when statisticians showed "low cycle" pitchers tossing no-hitters and Reggie Jackson pulling off his brilliant Series performance on a triple low cycle![31]

Much harder to down was the "god hypothesis." Many players sought divine help; a few, like Koufax, refused to play on holy days; but most players did take the field, having sought help from "the man upstairs" or "the great umpire in the sky." Enough seriously believed in the powers of religious objects and rituals to warn off detractors. Thus, few were now so bold as Birdie Tebbets, who once called time after a batter crossed himself to do the same, saying, "Now it's all even with God. Let's see who's the best man."[32]

With religious excitement sweeping the land, such drollery would be unwise. Organized religious meetings, like those of the Fellowship of Christian Athletes, were familiar locker room rites. The results were mixed: some players found succor, but the Fellowship was criticized for its conservative stands on unionism and racism, and was accused of toadying to owners. Some critics thought the meetings had a "numbing childish insipidity" about them. Such responses suggested that for baseball, the Christian millennium was rather remote. Besides, religious pluralism kept one dogma from triumphing over all. The era did produce one zealot manager in Al Dark, who tried to relay Christ's teachings to the A's. Dark went the way of ousted managers, however, for daring to assign Finley a spot in the underworld.[33]

Constant Threats From the Outside

With so many pressures, it was not surprising that players sought supernatural help or used earthy soothing aids like booze, drugs, and sex. Still, like eternal constants, impossible demands were made on players by managers, owners, fans, and media men.

Managers were not dictators, but they still set disciplinary rules and directed the courses of games, naturally imposing their diverse personalities, philosophies, and attitudes on their players. As foremen and "fall guys," they were powerful, and prudence dictated that a player "get to know" his manager. Players customarily drew fines for infractions like missing signs, ignoring curfews, engaging in locker room horseplay, or for sundry misbehaviors, such as violating dress codes or getting sunburned on off days. When Mayo Smith levied $200 fines on his sunburned Tigers, Gates Brown pointed to his black skin and quipped, "How about me?"[34] However, few managers were tyrants. Of course, they could bench players. In an extreme case, pitcher Ken Holtzman idled away two Yankee seasons because manager Martin refused to use him. However, because they were caught between powerful players and owners, managers learned to be circumspect. The players indeed worried more about aggressively assertive owners. According to one player representative, owners were regarded as "rich guys who don't like to be told what to do."[35] Indeed, some were economic conservatives who hated unions, begrudged every gain made by the Players Association, harassed player representatives, and tried to undermine attempts at player solidarity.

For a time some owners fought the Association by firing or trading away elected player representatives. When Miller took over the position, rumor had it that Robin Roberts had been blacklisted for recruiting him and that 48 player "reps" had been traded. Even after the Association's successful 1972 strike, the owners traded 16 player reps and frightened another 19 into resigning.[36] Owners waged a propaganda war against the Association, using inflated salary figures and exaggerated losses to inflame the public. Miller counterattacked, accusing the owners of browbeating young players into accepting low pay. Ironically, it helped the player cause when owners like Finley, Busch, and Ray Kroc behaved like petty tyrants. Kroc especially damaged the owner cause; the blunt hamburger king publicly called his players "dummies" and declared "I won't subsidize idiots."[37]

Such outbursts brought sympathy to player demands that they be treated as men. Owners had imposed dogmatic rules and punished violators with fines, pay cuts, suspensions, and dismissals for too long. They might instead have noticed that attitudes were changing. Some owners added long hair prohibitions to their list of infantilizing rules; in 1968 some even tried to fine players for refusing to play games on days set aside for national mourning of slain heroes Robert F. Kennedy and Martin Luther King.

Both sides of the confrontation between owners and players appealed for fan support. Thrust into the role of jurors, the fans appeared to support the players by responding to salary gains with increased attendance at games and higher ratings for televised games. Still, ballpark fans could drive players to despair with their relentless booing. Most players were jeered at occasionally; some were hectored constantly. Mantle was the Yankee scapegoat for years, but Roger Maris became the target when he arrived in 1959. Incredibly, while he strove for the homer record, Maris was booed in every city. At Yankee Stadium he was showered with Easter eggs, and he was grazed by a thrown bottle at Detroit. Others received similar treatment: Del Ennis and Dick Allen were targeted at Philadelphia, the local "boo birds" twice driving Allen out of town. Some profit-minded owners actually encouraged fans to vent their emotions. Finley reportedly instructed his organist to needle opponents with mocking tunes; others did the same, using scoreboard cartoons to incite jeers. A fad of the 1970s called for clubs to dress clowns in fantastic costumes to parade as totem-cheerleaders and hecklers. Thus, the "San Diego Chicken," the "Philly Fanatic," and the Chicago "Bleacher Creature" cavorted, arousing local fans and upsetting visiting players. Also, many players complained of headaches caused by orchestrated mass cheering. One of the worst of these ordeals came during a free bat doubleheader; not only did the games last ten hours, but fans constantly pounded seats and concrete with their bats. Pete Rose was a favorite target of boo birds everywhere; his "hell for leather" hustling incited fans to yell taunts like "---- Rose" and hurl bottles, ice cubes, and trash.

Sometimes death threats were hurled. In 1977 star players Steve Garvey, Dave Lopes, and Reggie Jackson were threatened, along with some umpires. At a time when terrorism and assassination were rife, such threats had to be taken seriously; indeed, one social scientist predicted that some player would be killed. If not on the field, this attack was foretold as occurring at some public place where players were targeted by insulting autograph seekers. The fans sometimes incited brawls, planted unexpected kisses, and prompted dousings with food and drink. For beating a boorish fan in a restaurant, Graig Nettles was slapped with a $100,000 lawsuit. Understandably alarmed, clubs now kept records of assaults and many players refused to sign autographs.[38]

A loss of privacy seems the inevitable price players pay for being public celebrities. The voracious public appetite for sports heroes was fed by media men, who would focus on some star and lay bare his life before discarding him for a new hero. But this was the way the celebrity-molding process worked.

No one really understood the celebrity-making process, but Edward Hoagland argued that sports fans needed heroes to worship. The fans seemed to crave some towering, lasting hero; what they got instead was a frustrating parade of episodic heroes, whose ready disposability made for a love-hate relationship between players and fans. It didn't help when fans were separated from their heroes by geographical barriers imposed by spacious new parks and by psychological walls, resulting from the salary revolution. Some critics argued that the mercenary, businesslike attitudes of many players incited fans, some of whom also harbored racist resentments. Increasing ballpark attendance and baseball televiewing cast doubt on this hypothesis.

Just what sort of hero the fans craved was the target of a 1973 study commissioned by product advertisers who used baseball to hype their sales. The study implied that fans mostly cottoned to stars like Musial, Mantle, and Berra. Only three blacks from all professional sports were listed among the top ten favored players. At any rate, sports fans preferred baseball stars over football players, race car drivers, and sports announcer Howard Cosell.[39]

Still, it was frustrating to be cast as a popular idol. Fans expected that a baseball demigod be chaste, temperate, clean-cut, and religious. Meeting such expectations demanded that a chosen player alter his personality. Give the fans what they want, advised Bob Feller, the one-time player unionist turned establishment spokesman. One player who heeded this advice, Pete Reichert, supported the Vietnam war, visited hospitalized veterans, and lectured students on the evils of drugs. Denny Doyle dutifully answered fan mail and visited sick children, while Greg Luzinski purchased blocks of seats for distribution among poor youngsters. While some chose this path, others like Reggie Jackson, Thurman Munson, Bill Lee, and Tug McGraw insisted on being themselves. But, in an age when consensus heroes were lacking, they, too, had their followings.

The mass media performed the touting of the heroes. Old-time sportswriters wielded inordinate power; this was evidenced by a *Life* journalist, whose 1939 feature story of Joe DiMaggio reeked with ethnic insults. He wrote that "Italians, bad at war, are well suited for milder competition"; that Joe "speaks English without an accent and is otherwise well adapted to most U.S. mores. Instead of olive oil . . . he keeps his hair sleek with water. He never reeks of garlic"; and that like "heavyweight champion Joe Louis, DiMaggio is lazy, shy, and inarticulate."[40] While such insults were unthinkable in the 1970s, a new permissiveness on social and sexual matters did allow writers to invade the private lives of players. Hence, a new breed of media men spun titillating tales about courtrooms, locker rooms, and bedrooms. Belittled and labeled "chipmunks" by old-time writers, these muckrakers were depicted as "stylists in stench," whose ghosted player biographies were described as "more ghastly than ghostly."[41]

Still, there was no stopping the trend. Americans now welcomed realistic, demythologizing probes into the private lives of celebrities, so such material was served with gusto. Maris certainly suffered from the hordes of prying writers who created stories which variously described him as decent, hot-tempered, low-key, easily agitated, home-loving, surly, cooperative, unselfish, trite, self-pitying, sincere, wonderful, petulant, honest, and morose.

Once burned by writers, the players naturally avoided the "poison pen guys," but the chipmunks persisted. They stirred controversies; yet they also created heroes. Still, the players resented forays into their private lives. After losing a tough World Series match, no team welcomed panning television cameras; upon spotting one, Johnny Bench of the Reds tore off his shirt, cast it over the camera, and angrily ordered the crew out. When chipmunks scurried after stories, even ordinary interviews became sparring matches. During a probing *Playboy* interview, Pete Rose deflected questions about his rocky marriage, his involvement in a paternity suit, and his use of pep pills, along with general probes into homosexuality and drug usage among players. Accused of being uncooperative, Rose retorted, "Look I know what you're gonna ask me and I ain't gonna talk about that ----. . . ." Asked if he meant the interview was over, Rose snapped, "----in' right it is."[42]

Not all writers were so easily dismissed. When three players filed suit in 1967 against "unauthorized and untrue" biographies, their case was dismissed by a New York State court on grounds that it lacked "sufficient reason" or "good and meritorious cause."[43] Therefore (and not surprisingly) some players refused interviews. Some took to hiding in clubhouses, while others lashed back, only to find that hot words could be grist for writers. Few dared to be so bold as Ted Williams, who once gave his recipe for writers: "Pour hot water over a sportswriter and you'll get instant ----." Instead, offended players bluntly refused to talk to any media men and boycotted certain journalists. Fred Patek would stare vacantly when confronted, while Amos Otis hung a sign over his locker which read, "No Interviews, A.O." Sometimes entire teams voted to bar writers and a few took Dave Kingman's advice: "It's easier to say nothing to the press. That way you never get yourself in trouble. They don't write about baseball. . . ."[44] The players were given Association backing to refuse interviews. This of course irritated writers, some of whom threatened to cut off coverage; these were hollow threats because writers needed subjects to keep their jobs.

Meanwhile, the players still battled their ancient enemies: the umpires. There were more of this group now, as four-man crews worked each game. They were better trained than their forebears; they were organized and they were in no mood to be bullied. As part of their new professional stance, the umps conceded that occasionally they erred; but as impartial judges, they demanded respect, dignity, and, above all, higher pay. To force concessions, umpires twice took to picket lines in the 1970s, winning union recognition, job security, and salary hikes. With those victories behind, the militant Major League Umpires Association moved against abusive players.

However, the players still treated the umps as scapegoats. Foul language was now commonplace and the players showered the "blues" with obscenities. Umpires retaliated by levying fines and tossing players out of games, justifying such actions in formal reports to league presidents. Although those punishments were upheld, the officials could only beg players to "strive for courtesy."

The Players Association took sharp issue with the umpires' fining power. Miller demanded in 1977 that all such fines be reviewed by an impartial arbitration panel. Warned that this would erode the umpires' authority, Miller retorted that if the umps didn't like it, they could "move to Communist China."[45] A power struggle ensued between organized players and umpires, and the 1970s ended with the struggle unresolved.

The End of the Dream

Most players avoided thinking of the day when they would be traded or released; that they were replaceable was understood. The owners were used to trading players and airily stating that they sought a strong arm, a right-handed bat, a great pair of hands, or a good set of wheels. Being treated as disposable objects was part of the game for players. Some coped by renting homes, hoping to cushion the impact of sudden moves on their families. Given their gypsy existence, a few, like Wes Parker, held off marrying until their careers ended, but married and single both resented being uprooted. Al Rosen recalled "It's a horrible feeling . . . I always thought they didn't give a damn." Years later as a Yankee GM, Rosen himself cut seventeen players from the 1978 Yankees.[46]

The problem worsened for players early in the expansion era, as GMs sought fame via the trade route. Over a three-year span of the 1960s, at least 400 players were swapped. Earlier, the New York to Kansas City trade route had been notorious, with 72 players shunted that way. Owners sometimes indulged in trading orgies; forty-two men were swapped in just one week during 1972. And if the Mets's third basemen seemed paranoid, it was understandable; 46 men were employed at this position during a 10-year period.

Castoff players often retaliated by assaulting the team that traded them. Proof of such a factor showed when pitcher Curt Simmons beat his former Phillies team 19 times and when Piersall batted .436 against his old Red Sox. Sometimes a player blocked a trade. Whitey Ford sabotaged Yankee plans to deal him by announcing that his arm was sore. Hawk Harrelson, Rusty Staub, and Woody Fryman (among others) simply refused to report to new teams; some players threatened to do the same if shipped to undesirable places. Ten-year vets could veto trades by the 1970s and restive players sometimes escaped cheap owners by denouncing them in interviews. Nevertheless, even satisfied players were desolated by the experience of being traded; Tug McGraw remembered; "It was like being thrown out of the house by your family. It was a terrible shock. Then I went to Philadelphia . . . and found out that foster parents can love you just as much."[47]

Officials gradually translated the message that the ruthless uprooting of players was no longer their inalienable right. At a time when organized American workers demanded security and freedom from arbitrary firings, players sought similar protection. Player resentment strengthened their Association and led to demands for long-term contracts; with shocking suddenness, in 1976 such contracts became a reality for many in the wake of the Seitz decision.

This latest freedom had furious owners denouncing their charges as disloyal mercenaries. Few executives had yet grasped the point that loyalty was a two-way street. The cruelest blow for a player came in the form of a dismissal notice. Even when he recognized that stints in the majors averaged less than five years, such announcements would hurt. One player described the jolt of a pink slip as "a sharp stick in the eye." Players struggled desperately to postpone dismissal; the last weeks of a season usually had marginals frantically battling to improve their statistics.

Players reacted in diverse ways when the axe fell. Some humbled themselves: pitcher Milt Pappas, who needed one more win to become the third pitcher ever to win a hundred games in each league, agreed to a $10,000 cut. Pappas hoped to buy time; but later the word came: "You don't fit into our plans."[48] Another pitcher, Carl Morton, made $100,000 a year when he was cut. To hold on, he contacted other clubs, but then he signed as a $14,000 minor leaguer. His hopes to make the Phils were extinguished by a pink slip. "I died," he recalled. "I'd lost my competitive edge." Years after receiving his dismissal notice, pitcher Jim Bouton remembered the very hour it came. Although he landed a good job in television, he brooded, accepted a low-paying minor league offer, and later came back to win one more big league game as a knuckle ball pitcher.[49] Pitcher Mel Stottlemyre, crippled at the shoulder, accepted the inevitable and found solace in the hefty pension he received. However, others failed to qualify for pensions. With attenuated minor leagues concentrating on youth, discarded major leaguers were less likely to find positions on minor league teams.

Thousands of players had passed through the majors since World War II, so many sad tales existed of final days. Thirty-seven-year-old Hank Bauer defiantly rejected a pay cut, demanding to play his last year at a respectable salary; Mike Andrews, cut by Finley for erring in a Series game, sued and won an out-of-court settlement; Art Shamsky, cut by the Mets at age thirty, angrily refused to join the team's Old Timers ceremonies. Some players chose to retire rather than be fired. One writer, noticing the spate of retirements in the early 1970s, suggested that clubs were weeding out veterans to save money. Naturally, most resented being told they were too old to play. Some sturdy oldsters performed well enough to challenge the myth that players were through at 35; yet hustling graybeards only delayed the inevitable hour. When it struck, some, like Billy Cox and Sandy Koufax, left with crippling ailments. Koufax's arm was crippled by arthritis, while Cox tended bar on legs "all swole and purple."[50]

The retired players faced the trauma of finding a new livelihood. Koufax, though provided with good income from investments, was bewildered and hurt when he failed as a sportscaster. Some glib veterans did very well behind microphones, and television now offered jobs for ex-players who could deliver "color" commentaries. This was one way of staying close to the game they loved; another method was to land a job as manager or coach, but such jobs were few and a nepotic "old boy" network limited opportunities.

Thus, most retired players faced the grim prospect of re-tooling their lives. Thanks to pension rights and athletic images, ex-players found their postdream lives easier than did their past cousins. By now, too, about fifty of them had served as subjects of biographies. For these chosen few, the comforting reminder of one's biography resting on a shelf gentled the wrench of retirement. At least these volumes were proof that one's baseball life had been no dream.

Chasing the Dream

An examination of the tension-ridden lives of major leaguers must not obscure the fact that making the "bigs" fulfilled a well-nigh impossible dream. Granted, more than 10,000 men played big league ball since 1876; millions of hopefuls, however, never realized this dream. Always, a ruthless attrition process crushed visions, and this force still applied in the talent-scarce year of 1976. Of the millions of boys who then played little league ball and began dreaming, fewer than one hundred survived the final sifting into the majors. Indeed, the six major professional team sports of that year accommodated only 3,500 players, and of these, only 1,740 were starters.

Those were indeed pitiful odds; some thought commissioner Kuhn did youthful dreamers a disservice in 1978 by publishing a sprightly pamphlet touting "Baseball, The Now Career." By stressing the rainbow's end with its cash and glory, romantic travel "to the most dynamic cities," and promised fellowship of "the baseball family," Kuhn's propaganda piece rather attempted to woo young athletes from rival sports.[51]

Nothing was printed of the bleak lives of minor leaguers or of the endless dedication to daily bat-swinging and body-punishing exercises that was demanded. Indeed, honesty required that catcher Bill Freehan's warning be spoken loudly: "If you don't think you can be a star, then don't try it."[52]

However, baseball was facing a talent shortage, mainly due to competition from rival sports. Indeed, at many schools and colleges, baseball was a minor sport and few of the once-plentiful sandlot leagues survived. Still, little leagues, junior leagues, American Legion leagues, and scholastic and college programs supplied talent enough—if properly exploited. While some officials applauded the systematic, formal instruction obtained from these sources, some stars, like Mantle, Roberts, and Lopat, preferred old-fashioned pickup games that afforded youngsters more throwing and swinging. Thus the debate—the grim facts showed that there were fewer amateur programs and a consequent shortage of organized opportunities for talented young players.[53]

This talent-scarcity threat hit baseball soon after World War II and forced scouts to invade the black leagues, comb Latin America, and engage in costly bonus baby bidding. In the search for talent, all the old stops were pulled and some new ones tried. Rickey staged his try-out camp scheme; also, in 1970 Royals owner Kauffman resurrected Wrigley's old baseball academy scheme. At a cost of $2 million, the Royal camp opened its doors to athletes who would face physical and mental tests so rigorous that only one of every 1,500 high school athletes could pass. Baseball knowledge was not required; that was gained through relentless cramming. Sadly, the experiment failed: after spending 4 million dollars and scrutinizing hundreds of hopefuls, only one, Frank White, made the majors. To recoup losses, the facilities were sold to the rookie leagues, a shared baseball enterprise for instructing draftees.

Talent hunters scraped for newer ploys; they dangled college scholarships, sought the sons of ex-players, and signed ex-convicts. Interestingly, the ploy of scouting sons of ex-players supplied nearly twenty players.

Obviously, the era of free enterprise talent hunting was over. By the 1960s most clubs recognized that the limited pool of players and the attendant problem of developing young talent must be shared by all. Thus, the old idea of a free agent draft, long derided as "socialistic" by talent-rich clubs, gained ground and then was adopted by owners in 1965. A frank imitation of pro football's annual college player draft, the first free agent draft of promising high school and college ball players took place that spring. Clubs selected players in turn, with first choice in each round going to clubs with the poorest previous records. From that year on, the annual drafts became the main source of new talent; these infusions supplied as many as 1,100 players in each draft. A winter draft was added in the 1970s to net any players not signed in the June draft.

Although this system shared the talent, its workings were costly and controversial. Because the system deprived young prospects of free negotiating rights, it was legally vulnerable; because draftees demanded bonuses for signing, the first five drafts cost clubs $24 million in bonuses. Indeed, "signability" was a key consideration in drafting a player, because if a youth refused to sign, the drafting club had wasted one of its selections. Ferreting out the best young prospects and assuring signability were new tasks for baseball scouts. However, seventeen clubs in 1974 sought to cut scouting expenses by subscribing to the Major League Scouting Bureau at a yearly cost of $118,000 per club. This common enterprise was later criticized as inadequate and double-dealing, and its membership shrank.[54]

The Phillies elected to use their own scouts. Using a streamlined system, the club employed twenty full-time scouts, with one National Scouting Director to assign the corps to cover five geographical areas. Of these five, California emerged as the great nursery of talent, with the South ranking second. For $16,000 plus expenses, a scout scurried about, grading youngsters on hitting, fielding, running, throwing, and power hitting; pitchers were ranked for their fast balls, curve balls, and sliders, and they were checked for control. When not evaluating prospects, Phillies's scouts appraised minor league players, including those of other teams. Also, scouts sometimes were assigned to investigate the strengths and weaknesses of major league rivals.[55]

While this approach solved the problem of talent scarcity, the knotty task of developing players remained. Unlike football or basketball players, it was a rare young baseball recruit who was good enough to play in the majors. Most prospects needed seasoning "in a teaching atmosphere" where they could hone skills by regular playing. Hence, the major leagues of the 1960s adopted a common player development program, which aimed at promoting quality college baseball programs and, above all, brought new life into the shattered minor leagues.

Clubs spent millions to finance college baseball scholarships and summer leagues—including a thriving Alaskan circuit! Still, thorns remained in relations with college coaches, as the latter insisted that no eligible player be drafted until his college career was over. Unwilling to go all the way, major league teams agreed to draft only seniors or 21-year-old players.

Revitalizing the half-dead minor leagues was far more difficult. In 1949 the minors reached a prosperity peak with 59 leagues, 448 teams, and some 40 million fans. Then there was a shocking decline: by 1956 only 28 leagues remained to draw twenty million fans; in 1963 fewer than 20 leagues drew crowds of less than ten million.[56]

Minor league officials blamed the majors for expanding into their territories, for indiscriminately drafting minor league players, and for upstaging minor league games with broadcasts and telecasts of major league games. These competing telecasts did the most damage. As Frank Shaughnessy explained, "Our fans heard nothing but prodigious feats of the major leaguers."[57] The majors even refused to share television revenue with the minors. Other blamesakes arrived as uncontrollable changes: the great popularity of television and rival sports, and the new leisure outlets, like stock car races, bowling, and various water sports. These new activities accounted for the talent shortage that vexed the majors and killed many minor leagues. Statistics compiled by writer Leonard Koppett told the grim story: the 400 major league players of 1950 were culled from 9,000 minor leaguers; whereas in 1975, the 600 major leaguers were picked from only 3,000 minor leaguers.[58] This was an astonishing turnabout; while it allowed major league players to wallow in complacency it also failed to speed the promotion of minor leaguers to the majors. Indeed, the adoption by the majors of the re-entry draft in 1976 further slowed the transition by giving major clubs the option of bidding for established veterans.

Meanwhile, the major leagues were trying to pump new life into the moribund minors. Under the Player Development Program of the 1960s, the majors voted to subsidize the minor leagues; because nearly all independent minor league operators had been forced out, this was the only viable choice. Thus, the minor leagues were reclassified into four levels: these included AAA (the highest class), AA, A, and the rookie leagues. Each major league team was now obliged to finance five minor league teams; this number was reduced to four in 1975 and included one team from each class. On the average, this cost each major team $1.5 million annually, most of which went for operating expenses and player salaries. The plan worked well enough to stabilize the minors at 17 leagues and 121 teams by 1977. Although some major league officials suggested scrapping the minors in favor of two large training complexes, most officials demurred, believing that trial by ordeal in the minors was good medicine for young prospects.

While life in the minors had always been nasty, brutish, and long, now it tended to be nasty, dull, and somewhat shorter. This limited gain came because personnel directors now regarded three years in the minors as time enough to judge if a prospect was good enough to make the "bigs." Still, for middle-class youths, a 3-year stint was a tortuous financial and psychological ordeal. Imagine a young player fresh out of college or high school, local plaudits still ringing in his ears, and a bonus payment feeding his dream, suddenly finding himself playing before sparse crowds and under primitive conditions for $500 a month and $5 a day meal money! This is the way it was for class A minor leaguers of the 1970s, and AAA players knew little better.[59]

Many dropped out, especially the married players. Those who hung on complained of inadequate instruction and playing time, of managerial favoritism, and of boredom, while black and Hispanic players added discrimination to the list of woes. Although the "bus leagues" were dying out, class A players of the mid-1970s were still seen riding long hours in hot, ancient buses.

Many of those major league stars who survived minor league hitches shudder to recall the experience. Six of eight interviewed agreed with Bud Harrelson that the life was "hard, low paying," lonely, and long. Hispanic Ed Figueroa and black players George Scott and Roy White contributed complaints of segregation and racism. While George Brett and Buddy Bell were fortunate enough to have close relatives with major league experience to encourage them, Sal Bando's bitter recollections centered on a meddling coach who tampered with his batting style. Only two of the eight, Jerry Koosman and Bobby Grich, enjoyed the experience. Koosman learned to throw a slider and "loved just about every minute," while Grich remembered the minors as a "nicer world" than the "business-like . . . materialistic" majors.[60]

Still, the eight were lucky enough to make the majors; even more fortunate was Bob Horner, who missed the whole ordeal. Doffing his college uniform for a Braves uniform in 1978, Horner homered in his first major league game and stayed on to star. Most, however, were unlucky. Some were like Pat Jordan, who never lived up to his promise and quit early; some were like Dave Turnbull and Tony Silicato, hanging on for nearly a decade with no hope; and some, like Jerry Rosenthal, were so put off by the adolescent environment that they decided life in a "kid's uniform" was too silly. While some "professional minor leaguers" remained—mostly short-term major leaguers who were sent down because of injuries or ineffectiveness—their numbers were few. The new policy of youngsters was inhospitable to aging, marginal players who were cut by major league teams.[61]

Those youngsters who dreamed on in baseball's Siberia saw encouraging signs that their lot was improving. Fearing that they could no longer risk losing these prospects, some owners introduced badly needed reforms, such as hiring capable teaching managers and paying better salaries. Thus, the 1967 White Sox were first to offer life and medical insurance for their charges. By 1979 Yankee owner Steinbrenner spent $3 million for better coaches and new uniforms, better travel conditions, and salaries; others, like the Phillies and Dodgers, followed suit.[62]

Encouraging as these trends were, the Players Association continued to ignore the plight of minor leaguers. These men could therefore only dream of baseball's cash and glory, though the reformist spirit brightened their outlooks as the 1980s dawned.

Of Fans, Owners, and Other Non-Players

F **The Changing Face of Baseball Fandom**
rom the start of the postwar era, the most arresting change in
baseball's following was its burgeoning numbers. To the delight of
owners, National League attendance in 1947 topped the 10 million
mark; when the American League followed suit, the majors exceeded the 20 million attendance mark and repeated the feat in
1949. The club owners now determined to make this the norm, but
the new attendance gospel was barely established when reversals in
1952 and 1953 dropped total attendance to 15 million.

This reversal inspired the first franchise shifts and all subsequent
expansions. Such medicine worked wonders; once the Dodgers and
Giants had arrived on the west coast, National League attendance
returned to the 10 million annual figure. Owner O'Malley soon
proudly hosted the largest World Series crowd in baseball history
when 90,000 fans crowded into the Los Angeles Coliseum on Oct. 3,
1959. The outclassed American League waited until 1961 before

regaining the 10 million mark. By then these owners had seen their rivals drawing 15 million fans a year. A new expansion round and a new ballpark-building boom combined to push 1969 attendance totals higher. Attendance for both leagues topped 31 million by 1976, and by decade's end, total major league attendance had passed the 40 million mark.

Such impressive totals established new norms for individual clubs. One million paid fans drawn each year of the 1970s was considered essential, two million was excellent, and the magic three million mark, topped by the 1977 Dodgers, was Olympian. Indeed, bragging rights belonged to the Dodgers, who owned seven all-time attendance records and hosted crowds of 50,000 or more sixteen times in 1977.

Like bullish stock market figures, such records were grist for Commissioner Kuhn's propaganda mills. In baseball's centennial year of 1976, Kuhn boasted that the one billionth patron since 1903 had passed through the turnstiles. The commissioner claimed this was a sign that baseball had regained its sporting pre-eminence; but sharp-eyed critics deflated his enthusiasm, arguing that the recent boom was an inevitable accompaniment of expansion, new parks, and rising public interest in all spectator sports. That baseball's share of the boom was actually modest was proven by comparing attendance figures of the 1970s with 1949 figures, when combined major-minor league attendance topped 60 million. Kuhn's credibility suffered even more when he played down rising attendance while attacking player salary increases.[1]

Ironically, just as fans settled into the newer parks, built to accommodate America's suburban populations, the price of gasoline shot upward. Higher prices at the pumps also increased the cost of attending games, and this simply added to the emotional expense of battling massive traffic jams in and around ballpark areas.

Indeed, rising ticket costs and other expenses taxed ballpark fans of the 1970s. The classic 50 cent seat was a blessed memory by 1974; the cheapest seat now ran at least a dollar, with choice seats going for $5.50 and more—only the Dodgers could boast of holding ticket prices to 1957 figures. By 1977 creeping inflation sent the average cost of a big league ticket to $3.45. Although owners argued that baseball tickets cost less than other sports' tickets, a patron still found a night at the park a costly venture. High prices for refreshments and souvenirs took their toll, as owners wrung more money from concession sales than from tickets. One writer reported that a night at Candlestick Park in 1976 cost $42.85 for his party of four, $20 of which was spent on food. Elsewhere, fans carped at higher refreshment prices, while an increase in ticket prices at Yankee Stadium had fans chanting "Baloney." On the other hand, wealthy firms willingly paid up to $19,000 a season to rent plush, sheltered suites where clients could relax on easy chairs, dine on gourmet foods, and look down on the game beneath them or watch it on closed circuit television.[2]

Beyond these costs, a trip to the park was physically taxing. Physicians warned heart patients who watched televised games to restrain their enthusiams, lest they suffer some fatal seizure. While stricter safety regulations protected fans from ballpark accidents, a fan still fell to his death at Philadelphia's virginal Veterans Stadium through an unguarded opening in the upper deck area; the club later paid a $550,000 judgment.

To keep the hordes of fans coming in spite of higher costs was the task of newly employed experts. Fans were now served a steady diet of night games; by 1950 one-half of all games were played at night and day games were later scheduled on weekends. Doubleheaders became increasingly rare; besides the owners' profit motive, fans actually preferred shorter outings. As a 1960s poll indicated, most fans thought three hours was long enough for a ball game.[3] Ladies Day games also gradually disappeared, a casualty of the rising equality movement, the increase in the number of working women, and the popularity of family outings. Acting on the assumption that families with kids were in the majority, promoters introduced giveaways, created picnic areas, and welcomed station-wagon tailgate parties in parking lots. However, park attendants still searched parcels, looking for forbidden booze and bottles.

The strategy of wooing families seemed so reasonable that most promoters blindly pursued the policy. That they were wrong was the verdict of Matthew Levine, a market consulting specialist, who interviewed 300,000 ballpark fans from 1974 to 1980. Levine discovered that 75 percent of these attendants came regularly to five games a year and that most were older people who seldom brought children. He also found that most were working-class people, who were vulnerable to price increases. Thus, the promoters' image of the typical fan as an affluent, middle-class family type darkened. Furthermore, Levine found that the most zealous baseball fans preferred watching televised games.[4]

This shocking revelation exposed the promotional specialists as mere dilettantes. Nevertheless, throughout the era promoters aimed giveaway schemes at families, and when it came to inventing these, Bill Veeck was the master. Veeck laughed off such ironic failings as giving a prize of 1,000 cigars to a child, 1,000 cans of beer to a teetotaler, and 150 cans of motor oil to a guy whose car broke down earlier for want of a single can! The promoters, imitating Veeck, aimed most giveaways at youngsters. By the 1960s, every club had its free bat and ball days, and later added cap days, batting helmet days, batting glove days, T-shirt days, and—most popular with the 1977 Phillies's fans—jacket days. The giveaways initially went to kids, but by the 1970s women were given hot pants, pantyhose, halter tops, and shorts. Adult fans were lured by the popular (but dangerous) cheap beer nights. Indeed, one disastrous Veeck experiment taught promoters to be wary of riots fueled by beered-up fans or by rock music buffs.[5]

Just why promoters failed to gauge the riotous consequences of some of their lures is understandable. Truthfully, no one knew much about crowd behavior; nor, for that matter, did social scientists know much more than they did back in 1896, when Gustave Le Bon proclaimed the 20th century to be "the era of the crowd."[6] Beyond recognizing that currents of unrest could turn ballpark crowds riotous, promoters were unable to predict both the circumstances and the timing of riots. Thus, these promoters led unbalanced lives: on the one hand, their jobs demanded that they entice huge crowds; on the other, they never knew when to expect calamitous outbursts from the same.

To the muddled art of understanding ballpark crowds, sportswriters added myths of "true fans." Supposedly "true fans" occupied cheaper seats and were more baseball wise, more rebellious, and more littering; another version of the myth held that the only true fans were those who watched preseason games in the small parks. Both versions, however, merely echo the Marxist notion of the goodness of the proletariat and both stubbornly cling to nostalgic myths of the superiority of old-time baseball.

Predictably, paranoid promoters adopted a "bad animal" view of baseball crowds. This notion depicted modern ballpark fans as more menacing than those of the past. One writer blamed night ball, television, mercenary "monsterized players" for this transformation. This assumed that night ball added to the evils of darkness, that television raised jealousies by glorifying the players, and that modern fans were intimidated by the largeness of modern athletes.[7]

Another observer believed that the new bad animal fan had scared off the "true" fans. He blamed television for turning fans into action-obsessed masses with cravings for entertainments, sideshows, music, fireworks, pregame shows, giveaways, and orchestrated cheerleading. Above all, modern fans were thought to be comfort-obsessed.

A smattering of limited studies suggested that 40 percent of the ranks of "typical" crowds were females; this prompted a psychologist to conjecture that the presence of so many women must upgrade decorum. Not only did this smack of wish fulfillment, but it merely echoed Harry Wright's forlorn dream of the 1880s.[8] These were fumbling attempts to plumb the character of expansion era crowds. Certainly this era was not the first visited by bad animal crowds; indeed, baseball history is pock-marked with ballpark riots. That a ballpark crowd is a differentiated mass had always been demonstrated by unique characters and groups at games. Among the throngs were celebrities vying for attention, showoffs, and cheerleaders. Pete Adelis was such an effective heckler of opponents that Phillies owner Carpenter gave him free passes, while seat mates bought him hot dogs, hoping to quiet him. Unfortunately for them, Adelis managed to yawp between bites. Among other characters were frenzied foul ball chasers, inveterate bettors, brawlers, drunks, and auto protection racketeers on the park's outside. San Diego's "tuba man" loaded his instrument with beer bottles, the contents of which soon inspired his blasts; Shea Stadium's "sign man" carried a stack of some 700 critical signs for situationally harassing players, owners, umpires, and other fans; Philadelphia's "umpire-baiter" was said to be the vilest of fans; and Atlanta's "rabble rouser" fired up fans much better than he did the forlorn Braves.[9]

While all parks had foul ball chasers armed with baseball gloves and butterfly nets, Chicago's Rich Buhrke was the reigning genius of the tribe. Positioning himself outside of Wrigley Field, Buhrke's equipment included only a small radio and a fielder's glove. Eighteen years of chasing balls driven out of the park even taught Buhrke to take wind direction into account. As of April, 1977, he had collected 876 balls, 830 of which were homers. Although valuing his collection at $3,000, Buhrke admitted that getting them cost him a dozen injuries from rival kids and dogs.[10]

Inside the parks, other characters chased after other trophies. Some dashed on the fields seeking player autographs, snatching caps, or menacing players and umps. Cincinnati fans in 1969 witnessed a new wrinkle in the appearance of a long-haired, curvaceous stripper, who styled herself "Morganna the Wild One." On five separate occasions in 1970, Morganna dashed onto the field to kiss a player as he waited his turn to bat. Her battle cry, "Kiss me for Christ's sake!" was as divinely compelling as her 44–23–37 figure and no quarry spurned her. Morganna's erotic reign came to an end at the 1970 All-Star Game when several of the fifteen extra guards hired to stop her threatened incursion, cornered, and arrested her. Even in defeat, she upstaged President Nixon, who attended the game.

Such episodes only confirmed the promoters' bad animal view. Club "security executives" in 1972 denounced modern baseball crowds as the worst ever! One suspects that thoughts of job security prompted this stand, but their fears are still worth considering. Maintaining that fan misbehavior was baseball's leading security problem, they opted for more policing and more body searches. Still, gate crashers, gamblers, and player molesters preyed on their minds, along with enthusiastic rooters.

Reports of misconduct mounted. Some stories singled out players who were most likely to inflame partisan crowds: Pete Rose for his aggressive play, Gaylord Perry for his alleged spitball, and Willie Montanez for his flamboyant style. Also, certain cities were pinpointed as habitats of notorious fans. Philadelphia's "boo birds" were judged the worst; their raucous heckling so frightened visiting teams that the players ran to shelter as soon as the final out was made. Enhancing Philadelphia's reputation were the Vet Stadium football fans, who once booed and snowballed Santa Claus as he rode upon a float. One Phillies executive publicly praised local fans for this and credited their "knowledgeable" and intelligent criticism.[11]

He might have argued that obstreperous fans were everywhere. Jeering "bleacher bums" at Wrigley Field wore yellow helmets, doused enemy players with drinks, and blew bugles, thus becoming the subject of a Broadway play. Exploding cherry bombs harried opposing players at Baltimore. Several parks installed mesh screens to prevent incursions. At Cincinnati, when an enemy player fell injured after crashing into a fence, fans poured beer on him; also, an umpire was once hit by a flying can of beer. At Detroit in 1960, flying objects struck so many players that the club threatened to jail offenders; but a dozen years later, players still dodged steel balls, firecrackers, frisbees, and pellets. Reggie Jackson was pelted with hot dogs and "Reggie" candy bars at Yankee Stadium in 1978. After hitting a third homer in the final game of the 1977 World Series, Jackson tremulously eyed fans perched ready to jump on the field at the final out. In a scene reminiscent of Hitchcock's *The Birds*, they swooped down and chased Jackson, who knocked down two of his pursuers before gaining the protection of a police cordon. The game ended with a sea of fans milling about the Stadium field.

Such "victory riots" were all too familiar. One of the most famous of these was the 1969 "Metomania" outburst that followed the Mets's Series win: fans burst onto the field, tearing up turf and seizing bases as magical talismans. Likewise, Yankee fans greeted their team's 1976 playoff victory with a memorable riot. As seen from the Goodyear Blimp overhead, the milling rioters resembled fire ants on a rampage. These outbursts lent credence to the bad animal theory, but stadium cops' behavior could sometimes add fuel to the fire. In 1972 their pointed surveillance was cited as one possible cause of a Yankee Stadium mob scene that pitted 700 cops against enraged fans.

Some thought that certain club policies, intended as innocent entertainment, actually had an opposite effect. A comely Phillies usherette reported that she was ordered to dress seductively, told to "make sure that her hot pants were short and tight at the thighs"—a policy that aroused ogling, leering fans. Organists at some parks were instructed to deride rivals with jeering tunes and to orchestrate local cheering and jeering.

Yet no promotion venture stirred more trouble than cheap beer night. If only owners had heeded Wrigley, one of their wiser colleagues, who never sponsored such sales nor offered free chewing gum. Instead, Cleveland promoters sponsored the memorable Cleveland Beer Night of 1974, drawing 25,000 fans. The lure of unlimited ten cent beers produced several unforeseen consequences: drunken fans turned riotous, attacked the visiting team, and hit the home team pitcher with a thrown chair. When many rioted on the field, the umpires forfeited the game to the visitors. While this ended cheap beer nights, a 1977 Los Angeles beer riot was charged by regularly priced beer. The ruckus began when fans in upper deck seats dumped beer on those below; when the latter battled back, the air became white with foam and all ended with riotous rancor. One pacifying cop caught a full cup of beer in his face.

Indeed, almost any item sold or given away at the parks posed a threat. Paper airplanes fashioned from scorecards littered the fields; free bats became nerve-wracking noisemakers; ice cubes were handy missiles; and crushed ice served as snowballs. The anonymity afforded by the crowd surely encouraged this wild behavior; some fans openly consumed illegal booze and dope, snatched purses and picked pockets, and set fire to banners. The national "streaker" craze had naked fans occasionally dashing across playing fields. Only rarely did a fan invent a new torment, like the one who buzzed Dodger Stadium in a plane and bombed the crowd with bottles and flour sacks, narrowly missing the shortstop's head.

Armchair advisors offered schemes to prevent such antics, but officials trusted their own insights. Thus Commissioner Eckert polled 5,000 fans in 1967, asking what they wanted. Returns indicated that fans much preferred high-scoring games, jazzy uniforms, new parks, and stricter security measures. Another study showed that fans resented phoney patriotic appeals and childish baseball myths. In letters to sports editors, some fans attacked overbearing owners, mercenary players, long-haired players, nocturnal Series games, childish sports stories, and the lack of patriotic displays.[12]

Such discordant feedback indicated that fans were no single-minded mass. Many, though, were eager boosters who formed clubs to lionize players; their tastes in heroes ran the gamut from prissy types to bumblers to errant types. Hordes of Detroit fans in 1976 warmed to Mark Fydrych, their beloved "Bird." Some sent the eccentric pitcher money because they considered him underpaid; the club returned these contributions. So popular was the "Bird" that when a sore arm sidelined him in 1977, he was hired to do color commentaries on national television, where a broad audience heard him excuse his brief absence thus: "I went out to the commode!"

To cultivate better relations between players and fans, Kuhn allowed a one-half hour's fraternizing time before each game. Some clubs tried to organize minority groups; indeed a positive approach was made to quell racial and ethnic tensions. Veeck spent $148,000 to refurbish Comiskey Park and improve its neighborhood.

Nevertheless, promoters seemed never to understand their clientele. That its face changed dramatically was evidenced by its many subcults. Fastest growing of these groups was the television audience, whose ranks swelled to over 60 million at World Series time and whose overall impact produced average windfalls of $2 million per team. Moreover, such familiar subcults as radio and newspaper fans were joined now by baseball researchers, collectors, and table game buffs. The latter group gained prominence in the 1950s when the APBA fad began; a table game devised by Richard Seitz, APBA was played with dice, a cardboard diamond, and computerized performance records of players past and present, all of which provided for realistic strategy. By 1968 hundreds of APBA zanies subscribed to newsletters and motored to annual conventions with bumper stickers that read, "If you play APBA, Honk three times!"[13]

More numerous than the table game freaks were the collectors. Resembling baseball pack rats, they collected and swapped baseball cards, books, journals, equipment, and a host of other memorabilia. Again, newsletters united them, guiding members to trading conventions. The most visible of the lot were the estimated 100,000 bubble gum card collectors, whose squirreling tendencies were stimulated by the Topps Bubble Gum Company, which put player picture cards in each pack of gum.

Smaller in numbers, but highly vocal were the baseball researchers, whose organizations included the 1,000-member Society for American Baseball Research and a strong wing of the North American Society for Sports History. In their ranks were professors and teachers who offered formal courses in American baseball.

Indeed, all pro sports attracted hordes of zealous fans. So numerous were these followers by the end of the 1970s that consumer advocates Ralph Nader and Ralph Gruenstine tried to organize them into a consumer group. To right the wrongs of promoters and to give fans a say in policy making was the campaign of Fight to Advance the Nation's Sports (FANS). Its prospectus attacked soaring ticket costs and food prices, shilling sportcasters, and rule changes and innovations. Unfortunately, FANS operated with the notion that all sports fans were alike. Perhaps this explained why so few became fellows and why the abstainers seemed better attuned to LeBon's warning: "The power of crowds is to be dreaded, but the power of certain castes is to be dreaded yet more."[14]

The Officials: Baseball's Militant Villains

One of baseball's clichés defines umpiring as "the only job in the world where you are expected to be perfect when hired and to improve as time goes on." Facing the "ultimate can't-win situation," these guardians of the game were always expected to be invulnerable, inviolate, and invisible; this ludicrous trinity collapsed amidst deafening boos as soon as the umps took the field.

So much for invisibility. To be inviolate meant to never have a call questioned, but this was impossible for a plate umpire who regularly ruled on about 200 plus pitches a game, or for a first base ump who might make 50 or more calls each game, or for the rest of a crew who probably averaged another 50 calls per game. In few other professions were workers so harshly and openly judged. Throughout the postwar era, umps were easily fired, poorly paid, and denied pensions—so much, therefore, for invulnerability.

Moreover, heaven needed to help the union-minded ump. For attempting to organize his ranks in 1948, American League ump Ernie Stewart was summarily fired by President Harridge. Then, after Commissioner Chandler sustained his ouster, American umps waited twenty years before trying again, and did so only after their bolder National colleagues showed the way.

Like their ancestors, postwar umpires were harried by fans and players. Under such pressures, all sports officials revealed thick-skinned temperaments and dominant, demanding, and strongly disciplined personalities. To be always criticized and almost never praised was their lot. Thus, Babe Pinelli—the "Lou Gehrig of Umpires," who worked twenty-two years in the National League without missing a game—wept in his dressing room after his last plate appearance in the Series game that saw Don Larsen pitch his perfect game. His tears came partly because his career was ending, but also because nobody had thanked him for his work that day. Upon retiring, Pinelli received a curt note thanking him for serving with "distinction."[15]

Improvements followed steadily after Pinelli's 1956 departure. By 1965 six umps had been enshrined in the Hall of Fame, including Jocko Conlan, who first dared to shed his coat while working the bases on a hot day, and Cal Hubbard, who was also enshrined in pro football's Hall of Fame. At least the early 1950s brought safety in numbers. With four-man crews working each game, an ump stood behind the plate every fourth game instead of daily, as Bill Klem had done for 13 seasons. Moreover, umpires were better trained, thanks to special schools run by their retired brothers. There they learned the rules, the proper signs and gestures, and the best field positions.

Because each league controlled its own umpires, American and National plate umps used different vantage points when crouching behind the catcher. American umps reportedly called "higher strikes," possibly because the more mobile National plate umps wore chest protectors under their coats while their American cousins still wore immobilizing inflated mattresses outside of theirs.[16] Still, any differences were overshadowed by demeaning similarities. Most complained of low pay; also umps were forbidden to drink in public, fraternize with players, gamble, or hold part-time jobs. Wearing glasses was long tabooed, and overweight umps might be expelled.

The umps were obliged to report instances of players fraternizing, to check balls for signs of illegal doctoring, and to investigate playing fields for evidence of groundskeeping chicanery. Their greatest tests, however, came in confrontations with hot-headed players and managers, including that notorious umpire-baiter, Leo Durocher.[17]

Probably no other manager matched Durocher's reputation as an umpire-baiter. Even in retirement Jocko Conlan and Bill Stewart frowned at his name; Conlan recalled how Durocher once incited a crowd to throw bottles at him, and Stewart remembered Durocher as the most vicious and foul-mouthed of all managers. Even a younger ump, Doug Harvey, despised Durocher, once saying, "Call me anything, but not Durocher." Indeed, Durocher had listed eight National League umps as his mortal enemies; in his ghosted autobiography he spewed contempt on four—Bill Stewart was weak-eyed, Lon Warneke was incompetent, Larry Goetz was spiteful, and Frank Dascoli was an ingrate. Durocher told how he once helped Dascoli, but "the ungrateful Dago" turned on him.

More power to the umps clipped the wings of chronic baiters. Backed by league presidents, umps ejected complainers and filed detailed reports that evoked fines. Some reports quoted such salty obscenities that one female secretary refused to read them. Finally, Lee Ballanfant was honest enough to add this postscript: "Boss: if you take his money . . . take some of mine. . . . I gave him as good as he gave me."[18]

Still, postwar umps were pitifully vulnerable. Vic Delmar was fired for allowing two balls in play at the same time; others lost out because of negative evaluations from managers; and all umps could be second-guessed by television cameras. Indeed, slow-motion replays shown on scoreboards were so irritating that one umpire crew left the field, refusing to return until this was stopped. This occurrence in 1975 prompted league officials to fine owners for using television against umps.

Such bold defiance by umps was unprecedented in baseball history. Hence, like militant players, the expansion era umps were a new breed, and their militant union made them strong. The road to this unionization was tortuous. As recently as 1969, ten-year veteran Bill Kinnanon earned only $10,000 a year. A *New York Times* reporter estimated the average umpire of the 1978 received wages far below the game average of football or basketball referees. Moreover, league officials still practiced age discrimination, insisting that umps conform to certain physical standards and that they retire at age 55.

Expansion era umps were better educated and more professional than ever before. As certified umpire school graduates, most were called to the majors after an apprenticeship under the new Umpire Development Program All umps sharpened their skills by spring training officiating and by attending seminars. Umps now viewed their roles as impartial, professional judges, whose chief qualifications were authority, dignity, and judgment. Moreover, they admitted to mistakes, but stoutly resisted being second-guessed.

Their greatest strength lay in their growing numbers. By the end of the 1970s there were 52 umpires, 28 in the American League and 24 in the National. In spite of owner attempts to cut back, four-man crews worked each game: each crew had its chief, and the four usually formed a compatible group, an essential element in their isolated lives. A candid, detailed view into the workings of one crew came from Lee Gutkind, who followed Doug Harvey, Harry Wendelstedt, Art Williams, and Nick Colosi in 1974. Their earthy revelations testified to the new spirit of freedom; as Wendelstedt put it, "I don't give a ----. It's about time people find out what umpires go through." Indeed, Wendelstedt's massive body has sustained the bumps of his calling, including a broken collarbone, broken elbow, smashed foot, broken toes, and the loss and replacement of each toenail. Wendelstedt's woes were typical.

The umpires' troubles still included autocratic officials and their own jealous rivalries. League officials could fire, but a jealous colleague could drive one to despair. It's no wonder that umpires treasured trusted buddies who shared their lives and helped them release steam. Fortunately, each league town seemed to have its "umpire freak," usually a friendly fan or sympathetic cab driver whose invitations were welcome. Thus, for all their vicissitudes, umps liked their lives. As Bruce Froemming noted; "Baseball! It's the greatest ----ing game in the world and umpiring is the greatest -------profession."[19]

Coming from this long-muzzled crew, such candor was incredible. Only unionization made this possible, but getting it was no easy accomplishment and winning bargaining rights from troglodyte owners was even harder. The turnabout came in 1963 when ex-ump John Reynolds, a Chicago attorney, established the National League Umpires Association. Reynolds persevered, even without the support of tremulous American umps, and within five years the Nationals outstripped their brethren in salaries and expense allowances; in 1969 he reluctantly accepted a contract which won National umps minimum salaries of $10,000 and a maximum of $26,500—far above the $17,000 maximum of the unorganized Americans.

That victory made unionists of American umps, although Al Salerno and Bill Valentine were fired in 1968 by league president Joe Cronin for organizing. Cronin's claims that the two umpires were incompetent, that he himself was no union buster, only stiffened resistance and developed the incident into a *cause celebré*. The umpires appealed to the National Labor Relations Board and won a ruling that the Taft-Harley labor law allowed them to organize if they chose. In December of 1969, therefore, Reynolds presided over the new Major League Umpires Association, whose ranks included all 48 major league umpires.

In the following season, Reynolds called a one-day strike that forced league presidents to recognize the Association and to negotiate the first formal labor contract. This document fixed minimum salaries at $11,000, sent average salaries to $21,000, provided more expense money, and won annual pensions and widows' benefits for retirees. It was Reynolds's finest hour; after ten years of service he retired in 1972, a hero to bluecoats.

His successor, Chicago lawyer John Cifeli, was also an experienced labor negotiator. However, Cifeli's six controversial years with the Association ended ignominiously. His clients demanded that he fight for increased pay, the end of the publicized ratings system, and the access to tenure rights; the 1973 contract that Cifeli negotiated fell far short. While average salaries rose to $23,000, Cifeli failed to win tenure or to stop the ratings system. His downfall came after he negotiated his second contract in 1977. Although the pact kept the four-man crews, increased salaries and fringe benefits, and won a vague promise of tenure, it was denounced as a sweetheart contract. Engaging in secret negotiations, Cifeli bound the men to a five-year pact, which none saw until a year later. The suspicious umps accused Cifeli of selling out and ousted him in 1978.[20]

His tough-minded successor, lawyer Richard G. Phillips, studied the pact and exposed its shortcomings. According to Phillips, the average salary of $31,000 and the daily expense allowance together failed to keep up with inflation. Phillips also discovered that the pact allowed a cashiered ump only ten days of severance pay. The lawyer seized the offensive, demanding that the dismissal provision be stricken and that the entire money question be reopened. He issued an ultimatum in July, 1978; when the owners ignored it, Phillips ordered a work stoppage. This second umpire strike lasted one day and forced owners to hire amateur and minor league umps to work the games. The hold-out ended when U. S. District Court Judge Joseph L. McGlynn issued an injunction against the umpires.

Still, the strike rocked the establishment and had Commissioner Kuhn questioning the umpires' integrity. Editor Johnson Spink of *The Sporting News* chimed in, comparing umpires with teachers and truckers, who also took abuse and spent days away from home. Spink sneered at the umpires' workload of 800 hours a year and voiced the tired refrain, "If you don't like it, get out."[21]

Association President Dave Phillips spoke out in defense of his namesake: "Not one umpire signed that [Cifeli] contract." Others backed what Phillips said and shouted, "I'm not married to baseball." Thus, surly umpires returned to work while Richard Phillips devised a new attack. The smug owners met in December to consider placing American and National umpires under a single set of standards. The two leagues indeed differed. They dressed in different costumes: in 1968 American umps stole a march on their National brothers, wearing gray slacks and doffing their blue jackets in hot weather; in 1971 the same group assumed maroon blazers. Later, umps in both leagues wore baseball caps emblazoned with capital letters to denote their league affiliation.

While owners debated matters of decorum, director Phillips was earning his $12,500 retainer. In September he negotiated a five-year endorsement that netted the Association $150,000, one-third of which went to Phillips. Surprisingly, no one complained about Phillips's cut; as one ump observed, "We got nothing before."[22]

Soon after this small triumph, Phillips found a way to circumvent Judge McGlynn's injunction. Noting that each ump signed a personal contract in the spring of each year, Phillips advised his clients to sign no 1979 contracts until told to do so. This shrewd gamble allowed the umps to stage a legal job action, unless, of course, the courts ruled their move a conspiracy.

Hard line owners, infuriated at this bold stroke, threatened to fire unsigned umps and used temporary hirelings to work exhibition games. However, when the owners asked McGlynn to reinstate his injunction, the Judge denied the motion, ruling that as individuals, umps had the right to refuse to sign proferred contracts. With the battlelines drawn, the third umpire strike began on the season's

opening day and lasted until May 18. While Association umps pick-
eted, amateur, semi-pro, and minor league umps worked the games,
to the general dissatisfaction of teams and fans. As the strike
dragged on, writers freely criticized the incompetencies of the replacements and chided Kuhn for doing nothing.

The commissioner and the owners now heatedly pressured league
presidents to settle, but Phillips's threat to use NLRB procedures to
force mediation was the decisive blow. Thus, the antagonists returned to the table and hammered out a new contract. This new
basic agreement ran for three years; its most important proviso, a
fixed salary schedule based on years of service, provided a starting
salary of $22,000 and stepped the maximum to $50,000 for those
with twenty years of service. For the 1979 season, umpires received
average raises of $7,500, plus $67 daily expense money. Just as
important as these money gains, the pact conceded that no ump
could be fired during the season, and if ever fired, he was to receive
one year's severance pay. Moreover, each ump now received two
weeks' paid vacation during the season, and if a players' strike occurred during the contract term, each idled ump was guaranteed up
to 45 days' pay.

This landmark victory transformed the lowly group of umpires
into a powerful professional force. Phillips crowed: "I am extremely
pleased, because we got more than we asked for. . . . We got an
average of $7,000 a man, plus an average increase of $3,000 in the
per diem, plus vacations. And a no-cut contract which the umpires
had never had."[23]

The returning umps were greeted warmly by teams and received
roaring ovations from fans. Mets Manager Joe Torre blamed their
incompetent replacements for this incredible reaction, while a Met
outfielder bluntly stated, "We need them." Writer Red Smith wryly
added, "After all, umpires are a lot like people."[24]

The aftermath of the strike, however, left a residue of bitterness,
prompted by the presence of eight "scabs" whom vindictive owners
insisted on keeping. Ordered to call them "new umpires," Association men insisted, "They *are* scabs." Thus branded, the eight pariahs
were barred from Association membership, were shunned and embarrassed on the fields. The eight pleaded that had they not grabbed
the opportunity, they would have languished in the minors—which
was true enough, since the Umpires Association did nothing to help
minor league umps.[25]

Such a lack of magnanimity ran afoul. After all, one victory did not make the campaign, and the umps were vulnerable on their flanks. On one of these wings stood the organized players, who had played throughout the strike and whose apparent goodwill masked deep hostilities. An embittered Players Association demanded arbitration of all fines, upheld their right to evaluate umps, and challenged the right of umps to decide on rain delays. The managers held a weak front. Once the most formidable of foes, they now were so impotent that umps evaluated them! One such evaluation pegged Dick Williams, Billy Martin, and Earl Weaver as the worst of the crew. Even a hello from Williams was sarcastic; umps were advised to keep both eyes on Martin; and Weaver's insults were known to sting the worst. Still, Durocher was right in mourning that managers could no longer battle for their players, but had to submit to the whims of umpires.

The club owners mounted a formidable threat against the umpires, while writers and sportscasters hectored and second-guessed.

Against all these forces the umps marshalled a strong union, probably the most exclusive professional organization in the land. Most of its 50-odd members were dedicates, awed by their responsibility of protecting "the quality of the game." Some, like Doug Haller or Ron Luciano, were highly respected stylists. However, when Luciano won fame for his flamboyant five-syllable "Safe" calls, he quit to become a highly paid sportscaster.[26] To a dedicate like Nestor Chylak, who collapsed from a heart attack while working, such a move might seem inexcusable. Of course, others might say that Luciano was only human.

Baseball's Emasculated Managers

As players and umpires gained wealth and power, baseball's field managers sank to the status of wretched scapegoats, whose ousters concealed the failings of club owners and their henchmen. Sacking the manager was a time-honored ploy; whenever the rumblings of fan discontent were detected, a manager was dropped. Indeed, each passing season from the 1880s through 1979 was littered with cashiered managers; records, in fact, showed only twelve seasons when none were fired.

By the postwar era, most managers accepted firings as a fact of life, to be borne philosophically or to be mitigated by gallows humor. If any dared to think that their shrinking status had touched rock bottom, they were deluded. In the years 1946 to 1966, continued firings reduced the average tenure of a manager to less than three years. Thus, as Walter Alston of the Dodgers (the most enduring manager of the age) served out his 23 seasons, some 85 colleagues read their walking papers.

Managers had every right to feel paranoid. On the one hand, their bosses expected them to win games; on the other, they faced the hopeless task of pleasing 25 highly individualistic players. To further worsen matters, the players steadily gained in power and wealth, until their salaries far exceeded those of most managers. This was a staggering blow to managerial prestige and authority, and continuing pressures from hostile fans and writers created a no-win situation that yielded soul-destroying consequences. It all added up to intolerable pressure from the combined assaults of owners, players, writers, and fans.

Surely, the worst of their troubles was the steady erosion of their authority. Some managers of the postwar era still attempted the dictatorial style of the late John McGraw, who made his men practice five hours before a game and who insisted on making all major decisions, sometimes even calling pitches. McGraw once spotted one of his men ogling a woman in the stands, whereupon he turned to a younger player and said: "See that? That cement head is thinking more about that girl than today's game. Remember this, son. One percent of ballplayers are leaders of men. The other 99 percent are followers of women."[27]

That brand of vainglory was passé. Granted, the postwar era harbored a few McGrawian disciples, who lorded over players and wore the number 1 on their backs; the archetype here, in the opinion of Jim Brosnan, was Leo Durocher, a hard-bitten, "I" type of manager. Such managers saw themselves as decisive factors in a team's success; others of this ilk included Charley Dressen, Eddie Stanky, and Gene Mauch.

Under pressure from owners and organized players, these managers faded and were replaced by emergent "We" and "They" types. Resembling high school guidance counsellors, the "We"s oozed concern for players and tried to win cooperation by downplaying their role. According to Brosnan, examples of this character were found in Walter Alston, Fred Hutchinson, Ralph Houk, Hank Bauer, Danny Murtaugh, and Sparky Anderson. Meanwhile, the "They"s operated by welding teams into tightly knit communities. They unloaded trouble-making players by insisting on conformity to team standards. This posture generally worked best with talent-rich teams or, as in the case of Connie Mack, if the manager also happened to be the owner. Joe McCarthy, Casey Stengel, Billy Southworth, and Al Lopez were all managers who fit into this category.[28]

The growing number of "We" and "They" managers underscored the era's diminishing powers of field management. Indeed, the importance of field managers was increasingly questioned. Veeck was one owner who believed that managerial strategies and tactics were minor factors in a team's success. Naturally, Durocher and Paul Richards disputed this, but not Yogi Berra, who once revealed to a reporter that he could hardly invent new plays! Players also challenged the myth of the manager, claiming that these men played no positive role in a team's performance, but might be a negative influence.

When it came to dispatching managers, however, no one matched Charles Finley. After firing a dozen of these underlings, Finley opined that any fan or smart monkey could do the job. Still, Wrigley was the only owner who tried to eliminate the post. In the 1960s he used a system of revolving coaches for six years before returning to the manager system. Although other clubs ridiculed this experiment, there was a definite trend toward excluding managers from such central matters as trade decisions, player discipline, and even strategic decisions.

Even with clipped wings the managers survived, especially those reputed to be good strategists or leaders. Such a mystique was still prized, and those who fit the mold were eagerly sought. In 1967 the Mets gave the Senators $100,000 and a pitcher to obtain Gil Hodges as their manager; the 1976 Pirates paid cash and catcher Manny Sanguillen for Chuck Tanner. Indeed, each of these golden fellows produced world titles. Few, though, were reputed geniuses. Most managers were hired to be fired; when sacked, they were paid off and sidelined until picked up by another club. This game of musical chairs sometimes became ludicrous, as in the early 1950s when three working managers drew double salaries, one from the current team and the other from the team that had sacked them. The presence of so many re-treaded managers also testified to the tentativeness of the job. Open season on managers began in earnest in that decade, with a record 58 replaced. Ninety were cashiered in the 1960s and 50 heads rolled in the 1970s.

Often the sacking of a manager defied reason. Two unfortunates were fired during spring training: owner Griffith dumped Sam Mele a year after his team lost a closely contested World Series and free-spending owner Autry dropped Bill Rigney in 1969 in an economic move. That same year Larry Shepard was fired by the Pirates for winning *only* 88 games, yet his successor, Danny Murtaugh, was later named Manager of the Year on the strength of 89 wins!

To further complicate matters, the managers discerned a growing tide of contempt directed their way; their jobs were described as "the most overrated . . . in professional sports." Indeed, expansion era owners seemed determined to upstage the managers by imposing themselves as decision makers. Most notorious of this crew was Finley, who routinely meddled. Later, Yankee owner George Steinbrenner's clashes with manager Billy Martin drew national attention, especially when Steinbrenner imposed a list of commandments which aimed at restraining the independent Martin. But Martin hung tough; he kept his independence in spite of six firings, two by Steinbrenner. Bloody but unbowed, Martin resurfaced in the late 1970s to work for Finley in baseball's Oakland snakepit. When the brash Martin lifted that sorry team to a flying start, he cautioned Finley to take no credit: "I've dealt with owners like that before. I didn't take it then, and I'm not gonna take it now. If it does happen, it's bye-bye Billy."[29] Luckily for Martin, Finley left baseball: no manager had ever satisfied this owner. During his five years with the A's, outfielder Rick Monday saw six skippers come and go, including hard-nosed "I" types like Dick Williams, several "We" counsellors like Al Dark, and a pair of "They"s, found in the aloof Bob Kennedy and the inept Luke Appling.

Second to prying owners, managerial authority suffered from the new breed of players. While admitting that expansion era players were able, managers generally regarded them as less dedicated and much tougher to discipline. Shielded by their Association, this affluent new breed resisted dogmatic authority, challenging training programs and demanding the right to ply their own regimens. Bench warmers demanded to know why they were seldom used and clubhouse lawyers criticized strategy and tactics.

By the 1970s all managers suffered eroding credibility and dugout treason. From sheltered retirement posts, ex-hard-line managers Jimmy Dykes and Billy Herman wondered how the moderns survived. In Dykes's opinion, the intolerables were opinionated players, interfering wives, and pampered specialists. After his ordeal with the 1966 Red Sox, Herman accused modern players of placing personal glory ahead of the team.[30]

As their lot worsened, manager Sparky Anderson complained in 1977 that only rookies responded to discipline and they, too, soon

Pennant-winning managers: Walter Alston of the Dodgers (*top left*); Alston's successor, Tom Lasorda (*top right*); Earl Weaver of the Orioles (*bottom left*); and Larry "Yogi" Berra of the Yankees and Mets (*bottom right*).

converted into pampered individualists. Martin joined Anderson in blaming the salary revolution for eroding his authority. Complaining that most of his players earned more than he, Martin urged owners to adopt pro football's policy of paying coaches higher salaries than players and of awarding to them long-term contracts. Meanwhile, Billy Rigney and Anderson complained that outside investments distracted players. Dealing with plutocrats was touchy—pushing a star too hard could cost a manager his job. This appeared to happen to Martin in his confrontation with Reggie Jackson; while tough, old Herman Franks quit in 1979, complaining of too many egotistical players.[31]

Some managers invoked team loyalty and "family" sentiments to survive this strange new atmosphere. A favorite of the "We" type, this stance required much patience and huge amounts of praise. When successful, noted Jim Bouton, the style produced nondescript managers like Ralph Houk, Ken Aspromonte, Tom Lasorda, Bill Virdon, and Whitey Herzog. In 1979 such types were crowding out authoritarians, but surviving bulwarks like Martin, Dick Williams, and Earl Weaver towered over all, their mystique establishing them as folk heroes.

While no expansion era manager matched Martin's electrifying style, none was more victorious than craggy-faced, stumpy Earl Weaver. Because he lacked major league playing experience, Weaver managed in the Oriole farm system where he suffered only one losing season. He nearly quit, however, because of quarrels with umpires. Called to manage the 1968 Orioles, he pulled a winning percentage over the next dozen seasons, ranking him behind Joe McCarthy and Frank Selee in effectiveness. Through 1979, his teams won six division titles, four American League pennants, and a world title. Only twice did he finish below second place.

His personality resembled that of his great rival Martin. Both were fierce umpire-baiters and both believed themselves vital forces for victory. Nothing was more important to Weaver than the duties of picking his squad, setting the lineup, and pitching rotation. He met his tasks ruthlessly, snarled at mental mistakes, and bullied malingerers. Sometimes his baiting led to fisticuffs, yet for all his haranguing his teams were generally harmonious. Weaver's players admired his winning ways and appreciated his scrappy battling on their behalf. Over the years, this notorious umpire-baiter was ejected from the diamond some sixty times. Umps feared him because he came on fuming, quoting chapter and verse from the rule book; once, he delighted a crowd by tearing a rule book in front of an ump. When ejected, he defended himself, saying, "You gotta get your beef in . . . or else they will walk all over you."[32]

Observers were impressed by Weaver's ability to continue winning, despite constant losses of stars to the re-entry drafts. The Orioles were hit hard when they refused to pay huge salaries, but the club's efficient farm system saved Weaver, who plugged the vacant ranks with able rookies. Many stepped right into key roles because of his 88-page manual on playing tactics, which was used by all Oriole farm clubs.

Frank Robinson, who both played and coached under Weaver, called the little man the "most complete manager" he knew because Weaver used all 25 of his men. Another admirer credited Weaver for keeping his pitching staff always trim and ready for the September stretch drive. Certainly one measure of a manager's greatness is the quantity and quality of his lieutenants. Like Lord Nelson's captains, who carried on "the Nelson touch," men who had coached under Weaver—Robinson, George Bamberger, and Jim Frey—were stamped with his influence and went on to become managers.

Hard-nosed managers like Weaver and Martin advanced because of their winning ways. Bouton thought that the ideal manager must embody an impossible mixture of virtues: Joe Schultz's salty vocabulary, Yogi Berra's luck, Charley Dressen's *chutzpah*, Durocher's cosmopolitanism, Herzog's skin pigmentation, Harry Walker's mouth, Houk's dream world, and Rocky Bridges's earnestness. Genius was missing, perhaps because Bouton agreed with statistician Walter Lapp's thesis that the vaunted managerial "book" was a hoax. According to Lapp's findings, a manager's stratagems—like choosing pitchers, and lineups, and making tactical moves—rarely effected the outcome of a game.[33]

Studies like Lapp's furnished ammunition for a manager's arch enemies, the writers. Writers often attacked managers by siding with players; they stirred trouble by uncovering shortcomings and thus speeded a manager's dismissal. Journalists exploited every rumble of Martin's Yankee ordeal; because Martin had a history of releasing steam and being fired for it, writers hung on his words and used them to attack. Even phlegmatic managers like Danny Ozark of the Phillies were targeted; a year-long campaign mounted by local writers ended with Ozark's 1979 dismissal. In 1972 badgering Chicago scribes hectored Durocher, finally wearing down owner Wrigley's stubborn insistence that no "reporter SOB" will "run my ballclub."[34]

The power of writers to destroy was dramatized by Martin's 1978 ordeal. Before the axe fell, New York papers rang with stories of Martin's troubles; but when Bob Lemon succeeded Martin, a providential New York newspaper strike blacked out all baseball news for the rest of the campaign. Thus, Lemon regrouped the team amidst blissful silence and drove it to a miracle triumph.

Finally, the umpires drew the cruelest cut of all. Long the managers' whipping boys, the umps turned tartars behind their Association, winning protection from harrying managers. No longer were umpires scapegoats, for the shoe was on the other foot. Umpire Tom Gorman freely taunted managers in his book, recalling his recent visit to the hospitalized Leo Durocher. "I came," said Gorman, "to see if you were dying."[35]

Baseball's Harried Robber Barons

Postwar era owners passed on, and as expansion swelled the number of fiefs to 26, a new cast of characters controlled the fortunes of baseball. Like the previous owners, the new lot posed as gentlemen sportsmen and claimed to be motivated by civic pride and devotion to the "national game." As always, their claim was spurious: most were wealthy businessmen, set on enhancing their outside interests and upgrading their social status through baseball affiliations.

In a land where millionaires numbered in the tens of thousands, social recognition needed the kind of publicity boost that club ownership provided. Certainly, the ego factor ranked higher than the profit motive; *Forbes* magazine in 1977 called baseball ownership the world's worst investment.[36] Although the profit potential was poor and the economics capricious, there was no proven instance of any expansion era owner going broke because of his baseball investment. Indeed, until 1976, the tax shelter advantage "changed the character of ownership . . . from real baseball people to real businessmen" by allowing an owner to depreciate the value of a player's contract 100 percent over five years.[37] Moreover, television income, cash bounties from expansion moves, subsidized ballparks, and the rising value of franchises were powerful lures. Thus, not until the late 1970s did the glittering fade, and burgeoning player salaries and inflated operating costs then dimmed the prospect. Nevertheless, whenever new franchises were floated or old ones placed on sale, buyers lined up to offer as much as $20 million and enter into the world's worst investment.

Like Marley's ghost, expansion era owners dragged a heavy chain of self-made problems. Perhaps the heaviest link was their excessive individualism. The robber baron mentality had each owner lording over his own manor and refusing to share income; the Lords of

Baseball functioned as "a loose confederation of carney operators with a small sprinkling of enlightened statesmen thrown in."[38]

Indeed, one would be hard put to find many statesman in this group. Generally, each owner went his own way, meeting with others semi-annually to vote on matters of general importance. Most of the policies were shaped by key committees; this allowed the zealous O'Malley to wield his inordinate influence.

As owners fought among themselves and blunderingly alienated fans with their carpetbaggery, they faced a fearful credibility problem. While patrons still accepted the notion of franchise ownership by rich men, critics boldly questioned the custom. Television sports impressario Roone Arledge thought baseball promotion so important that each owner should submit to governmental licensing, demonstrating his ability to run his franchise as a public trust. Journalist Mel Durslag faulted owners as dangerous dilettantes; because all benefited from public subsidies, Durslag recommended licensing, along with psychological tests, to weed out misfits.[39]

Such radical proposals needed time to sink into the public mind. Meanwhile, the 1970s owners defended themselves against charges of absenteeism, self-aggrandizement, stupidity, and poverty-pleading. Almost every owner refused to open their ledgers to the public; therefore, published statements of earnings and losses were suspect. Pieced together, annual attendance figures and data on radio and television income can give a rough picture of baseball's financial growth. By comparing overall ticket and media income of 1950 with that of 1977, one can see an astounding growth. In 1950 the 16 clubs earned an estimated $32.3 million, $5.3 million, or 16 percent, of which paid player salaries. By 1977 the 26 clubs took in $263 million from these sources, $50 million, or 19 percent, of which went for player salaries.

Of course, the value of franchises increased markedly. In 1961 the four newly admitted expansion clubs brought $2 million apiece; two new National franchises fetched $10 million each in 1969, while each of the new American franchises went for $5.6 million. Two more American franchises sold in 1977 for $6 million each. This new money was always distributed among the established clubs as a windfall profit. Accordingly, when put on the block, the established clubs fetched ever higher prices. In 1950 O'Malley landed the Dodgers for $4 million; Busch bought the Cards in 1953 for $3.75 million; John Fetzer got the 1956 Tigers for $5.5 million; and Finley obtained the A's for $3.9 million in 1961. Sale prices climbed much higher in the 1970s. In 1976 Stoneham sold his Giants for $8 million, the same price that the 1972 Indians had fetched. However, the 1977 Red Sox went for $16 million, and in 1979 the golden Mets were sold for $21.1 million.

Such frenzied market activity yielded a new lineup of owners. Some were dedicated to baseball though none matched the zeal of O'Malley, who made his fortune from the game. Much less successful, financially and artistically, were Horace Stoneham of the Giants and Cal Griffith of the Twins, both of whom depended on baseball income for their livelihoods. Other owners enjoyed outside wealth; this group included Philip Wrigley, Tom Yawkey, John Fetzer, Gene Autry, George Steinbrenner, John Galbreath, August Busch, Ruly Carpenter, Ted Turner, Mrs. Joan Payson, and Ray Kroc. Most of these persons were absentee owners who generally delegated authority to executives or minority stockholders.

Some clubs, like the Reds, Indians, Astros, and White Sox, came under syndicate ownership. More often than not, their investors were preoccupied by outside business interests. Other wealthy owners were more assertive; Steinbrenner, Finley, Edward B. Williams, Brad Corbett, Bud Selig, Ewing Kauffman, R. Howard Webster, and Charles Bronfman are a few from this group.

Finley was the most controversial and the most successful of the wealthy commanders. A continual meddler, he pushed his Oakland team to three world titles; but when attendance fell off and rising salaries strained, he fielded a poorly paid team of losers while still earning profits. Using ruthless cost-cutting practices, he succeeded in cutting expenses to the bone and drawing on his share of gate receipts from road games. He sold the club in 1980 for $12.7 million, leaving with $8 million more than he had originally paid. He walked out amidst damning farewells from fellow owners; Red Smith wryly suggested that he should have been sued for "practicing witchcraft." Still, Finley gave as good as he got, and as a robber baron, he was in a class by himself.

Indeed, all the owners of this age lived in a mist of controversy. Each seemed fated to bear the onus of the accumulated wrongdoings of past owners and, thus, the bright promise of public esteem turned to ashes. Having entered baseball as rich men, the owners

Opposite: Baseball club owners of the expansion era: (*top row*) Thomas Yawkey, Red Sox; Charles Finley, Oakland A's; Joan W. Payson, Mets; (*center row*) Edward B. Williams, Orioles; Gene Autry, Angels; George Steinbrenner, Yankees; (*bottom row*) Ray A. Kroc, Padres; Cal Griffith, Twins; Ted Turner, Braves.

naturally expected they would wield the same power and command the same prestige of their forbears. Instead, they found themselves embroiled in controversy with organized players and umpires, with angry fans from abandoned cities, and with critics who questioned their right to exist.

They could not win in the realm of franchise movements and league expansion. The first shifts stirred complaints, and when the Giants and Dodgers moved west, the ensuing storm of opposition soon forced expansion. The three expansion movements fueled the controversy, especially when several carpetbaggers jumped again. Later, damage suits filed by the cities of Milwaukee, Kansas City, and Seattle forced owners to return franchises to these abandoned sites. Ironically, these civic-minded poseurs were pressured to demonstrate their altruism. Every club but the Dodgers played in publicly financed stadiums by 1980, and even the Dodgers had accepted a public land grant. The loss of ancient powers was a bitter draught to swallow. Organized players assumed more rights and legal restrictions limited the owners' control over their clubs. It's no wonder that some like Busch screamed "socialism" and forecast an approaching doomsday for baseball.

Such bleatings, however, were hard to believe because as the owners lost their power, baseball experienced unprecedented prosperity. This economic rise was both a challenge and an opportunity for the owners. Should they choose to unite in a commonwealth organization and accept empowered players and umpires as legitimate constituencies, they would better themselves and baseball. On the other hand, should they cling to their usual ways, then Miller's prophesy that owners are "unnecessary" might come to pass.

Baseball's Tottering Czars

Among the crestfallen, the would-be baseball czars evoked the loudest mockery from critics. Like the fetish kings of West Africa who were thought to make the winds blow, the high Commissioner was believed to order the game of baseball. This magical myth was spun by Landis; few expansion era owners believed it, nor were they willing to put Humpty Dumpty together again.

The last thing the owners wanted was another czar. When Frick retired in 1965, his employers dazzled the public briefly with their promise of a Landis-like successor; they just as quickly reneged. For a few days newspapers reported that the search committee was considering national figures, like generals Curt Le May and Maxwell

Taylor and politicos Robert F. Kennedy and Richard Nixon, among 150 nominees. Later stories had the list whittled to twenty and one owner reportedly said, "We want a guy who won't be too big."

Indeed, this wish came true. At a secret November meeting, the owners elected retired Air Force Lieutenant General William Dole Eckert, a complete unknown to both baseball people and military historians. Upon hearing of Eckert's election, sportswriter Larry Fox quipped, "Omigod, they've hired the unknown soldier!"

In fact, it was General Le May who had first suggested "Spike" Eckert's name. The retired Lieutenant General had taken a consulting job with a contracting firm. When tapped for the commissionership, the 56-year-old Eckert allowed that his business background and administrative skills were his best qualifications. Cynics viewed the Eckert election as a strategic victory for kingmaker O'Malley; one grouser snarled that television ran any areas of baseball not ruled by O'Malley. That Eckert was a figurehead was apparent from the start as the owners soon named a four-man cabinet to handle Eckert's major chores of administration, public relations, records and finance, and liaison with the minor leagues.

This was just as well because Eckert was a bumbler. He knew, and learned, little about baseball, and he feared his masters. A baseball historian once told Eckert of his interest in owner carpetbaggery; Eckert blanched as he listened, then protested tremulously: "The owners are gentlemen—you can't call them carpetbaggers!"[40]

Such ineptide eventually undid any loyalties. Soon after his election, Eckert addressed a gathering of baseball men and writers: he began to deliver a speech intended for another group on another subject. Although one of his advisors rescued him, the damage was done.

Obviously, he was no czar; yet leadership was sorely needed in 1968, as falling attendance, inter-league wrangling, and strike threats swirled round baseball. Confronted with such trials, even a trimmer like Frick might have stirred, but Eckert could not even decide whether to cancel games out of respect to assassinated heroes King and Kennedy. Convinced at last that a do-nothing king was fatal, a dozen owners moved that fall for Eckert's ouster. They made their way firmly, and on the night of December 6, 1968, the defeated Eckert read his resignation. It was a brutal hatchet job; most owners avoided looking at him and few believed his pleading words: "In no sense was I fired." Club owners told the press that Eckert had resigned to facilitate a "bold and imaginative restructuring" of his office and that they reluctantly agreed to "the General's wishes." Whatever had happened, the unknown soldier, who "barely kept the chair warm," was out of baseball; his passing was eased by four years of severance pay, which he was still drawing when he died in 1971.

The masters now fought over his replacement. Two factions locked horns; O'Malley's claque touted Chub Feeney of the Giants while a "young Turk" faction backed Mike Burke of the Yankees. Suddenly the clamor ended and the unanimous choice was announced; Bowie Kuhn would serve as "Commissioner *pro tem.*"

The Princeton-educated Kuhn had practiced law with a New York firm that long had handled National League business. The tall, portly Kuhn loved baseball, though he was not athletic himself. Owlish-looking behind his glasses, he introduced himself to the press as "the unknown lawyer" and grandly promised "by persuasion and force of personality" to bring harmony and greater popularity to the game.

This was blowzy rhetoric even for a Princetonian; Kuhn was quickly brought to earth when he laid his master development plan for baseball before his masters. The Commissioner's study, completed at a cost of $100,000, urged that league presidents and minor league officials come under his control. Moreover, he requested authority to nominate league presidents, appoint committee chairmen, set the agenda for owners' meetings, and personally direct the all-powerful executive committee. His final shot suggested that he be re-elected by only a two-thirds vote.

That Kuhn spent so much money and came forward with a personal power play boggles the imagination. He certainly recognized the obvious—that the two league presidents labored at cross purposes, each trying to exalt his circuit over the other. In 1979 the American League harbored fourteen clubs to the National's twelve, while the latter still rejected the American's DH rule. The owners bristled at Kuhn's plan and resoundingly rejected it, accusing the Commissioner of wasting their money. Kuhn accepted the rebuff silently. Then, in 1970, he blundered again. Acting as the league's lawyer in the Flood case, Kuhn conceded that the reserve clause controversy might be thrashed out in labor negotiations—a concession that owners rightly feared would cost them dearly.

The Commissioner was criticized and benched as the owners' legal representative. This time, however, Kuhn's capacity for shedding criticism was impressive; asserting his dignity and optimism amidst all the strike calls and lawsuits of the turbulent 1970s, he airily ignored threats and accusations of his own impotence. Kuhn exulted

Baseball Commissioner William Eckert (*left*) lasted only three years in office; in 1969 he was succeeded by Bowie Kuhn (*right*).

over baseball's global expansion and moved his streamlined office to plush, new quarters. On the eve of his re-election, he crowed his accomplishments and made proposals for changing the game.

Kuhn needed this rosy optimism in 1975 when a "dump Bowie" movement was supported by players and a cabal of owners. A straw vote in July called for his ouster; it took a night of frenzied negotiations, led by O'Malley and Galbreath, to convince two hostiles to change their votes, thus securing Kuhn's re-election for another seven years at a salary of $150,000 per year. Certainly, this was a Pyrrhic victory; Kuhn was now described by journalists as O'Malley's tool, a stuffed shirt, a weak disciplinarian, a publicity hound, and the best commissioner since Eckert. Still, Kuhn dismissed "hateful criticisms" and prided himself on his dignity.[41]

Nevertheless, the commissioner's role as the defender of policies, set forth by the O'Malley-dominated Executive Committee, was exposed. Thus, when strikes loomed and salaries rose, Kuhn led the opposition. From 1976 onward, his annual "State of the Game Message" carried a doomsday song that blamed greedy players for driving owners to bankruptcy. Although some believed these diatribes, astute writers like Koppett and Smith skewered Kuhn's logic, while Marvin Miller routinely derided "Bowie's annual poor-mouth speech, which he feels impelled to give. . . ." Observing the skyrocketing prices of available franchises, Miller sneered: "Bowie would have us believe these buyers are lunatics."[42]

Kuhn was anathematized by the players. Some called him a disaster; the retired Hank Aaron snubbed his invitation to appear at a ceremony commemorating his homer mark, noting that the Commissioner had not bothered to attend the game when Aaron hit the record-setting homer. Pitcher-columnist Bill Lee regularly potted the "Bowie of Kuhn" and once donated a buck to his own "Oust Bowie" fund. While Kuhn seemingly heard none of this, the low state of the commissionership worried owners. They agreed to allow Kuhn the power to fine owners for tampering with players and he was unleashed against Finley, the leader of the "dump Bowie" movement.[43]

The Kuhn-Finley vendetta dated back to 1972, when Kuhn twice had fined Finley for misbehavior. Finley retaliated by trying to dump "the nation's idiot," but his abortive coup left him vulnerable. Kuhn later hit the straitened Finley in the wallet by negating his 1976 player sales. Finley's chance to make $3.5 million from the sales were voided, as Kuhn termed them "devastating to baseball's reputation." However, the Commissioner's actions ignored several precedents, and thus drew fire from writers, players, and some owners. Finley filed suit and the case came before U.S. District Court Judge Frank McGarr in Chicago. Kuhn argued that his "awesome" powers allowed him to act, and owners O'Malley and Kauffman backed him, stating that he had acted with the approval of the executive committee. McGarr stunned the baseball world by upholding Kuhn's owner-given power. The vindicated Kuhn exulted, "The McGarr decision is my most important victory." Later, he imposed a $400,000 cash ceiling on any future player sale.

Unfortunately for Kuhn, another court case went against him. Kuhn had fined Busch a mere $5,000 for tampering with a player's contract, but when Ted Turner did the same, he received both fine and suspension. Turner took umbrage at this piece of discrimination and sued. The case came before Judge Newell Edenfield of the U.S. District Court in Atlanta. Edenfield noted the inconsistency of the two punishments and got Kuhn to admit that he had hit Turner harder for doing his tampering at a cocktail party! Although Edenfield upheld Kuhn's action, he took a limited view of Kuhn's powers, stating that his ruling dissented from McGarr's interpretation of the commissioner's powers. This decision not only clipped Kuhn's wings, but it also portrayed him as the tool of a small ruling class of owners.

Kuhn's illusory powers were evidenced each time an owner negotiated labor pacts with players or umps and the Commissioner was "benched" in favor of hired negotiators like John Gaherin or Ray Grebey. He still, however, provoked the players. Kuhn rejected a shaving lotion firm's offer of $1,000 a game to the player with a season's longest hitting streak; his action again ignored a dozen precedents. When one umpire suspended a player for fifteen days, Kuhn did nothing.

In 1979 Kuhn ordered ex-player Willie Mays to sever his connection with the Mets because Mays held a public relations job with a gambling casino. However, he was forced to back down when a Canadian court quashed a player's drug possession charge and Kuhn tried to punish the player under "baseball law." Recourse to "baseball law" had been a favorite disciplinary ploy of Landis, but Kuhn's brandishings ran afoul of weightier civil rights laws. Even his baseball boosting fell apart when Kuhn engaged NFL Commissioner Pete Rozelle in a debate over which sport was the nation's favorite. When Kuhn returned All-Star game voting to fans, the patrons used easily available ballots to stuff votes for local favorites. The Commissioner felt let down by the fans; however, sportswriter Red Smith faulted him for subordinating the interests of ballpark fans to those of television watchers by his decision to allow nocturnal World Series games.

Thus, the woebegone heirs of Judge Landis sank to the status of owner puppets. Indeed, Kuhn's posturing raised the sane question: would baseball continue to abide a fetish king who no longer made the winds blow?

New Vistas for Baseball

Television Baseball

Television was the most important of all the forces that molded major league baseball in the expansion era. The one-eyed monster, controlled by "the powers of darkness," stirred the forces of baseball expansionism, unionism, and mercenariness. Television transformed the game into an entertainment and the ballplayers into celebrity-entertainers.

By bankrolling expansion and deluging the nation with broadcast games, the television industry enriched all major sports. Indeed its marriage with sports was a mutual blessing; as watching the video box became the nation's leading pleasure pastime, sports events became the most popular of televised programs.[1] This vogue was dramatically enhanced when Roone Arledge, the innovator of sports programming, turned the struggling American Broadcasting Corporation of the early 1960s into a leading television network.

The popularity of Arledge's "Wide World of Sports" show demonstrated the profit potential in televised athletics. Arledge determined to "take the game to the fan," annoying conservative baseball moguls, who held that television fans should view baseball as though stationed in the worst seats of a park. Undaunted, Arledge ordered film crews to find the best possible shooting angles and to take cameras and microphones into such former no-mans' lands as dugouts, bullpens, and locker rooms. It was a brilliant success; the mobile, hand-held cameras offered television fans a better view than the ballparkers enjoyed. Arledge pushed for more innovations: instant replays, isolation shots, and superimposed player names and statistical data. In 1965 he introduced Howard Cosell as ABC's chief sportscaster, and the grating, ever-critical commentator soon became the most hated and best-known of all sportscasters. Indeed, Arledge turned sports broadcasts into lavish entertainments, dramatically staged, colorfully described, and celebrity acted.

The marriage of sports and television was a lucrative one. The media producers gained from the match, with product advertisers paying as much as $765 a second to display their wares. Unfortunately, the producers soon demonstrated a desire to alter the sports they televised. By influencing schedule formats, league structures, club locations, game rhythms, and even the game rules, they changed the geography, economics, esthetics, and the spirit of the sport they sponsored.

Television beckoned baseball owners to new urban areas, spurred expansion moves, fostered postseason playoff campaigns, encouraged night games in prime time slots, demanded breaks in the action for commercials, and goaded officials to change game rules in order to maximize dramatic action.[2]

Professional golf in the 1960s had substituted medal or stroke competition for its time-honored match play format to accommodate television. Lured by attractive revenue, tournament officials scheduled four-day tourneys, timed to finish on Sunday afternoons, which pitted professionals in head to head competition for the top cash prize. The purists raged, but this format rewarded top golfers with purses worth more than $100,000 a year by 1969. Likewise, television reshaped football, basketball, hockey, and baseball schedules, so that more attention was focused on postseason playoff games, climaxed by a "world championship."

Although this new groom changed much of the maiden's estate, no tears should be spent for the happy bride. Certainly all constituencies of pro sports benefited from the union. Placed "on stage" by television cameras, players became national celebrities; many were able to command six-figure salaries by the late 1970s, while an elite few received more than one million dollars a year by 1980. The fans now had more games to see and the owners watched as television revenue dramatically enhanced the value of their franchises.

By 1979, in accordance with the league policy of sharing television revenue, each football club landed $5.2 million before the season's start. Each baseball club received only $1.8 million from national television deals, a result of baseball's policy of televising games locally. Profits derived from local television contracts ranged widely, from a Kansas City low of $500,000 to a maximum $6.3 million for the Montreal Expos. The Expos, Yankees, Phillies, White Sox, and Cubs were more fortunate than other clubs, being housed in lucrative media centers. Since their owners were unwilling to share such monies, the rift between the haves and have-nots grew wider in the baseball–television marriage.[3] Naturally, the have-nots wanted more of the national network income, now shared equally. Commissioner Eckert was hotly criticized in 1966 for netting only $9.75 million a year from NBC for television rights to the World Series, All-Star Game, and nineteen "Game of the Week" telecasts. Eckert was "benched," and the following year a special owners committee managed to negotiate a $50 million, three-year pact for the same events.

In 1971 Commissioner Kuhn negotiated a $70 million, four-year national network package that gave NBC the rights to televise these same events, plus ten Monday night games, six additional "Game of the Week" shows, and the postseason divisional playoffs. The have-not owners and the Players Association, enraged at having to give so much away and then profiting only one million per year more, called for Kuhn's ouster. Instead, Kuhn was saddled with a "marketing and broadcasting" specialist, who handled future rounds of negotiations. Thereby, a four-year pact negotiated in 1976 resulted in a $23.2 million annual pie to be divided among all clubs.

The constant squabbling over television income not only undermined the commissioners, but also incited bickering among the owner ranks. Opponents of the local television policy rightly complained that neither the national nor the local television incomes kept pace with inflationary spirals of the 1970s. The 1979 national income was 19% above that of 1971, while local income over the same period increased only 10%. For this reason, the combined television revenues of the best-endowed club generally lagged $1.5 million behind that of any pro football team.[4]

Baseball fans were also at the mercy of the bewildering quilt of local television policies. Some clubs generously televised one hundred or more games; others adopted a middle-of-the-road policy, televising half that number; while several clubs showed no home games at all. The gods kindly favored these last blunderers with opportunities for redemption; by 1979 owners cited potential profits from cable television. The prospect for profits was so dazzling here that one baseball executive proclaimed, "Pay TV is the future of baseball," while another predicted that baseball would no longer be a free television show. Tom Villante, baseball's broadcasting director, advised clubowners in 1981 that selling subscription baseball to the millions of homes being cabled would be the "purest form of expanding your box office," with teams likely to net $16 million a year in future television income.[5]

While the cable revolution promised to lessen baseball's heavy dependence on local television contracts, owners worried that television's "glamorizing" of the players would escalate salaries and turn these new celebrities into plutocrats. And why wouldn't it? Players could not be denied salaries commensurate with the highest paid television entertainers and news anchormen. By 1979 their soaring salaries had increased baseball's appeal.[6]

The threat of baseball becoming a form of media entertainment was ever-present. More weekend and prime time night games were scheduled to fit into the television format which, in turn, focused on rival sports to the detriment of baseball. Certainly television changed the character of all sports by forcing rule changes and disrupting the action. Football, soccer, and hockey games were interrupted by time-out calls to allow for commercial messages. Luckily, baseball suffered less, thanks to its natural between-innings breaks.

Commissioner Kuhn allowed nocturnal World Series matches and continually proposed inter-league games, with an eye towards matching regional rivals. Television producers meanwhile sought a shortened baseball season, limited mostly to weekend games. Such notions appealed to all profit-minded factors. The dangers to baseball were obvious to few; one baseball purist, owner Ray Kroc, warned: "Baseball has prostituted itself. We're making a mistake always going for more money."[7]

Television Phobia

Multi-millionaire Kroc was naive if he thought that his colleagues would place esthetic considerations ahead of cash. On the contrary, most owners only worried about the television threat after collecting their profits. Still, none could deny that the medium was a demanding provider.

To review thirty years of television baseball caused concern for many. Some critics of the 1970s thought the medium resembled a Trojan horse disgorging destructive elements. In addition to fomenting the salary revolution, restructuring the game, and pitting owners against each other, some officials feared that television might one day run major league baseball. Indeed, pessimists already saw baseball as an extended soap opera, one of television's stock products. Optimists compared this view to the old alarum raised against newspaper and radio coverage; not only did those extensions of baseball prove harmless, but both boosted attendance and cultivated new fans. This group believed that, given the chance, television would also boost baseball into more profitable uplands.

Any wise owner would consider what the medium had done to the majors, the minors, and the players. That it affected live attendance was evident, and with 162 games to play in a season, all clubs depended heavily on ballpark crowds. Although live attendance dipped alarmingly in the 1950s and 1960s, the totals after 1975 soared to new highs. To blame television for dipping attendance was simplistic, since the aging of parks, the Yankee domination, the hitting famines, and the competition from rival sports also took their toll. Television in fact deserved credit for encouraging new park construction, game expansion, and more exciting races.

Owner O'Malley allowed the fewest number of televised games and defended his policy by pointing to his club's all-time attendance records. At the same time, generous television purveyors like the Yankees, Red Sox, and Mets also enjoyed high attendance. Any conclusions drawn from this stand-off of policies were muddied by the Oakland A's, who won three world titles but did poorly both at the gate and in local television ratings. The debate over television's impact on attendance therefore continued, but a majority of observers credited the medium for converting viewers into paying fans. Writer Len Koppett disagreed; he argued that the attendance upsurge of the 1970s was disappointing, that with increasing population, new parks, and exciting races, the live attendance totals should have been much higher.[8]

Koppett's argument carried a whiff of the nostalgic bias for live gates that was rife among reporters. In past times this attitude had damned telegraph board and radio fans, yet each of these groups had been accepted. Why not now accept television fans as the latest species? To denounce this horde was foolish, especially after an estimated 75 million viewed the last games of the 1975 World Series. Still, one critic of the television viewers, writer Red Smith, demanded that live fans should see more than the television freeloaders. Smith sneered at these "second rate" followers and insisted that "at the gate is baseball's fate."[9]

There was substance to the charge that television producers stealthily molded baseball into a form of entertainment. An epidemic of television-phobia had swept the baseball world in 1964, following the purchase of 80 percent of the Yankee club by the giant Columbia Broadcasting System for $11 million. CBS defended this move as being one leg of an overall diversification scheme, which also saw the network acquire a profitable guitar manufacturing firm. That guitars outprofited Yankees hardly assuaged owner fears of this corporate giant; the resulting protests were loud and included threats of antitrust action by the U.S. Senate. By late fall the protests faded and the deal was quietly consummated. Given an opportunity to reject the sale, American League owners dutifully approved by an 8–2 vote.

Over that winter, CBS lawyers easily defended the purchase before a Senate committee. Not only were the firebrands silenced, but some senators suggested that other networks buy clubs and bring corporate money into baseball. However, it turned out that CBS had little effect on baseball's power balance. True, the corporation had played up the Yankees in 1964 and 1965, and in 1965 the Mets had complained when CBS bought their local television outlet, leaving them temporarily without coverage; but these were the worst deprivations. Owner Gene Autry proved that the giant could be managed, prodding CBS to approve Finley's move to Oakland by threatening to withdraw his own profitable business.

During its ten-year ownership stint, CBS appointed one of its many vice-presidents, dapper Mike Burke, to head the Yankees. Burke tried his hardest to refurbish the Yankee image. In 1967 he tidied up the deteriorating stadium and improved ushering and food service, while vainly vying for league powers outside. However, the Yankees were destined to fall. Fielding a loser was bad for the CBS corporate image, so, despite tax advantages, the network sought to unload its pig-in-a-poke. Upon selling the team for a mere $10 million in 1973, one CBS official explained: "I think that sports franchises really flourish better with people owning them." Burke was given the option of purchasing the team, but chose instead to oversee the sale.[10]

The departure of CBS didn't eliminate the television menace. Regional television moguls like Autry and Atlanta's Ted Turner remained; Turner challenged the networks and alarmed his colleagues by televising the Braves games on his far-reaching cable system. Meanwhile, little sentiment was spent over the wasting of the minor leagues, speeded along by national and local televising of major league games. By the mid 1970s nearly every independent operator was gone, leaving a shrunken network of leagues as wards of major league owners. Subsidized in a limited fashion, each minor league team received $5,000 a year from television income.

While television savaged the minors, it glorified major league players, changing them into plutocratic celebrities. The club owners would have been wise to take heed when writers first noticed the players "mugging" for the cameras. The roving eyes caught many offensive displays, including obscene finger gestures, spitting and brawls, and confrontations with umps that horrified lip readers. Some squeamish fans took umbrage at players with cheeks swollen by cuds of tobacco.

While fans eventually grew accustomed to such sights, players were modeled idols as never before, and their celebrity statures inspired higher salaries. The Association always had claimed a share of national television revenue; in 1971 Miller asked to be let in on network contract negotiations. Though this was denied, Miller never lost sight of the fact that television income exceeded that of ticket sales.

At the same time, however, the medium also exposed baseball's weakness as an entertainment. From a producer's perspective, baseball was not very photogenic; viewers got at best a knothole view of the game as played between pitcher and batter. Despite innovations like big and split screens, holographs, wide angle cameras, and instant replays, baseball coverage was still segmented. The two-dimensional screen was a major problem; without depth perception, viewers could not tell if a batted ball was foul or fair. One critic wondered if baseball was not "too artful, too individualistic . . . too gentle, to survive" the television screen.[11] Producers complained that baseball games made the television industry look bad!

By the 1970s a new controversy surrounded sportscasters, who were often accused of promoting the home teams and catering to product advertisers. Their between-innings commercial messages, pushing cigarettes, cars, gasoline, razors, beer, and other "masculine" products, substantiated complaints that television had tainted the game with sleazy commercialism.

A Babble of Baseball Announcers

Instead of attacking the advertisers who bankrolled baseball, critics of the new commercialism cited the enemy in the sportscasters. These highly visible wretches were easier prey. Their tormentors, riled by their cheerleading repartee, derided sportscasters as "gee-whiz, smiling toothed," home team touts, as cliché-riddened "cotton-mouth announcers," or as bland cowards, wary of controversial issues. Probably most of the group were guilty as charged; but as hirelings of the owners, most were obliged to emphasize the positive, to empower the players with god-like abilities, to enliven routine games with phoney dramatics, and to always eliminate the negative. These retreaded radio announcers most certainly knew how to hype.

Improved camera work allowed the fans to take offense at those announcers who used the windy, exaggerated style of the radio era. If they belabored the obvious or glossed over poor play or sportsmanship, bad weather, or weak attendance, they were now likely to be assaulted by a bevy of critics.

Although local sportscasters were more subservient to owners, national network crews also felt the increasing pressure. For failing to discuss the controversies of the 1971 All-Star Game, Curt Gowdy and Tony Kubek were stormed upon by critics. ABC coverage of the 1978 World Series was judged a "gruesome sight" by one Chicago writer, who accused camera crews of focusing more on fans than on players.[12]

Most sportscasters chose to call games as their bosses prescribed rather than as they saw them, and for failing to give fair and honest accounts, they risked investigation by the Federal Communications Commission. This 1973 threat resulted in no official policy and, in fact, it freed the network sportscasters. But locals continued to lick the hands that fed them, despite stinging reminders such as by Herbert Bayard Swope, who wisely noted that "Sometimes the events you cover carry their own excitement."

The sportscasters did not lack professional pride; rather, they feared losing their jobs. This fear was proven valid by a long list of independent-minded sportscasters who were sacked. Mel Allen and Red Barber were among this group; Barber still lamented that Yankee owners wanted a voice who could con listeners into thinking that the team still had Ruth and Gehrig.[13]

Surviving sportscasters caught the message that their dismissed brothers were easily replaced and speedily forgotten. Barber received only 250 letters of condolence following his ouster. Owner Finley underscored the lesson, "don't count on fickle fans," by regularly axing announcers. From 1961 to 1973 he dropped thirteen, including stars like Jim Woods and Harry Caray. The latter was aghast when Finley told him to change his famous "Holy Cow" exclamation to "Holy Mule," in deference to the owner's mascot. Bill Veeck redeemed Caray by bringing him to Chicago and complimented him with a bonus clause tied to attendance. Still, there were few charismatic Carays and even fewer redeeming Veecks; in a year-long reign of terror beginning in 1975, seventeen local television sportscasters were fired. Not all of the castoffs went quietly. Shown the gate by owner Short, Shelby Whitfield roasted his former boss in a sizzling exposé. The fired duo of Bob Prince and Nelson King joined street demonstrations staged by their Pittsburgh partisans.

While most of the fired sportscasters were locals, some national network announcers were threatened. When Tony Kubek commented on Steinbrenner's meddling, the owner demanded the sportscaster's head; when rebuffed, Steinbrenner threatened to fine any Yankee interviewed by Kubek. Some network sportscasters weren't as fortunate. Curt Gowdy was reportedly dropped by NBC in 1975 for being too versatile. Belonging to the vanishing species of all-around sports announcers, Gowdy was replaced by Joe Garagiola, who would concentrate only on baseball. One critic who mourned Gowdy's passing lamented, "The era of the man for all seasons is fading."[14]

That dirge ignored the mighty presence of Howard Cosell. Throughout the 1970s, the balding Cosell, star sportscaster for the ABC network, hosted for a variety of sports, including baseball games and the World Series. Whichever sport he worked, Cosell narrated with such animation that often he upstaged the game.

Sports fans either liked or hated this grating announcer from the Bronx. A 1978 opinion poll was conducted to find the most liked and disliked sportscasters: the results showed that Cosell led on both ends. Twenty percent of the voters thought he was the best; 39 percent judged him the worst. Yet Cosell's glory was that no other sportscaster was so well known.

Cosell entered the baseball world in 1953 when he incorporated

little league baseball in New York State and shortly thereafter narrated a little league feature program on ABC. His performances
won spot ABC assignments for Cosell, and in the early 1960s he
conducted pre- and postgame shows for the New York Mets. When
Roone Arledge became ABC sports director in 1965, he chose Cosell
to narrate several major sports shows, including baseball games, and
by 1969 Cosell's was a familiar voice on sports telecasts.

Many of his critics thought he could do no right, but his advocates,
including writers Smith, Twombly, and Povich, welcomed his critical
voice amidst a flock of toadies. They praised him for bringing "the
tenets of good journalism to TV." This "puncturer of heroes" and
defender against "pretentious boobery" refused to accept official
press releases. "If a game stinks, I say it stinks," he boasted, and
boldly directed his abrasive wit at officials and owners. Once, while
addressing a gathering of newspaper publishers, Cosell called sports
"the single most corrupting influence in American society." He often
seared his colleagues for glorifying "guttural illiterates who can hit
46 home runs in a season."[15]

Though more than a little vainglorious, Cosell rode out the decade as the nation's best-known sportscaster. He was assigned to
cover major events, including all the decisive baseball games. Many
local announcers resented Cosell's stature and owners grimaced at
his cutting descriptions. Kuhn once reportedly sought his ouster for
attacking the owners and downplaying the games, but Cosell was too
large a television celebrity to dislodge. Indeed, he fed on criticism
and grew stronger.

At times Red Smith and others took him to task for unsupported
criticisms; though Cosell never seemed to slip, no rival loomed, and
none dared imitate his audacious style. Cosell's genius was his real-
ization that fans wanted exciting games; if it wasn't there, Cosell
stirred his own fire.

Fearing that their own house announcers could not match Cosell,
the club owners began to hire ex-players as "color men" to perk up
telecasts. A lack of professional experience, however, produced crippling stage fright for some, while the earthy vocabulary of others
had the owners sitting on needles. The famous Dizzy Dean was
forced into retirement in 1965 by NBC and the network chose ex-
catcher Joe Garagiola to fill his place. Garagiola was witty and anec-
dotal, and he had experience working Yankee games. His sing-song
voice, striving always to make an event of an ordinary game, soon
annoyed some critics. One observer reported that Garagiola came to

work armed with a list of anecdotes to use no matter what transpired. In time NBC promoted him to the sports position on its popular "Today Show."

Although Garagiola was living proof for Cosell that ex-players made poor announcers, the major networks and local stations still scurried to sign them. Ex-Yankee Tony Kubek joined the NBC crew, and when Cosell covered World Series matches for ABC, he was partnered with active players like Tom Seaver and Reggie Jackson, who were hired as part-time experts.

As local stations took on more ex-players, the morale of professional announcers sank. The retired Barber complained that ex-players landed jobs "because television and the sponsors want big names. . . . I tell young people who want to get ahead . . . in sportscasting that the only way they can make it to the top is either hit .315 or win 20 games."[16] Barber also accused player-announcers of cheerleading and inept reporting, and ex-player Duke Snider admitted the same: "I had to learn a lot . . . I found myself hollering and cheering . . . as if I were a third-base coach, which I was just before I went into broadcasting. Now, I've learned to be a reporter."[17]

Fans in 1980 listened to more than twenty ex-players and even an ex-ump, Ron Luciano, behind microphones. Most were hired by the former teams and hoped to cash in on their popularity. Thus, the Phillies used Richie Ashburn and Tim McCarver; the Yankees, Phil Rizzuto; the Red Sox, Ken Harrelson and Rico Petrocelli; the Orioles, Brooks Robinson; the Reds, Joe Nuxhall; the Tigers, Al Kaline and George Kell; and the Indians, Herb Score. Only a few of the announcers were blacks, although Bill White teamed with Rizzuto, and Bob Gibson served briefly for the Cards. Interestingly, Wendell Smith, the crusading reporter who had fought in Jackie Robinson's behalf, was the first black announcer, hired by WGN-TV in Chicago.

While the fans enjoyed the player-announcers, few were heard outside of local environs. Ex-Yankee Jerry Coleman was one who gained a considerable reputation, mostly for his many malapropisms. He told fans of a pitcher with a Karl Marx hairdo; of a rookie who pitched the best game of 1979, "maybe even for that year"; of a relief pitcher "throwing up in the bullpen"; of an outfielder losing "a sun-blown pop up"; and of a runner "sliding into second with a standup double!"

One former star, Richie Ashburn, deserved a wider audience than his Philadelphia area. Not only was Ashburn a tough-minded reporter, but he also displayed Cosellian independence *without* the abrasiveness. When he saw a botched play or an ump's poor call, Ashburn reported it frankly and knowingly. Although baseball needed more announcers like him, Ashburn at least flavored Philadelphia.

Chipmunk Journalism

Like the baseball announcers, who endured both the fair and foul judgments of their audiences, baseball writers both delighted and affronted fans with their spritely reportorial style. These "chipmunks" emerged from the Pandora's box of television when writers probed the inside stories of the final scores. They churned out tales of authoritarianism, racism, sexism, unionism, drug abuse, and other issues.

Even veteran Dick Young admitted that the chipmunks now dominated baseball writing; he and other oldsters criticized the new breed's habits of straining for offbeat stories and emphasizing always some critical facet of the game.[18] Still, criticism or no, the new probing style swept the country, converting former "gee whiz" romantics like Wells Twombly along the way. Twombly took the readers to places where no television camera could go, thus gaining fame as an analyst. Upon his death in 1977, *Newsweek* named him as a pioneer of the new style, one who saw sport as "a minor event in a real world, a spectacle frequently entertaining, produced by businessmen."[19]

Of course, the new breed did more than skewer baseball's sleazy aspects. The best of the lot wrote fine descriptions, blending the flavor of the "Gee Whiz," "Aw Nuts," and "On the Button" schools into appealing stories. Assuming that their readers were sophisticated, the new breed probed the peripheral dimensions of baseball, moving into courtrooms, board rooms, locker rooms, and bedrooms. The readjustment was harrowing for some seasoned journalists; others changed almost without knowing it. Leonard Koppett now spent so much time in courts, interviewing lawyers, judges, player representatives and officials, that he became more an authority on baseball law and economics than a reporter of games.

Bob Lipsyte of the *New York Times* credited the reformist spirit of the 1960s with reshaping his approach; Lipsyte was convinced that the players' cause had much merit and that official propaganda was rampant. Likewise, Larry Merchant of the *New York Post* potted owners, criticized patronizing sportscasters, and ridiculed the phoney patriotic stance of baseball.

While the chipmunks reported the racial, ethnic, and sexual biases of others, they were equally advised to look at themselves. Many in the group resented female baseball writers, and especially their newly won access to locker rooms for postgame interviews. The players harried these reporters with sexist remarks and occasional naked confrontations, all to the amusement of the male journalists. However, backed by equal opportunity laws, these new scribes survived and in 1974 most sportswriting staffs had at least their token female writers.

Some writers also gibed at the few ex-convict players, including Ron LeFlore, whom they depicted as wearing Tiger "stripes" and leading the team "in what else?—stolen bases!" Although some abstained from such sick humor, many were accused of discriminating against black or Hispanic players.[20]

Furthermore, the chipmunks inordinately played up money and sex to perk reader interest. While disclosures of big salaries produced good stories, sexual allusions worked even better—though editors still tidied up obscenity-studded quotes. Most copy-editors of the daily newspapers routinely changed or "bleeped" words, but when doing magazine articles or ghosted biographies, writers freely quoted obscenities and gave full-bodied accounts of behavior.

At their worst, the chipmunks pandered to reader emotions and sometimes indulged in cruel humor; one described a batboy with prosthetic hands as unlikely to major in math "because he has no fingers to count on."[21] At their best, these freshmen turned out informative, funny articles that charmed readers. No longer on team payrolls, writers were warned by editors to refuse even offers of free drinks from teams. Although this sacrifice promoted objectivity, writer salaries lagged far behind those of the players. For $23,000 a year plus expenses, Peter Gammons of the *Boston Globe* annually covered 165 games, filled a weekly column, and supplied weekly feature stories.[22]

Luckily, murderous work schedules were meat and drink to zealous writers, who delighted in well-turned phrases. In one memorable outburst, Mike Barnicle of the *Boston Globe* poured out his rage at the fallen Red Sox: "What has 18 legs and no arms? What turns pale yellow in the fall? What folds easier than toilet paper? What baseball team can impersonate the main dish at a Thanksgiving Day dinner? The Red Sox could qualify for a group rate on a heart transplant . . . . "

Even more inspired was Jerry Flemmons's portrayal of the woebegone Texas Rangers. Flemmons uncorked his "Tales of the

Strangers" in the *Fort Worth Star Telegram*. In one hilarious episode, the team's 92-year-old club owner fell to his death after failing to release the ceremonial opening-day ball, which he tossed from the skytop mezzanine. Play was delayed twenty minutes to allow his 23-year-old wife to recover from her grief. In the following game, the Stranger pitcher nursed a no-hitter until felled by his allergies to the resin bag. From then on reliefer Tan Tham Hoang, the "Yangtze Clipper," allowed 26 runs![23]

Flemmons was indeed one of a kind, but other chipmunks were unique, too. So individualistic were expansion era writers that not many readers and critics saw their mass as a dangerous cultic threat. Still, several mossback writers characterized chipmunks as messenger boys who haunted locker rooms searching for inane quotes. Octogenarian Ed Kemp thought they were idiots: "I'll be a *SOB* if I know what they're thinking about. They're not writing sports. They're telling the manager who to hire, who to fire, how to coach, who to play."[24]

Dick Young seconded such criticisms. This veteran baseball journalist for the *New York Daily News* and weekly columnist for *The Sporting News* made his mark on the sports world by catering to the conservative tastes of his readers. While Young's bullying style angered players and many of his own colleagues, the writer continued his attacks on long-haired players, militant blacks, war protesters, high salaries, and unions. In 1977 Young stirred a fiery debate over Mets pitcher Tom Seaver's salary demands by supporting director Grant's refusal to yield and by castigating the pitcher in print. When New York *Post* writer Maury Allen accused Young of driving Seaver out of town and suggested that Young was motivated by the presence of a son-in-law in the Mets office, Young bit back hard and a name-calling match ensued. The testy Young's popularity fed on such controversy and his labors earned for him a Spink Award in 1978 and a place alongside 25 writers enshrined in the Hall of Fame.

With hard-shell tortoises like Young around to uphold conservative standards, any danger that a single style of baseball writing would become dominant was remote. Although this breed of writers appeared more independent than any other, writers remained clustered together under the Baseball Writers Association, the recognized custodian of all major league pressboxes. Access to the boxes was a privilege enjoyed only by card-carrying Association members.

Baseball magazine assayed the ten best-known and most influential contemporary baseball writers thus: Dick Young, Phil Pepe, and Jack Lang of the *New York Daily News;* Murray Chass of the *New York Times;* Pete Gammons of the *Boston Globe;* Jerome Holtzman of the Chicago *Sun-Times;* Bob Broeg of the *St. Louis Post-Dispatch;* Joe Falls of the *Detroit News;* Hal Bock of the Associated Press; and Milt Richman of United Press International. All were full-time baseball writers (which explains the absence of men like Red Smith or Len Koppett from the list), all wrote syndicated columns or contributed weekly columns to *The Sporting News,* and most authored popular histories and player biographies.[25] These men displayed their widely dissimilar interests and styles through their printed matter. Broeg produced nostalgic columns and historical sketches; Holtzman published annual histories; Richman, Young, and Bock specialized in gossipy scoops; and Chass penned interpretive articles on baseball's legal, labor, political, and financial fronts. Fred Lieb was missing from the list. A green vine who insisted on growing, Lieb kept himself from falling into the "old sports writer" rut. This stickler for facts authored eighteen books, mostly team biographies, but he also drafted an exceptional ghosted biography of Judge Landis. His autobiography celebrated the uniqueness of each passing decade in baseball. As a seven-decade writer, Lieb refused to fault modern players, finding them as tough, efficient, and earthy as old-timers, but more sophisticated and freer to be themselves. He would not toady to owners and could cite no altruistic owner at any time. Lieb maintained his wonderful capacity for absorbing change and his sharp eye for noting the timeless qualities of American baseball.[26]

Meanwhile, writers continued to probe freely, although forays into player lives, team morale, owner policies, and managerial tactics now meant paying the piper. Thus, many players refused interviews, including pitcher Steve Carlton who held out for several years. Such boycotts hurt writers but injured them less than the occasional physical assaults. Journalist Harold Kaese recounted in 1973 a string of incidents which dated back to 1946 and encompassed assaults, insults, and chilling practical jokes.[27] Writers serving as official scorers also met abuse, as controversies caused by their rulings on hits and errors grew so severe that leading papers in five cities ordered their scribes off the jobs. As a result, officials seriously considered using trained umpires to handle scoring.

On another front the all-knowledgeable fans faulted the writers' choices of Hall of Fame entrants and regularly criticized journalist selections for MVP and Cy Young winners and Rookie of the Year awardees. The writer-voters were rendered vulnerable by the vast outpouring of published baseball statistics. *Baseball Encyclopedia* became a powerful weapon in aiding the fans' game of second-guessing writers. Even more bothersome though were the statisticians, whose nit-picking grated on writers. The current tribe of "stat. freaks" proposed the installation of computer terminals in each park, and some, brazenly ignoring historical canons, proposed the standardization of all baseball records in terms of the present.[28]

The baseball writers did little to blunt these excesses, but, rather, continued to print lengthy columns of statistics. When the sportscasters successfully employed these numbers to enhance their own babble, the embittered writers finally longed for the old days when the scribes had ruled the world of baseball information. To further worsen matters, an increasing number of alien writers challenged these veterans for their worn turf.

Literary Baseball

The popular writers may have wondered where the literary artisans came from, but the new crew rode in on a century-long trend. In past years, fiction writers like Ring Lardner, Thomas Wolfe, James T. Farrell, and James Thurber had engaged baseball themes; Bill Veeck had drawn upon Thurber's short story, "You Could Look It Up," for his caper of playing midget Eddie Gaedel.

Although Veeck's ploy was an abortive one-night stand, other writers could not be stayed from dipping into baseball. Story-tellers of the 1950s and onward produced a catch-bag of works, realistic and farcical, fantastic, and even pornographic. The realistic heritage, passed on by Lardner, Wolfe, and Farrell, inspired newcomers Mark Harris, Eliot Asinof, and Martin Quigley. In 1953 Harris published *The Southpaw*, the first of a trilogy based on the life of pitcher Henry Wiggin. Harris's knowledge of the major league game was sound; his presentation, vividly realistic. The much admired second volume of the trilogy, *Bang the Drum Slowly*, depicted the last hurrah of a third string catcher who was dying of Hodgkin's disease.

Also included in this class of realistic fiction is Quigley's *Today's Game* and Asinof's *Man on Spikes*. Quigley's novel offered a candid view of managerial tactics and strategy. Ex-minor leaguer Asinof drew on personal experience in describing the laborious life of a player who never made it to the "bigs."

At the same time the vogue of light entertainment fiction was given life in the works of H. Allen Smith, John Craig, and James F. Donohue. Smith's *Rhubarb*, a sexy farce about a cat who inherited a ball club, was a big success when published in 1946. Later, Craig's fast-moving piece, *All G.O.D.'s Children* (1975), described the life of the first female major leaguer, with plenty of sex and a parody of owner Finley supplied. *Spitballs and Holy Water* (1977), Donohue's offering, was an artful tale of magic and nostalgia, centered about a black baseball team and its guru nun.

Symbolic fiction writers used similar techniques of magic and myth to explore the tragedies of the human condition and other serious issues. Works by novelists Bernard Malamud, Philip Roth, and Robert Coover shone brightly among this group. In his much acclaimed novel, *The Natural* (1952), Malamud parodied the leading myths of baseball by following the career of Bunyanesque hero, Roy Hobbs. Blessed with his magic bat, "Wonderboy," Hobbs rose to great heights, only to fall by yielding to earthy pleasures. Roth also used baseball themes and parody to air weighty issues in *The Great American Novel* (1973). Its humorous story recounted sportswriter Smitty's odyssey with a depression era ball team and its mercurial star pitcher, Gil Gamesh—a Babylonian-American!

Academicians were impressed by Coover's *The Universal Baseball Association, J. Henry Waugh, Prop* (1968). This story used baseball as an analogue to the Book of Job's eternal message that God's logic is unfathomable and that God has problems of His own. Coover's protagonist, J. H. Waugh (JHWH), invents a table baseball game played with dice and complete with teams, records, and a superstar pitcher, Damon Rutherford. Creator Waugh's dilemma is godlike, raising, for example, the question of what a creator must do when his own laws demand his hero's death. By raising such issues, Coover excited scholarly attention, while ordinary fans accepted the work as a rattling good story.[29]

Naturally, essayists found inspiration in baseball. Among the best of these published volumes, Angell's *The Summer Game* (1973) still serves as the bible of baseball. This book attracted great attention for its sensitive probings into baseball's esthetic, ritualistic, and tradition-supporting significance. Angell's later effort, *Five Seasons: A Baseball Companion* (1977), resembled an anthropologist's report of the major league scene from 1972 to 1976. Angell's descriptions paint a mural of teams and players, technological advances, and rule changes and their effects.

Likewise, Roger Kahn's *Boys of Summer* (1972) rendered a sensitive account of the Dodger players of the 1950s and recounted the grim afterlives that several endured in adapting to postbaseball exigencies.

While writers like Angell and Kahn were sideline observers, essayist George Plimpton posed as a participant in an attempt to give his readers a staged view of professional athletics. Plimpton's approach called for him to perform briefly; he pitched against major league batters, boxed with a heavyweight, fought a bull, battled a professional tennis ace, and quarterbacked a pro football team. The gangling Plimpton, a former high school pitcher, hurled in an exhibition inning against major league stars. After getting one batter out, he was brutally shelled. From an inning's work, he told the exhausting tale of pitching in his book, *Out of My League.*[30]

One magazine of the era continually attempted to probe the inner dimensions of pro sports with literary èlan. The first issue of *Sports Illustrated* took a swipe at sportswriters upon stating that their intention was to cover the sports without "cant or clichés." Still, readership was slow in building, and in the first year publisher Henry Luce, the *Time* magazine magnate, lost $6 million. In a narrow field where only a time-honored and baseball-dedicated journal like *The Sporting News* survived, this headier vehicle seemed doomed. Snobbish critics ridiculed the effort; Ivy League parodists had a field day with its *Sports Illiterate* spoof, while *Playboy* parodied the weekly by introducing a nude female reporter, Jacqueline Strop.

Not until the 1960s did the strange child make money, and by 1969 this solid teenager boasted a circulation of 2 million. The force of its penetrating, intelligent essays—covering not only sporting events but also sports-related movies and books, environmental issues, recreation, travel, and sedentary games—had finally been felt and its worth appreciated.

Sports Illustrated celebrated its 25th anniversary in 1979, having outlasted its mighty stablemate *Life* magazine. To baseball historians *Sports Illustrated* is a valuable tool, as it monitors sports seasons clearly and critically, regularly features stars, and grapples with important current issues. That same year *Newsweek*, *Time*'s rival, launched *Inside Sports*. Its editor admitted that readership would probably be *Sports Illustrated* devotees and, sadly, the weekly indeed suffered a rocky debut.

Magazines devoted completely to baseball rode the crest of the game's popularity boom. The monthly *Baseball Digest*, launched in 1942, endlessly reprinted articles from baseball writers. Other peri-

odicals appeared in the 1970s, including the *Baseball Quarterly* and
the reborn monthly, *Baseball* magazine.

Baseball writers found free-lancing opportunities in these journals; by the 1970s writers ghosted and co-authored team histories,
player biographies, and "autobiographies." Publishers no longer
viewed baseball books as poor risks, and so a torrent of these books
poured down on the public. The popular biography enterprise was
given a big boost when writers were freed to cover their subjects
without obtaining approval. This version of press freedom followed
a 1976 U.S. Supreme Court decision in which the judges retracted a
lower court's $10,000 damages award to pitcher Warren Spahn, who
had protested an unauthorized biography. The court upheld the
author's rights, ruling that as long as a book was in the public interest and was written without reckless disregard for truth, a state's
right-to-privacy laws could not be used to bar its publication. The
decision muffled similar suits by Don Drysdale, Hank Aaron, and Ed
Mathews.[31]

However, baseball scribes now faced competition from scholarly
writers who were moving into sports studies. Sportswriters resented
these smug "poachers," some of whom dismissed journalists as myth
mongers, whose works at best supplied some useful data. Thus, academics and baseball scribes locked horns in confrontation, with hostilities usually taking the civilized form of a studious ignorance of
each other's works or a blasting of them in published reviews.

Several blessed peacemakers sought to heal the breach. Lee Allen,
a former Cincinnati scribe who became historian of Baseball's Hall
of Fame, was one to welcome and support the academics. The scholarly Allen gave students access to his huge collection of statistics and
inspired academics with his book *The Hot Stove League*.

The many works of university scholars in time enriched baseball
literature. Some colleges and universities offered courses in the
American baseball culture, and professional organizations like the
Popular Culture Association and the North American Society for
Sports History devoted regular sections to baseball studies at their
annual meetings. Among the torrent of academic works were doz-
ens of doctoral dissertations, including those of historians Steven
Riess, Richard Crepeau, and Larry Fielding. These academic baseball historians followed a course earlier plotted by Harold Seymour,
whose dissertation was later published as two volumes of major
league history.

However, because baseball is so much a part of any American's experience, no single writer nor discipline can claim the field. The possibilities for varying insights are limitless; this was shown in 1966 when economist Larry Ritter produced a valuable work engendered from his taped interviews of turn-of-the-century players. Ritter's *The Glory of Their Times* spawned an excellent documentary film and inspired others, like Don Honig and Larry Gerlach, who published invaluable interviews with players, managers, and umpires.

One senses, however, a jealous note in baseball writer Bob Lipsyte's warning against the over-intellectualizing of baseball. Lipsyte wanted baseball to remain "a kind of comfort station" in the world,[32] but few academics were warned off. By 1974 a vanguard of social scientists—psychologists, anthropologists, sociologists, political scientists, and economists—had published inquiries into baseball.

English professors were likewise stirred to action. A compilation by Professor Kevin Kerrane with Richard Grossinger, entitled *Baseball I Gave You All The Best Years of My Life*, offers a sampling of their works. Amateurs joined the movement, too. The Society for American Baseball Research was formed, and by 1980 their members numbered over 1,000. This sturdy club boasted a journal, regularly scheduled meetings, and a variety of useful monographs published on baseball subjects. In time, SABR researchers also annoyed baseball writers by second-guessing the selections for Hall of Fame memberships. Nor did sportswriters take kindly to John Holway's studied accusations that they ignored the records of the great black leagues and their players.

America's torrid love affair with baseball benefited from one other member of the mass media. Baseball movies had long been regarded by producers as box office poison. The belief was generally valid for prewar films, with the possible exception of *The Pride of the Yankees*. Several better-than-average baseball films were released in the 1970s, including *Bang the Drum Slowly, Bad News Bears, It Happens Every Spring, Angels in the Outfield,* and *The Bingo Long Traveling All-Stars and Motor Kings*. Also, filmed biographies like those recalling the lives of Jackie Robinson, Jim Piersall, Roberto Clemente, and Ron LeFlore were widely applauded. Unfortunately, such films were still modest money makers.

The same profitless reputation followed legitimate theatre's use of baseball themes. Except for *Damn Yankees*, a Broadway musical adaptation of Douglas Wallop's satire, *The Year the Yankees Lost the Pennant*, none of these productions fared well. However, Jonathan Reynolds's *Yanks 3 Detroit 0 Top of the Seventh*, a play that blended satire and pathos, was a critical and artistic success at New York's American Palace Theatre in the summer of 1975.

Baseball inspired other media as well. Artists now used baseball themes in painting, sculpture, and photo art. The latest computer technology titillated fans with entertaining simulations of games or all-star matchups. Computerized scoreboards at the ballparks posted current statistics, simulated pictures of players, and offered visual entertainments with musical accompaniments.[33]

Such vast enthusiasm for major league baseball remains awesome. Knowing that the game is so strongly entrenched in the minds and hearts of Americans emboldened those who guided the way into the 1980s. Knotty issues like salary escalation, league expansion, unionism, and television's encroachment did threaten stability and demand solutions; however, baseball's manifest popularity justified optimism. Hence, like the ten wise virgins of the Bible, baseball constituencies moved confidently forward, though caution called for keeping lamp wicks well trimmed.

Or, Striking Out in the 'Eighties?

The Gathering Storm

When the 1980s arrived, optimistic calls for greater popularity for major league baseball were muffled by rancorous threats. The bells of New Year's Day sounded another match of strength, owners against players. This test promised to be a donnybrook, one that might dwarf the 1972 strike and perhaps rival the big brawl of 1890.

At issue was the new labor contract, set to replace the fourth basic agreement, which expired on December 31, 1979. The defunct contract stuck in the owners' craws like a fish-hook. The re-entry draft concession was the major irritant because it undercut the reserve clause, freed players to move, and made plutocrats of many stars. As if this wasn't painful enough, those owners who lost valuable players in re-entry drafts fumed at receiving untried amateur prospects in return. The owners wished to reverse that situation, and would have been happier yet if a smashing blow could have been leveled at the Players Association by forcing the issue.

United at last by this principle of aggressive action, the owners moved toward a showdown in 1980. Tough-minded Ray Grebey handled negotiations and worked to force players to relinquish some of their re-entry rights. The owners obeyed a strict gag rule cast over war plan discussions with outsiders; a careless mouth would be penalized by a $500,000 fine.[1]

No new basic agreement had been reached by spring. Grebey refused to budge on the stern demand that the re-entry draft procedure be modified to force a club which signed a premier player (defined as one from the top 50% of performers) to compensate the yielding club by sending one of its own major or top minor league players in return. Here then was the central issue—the owners demanded that players "give back" a concession previously granted and legally approved. Marvin Miller responded with equal resolve, refusing to concede. As the issues stalled the negotiations, players seethed at the prospect of playing without a contract.

In early March the players voted 967–1 to strike if an acceptable agreement wasn't reached by opening day. On April 1 they underlined this threat by voting to boycott the last week of spring training, and they sent a specific warning to the owners—if a satisfactory agreement wasn't reached within six weeks, a strike would begin on May 23. The players extended one compromise: the negotiators were to continue in their attempts to settle less controversial contract matters, like increasing the pension fund, raising the minimum salary, and redefining arbitration procedures. With these matters settled and the compensation issue cooling on a back burner, perhaps further study would yield a peaceful solution. The negotiators indeed quickly settled all other issues; among these accounts, the owners' pension payment climbed to $15.5 million annually and the minimum salary was slated to rise to $35,000 by 1984.

The owners stood firm over the compensation issue, stonewalling right up to the deadline. Federal Mediator Ken Moffett kept both sides talking, but despaired of reaching agreement. The owners were seemingly testing the solidarity of the players, hoping that their brinksmanship strategy would turn greater player plutocrats against lessers, thus undercutting Miller's strong position.

Ultimately they were disappointed. Not only did the players hold firm, but upon finishing the games of May 22, most began packing suitcases and booking transportation home. It appeared that the 13 games scheduled for May 23 would be canceled and the rest of the calendar suspended. Anxious negotiators talked until the early morning hours of May 23. A small breach in owner ranks sustained their hopes; newcomers Edward Bennett Williams of the Orioles and John McMullen of the Astros, both critical of Grebey's all-or-nothing tactics, persuaded hardliners to table the issue. They proposed that a committee of players and GMs meet to study the compensation issue, and then report back, jointly or singly, by January 1, 1981. Any recommendations would become part of the new basic agreement; if no solution was reached, the owners could implement their own plan a month later. If the players rejected this *diktat*, they could announce their intent to strike by March 1,1981.

This compromise salvaged the 1980 season. Commissioner Kuhn called it a miracle. Most fans preferred news of an armistice to the gloomy strike headlines of sports pages, which had damaged attendance (though only slightly) and overshadowed the close races shaping up in both leagues. Obviously, however, some fans had been spooked and the wise adversaries should have heeded this sign.[2]

Miracle in Philadelphia

Baseball men were neither the first nor the last mortals to ignore omens, and the storm that passed by baseball was not the only fateful sign. Indeed, as the two sides muddled toward their shaky truce, Bill Veeck bade the game farewell. Worn by age, infirmities, and financial woes, this baseball giant left a lonesome void and was fittingly mourned. The same was not true for Charley Finley; his passing evoked gibes of good riddance as he sold his A's to a trouser manufacturer. Still, in his erratic way, Finley was also an innovative force.

Small omens like these passings were understandably ignored, but more dramatic signs appeared as the season unfolded. What they foretold was a drastic change in the power balance. This was the year that downtrodden teams turned tartars, bringing championship glory to pennant-starved fans.

There was every reason to suppose that the swashbuckling Pirates would continue their winning ways in the 1980 season. Although pitcher Bruce Kison and infielder Rennie Stennett had been lost in the latest re-entry draft, their otherwise powerful team was intact. Manager Chuck Tanner had received a five-year contract for landing the 1979 world title, a tribute unprecedented in National League history. With sluggers like Stargell and Parker, steady hitters like Madlock, speedsters like Moreno, and ace reliefer Tekulve in fold, the team was touted to win again.

Only the Expos in the Eastern National seemed to bar the way. Behind Dick Williams, 1979's Manager of the Year, the Expos mounted a well-balanced offense and the league-leading defense. Although slugger Tony Perez, infielder Dave Cash, and pitcher Rudy May were claimed by the re-entry draft, the same route had lured outfielder Rowland Office and pitcher Fred Norman to Montreal. Ex-Tiger Ron LeFlore contributed his base-stealing acumen, and the outfield of Andre Dawson and Ellis Valentine was formidable, while the infield of Warren Cromartie, Chris Spier, Rod Scott, and slugger Larry Parrish was just as tough. Catcher Gary Carter was the league's best—an effective handler of starting pitchers like Steve Rogers and Scott Sanderson and relievers like old Woody Fryman.

South of Montreal, the league's highest salaried team seemed to be aging. The Phillies, now managed by Dallas Green, were a standpat team of veterans, augmented by rookies like pitcher Bob Walk and catcher Keith Moreland. Because owner Carpenter spent heavily to acquire Pete Rose in the 1978 re-entry draft, he passed on the most recent round. Thus, the Phils would return with the seasoned corps of Pete Rose, Manny Trillo, Larry Bowa, and Mike Schmidt to the infield. Veterans Maddox, McBride, and Luzinski roamed the outfield, though youngsters Lonnie Smith and Greg Gross and veteran Del Unser were summoned to cover for Luzinski's batting decline. Catcher Boone was an adequate handler of capable starters like Steve Carlton and Dick Ruthven, and when other starters needed help (which was often), Tug McGraw and Ron Reed headed a strong bullpen crew.

Many observers were surprised when the Eastern race developed into a grim war of attrition. The Expos led most of the way, but the Pirates, handicapped by injuries, suspensions, and poor pitching, still hung close. At times they seemed about to take charge. They thrashed the Phils in a mid-August doubleheader and were only 4½ games behind one month later. Still, this threatened charge never materialized, and they finished third, eight games off the pace.

The Phillies's double loss in Pittsburgh inspired a monumental tirade by the hot-tempered team manager. Not even locked clubhouse doors could muffle Green's chords. One *Inquirer* reporter taped the "Pittsburgh Address" and judged it the most "screeching, screaming, vulgar" blast he ever heard. The players also listened, though in stunned anger. They reacted by beating the Cubs two out of three games in Chicago and then dashed Met hopes by thrashing them five times. Six games behind at the time of Green's speech, they won 21 of their next 28 road games. As the season waned in late September, they led by half a game; then the Expos came to town and seized the lead, downing the Phils in two of three.

Green's men rebounded, socking the Cubs four times. Next they traveled to Montreal for the three games which would decide the pennant. With McGraw pitching stoutly in relief, the Phillies clinched a tie by winning 2–1. Then, on a rain-soaked field, the jittery Phils shook off five errors and used Schmidt's homer with Rose on base in the 11th to take the divisional title with a 6–4 victory.

Pitching was the Philadelphia story. Their staff was the best in the East; Carlton's 24–9 (2.34 ERA and 286 strike-outs) earned the 35-year-old veteran another Cy Young Award, and starters Ruthven (16–10) and Walk (11–7) lent solid support. Rookie Marty Bystrom's late season 5–0 performance finally carried the day.

The Phils's .270 batting ranked second to the Cardinals, whose .275 mark failed to compensate for horrendous pitching and held them 17 games back. Leading the team's offensive attack was Schmidt, whose league-leading 48 homers and 121 RBIs on a .286 average produced 17 game-winning hits. His one-man war easily earned MVP honors. This newly matured infielder was now a straight-away hitter and appeared more relaxed at his tight third base. Among his mates, the quintet of McBride, Trillo, Rose, Smith, and Moreland accounted for nearly 50 game-winning hits.

The Expos suffered another agonizing defeat, their losing road record overriding a home field domination at Olympic Stadium. The team was so injury-cursed that Williams only managed to play his best men 23 times. The crusher came later in the season when LeFlore fractured his wrist; his 91 steals at that time led the majors.

Though the Eastern race was exciting, the Western was closer. The leading division contenders, the Astros, Dodgers, and Reds, waged a bitter three-way race that ended with only a 3½ game separation.

Winless since joining the league in 1962, the 1979 Astros finished a close second to the Reds. They now turned to the re-entry draft for added strength and outbid all others for fire-balling Nolan Ryan, who signed a guaranteed three-year contract, making him baseball's first million-dollar-per-year man. Ironically, this coveted starter owned a mediocre win-loss record, but as a stellar gate attraction, he proved himself valuable to the 1980 Astros. Ryan joined an already strong pitching staff that included towering J.R. Richard, who was equally as fast as his new mate, Ken Forsch, knuckle-balling Joe Niekro, and ailing Vern Ruhle, whose recent back surgery made him a doubtful factor. Supporting these starters was a capable relief crew headed by Joe Sambito, Frank LeCorte, and Dave Smith.

Offensively, manager Bill Virdon's team was suspect. Their 1979 homer output was a laughable 49. Virdon resorted to collecting runs by the old-fashioned hit-run and base stealing method. This was nerve-wracking baseball, but the Astros were tough in their enclosed Astrodome. Outfielders Terry Puhl, Jose Cruz, and Cesar Cedeno were consistent hitters, as was infielder Enos Cabell, but Virdon juggled the rest of the infield and played four first basemen.

Meanwhile, the Reds lost Pete Rose and Joe Morgan to higher bidders. Fortunately, the club's player development program produced good youngsters to bolster veterans like Ken Griffey, George Foster, Dave Concepcion, Dan Driessen, and Tom Seaver. In 1979 these vets came from ten games behind in September to overtake the Astros; but pitching still plagued, and this year fifteen assorted hurlers allowed a generous 3.85 ERA, neutralizing the team's .262 batting.

The Dodgers were somewhat luckier, having decided this year to use the re-entry draft. They gained a pair of solid pitchers in Dave Goltz and reliefer Don Stanhouse and bought outfield strength in Jay Johnstone. Goltz and Stanhouse joined a versatile pitching staff that included Don Sutton, Burt Hooton, Charley Hough, Doug Rau, Terry Foster, Bob Welch, Jerry Reuss, and 1979's Rookie of the Year, Rick Sutcliffe. Catchers Joe Ferguson and Steve Yeager were proven veterans, and no infield in baseball history played together longer than Steve Garvey, Dan Lopes, Bill Russell, and Ron Cey. Likewise, the outfield of Reggie Smith, Rick Monday, and Dusty Baker was battle-tested and backed by newcomers Pedro Guerrero, Ron Roenicke, and Johnstone.

This veteran team made the Western race a three-way fight, with the Astros nursing a shaky lead in the early going. Through July, J.R. Richard was a pitching terror, posting ten wins and a 1.89 ERA, but late that month he collapsed from a stroke as he was practicing. At first the attack threatened his life, then a slow recovery cast doubts over his future pitching career. Stunned by the loss of Richard, the Astros went into a tailspin, losing three to the Giants. Vern

Opposite: Nolan Ryan of the Astros pitching in the fifth no-hitter of his career—an all-time record.

Ruhle, recovering from surgery, now joined the starting staff and won fourteen; Morgan, shaking off a slump, batted .300 in the stretch and emerged as a team leader. Catching fire in late August, the Astros won ten straight; Cedeno and Cruz carried the offense with superb batting, Niekro went on to win twenty, and the bullpen saved some forty games.

Leading the Dodgers by three games with as many left to play, the Astros journeyed to Los Angeles expecting to apply the lethal stroke. However, noisy crowds of more than 50,000 at each game rallied the crippled Dodgers. The Astros lost all three games by one run, horrifying Houston fans. The Dodgers, down 3–0 in the last, battled back on Cey's homer and a key pinch hit by coach Mota. Stepping to the plate for only the seventh time this year, Mota punched his 150th pinch-hit to swell his all-time record.

The Dodger victory deadlocked the race and forced a playoff, the fifth such encounter in National League history. Ironically, the Dodgers had been involved in each, yet only once did they win. A sudden death single game scheduled for Dodger Stadium on October 6 now rekindled that old jinx. The Astros sent Niekro to the mound against Goltz, whose 7–10 record spelled doom. The Dodger did not redeem himself, as the Astros, aided by two first-inning errors, scored twice in the first and mounted a 7–0 lead after four. With the outcome assured, Dodger tempers flared and brawls erupted, abetted by fans who hurled debris on the Astros until cautioned by officials. The finish arrived with a 7–1 Astro victory, a 20th win for Niekro, and a first divisional title for the Houston team.

Given no time to savor the victory, the Astros jetted east to Philadelphia to open the five-game championship series. Though dismal enough facing the rested Phillies in their home park, the task was made more difficult by a league decision allowing the Phils to use pitchers Marty Bystrom and Kevin Saucier in place of veterans Nino Espinosa and Randy Lerch. Indeed, some groused that Lerch's 4–14 mark was his only disablement.

The Phils drew first blood, winning 3–1 behind Carlton's shaky pitching and McGraw's relief work. Luzinski's two-run homer off Forsch carried the day, but the smug Philadelphia fans were hardly prepared for what came later. In the most dramatic playoff series yet waged, the embattled teams struggled through four extra-inning games. In the first of these matches, a 2–2 deadlock was broken in the eighth by the Astros, capturing the first earned runs scored off of McGraw in seventeen games. They went on to win 7–4 in the tenth.

The Astros seized the advantage by evening the series in Philadelphia. The remaining games would now be played in the Astrodome, the backdrop for 55 Astro wins. Local fans rousingly welcomed them back from their six grueling road games. With Christenson matched against Niekro in the first game, neither side scored through ten innings. McGraw yielded a triple to Morgan in the 11th, and the winning run scored on a sacrifice. However, the victory was costly, as Cedeno injured his ankle and was lost for the series.

The Astros needed but one more win, and that prospect seemed likely when a bizarre play killed a Phillies rally in the next game. At the plate in the fourth inning, Maddox hit a tap ball which baffled umpires, who could not call it a catch or a grounder. Eventually, a catch was ruled and a double play allowed, but the Astros demanded a triple play and the Phils a single out. A 20-minute argument ensued before the issue was decided and both teams lodged protests. The long delay apparently unnerved Carlton and the Phils fell behind. They rallied with three in the eighth to lead and might have had more when another umpire's ruling on a possible trapped ball went against them. The Astros evened the score in the ninth, but Rose singled in the tenth and Luzinski pinch hit a double, pushing Rose home. Trillo doubled to add another, and the 5–3 win deadlocked the series.

Sixty million television fans watched the ten-inning donnybrook which followed. In this single deciding game, the Phils fell behind 5–2 after seven, but turned on Ryan and rallied for a 7–5 lead in the eighth. Ryan botched a double play, misplayed a bunt, and walked a run in. McGraw, summoned for the fifth time in the series, now allowed the Astros to tie the game in the eighth at 7–7. The stalemate remained until the tenth, when doubles by Unser and Maddox produced the winning run; starter Ruthven then protected the lead with brilliant relief work. The victory faded the Phillies's losing reputation and sent the newly crowned league champs into the World Series.

Meanwhile, the American League housed one close race and interested fans in another with heroics of a different kind. The royal battle took place in the East, as the Yankees and Orioles locked horns. The Yankee restrengthening from their 1979 collapse was aided by owner Steinbrenner's spending in the re-entry draft. For $2.1 million, he acquired Bob Watson for four years and another million brought left-handed pitcher Rudy May from Montreal.

Each newcomer proved his own worth. Watson batted .307 and

delivered thirteen homers, and May's 2.47 ERA on a 15–5 mark led the league. Such acquisitions justified Steinbrenner's spending strategy; he calculated that each Stadium fan spent $8 on the average, of which the Yanks kept $6. Furthermore, not only did home attendance better the old American League record, but Yankee-hating fans on the road came in flocks. To gross receipts of $15 million from live attendance, Steinbrenner added the team's hefty television–radio income. None dared call him mad.

The fans cheered for a team made of some of the same stars that won the world title in 1978. Thurman Munson was gone, but Rick Cerone filled in as a good fielding catcher who batted .277 with fourteen homers. Star pitchers Tommy John and Ron Guidry were supported by reliefer Gossage, who notched 33 saves. This strong Yankee pitching, ranked second in the league, compensated for a mediocre .267 batting attack, although the team's 189 homers stood second only to the 203 of the Brewers. At least Reggie Jackson's 41 slams tied Brewer Ben Oglivie's total for the league lead, and Jackson batted .300 and drove in 111 runs. The team had depth at most positions, and not even Graig Nettles's absence because of hepatitis could stay rookie manager Dick Howser from driving the Yanks to 103 wins, the best record in baseball this year.

Only the Orioles challenged. Despite the loss of star reliever Stanhouse in the re-entry draft, Baltimorean pitching was strong. Steve Stone's 25 wins piloted the league and brought him the Cy Young Award. Scott McGregor added twenty more victories. Furthermore, Oriole batting at .273 outdid the Yanks, although homer output stood some thirty-odd shy.

The Yanks jumped to a fast start to build a 9½ game lead, but squandered it in the stretch. The Orioles closed in late, edging to within half a game and clinging that close for five matches. They challenged until the final week, then with three left, the Yankees downed the Tigers 5–2 to clinch. Still, Earl Weaver's challenge, which produced a hundred wins, had given their conquerors a full measure of worry.

The Royals, however, posed an even greater threat to the Yankees by making a shambles of the Western division race. Rookie manager Jim Frey welcomed newcomers Willie Mays Aikens at first base and young relief star Dan Quisenberry. Otherwise, this was mostly the same Royal team that dogged the Yankees in the late 1970s.

Although Quisenberry saved 33 games to tie Gossage, the soul of the Royals lay in its offense. Frey platooned an outfield of Jose

Cardenal, Clint Hurdle, Amos Otis, and John Wathan, playing only young Willie Wilson regularly. This was an astute decision because the switch-hitter, batting 705 times, punched a record 184 singles, stole 79 bases, and batted .326. Infielders Aikens and George Brett were even more productive. Aikens drove in 98 runs and racked up 20 homers, but Brett terrorized the league. Though nagged by injuries, he flirted with a .400 average all season and finished at .390, baseball's best since Ted Williams batted .406 in 1941. With this powerful duo at the corners, slick-fielding Frank White at second, and U.L. Washington at short, the Royal infield was the best in the west.

They won eight of twelve decisions against the Yankees; in seasonal play, they were bested by only the Twins and the A's. The A's, managed by Martin, delighted fans with their "Billy Ball" fashion of play. Even more than the Astros's, this was old-fangled hit-run and steal action. Rickey Henderson stole 100 bases for a new American record. Furthermore, their daring team manager defied prevailing pitching theology by allowing starters Mike Norris, Brian Langford, Matt Keough, and Rick McCatty to pitch all the way, posting 94 complete games. This heresy produced the league's best ERA mark and helped name Martin Manager of the Year.

Still, the Martin touch left the A's 14 games behind the Royals's winning gait. By mid-season the Royal stranglehold was so tight that only "Billy Ball" and Brett's heroics sustained fan interest in the A's. Kansas City's eventual failure to win 100 games was blamed on late season injuries and Quisenberry's slump.[3]

Winless in three previous playoffs against the Yankees, the Royals rose this time with a vengeance. Opening at home, they downed the Yankees 7–2, the New Yorkers blaming the afternoon sun for their poor showing. The versatile Royals then hung a nocturnal 3–2 loss on the Yanks, which Steinbrenner blamed on the poor judgment of his third base coach. Steinbrenner held a strategy session when the action shifted to Yankee Stadium, only to meet defeat again, as the Royals pulled a 4–2 victory and a sweep. While Brett's three-run homer off Gossage in the seventh was the crusher, White was the hero, batting .545 and fielding brilliantly.

However, the jubilant Royals met a swift comeuppance. The team was paired against the Phillies in the World Series and this matchup was touted as the first duel between non-winners in sixty years, with the Philadelphia drought almost a century long. The rested Royals might have thought their rivals were spent or perhaps the Phillies were simply hungrier. Maybe the gods liked the Phils, as astrologist Jean Dixon prophesied.

Any conjecture notwithstanding, Manager Green took note of his spent pitchers and elected to send rookie Bob Walk into the Philadelphia opener. Despite yielding a pair of two-run homers to Aikens, Walk indeed emerged the winner of the 7–6 struggle, with thanks extended to reliefer McGraw. The Phils rallied again in the second game to overcome a 4–2 deficit and club Quisenberry for a 6–4 win.

Behind by two matches, the Royals returned home. George Brett, back in action after minor surgery, homered in the first inning and inspired his mates to a 4–3, ten-inning victory. The Royals evened the Series the next night, as Aikens again clubbed a pair of homers to insure the 5–3 victory. This, however, was the crest of the Royal surge. In the finale at Kansas City, the Phils overcame a 3–2 deficit by scoring two off Quisenberry for a 4–3 win. Next, they delighted a capacity Philadelphia crowd—restrained by a corps of police who held attack dogs in leash—with a 4–1 victory that brought the world title to the Quaker City.

The winning Phils had batted .294, paced by Boone's .412 effort, Schmidt's .381, and Unser's three timely hits. Rose's back-up catch of a Boone muff was one of the fielding gems of the Series. Pitcher Carlton won twice, and McGraw earned one and saved another. These highlights shone brightly as Philadelphia shook off their "city of losers" tag. There was toasting and parading, and it *was* a glorious season for the game.

The Great Strike of 1981

Had the Lords of Baseball studied the results of the last divisional races, they would have seen that there were no repeat winners. Hence, who could say that the re-entry draft was undermining the game's competitive balance? Indeed, such turnover kept attendance high and fan interest at fever pitch.

Also, if owners had consulted baseball history, they might have been forewarned of the folly of waging strikes. Certainly the 1889 season furnished a parallel; then, a successful year followed by the greatest of player strikes had spawned a decade of profitless seasons.

However, modern owners could easily draw a different meaning from the 1890 strike. The owners of the past had been opposed by a battalion of organized players, but they had prevailed, destroying the union and cowing players for the next 75 years. The modern owners, looking to their older brothers, seemed bent on doing the same to the Players Association. Therefore, when the study committee failed to reach an agreement by the end of the 1980 year, the owners imposed their own compensation plan on February 19, 1981. This fateful imposition provoked baseball's second longest strike.

Negotiator Grebey rejected Miller's conciliatory proposals, including the one that eventually became the accepted compromise, and the owners girded for a strike, believing that their position was strong. In addition to $15 million squirreled away in a strike fund, they paid Lloyds of London $2 million for $50 million worth of strike insurance; in the event of a strike, the policy would eventually pay $100,000 for each lost game over a six-week period. Lloyds was indeed the final loser of this deal.

This prop immediately put the owners at a great advantage over the players, whose vote to strike in June most certainly crushed their hopes of obtaining insurance. Thus, the great majority of players stood to lose hefty portions of their salaries. The umpires, on the other hand, wielded contracts which guaranteed full wages for 45 days of player strike inactivity.

The players determinedly planned to strike on May 29, but the deadline slipped by as a National Labor Relations Board counsel filed an unfair labor practice suit against the owners. This faint hope faded when a federal court disallowed the petition, and a new deadline was set for June 11. It was now clear that the time of power struggling had arrived. All games were cancelled after the deadline passed, and for fifty days there was no major league baseball. In all, 706 games went by the boards.

Once started, the strike fed on momentum. Tempers raged at summit meetings and Federal Mediator Ken Moffett struggled to reach a rapprochement. It seemed that representatives Miller and Grebey fought a personal duel, and eventually Grebey lost the support of a trio of moderate owners, who forced him to compromise. At one point Miller faced a similar threat, but somehow he gained renewed support.

Unable to break the player ranks, the owners were compelled to yield.[4] Also, by late July this profit-minded group was sobered by the apparent damage done to the game's image. When the strike threatened to end the 1981 season, Miller exploited their fears. He cannily raised the possibility of players starting their own league in 1982, and if this prospect did not pan out, the chance of a massive talent shuffle waited right at hand.[5] The possibility of lawsuits from individual players and organized umpires posed another threat. In the early weeks of the strike, the Umpires Association had filed to restrain Lloyds from paying owners, but the suit was dismissed in a district court for want of precedent. Nevertheless, the owners realized that the strong legal position of the players derived from the Federal Circuit Court ruling that upheld the re-entry draft system.[6]

Most frightening of all was the possibility of irritating the fans. Many sportswriters criticized the players, but some stalwarts like Red Smith struck hard at the owners, and *Sports Illustrated* proclaimed their stance with a stark cover headline: "STRIKE! The Walkout The Owners Provoked."[7]

A *New York Times*/CBS poll indicated in early July that such attacks were winning support for the players, if only by a slim margin. These backers were the younger, poorer, less-educated fans, while generally the older and richer patrons favored the owners. One-third of those polled either resented both or simply did not care. In a letter to the *Times,* President Giamatti of Yale University sounded a harsh "plague on both their houses" sentiment, urging both sides to return to their jobs because the "enduring institution" of baseball was "quintessentially American." Meanwhile, *Time* magazine bluntly claimed that the strike was alienating fans.[8]

The end came as the Lloyds policy was about to expire. On July 31 the strike was 50 days old, and barely enough time remained for a credible resumption of play. Both sides were bloodied; the players had forfeited an estimated $4 million a week in salaries, while the owners sustained a total loss of about $72 million. The Dodgers alone claimed a loss of over $7 million. League cities also forfeited tax revenue and baseball-generated commerce; New York claimed an $8.4 million dip, Cincinnati missed $900,000, and Philadelphia mourned a loss of $100,000 for each cancelled home game. Income cuts for vendors and summer ballpark employees hurt sorely.

The settlement that followed the strike handed owners a limited victory on the compensation issue. Beginning with the 1981 re-entry draft, clubs that lost ranking free agents were to receive a major leaguer or top minor leaguer in return. Wringing this giveback from players was a limited victory, though, since players won their demand for a compensation pool in which all clubs were required to participate. The pooling arrangement allowed each team to exclude their best 24 men; clubs not participating in the draft were permitted to protect 26. This allayed player fears that lucrative salary auctions might cease if participating clubs were forced to surrender players directly.

With the compensation stumbling block removed, other issues were easily solved and a basic agreement was promulgated. Players kept their pension continuity and their re-entry draft rights suffered no penalty because of strike time lost. They also were granted a week's time to get back into playing shape. Thus, with earlier agreements added on, the fifth Basic Agreement was shaped. Extending until the end of the year 1984, it afforded three full seasons of peace.

"Baseball's Dishonest Season"

From his October seat, writer Red Smith judged the strike-pocked 1981 year to be "baseball's dishonest season." This view was shared by most baseball observers, including fans and horrified statisticians.

Fortunately, the gathering strike storm had failed to dispel the optimism of the contending teams of 1981. The owners had plunged into the 1980 re-entry draft and spent lavishly to beef up teams, the upshot being a quick salary spiral and a new batch of player plutocrats. That fall fourteen players opted for re-entry, and of these, five signed contracts worth more than $500,000 a year. Dave Winfield of the Padres signed a 10-year Yankee contract worth an estimated $20 million when cost-of-living escalations were figured in. With a base salary of $1.5 million for 1981, Winfield became the reigning millionaire. However, he was not the only rich man. Fred Lynn left Boston to become a millionaire Angel, while Andre Dawson of the Expos, Phil Niekro of the Braves, and George Brett of the Royals each stayed at home to sign pacts worth one million a year.

Certainly, the fear of losing home favorites in the re-entry draft prompted clubs to pay more to keep their sons. Occasionally, this fear inspired dramatic trades, such as the Red Sox sending Rich Burleson, Fred Lynn, and Butch Hobson to the Angels for Carney Lansford, Joe Rudi, and Frank Tanana. The weightiest trade had the Brewers dealing outfielders Sixto Lezcano and Dave Green and pitchers Larry Sorenson and Dave LaPoint to the Cardinals for reliever Rollie Fingers, starter Pete Vuckovich, and the hard-hitting catcher Ted Simmons. Added to the powerhouse of Paul Molitor, Cecil Cooper, Ben Oglivie, Robin Yount, and Gorman Thomas, these additons threatened to upset the power balance in the American League East.

As the salaries of bartered players kept pace with those of free-agents, Kuhn predicted bankruptcies, pennant monopolies, and fan disenchantment, although these phenomena were not evidenced as the season unfolded. On the contrary, as the 1981 division races progressed and the June 11 strike date was reached, all races were hotly contested. Fans continued to warm to the competition, the crowd totals averaging nearly 20,500 a game.

The false season indeed provided enough heroics to stir the fans. At Los Angeles, a chubby, 20-year-old Mexican pitcher helped the Dodgers to a sprightly start by winning his first eight games with a fantastic 0.50 ERA! Although Fernando Valenzuela had cooled to 9–4 by strike time, his team's 26–9 mark by May 17 enabled the Dodgers to hold a half-game edge over the Reds when the storm clouds gathered.

Meanwhile, in the National East, the revamped Cardinals broke fast, leading the Phillies and Expos in the early going. Then Carlton's 9–1 pitching, Rose's .330 and Matthews' .300 hitting, and Schmidt's 14 homers spurred a Phillie charge that opened a 1½-game lead over the Cards at strike time. Just before the curtain fell, Rose electrified Philly fans by banging his 3,630th hit off Ryan of the Astros to tie Musial's league-leading record. The stealthy Expos closed to within four games of the lead on the sensational exploits of rookie outfielder Tim Raines. This converted infielder switch-hit for a .322 average and led the majors with 50 base thefts in 55 games. With millionaire Dawson batting .328 and poling 13 homers, Montreal fans eyed a pennant.

The American League had written the same story. The Yankees started slowly and fell behind Cleveland and Baltimore in the Eastern race. Cleveland fans were treated to a perfect game by fire-balling Len Barker, the first such masterpiece in the junior circuit since 1968. The Yankees rallied to come from four games back in mid-May and won 15 of their next 23 outings, snatching a two-game lead over the Orioles and three over the Brewers by strike time. Newly arrived plutocrats Winfield and Mumphrey led the New York batting attack.

The Western race was even more dramatic. Billy Martin drove the A's to the best start in modern baseball history, winning 11 straight before losing. Once again, Martin's tireless starting pitchers dominated rivals, like the hard-hitting Rangers. From a peak of 20–5, the A's skidded to 37–23 by strike time, though they still held a 1½-game lead over the Rangers and outstripped the slumping Royals by 12.

Baseball rebounded after the 1981 strike because of interest generated by stars like
Dave Winfield (*left*), the high-priced Yankee slugger, and Fernando Valenzuela (*right*),
the Dodgers's young pitching sensation.

At this point the strike threatened to end the 1981 season, leaving
these four leaders to reap whatever scant glory they could muster.
When the strike was over, the owners sought the most credible way
of resuming play. Kuhn headed a group charged with modifying the
seasonal format in the interest of salvaging profits. The group
quickly decided to split the season, allowing each team a fresh beginning in August. While such a plan was not unprecedented—having
been long used in the minors and once by the single "big league"
during the profitless 1890s—its implementation was a clumsy move.
Indeed, this much criticized scheme earned Red Smith's handle "the
dishonest season."

The scheme named the four prestrike leaders as first half winners,
who would compete against the victors of the upcoming second half
in a five-game playoff series for divisional honors. The sneaky pitch
was that no first half winner could repeat—a ploy which killed the
early winners' incentives until the playoffs. So ill-contrived was the
plan that it appeared as if first half leaders might help their playoff
chances by battling harder against dangerous rivals, in the hope of

blocking them from winning the second half. The possibility also existed that a badly beaten first half team might win the second half and go on to world honors with its shabby record. Perhaps the worst turn of this deal was the likelihood that teams with excellent overall records could get nothing from the season. In sum, this was a catch-penny format, and few believed Kuhn's lame explanation: "It has some warts, but no integrity warts."[9] To further worsen a bad situation, all teams resumed play under the regular schedule, giving some inordinate home field advantage over others. The Cardinals, for instance, played 30 of their 52 games on the road.

Predictably, such factors discredited the second half of the season. Three preseason leaders, the Phils, Dodgers, and Yanks, played so poorly that each would have failed to win its division had overall records counted. The Oakland A's, however, just missed winning again. The Royals eked out this lead, their overall 50–53 mark flirting with the possibility of their becoming history's most tainted world champs. Other predicted horrors came home to roost. Cincinnati posted the best overall record in baseball, but because Houston beat them by 1½ games in the second half, they received only the grim satisfaction of raising a homemade pennant. The Cards were also thwarted; with the best overall record in the National East, they lost the second half to the Expos by half a game—a schedule quirk had allowed the Expos one more game, which they won. Likewise, the Orioles in the American East went unrewarded after losing the fewest games, and the winning Texans in the West saw the Royals crowned second half victors.[10]

It was no surprise then when angry fans turned away. Despite close second half races in all divisions, won by Milwaukee and Kansas City in the American and by Montreal and Houston in the National, attendance sagged in 17 of 26 cities and television ratings fell off sharply.

Of course, the latter season had highlights. Kicked off by the All-Star Game played at Cleveland on August 9, a record 72,086 fans turned out to watch the Nationals win their tenth straight dream game and their eighteenth of the last 19 played. The second season opened the following day, with clubs staging special promotions to cool fans. San Diego's free admission lured a crowd of 52,000, but the Phils drew almost as many paying patrons. The Philadelphians wanted to see Rose top Musial's National hit record, and the slasher came through.

In fact, there were many highlights. Ryan of the Astros pitched his record-breaking fifth no-hitter; Tim Raines of the Expos stole 71 bases overall; Schmidt of the Phils poled 31 homers and drove in 91 runs to win another MVP honor; reliefer Rollie Fingers of the Brewers saved a total of 28 games—this added to a 1.04 ERA to earn both Cy Young and MVP honors in the American League; young Valenzuela of the Dodgers touted a 13–7 record to take both the Cy Young and Rookie of the Year honors in the Nationals (although Seaver of the Reds led the majors with an overall 14–2 pitching record). These records considered overall performances for both "seasons"; their stark comparison with past full season marks confounded statistical and trivia filberts. For example, seasonal batting titles went to Carney Lansford of the Red Sox (.336 with 399 at bats) and Bill Madlock of the Pirates, whose .341 mark was reckoned on a mere 279 at bats, four more than the minimum allowed this year.

On the other hand, this dismal season left a trail of ugly incidents. The bitter carping over the format never ceased. Players and owners sniped at one another, the players chortling at the owners' inability to break their union. Steinbrenner showed the greatest display of owner wrath, railing at players and firing manager Michael to bring on Bob Lemon once again. Predictably, the fans roundly booed the players. In one incident, shortstop Gary Templeton returned an obscene finger gesture to a provoking fan, earning a fine and a suspension. Cesar Cedeno went so far as to attack a fan in the stands, and one Yankee Stadium fan assaulted an umpire. There were times when the fans did react supportively or with friendly irony; thus, Reggie Jackson was repeatedly showered with coins and dollar bills in late season games.

While all baseball constituencies complained, few had more right to gripe than veteran players who, like some in past wars, missed out on one-time career chances. Rose lost irretrievable ground in his assault on Cobb's all-time hit record. The middle-aged Gaylord Perry missed notching his 300th pitching victory by three games, while others neared that mark: Seaver, Jenkins, Kaat, and Carlton. Youngsters just beginning their careers also suffered; some who were called up from the minors just before the strike went unpaid, while those sent to the minors at strike time had at least the satisfaction of drawing their salaries.[11]

Mercifully, the dismal season drew to a close in early October, with the eight winners of the two "seasons" meeting in playoffs to determine the divisional championships. The owners counted on extra television revenue from these series to curtail some losses. In the

American League West, Martin's A's speedily dispatched the Royals, winning three in a row on mighty pitching which held the Royals to two runs and one extra base hit. The Yankees in the East were treated roughly by the hard-hitting Brewers. After taking the first two in Milwaukee, the Yanks were matched by the Brewers, who rose to tie the series with 5–3 and 2–1 victories at Yankee Stadium. The Yanks then won the decisive game 7–3, on homers by Jackson, Gamble, and Cerone.

The National playoffs were just as competitive. In the East, the Expos beat the Phils in the first two games at their own Olympic Stadium, but back at home the Phils rebounded with 6–2 and 6–5 victories to tie. In the finale, Steve Rogers of the Expos blanked the Phils 3–0, hanging a second series loss on Carlton to the joy of Montrealers. Indeed, one of Quebec's independence champions mourned that "the Expos are killing . . . Quebec more efficiently than Prime Minister Trudeau. . . . We can fight Mr. Trudeau. How can we fight the Expos?"

Meanwhile, the Astros and Dodgers of the National League West carried on their bitter rivalry of 1980. The Astros looked like champions as they beat the Dodgers 3–1 and 1–0 at Houston. Then, the Dodgers repeated their last-ditch 1980 uprising at Dodger Stadium, thrashing the Astros three times to win the right to face the Expos for the league championship series.

This duel put Dodger staying power to the test once again. Opening at home, they topped the Expos in the first game, but dropped the second, as Ray Burris blanked the Dodgers, 3–0. Next, Rogers won a 4–1 decision at Montreal to move the Expos to within a game of the title. The Dodgers now halted the home team's progress, winning the fourth game 7–1 and following with a rain-delayed 2–1 victory. The final game ended amidst snow flurries, as Rogers, pitching in relief, yielded Cey's winning homer.

While these teams staged their French and Indian war, the Yanks and A's met in the American title series. A's manager Martin fielded some equally vengeance-minded ex-Yankees in his lineup, and so a vendetta seemed likely. Still, the Yanks swept the A's, winning the first two games at home, 3–1 and 13–3. When play moved to Oakland, the Yanks applied a 4–0 crusher, paced by Righetti's pitching and Nettles's three-run double. The Yankee triumph was marred, however, when a heated argument between Nettles and Jackson broke the peace at the victory party.

That rumble and one which followed signalled the reversal of

Yankee fortunes and provided the final stage for a lamentable season. World Series time had finally arrived; the action began at Yankee Stadium in late October. The Yankees methodically dropped the Dodgers in the first two games by scores of 5–3 and 3–0, carried off by the sturdy pitching of Guidry, John, and Gossage. With Nettles fielding brilliantly, the Yankee star of empire rose. When action shifted to Los Angeles, a medium-sized earthquake sounded another omen. Young Valenzuela took the rumble in stride and checked the Yanks 5–4, the loss tossing Yankee reliefer George Frazier into the first wave of his sea of troubles.

The Dodgers won the next game, an 8–7 madcap. Frazier lost again when freakish Dodger hits combined with Yankee errors and stranded runners. With the Series tied, the Dodgers won a third straight game, Reuss outdueling Guidry. The loser yielded consecutive homers to Guerrero and Yeager in the seventh, to go down 2–1. The desperate Steinbrenner snarled at his men. His rage increased when he suffered a broken wrist in an elevator fracas with a pair of Dodger fans. Cynics have opined that the fracas never happened and that the head Bronx Bomber relished the macho image it supported. Whatever the story, his discomfiture failed to rally the Yanks. Returning home, they lost the sixth game 9–2, Frazier losing again and becoming the first pitcher ever to lose three Series games.

The Yankee defeat has been blamed on the absence of the DH rule this year. The Dodgers effectively used pinch-hitters and the Yanks did not; indeed, Yank pitchers failed to hit in fourteen at bats and stranded thirteen runners. But that's partly hindsight wisdom; if the Dodger pinch-hitters had failed to deliver, manager Lasorda would have been called a bum. Overall, Steinbrenner's goading added a sour note. In defeat, he publically apologized to Yankee fans, prompting a footnote from Jackson, who proclaimed, "I don't have anything to apologize for. I played my best."

On that sad tune and with somewhat tarnished glory to the Dodger winners, who thrice rebounded from adversity, the "dishonest season" ended.

Fair Skies For the 1980s?

After all the blunders and animosities of 1981, baseball emerged cocky, hale, and hearty, ready for business as usual in 1982. It seems incredible that fans should so easily forget the past until we recall the unorganized nature of this audience and the gluttonous national appetite for sport. Clearly, baseball's good fortune stems from its strategic position as America's premier summer sports spectacle, a spot that seemingly assures hefty television incomes for ball-diamond promoters. The television money mine was so promising in the early 1980s that optimism seemed justifiable. Certainly millionaire Yankee outfielder Dave Winfield knew what he was talking about when he spoke these words during the dark hours of the 1981 strike: "Free agency and compensation aren't the only issues involved in our future and not the most important. Television and Cable TV will be very important down the line. For what's at stake we may have to change the entire player-owner relationship as we know it."[12]

Indeed, as the 1982 season unfolded, there were signs that the owners also saw things in that light. Even as a deeply rooted national recession idled more than nine million American workers, advance ticket sales matched those of baseball's best years. Moreover, the National Football League's multi-year, $2 billion television package was an inspiration to baseball promoters, a reminder to owners and players that television was the superstar factory, and the source and justification of huge salaries.

Any fears that the strike settlement would stunt the upward salary trend proved groundless. Instead, fall and winter salary negotiations awarded even heftier contracts to the players. Now stars like Gary Carter, George Foster, Ken Griffey, Bill Madlock, and Mike Schmidt joined the million-plus-per-year club, with others like Ron Guidry and Reggie Jackson close to that mark.

After the 1982 preseason round of contract signings, the average player salary approached $250,000. Owner generosity was attributed to the fear of losing stars in re-entry drafts. In short, rather than risk losing stars to the draft, owners either paid men like Carter, Schmidt, and Guidry the new going rates to keep them at home, or, like the Cincinnati Reds, they traded stars like Griffey, Collins, and Foster to teams like the Yankees and Mets, where owners willingly paid the higher pricetag.

Unquestionably, owner fears now worked as effectively as the re-entry draft to enrich players, and, ironically, the compensation question was hardly a factor in the 1981 draft. Incredibly, only one case called for compensation. When White Sox reliefer Ed Farmer signed with the Phillies, his former team eagerly plucked a promising young catcher from the pool of 2,000 eligibles. In this case the White Sox gain spelled a Pirate loss, but such was the way of the new compensation procedure. This bright outcome made the cause of the player strike seem absurd, though Marvin Miller disagreed. Suspicious of possible owner evasions of the rights of draftees, he filed a grievance procedure against two clubs, alleging under-handed violations.

Yet, when contract settlements proceeded so smoothly, the fans had to question what all the fuss of the past year had been about. True, many players were displeased by club offers, but of the hun-dred cases of players threatening to go to arbitration, the vast major-ity were settled before they reached that point. In fact, one peti-tioner hastily withdrew his claim upon learning that the club offer topped his demand by $15,000. The latest crop of plutocrats cer-tainly incited envy among stars still laboring under lesser contracts. Seaver, Garvey, and Cey at $400,000 and Carlton at $600,000 were among the grumblers. Dodgers Garvey and Cey knew that club pol-icy was to hold the line on salaries, but young Valenzuela assaulted the rule, staging an old-fashioned hold-out. Having received $75,000 for his fabulous 1981 achievements, Valenzuela now spurned an offer of $350,000 and returned to Mexico. However, threats from the Immigration Department to lift his visa and a fai-lure to qualify for arbitration prompted his return. He still refused to sign his contract, preferring to take his usual salary and to file for arbitration when he qualified in the next autumn.

Widely publicized accounts of disgruntled players no longer seemed to arouse the ire of envious fans or sportswriters. One journ-alist hailed Schmidt's six-year, $1.9 million-per-year contract as be-ing the player's just reward. Although some observers still predicted that multi-year contracts at high pay would produce complacent players, fans and writers appeared to accept player plutocrats for what they were—television celebrities who were exciting to watch. When they played well, they would be lionized; when they faltered, they would be booed.

Enough drama played on the current baseball stage to make the most cynical fans forgive and forget the immediate past. Raines and Henderson stood ready to resume base stealing, and the Tigers touted Kirk Gibson as the next Mantle. Oldsters Pete Rose and Gay-lord Perry were reaching for immortality. The doughty Rose passed Hank Aaron into second place on the all-time hit list. Still to be surmounted was Cobb's lofty record, but Rose's timetable seemed to indicate that he would pass that in 1984. Perry quickly got the three wins he needed to join the 300 club and then went after the 172 strike-outs he needed to break Johnson's all-time mark of 3,508.

There were also problems. The events of the 1981 World Series had strengthened the belief that the DH rule should be made uniform. The American League's string of All-Star Game losses and its three-game losing streak in Series matches suggested that parity with the Nationals should come quickly, lest the junior circuit be junior in fact as in name. Also, George Steinbrenner was enhancing his reputation as the *enfant terrible* among owners, as he pressured his affluent Yankees to report early to spring training and there submit to rigorous training in fundamentals. True to form, before the new season was warm, he had sacked manager Lemon and returned the prodigal Michael as another temporary field general.

At least the owners were wise enough to resist restructuring the game in the fashion of the NFL format. The proposal was made that the teams be divided into three divisions, with the three winners and three "wild cards" (those with second best records) squaring off in a round of playoffs. This would have netted a tidy windfall from television, but at the cost of debasing the playing season and arousing fans. This scheme was laid to rest, at least for 1982.

Backing that idea was Commissioner Bowie Kuhn, whose checkered career as high commander seemed likely to end with his personal "restructuring" in 1982. It was too much to hope that his possible dismissal might lead to a revamping of the game's leadership structure along the lines envisioned by Winfield. If Kuhn's possible departure seemed likely to be mourned by few, Red Smith's death was mourned by many. The dean of sportswriters was considered irreplaceable by millions of fans. So, too, for hundreds of players, was Marvin Miller. The impending retirement of the "players' commissioner" signalled the end of an era. He was the last of the great trio which shaped this era; Robinson and O'Malley were dead, and Miller's retirement would kindle speculation over the identities of the next great shapers of baseball history. Perhaps a television mogul would be involved, what with the vast potential promised by cable television. Maybe a statistician would be present, such as the one who devised and touted the revolutionary Total Achievement measurement for evaluating players; if adopted, this scheme would replace batting averages and homer marks, and possibly lead to objective standards for pricing players. A new leader could possibly be a technocrat, like the Japanese designer of the electronic catcher glove, now hawked as a fool-proof device for signalling pitches.

Obviously, baseball in the 1980s faces a crisis of leadership, but the threat hardly calls for apocalyptic rhetoric. After all, like the boy who cried "Wolf" once too often, the question of "Where does base-ball go from here?" has too often been sounded in this century to stir serious beliefs of the game's impending extinction. True, base-ball now faces formidable challenges in seeking to housebreak televi-sion interests, plutocratic players, and baronial owners, while also fending off incursions from rival sports and chasing after the will-o'-the-wisp of competitive balance. While much is new in these tests, baseball history reminds one that similar challenges have been met before. Indeed, baseball's strength resides in its historic continuity, a binding force which has enthralled fans of yesteryear and those of today. Thus, one might say, we have met baseball's future and it is rooted in the game's elegant past.

Notes

Introduction: American Baseball at Mid-Century

1. "Back to the Unfabulous '50s," *Time*.
2. Goldman, *The Crucial Decade—And After*, pp. 12–13, 47–50, 91–100, 138–45; Galbraith, *The Affluent Society*, passim; Keats, *The Insolent Chariots*, passim; Whyte, *The Organization Man*, passim. For a pictorial depiction of the era, see Barbara and Sy Ribakove's *The Nifty Fifties*, pp. 8–44, 71–100, 216–23.
3. Kennedy, "Oh, What an Era!"
4. Smith, *Baseball in America*, pp. 223–38; Andreano, *No Joy in Mudville*, pp. 79–100.
5. *Baseball Digest*, Nov. 1950.
6. *Baseball Digest*, July 1957, Apr. 1975; *Philadelphia Inquirer*, June 22, 1980.
7. *The Baseball Encyclopedia* (1st ed.), pp. 2335–36.
8. "Ballparks," *Baseball Quarterly;* Shannon and Kalinsky, *The Ballparks*, pp. 9–12, 243–53, 259–65.
9. Oriard, "Sports and Space."
10. *Baseball Digest*, Jan. 1949, Nov. 1950; *The Sporting News*, Aug. 14, 1971.
11. Appel, "It's A Whole New Ball Game"; Shannon and Kalinsky, *The Ballparks*, pp. 9–12, 243–53, 259–65.
12. *Baseball Digest*, Aug. 1950.
13. Personal interview with Brandy Davis.
14. *New York Times*, June 15, 1980.
15. Wind, *The Gilded Age of Sport*, pp. 52–54.
16. Rosenthal, *The Best 10 Years of Baseball*, passim.
17. *Baseball Digest*, July 1956, Sept. 1956.
18. *The Sporting News*, Nov. 2, 1933, Feb. 22, 1934, Dec. 2, 1943, Jan. 13, 1944, Aug. 23, 1945, Aug. 31, 1949. The last citation tells of an elaborate plan to move the Browns to Los Angeles in 1941.
19. *The Sporting News*, Nov. 28, 1970; "Westward the A's," *Time*.
20. Henderson, "Los Angeles and the Dodger War, 1957–1962."
21. Wind, *The Gilded Age of Sport*, pp. 52–64.

Chapter 1: The Postwar Campaigns: The American League

1. Allen, *Where Have You Gone, Joe DiMaggio?* pp. 89–90.
2. Reichler, *Baseball's Great Moments*, pp. 24–27; *Baseball Digest*, Feb. 1951.
3. Berry, *Boston Red Sox*, pp. 114–17; *The Sporting News*, Oct. 16, 1976.
4. *New York Times*, Oct. 10, 1928.
5. *Baseball Digest*, Aug. 1978; Allen, *Where Have You Gone, Joe DiMaggio?* pp. 105–7.
6. Reichler, *Baseball's Great Moments*, pp. 35–39.
7. Allen, *Where Have You Gone, Joe DiMaggio?* pp. 117–18, 132.

8. Golenbock, *Dynasty*, pp. 54–79; Cohen et al., *The World Series*, pp. 245–48.
9. *Baseball Digest*, Feb. 1957, Feb. 1959; *New York Times*, May 8, 1957.
10. Golenbock, *Dynasty*, pp. 279–307; *Baseball Encyclopedia* (1st ed.), pp. 412–15; Golenbock, "1961—A Year to Remember."

Chapter 2: The Postwar Campaigns: The National League

1. Allen, *The National League Story*, pp. 240–42; Honig, *Baseball When the Grass Was Real*, pp. 193–206; Reichler, *Baseball's Great Moments*, p. 10.
2. *New York Times*, Mar. 1, 1979; Kahn, *The Boys of Summer*, pp. 352–73, Robinson and Duckett, *I Never Had It Made*, p. 61.
3. Kahn, *The Boys of Summer*, pp. 102, 352–73.
4. Cohen et al., *The World Series*, pp. 225–29.
5. Kiernan, *The Miracle at Coogan's Bluff*, pp. 124–27; *Baseball Encyclopedia* (1st ed.), pp. 374–75; Durocher and Linn, *Nice Guys Finish Last*, passim.
6. Kiernan, *The Miracle at Coogan's Bluff*, pp. 133–46.
7. Reichler, *Baseball's Great Moments*, pp. 48–54; Dark and Underwood, "Rhubarbs, Hassles, Other Hazards."
8. *New York Times*, Oct. 9, 1971.
9. Kiernan, *The Miracle at Coogan's Bluff*, pp. 148–49.
10. Honig, *The Man in the Dugout*, pp. 100–11.
11. Alston and Burick, *Alston and the Dodgers*, pp. 76–86; *Baseball Digest*, Mar. 1978; Honig, *The Man in the Dugout*, pp. 100–11; *New York Times*, Dec. 9, 1955; *Baseball Encyclopedia* (1st ed.), pp. 390–91.
12. Cohen et al., *The World Series*, pp. 254–58.
13. Ibid., pp. 270–74.
14. Kahn, *The Boys of Summer*, pp. 125ff., 347; Reichler, *Baseball's Great Moments*, pp. 83–85.
15. Cohen et al., *The World Series*, pp. 275–80.
16. Ibid., pp. 281–86.

Profile: Jackie Robinson, Equalitarian

1. Chalk, "The Black Professional Athlete in Major Sports"; Holway, *Voices From the Great Black Baseball Leagues*, pp. 1–12.
2. *The Sporting News*, Sept. 24, 1977; Holway, "Only the Hall Was White"; Peterson, *Only the Ball Was White*, pp. 130–33, 254–55.
3. Voigt, *America Through Baseball*, pp. 114–15; Holway, *Voices From the Great Black Baseball Leagues*, pp. 11–14.
4. Frick et al., "Race Question."
5. Holway, "Only the Hall Was White"; Rosenblatt, "Negroes in Baseball."
6. Holway, *Voices From the Great Black Baseball Leagues*, p. 14.
7. *New York Times*, Apr. 9, 1968; *The Sporting News*, Nov. 1, 1945, Nov. 15, 1945.
8. *The Sporting News*, Nov. 1, 1945.
9. Holway, *Voices From the Great Black Baseball Leagues*, pp. 14–15.
10. Voigt, "Jack Roosevelt Robinson."
11. *New York Times*, Apr. 9, 1968; Woodward, *Sports Page*, pp. 82–83, 134–38; Robinson and Duckett, *I Never Had It Made*, pp. 9–12, 35.
12. Robinson and Duckett, *I Never Had It Made*, pp. 62–67; Olsen, "The Black Athlete—A Shameful Story."
13. Robinson and Duckett, *I Never Had It Made*, pp. 75–119, 137; Kahn, *The Boys of Summer*, pp. 300, 352–61.
14. Olsen, "The Black Athlete—A Shameful Story."
15. Robinson and Smith, *Jackie Robinson: My Own Story*; Roeder, *Jackie Robinson*; Robinson and Rowan, *Wait Till Next Year*; Robinson and Dexter, *Baseball Has Done It*;

Robinson and Duckett, *Breakthrough to the Big Leagues;* Robinson and Duckett, *I Never Had It Made,* pp. 9–12, 29–64.
16. *New York Times,* Oct. 25, 1972.
17. "The Black Dominance," *Time.*

Chapter 3: Born Out of Time: Players of the Postwar Era

1. Allen, "Major League Recruits"; *Reading Eagle,* Aug. 12, 1973; *The Sporting News,* June 18, 1977.
2. Holway, "Only the Hall Was White"; Peterson, *Only the Ball Was White,* p. 133; Rosenblatt, "Negroes in Baseball."
3. Golenbock, *Dynasty,* pp. 138–39.
4. Ibid., pp. 134–43; *New York Times,* Feb. 21, 1981.
5. *The Sporting News,* Oct. 30, 1970; *Baseball Digest,* July 1957; Rosenblatt, "Only the Hall Was White."
6. Veeck and Linn, *The Hustler's Handbook,* pp. 211–30.
7. Schrag, "The Age of Willie Mays."
8. Ibid.; Kempton, "The Homecoming of Willie Mays."
9. *Baseball Digest,* May 1947, Oct. 1952; Allen, "Major League Recruits."
10. *Baseball Digest,* Sept. 1950, Nov. 1950, July 1956.
11. Ibid., Aug. 1950, Mar. 1951, Oct. 1953; Allen, "Major League Recruits."
12. Allen, "Major League Recruits"; Allen, *The Hot Stove League,* pp. 51–72; *Baseball Digest,* Aug. 1956, Sept. 1957; *The Sporting News,* Nov. 27, 1976.
13. *Baseball Digest,* Oct. 1952, Apr. 1957; Andreano, *No Joy in Mudville,* pp. 126ff.
14. Haerle, "Member of the Team, But Uniquely Alone"; Brosnan, "It's a Long, Long Season."
15. Allen, *The Hot Stove League,* pp. 51–53; *Baseball Digest,* Mar. 1951, Oct. 1953, Mar. 1954, July 1959.
16. Durocher and Linn, *Nice Guys Finish Last,* pp. 280–86; Veeck and Linn, *The Hustler's Handbook,* p. 154.
17. *Baseball Digest,* May 1948, Aug. 1950; Voigt, "Sex in Baseball."
18. Voigt, "Sex in Baseball"; *Baseball Digest,* Aug. 1950, Feb. 1951, May 1955, Nov. 1954; Higbe and Quigley, *The High Hard One,* pp. 116–23.
19. *Baseball Digest,* Mar. 1951, Oct. 1953, Jan.–Feb. 1957; *New York Times,* May 17, 1967.
20. *Baseball Digest,* Oct. 1953, Mar. 1954, Apr. 1957, Aug. 1967, July 1973.
21. *Baseball Encyclopedia* (3rd ed.), p. 746.
22. *Baseball Digest,* Nov. 1946, Apr. 1959, Mar. 1966; *The Sporting News,* Oct. 29, 1958; Povich, *All These Mornings,* pp. 211–13.
23. *The Sporting News,* Apr. 22, 1972.
24. *Baseball Digest,* Aug. 1950; Seaver and Smith, *How I Would Pitch to Babe Ruth,* pp. 251–68; Williams and Underwood, *My Turn at Bat,* passim. *My Turn at Bat* was serialized in *Sports Illustrated,* June 10, 1968 to July 8, 1968.
25. *Baseball Digest,* Nov. 1946.
26. Ibid., July 1958, July 1959; *The Sporting News,* May 25, 1974, Apr. 9, 1977; Seaver and Smith, *How I Would Pitch to Babe Ruth,* pp. 186–97.
27. Durocher and Linn, *Nice Guys Finish Last,* p. 385; Honig, *Baseball When the Grass Was Real,* pp. 265ff.; *New York Times,* Feb. 1, 1976.
28. *Baseball Digest,* Mar. 1954, Sept. 1956, July 1959, Oct. 1972, Feb. 1976; *New York Times,* Dec. 27, 1975; *Philadelphia Inquirer,* Sept. 25, 1977.
29. *Baseball Encyclopedia* (1st ed.), pp. 249–353; *The Sporting News,* Sept. 4, 1977.
30. *Baseball Digest,* Feb. 1969, Nov. 1975, Oct. 1978; Angell, *The Summer Game,* p. 24.
31. *Baseball Digest,* June 1956.

32. Ibid., June 1956.
33. Ibid., Feb. 1951, Apr. 1951, Oct. 1952, Mar. 1954; Lincoln, "First You Learn Where the Mound Is."
34. *Baseball Digest*, Jan.–Feb. 1957, July 1958, Feb. 1959, Oct. 1970.
35. *Philadelphia Inquirer*, July 17, 1977.
36. *The Sporting News*, Mar. 31, 1979.
37. Allen, *The Hot Stove League*, pp. 233–39; *Statistical Bulletin*, Aug. 1975; Kahn, *The Boys of Summer*, passim.
38. *New York Times*, Jan. 5, 1967, Dec. 8, 1967, Feb. 13, 1969, Jan. 1, 1970, Mar. 29, 1970, May 24, 1971, May 28, 1972; *Baseball Digest*, June 1978.
39. Tracy, *The Psychologist at Bat*, pp. 29, 52, 89, 109, 154–55; *The Sporting News*, Aug. 17, 1974; Golenbock, *Dynasty*, pp. 177ff.

Chapter 4: Postwar Potpourri

1. Veeck and Linn, *Veeck-as in Wreck*, p. 325.
2. "Big League Baseball," *Fortune*.
3. Voigt, "Cornelius McGillicuddy."
4. *New York Times*, Sept. 20, 1966; Veeck and Linn, *Veeck-as in Wreck*, p. 257.
5. Veeck and Linn, "Back Where I Belong."
6. *Philadelphia Inquirer*, Aug. 22, 1980; *New York Times*, Aug. 13, 1980, Aug. 30, 1980; Veeck and Linn, *The Hustler's Handbook*, pp. 301–40.
7. *The Sporting News*, Jan. 3, 1976, Feb. 21, 1976; *Sports Illustrated*, Mar. 28, 1977; *New York Times*, Dec. 11, 1975.
8. *Boston Herald American*, Dec. 23, 1979; Onigman, "Tom Yawkey"; *New York Times*, Sept. 30, 1977, Nov. 20, 1977.
9. Furlong, "P.K. Wrigley"; Kowet, *The Rich Who Own Sports*, pp. 11–25; Chass, "The Cubs: A Legacy of Losing Seasons"; *New York Times*, Apr. 13, 1977; *The Sporting News*, Apr. 30, 1977.
10. *Baseball Digest*, June 1959.
11. Angell, *Five Seasons*, pp. 259–78, 335–36; *The Sporting News*, May 31, 1975, Jan. 3, 1976, Mar. 13, 1976, Apr. 3, 1976; *New York Times*, Mar. 8, 1975.
12. *The Sporting News*, Jan. 10, 1970; Reed, "He's Still Filling His Horn of Plenty."
13. *New York Times*, June 18, 1967; *Baseball Digest*, Feb. 1959.
14. *New York Times*, Oct. 9, 1971, Sept. 30, 1976.
15. *Baseball Digest*, Aug. 1956, June 1959, Jan. 1975; *New York Times*, Apr. 7, 1978; Lane and Madden, "Why I Traded Bobby Bonds."
16. Voigt, "Kenesaw Mountain Landis."
17. *The Sporting News*, May 3, 1945, Aug. 2, 1975; Povich, *All These Mornings*, pp. 174–75.
18. Chandler and Underwood, "How I Jumped From Clean Politics Into Dirty Baseball."
19. *The Sporting News*, Oct. 28, 1943; Veeck and Linn, *Veeck-as in Wreck*, pp. 240–43.
20. Frick, *Games, Asterisks, and People*, pp. 1–25, 208–20.
21. *New York Times*, Nov. 6, 1964, Nov. 13, 1965, Nov. 18, 1965.
22. Veeck and Linn, *Veeck-as in Wreck*, pp. 240–51.
23. Ibid., p. 251; *New York Times*, Nov. 6, 1964, Nov. 18, 1965, Apr. 10, 1978, Apr. 11, 1978; *The Sporting News*, Apr. 22, 1978; Frick, *Games, Asterisks, and People*, introduction and p. 220.
24. Woodward, *Sports Page*, pp. 3–4, 26, 35, 45–49.
25. Lieb, *Baseball as I Have Known It*, p. 20; Holtzman, *No Cheering in the Press Box*, pp. 163–68.
26. Holtzman, *No Cheering in the Press Box*, pp. 1–14, 230–42, 273–87; Veeck and

Linn, *Veeck-as in Wreck*, p. 316; *New York Times*, May 10, 1973, Dec. 7, 1973, July 2, 1978.

27. Reamer, *The Best of Red Smith*, foreword and pp. 120–22, 169–73; Smith, "My Pressbox Memoirs"; Stein, "Sportswriting's Poet Laureate"; Holtzman, *No Cheering in the Pressbox*, pp. 244–59; *New York Times*, Nov. 22, 1978; *The Sporting News*, Dec. 4, 1976; Yardley, "Everybody Knew Me, Al."

28. Shecter, *The Jocks*, p. 23.

29. Cartwright, "Confessions of a Washed Up Sports Writer."

30. *The Sporting News*, June 20, 1970, June 30, 1973, Nov. 23, 1974, July 30, 1977; Holtzman, *No Cheering in the Press Box*, p. 305.

31. *Philadelphia Inquirer*, June 15, 1979; *New York Times*, Nov. 21, 1971.

32. Kennedy, "Oh, What an Era!"

33. Johnson, *Super Spectator and the Electronic Lilliputians*, pp. 6–17; *Baseball Digest*, Apr. 1951.

Chapter 5: Plastic Baseball

1. *New York Times*, Aug. 2, 1959, Dec. 8, 1974.

2. Angell, *The Summer Game*, pp. 96–100; *New York Times*, Dec. 3, 1967, Apr. 7, 1968.

3. *New York Times*, June 2, 1968; *Baseball Digest*, Dec.–Jan. 1969; *The Sporting News*, Apr. 14, 1969, Oct. 23, 1973.

4. *Baseball Digest*, Nov. 1976; *The Sporting News*, Mar. 22, 1976, Dec. 10 and 17, 1977; *New York Times*, June 4, 1972, Jan. 17, 1975, Feb. 21, 1976, Apr. 17, 1976, Aug. 13, 1976, Feb. 6, 1977, Mar. 24, 1977.

5. *New York Times*, Oct. 9, 1966, Apr. 12, 1967, Feb. 9, 1969, Aug. 22, 1975.

6. Papanek, "There's an Ill Wind Blowing for the NBA."

7. Durso, "What's Happened to Baseball?"; *New York Times*, Mar. 20, 1979.

8. Appel, "It's a Whole New Ball Game."

9. *New York Times*, Mar. 13, 1980.

10. Ibid., July 1, 1979; Shannon and Kalinsky, *The Ball Parks*, pp. 9–12, 243–65; Oriard, "Sports and Space"; Surface, "How Much Are Sports Arenas Costing the Taxpayers?"; Riess, "Civic Financed Stadiums."

11. *New York Times*, Sept. 30, 1973, Feb. 13, 1978.

12. *The Sporting News*, Oct. 14, 1978, Jan. 13, 1979, Mar. 3, 1979, May 5, 1979; *Baseball Digest*, June 1979.

13. Keith, "They're Knocking the Stuffing Out of It"; Fimrite, "Pinning Down the Voodoo Ball"; *The Sporting News*, Apr. 13, 1974, July 12, 1975.

14. *Sports Illustrated*, June 7, 1976; *The Sporting News*, Mar. 8, 1969, Feb. 27, 1971; *New York Times*, Oct. 11, 1976; *Reading Eagle*, June 13, 1971.

15. *Time*, Apr. 30, 1973.

Profile: Walter O'Malley, Expansionist

1. *New York Times*, July 24, 1977.

2. Interview with Roone Arledge, *Playboy;* Parrott, *The Lords of Baseball*, p. 265; *The Sporting News*, Feb. 14, 1976.

3. Chandler and Underwood, "How I Jumped From Clean Politics Into Dirty Baseball"; *Sports Illustrated*, Apr. 26, 1971, May 3, 1971; *New York Times*, Apr. 17, 1946, June 6, 1949.

4. Stump, "On Deck for the Dodgers"; Kahn, *The Boys of Summer*, pp. 383–91.

5. U.S. House of Representatives Report, "Organized Professional Team Sports," pp. 1359–72, 1860–61.

6. *New York Times*, Oct. 13, 1974; Kennedy and Williamson, "Money—the Monster Threatening Sports."

7. *Baseball Digest*, May 1969; Stump, "On Deck for the Dodgers"; *The Sporting News*, June 22, 1974; Parrott, *The Lords of Baseball*, pp. 10–19; Kennedy and Williamson, "Money—the Monster Threatening Sports."

8. *The Sporting News*, Feb. 19, 1977.

9. *New York Times*, Jan. 12, 1977.

10. Ibid., Nov. 25, 1965, Jan. 30, 1968.

11. Parrott, *The Lords of Baseball*, pp. 10–29, 46–49.

Chapter 6: Expansion Baseball: The National League

1. *Baseball Encyclopedia* (1st ed.), pp. 427–29; *New York Times*, Sept. 18, 1976; Reichler, *Baseball's Great Moments*, pp. 109–11, 143–45.

2. *Baseball Encyclopedia* (1st ed.), pp. 438–39; *The Sporting News*, Sept. 3, 1977; *Baseball Digest*, Dec. 1975.

3. Manchester, *The Glory and the Dream*, pp. 1005–123; Trippett, "The '70s, A Time of Pause"; Reich, *The Greening of America*, passim; Toffler, *Future Shock*, passim.

4. Flood and Carter, *The Way It Is*, pp. 172–84.

5. *New York Times*, Dec. 21, 1969; *Philadelphia Inquirer*, Apr. 28–30, 1974; *Baseball Digest*, Jan. 1970.

6. *New York Times*, July 28, 1969, Oct. 17, 1969; *Philadelphia Inquirer*, Apr. 28–30, 1974.

7. Vecsey, *Joy in Mudville*, pp. 161, 167, 185–86, 202–49; *Baseball Encyclopedia* (3rd ed.), pp. 533–36; Reichler, *Baseball's Great Moments*, pp. 177–84.

8. *Baseball Encyclopedia* (3rd ed.), p. 2093; *Baseball Digest*, Jan. 1970; *New York Times*, Oct. 11, 1969.

9. Trippett, "The '70s, A Time of Pause."

10. *New York Times*, Oct. 13, 15, and 19, 1971; Cohen et al., *The World Series*, pp. 335–39; *Philadelphia Inquirer*, Oct. 20, 1971; *Pittsburgh Press*, Oct. 18 and 19, 1971.

11. *New York Times*, Apr. 16, 1979, July 6, 1979; Cohen et al., *The World Series*, pp. 345–50.

12. Cohen et al., *The World Series*, pp. 351–54; Angell, *Five Seasons*, pp. 147–94.

13. Deford, "Watch on the Ohio"; *Sports Illustrated*, Sept. 29, 1975; *New York Times*, Nov. 25, 1976; *Philadelphia Inquirer*, Oct. 13, 1976.

14. *New York Times*, Nov. 25, 1976, Oct. 24 and 25, 1977.

15. *Baseball Bulletin*, Dec. 1978; *Time*, Oct. 23, 1978; *New York Times*, Dec. 11, 1978; Fimrite, "The Battle is Rejoined."

16. *Sports Illustrated*, May 8, 1978, Oct. 9 and 16, 1978; *The Sporting News*, Sept. 2, 1978; *Reading Eagle*, Oct, 2, 1978; *Philadelphia Inquirer*, Oct. 8–18, 1978.

17. *The Sporting News*, Oct. 13, 20, and 27, 1979, Nov. 3, 1979; *Washington Post*, Oct. 7, 1979; *New York Times*, Oct. 3–7 and 13, 1979, Nov. 22, 1979; *The Sporting News*, Nov. 3, 1979.

Chapter 7: Expansion Baseball: The American League

1. Golenbock, *Dynasty*, pp. 351–70; *Baseball Encyclopedia* (1st ed.), pp. 430–32; Cohen et al., *The World Series*, pp. 302–6; Mann, *The Decline and Fall of the New York Yankees*, passim.

2. Koppett, "A Yankee Dynasty Can Never Come Back."

3. *Baseball Encyclopedia* (3rd ed.), p. 2094; Cohen et al., *The World Series*, pp. 326–29.

4. *New York Times*, Oct. 19, 1971; Deford, "Best Damn Team in Baseball."

5. *New York Times*, Oct. 3, 1976; Clark, *Champagne and Baloney*, pp. 8–29; Jackson and Libby, *Reggie*, pp. 5–17, 116; Honig, *The Man in the Dugout*, pp. 208–10.

6. Jackson and Libby, *Reggie*, p. 17.

7. Ibid., p. 68.

8. Ibid., pp. 4–32, 68; *New York Times,* Oct. 20, 1974.

9. Kuenster, *From Cobb to Catfish,* p. 32; *New York Times,* Oct. 20, 1974; Clark, *Champagne and Baloney,* pp. 186–239.

10. Jackson and Libby, *Reggie,* pp. 256, 263. See also Clark, *Champagne and Baloney,* 252–53.

11. *Baseball Encyclopedia* (3rd ed.), pp. 571–73; *New York Times,* July 8, 1975, Aug. 29, 1975, Oct. 3, 1976; Reed, "Again, A Hub of Anxiety"; *Philadelphia Inquirer,* Oct. 9, 1975; *Baseball Digest,* Mar. 1979.

12. *New York Times,* June 2, 1965, Apr. 7, 1966, May 9, 1966; *The Sporting News,* Sept. 16, 1966, June 27, 1970, Feb. 20, 1971; *Baseball Digest,* May 1969, Feb. 1970; Koppett, "A Yankee Dynasty Can Never Come Back."

13. *New York Times,* July 19–20, 1979; Kornheiser, "That Damn Yankee."

14. *New York Times,* Dec. 2, 1976, Mar. 19, 1979; *Baseball Digest,* Mar. 1977, Apr. 1978.

15. *New York Times,* June 20, 1977.

16. Lyle and Golenbock, *The Bronx Zoo,* p. 217.

17. *The Sporting News,* Sept. 23, 1978; Gammons, "The Boston Massacre."

18. *Baseball Digest,* Oct. 1979; *The Sporting News,* Oct. 20, 1979, Nov. 10, 1979. At one point 55 major league players were on disabled lists.

19. *Baseball Digest,* Jan. 1979; *New York Times,* Oct. 1, 1979; *Time,* Oct. 8, 1979.

20. *Baseball Digest,* Dec. 1979; *The Sporting News,* Dec. 15, 1979; *New York Times,* July 30, 1979, Nov. 22, 1979.

21. *Baseball Digest,* Oct. 1979; *Washington Post,* Oct. 7, 1979; *The Sporting News,* Oct. 13, 20, and 27, 1979.

Profile: Marvin Miller, Emancipator

1. Evers and Fullerton, *Touching Second,* pp. 42–45; Voigt, *America Through Baseball,* chapter 8; *New York Times,* Aug. 7, 1974.

2. *The Sporting News,* Nov. 9, 1944, Feb. 13, 1945, Nov. 13, 1946; *Baseball Digest,* Nov. 1945.

3. *Baseball Digest,* May 1947; *The Sporting News,* Nov. 9, 1949.

4. *New York Times,* Dec. 30, 1975.

5. Ibid., Feb. 2, 1947; *The Sporting News,* Apr. 25, 1946, June 19, 1946, Aug. 28, 1946, Nov. 16, 1949.

6. U.S. House of Representatives Report, "Organized Professional Team Sports," pp. 1309–11, 1356; *New York Times,* July 13, 1954.

7. *Washington Post,* Dec. 2, 1967; U.S. House of Representatives Report, "Organized Professional Team Sports," pp. 1336ff.; *New York Times,* May 22, 1976.

8. *Baseball Digest,* Aug. 1950, Sept. 1950, Feb. 1951, Mar. 1951, Oct. 1953, July 1956; Reichler, "Fines"; *New York Times,* June 20, 1965, Nov. 11, 1968.

9. *New York Times,* Aug. 24, 1966, Dec. 2, 1966, Feb. 26, 1973.

10. Parrott, *Lords of Baseball,* p. 17.

11. *New York Times,* Feb. 13, 1966; Boyle, "This Miller Admits He's a Grind."

12. Boyle, "This Miller Admits He's a Grind"; *Reading Eagle,* Nov. 18, 1976.

13. *New York Times,* Aug. 24, 1966, Dec. 2, 1966; Boyle, "This Miller Admits He's a Grind."

14. *New York Times,* Feb. 9, 1969; *Reading Eagle,* Feb. 9, 1969; Smith, "Baseball Needs a New Pitch."

15. *New York Times,* May 26, 1970.

16. Ibid., Nov. 26, 1972, Feb. 26, 1973; *The Sporting News,* June 6, 1970; Flood and Black, "The Legacy of Curt Flood"; Flood and Carter, *The Way It Is,* pp. 14–15, 41–57, 134–44; *Philadelphia Inquirer,* June 12, 1978; Lowenfish and Lupien, *The Imperfect*

Diamond, pp. 212–13. The court ruled that the reserve clause was "unusual" and suggested that it be reformed either by clubs and players or by the U.S. Congress.

17. Voigt, *America Through Baseball,* pp. 136–38.
18. *New York Times,* Feb. 26, 1973, Mar. 2, 1973.
19. *The Sporting News,* Jan. 26, 1974, Mar. 16, 1974, Feb. 14, 1975, Feb. 21, 1975.
20. *New York Times,* Oct. 14, 1974, Dec. 16–19, 1974, Mar. 24, 1978.
21. Ibid., Oct. 24, 1974.
22. Ibid., Oct. 26, 1975, Nov. 22, 1975.
23. Ibid., Dec. 24, 1975, Dec. 10, 1977.
24. Ibid., Mar. 5, 1978.
25. Good, "The Year the Mets Lost 'The Franchise.' "
26. Parrott, *The Lords of Baseball,* p. 265.

Chapter 8: A New Breed of Ball Players

1. *The Sporting News,* Sept. 9, 1972, Mar. 23, 1974, Apr. 26, 1975, May 1, 1976; *Baseball Digest,* Nov. 1974; *Sports Illustrated,* Apr. 24, 1978.
2. *Baseball Digest,* Aug. 1970, Nov. 1974, Oct. 1976.
3. *Sports Illustrated,* Apr. 21, 1975; *New York Times,* Dec. 19, 1976.
4. *Sport,* Oct. 1979; *Baseball Digest,* Nov. 1975.
5. *New York Times,* Aug. 22, 1970, Oct. 3, 1970; Jackson and Libby, *Reggie,* pp. 10–11, 17; McLain and Diles, *Nobody's Perfect,* passim.
6. Scholl, *Running Press Glossary of Baseball Language,* passim; *Baseball Digest,* June 1979; *New York Times,* Apr. 28, 1974, Apr. 11, 1978; *Sports Illustrated,* Feb. 25, 1974.
7. Ralbovsky, *The Namath Effect,* pp. 5–39, 61–71, 98, 102–11, 154–57, 179–81; Veeck and Linn, *The Hustler's Handbook,* p. 154.
8. Brosnan, *The Long Season,* pp. 5–19, 25–28, 53–59, 71, 86, 98–103, 160, 192–93, 287.
9. *New York Times,* May 4, 1976, Dec. 27, 1978.
10. *Baseball Digest,* Aug. 1950, Apr. 1951, Aug. 1956; *The Sporting News,* Feb. 22, 1950, Oct. 3, 1970, May 29, 1976.
11. *The Sporting News,* May 28, 1952; U.S. House of Representatives Report, "Organized Professional Team Sports," pp. 1413–14; Andreano, *No Joy in Mudville,* p. 140.
12. *New York Times,* Sept. 23, 1977; *Baseball Digest,* Apr. 1957.
13. *Philadelphia Inquirer,* Aug. 15, 1978.
14. Kennedy and Williamson, "Money: The Monster Threatening Sports"; *The Sporting News,* Jan. 28, 1977, July 2, 1977, Mar. 31, 1979.
15. *New York Times,* Mar. 28 and 31, 1966, Apr. 1, 1966, May 21, 1970.
16. *Reading Eagle,* March 21, 1969; *Time,* Apr. 19, 1968.
17. *New York Times,* Mar. 2 and 16, 1966, Apr. 6, 1966, Feb. 27, 1969; *The Sporting News,* July 11, 1970, Feb. 27, 1971, Mar. 20, 1971, Apr. 17, 1971, June 5, 1971.
18. *Look,* Apr. 21, 1970; *The Sporting News,* Apr. 12, 1970.
19. Kennedy and Williamson, "Money: The Monster Threatening Sports"; Kahn, "Of Galahad and Quests That Failed"; *New York Times,* Feb. 23, 1973, Nov. 17, 1974, Feb. 14, 1979; *The Sporting News,* May 29, 1976, Apr. 16, 1977, July 2, 1977, Jan. 28, 1978.
20. *New York Times,* Feb. 23, 1973; *The Sporting News,* May 29, 1976, Feb. 14, 1979.
21. *The Sporting News,* Apr. 8, 1972, Aug. 5, 1972; *New York Times,* May 10, 1972, Feb. 10, 1973, Mar. 7, 24, and 31, 1973.
22. *New York Times,* Mar. 5 and 24, 1978; *Sports Illustrated,* July 17, 24, and 31, 1978; *Philadelphia Inquirer,* Sept. 1, 1979; *The Sporting News,* April 23, 1977, July 21, 1977.

23. *New York Times,* June 5, 1977, July 10, 1977.

24. *The Sporting News,* Nov. 5, 1977, Jan. 28, 1978; *Philadelphia Inquirer,* Nov. 6, 1978.

25. *New York Times,* Jan. 27, 1979; *The Sporting News,* Mar. 10, 1979, Sept. 29, 1979. In 1978 Oakland's $49,000 salary average was baseball's lowest.

26. *The Sporting News,* Dec. 15, 1979.

27. *Sports Illustrated,* July 31, 1978. Average attendance at a major league game in 1967 was 17,187; in 1977 it was 19,991. In 1967 nationally televised games were viewed in 9.5 million households; in 1977 the total was 10.1 million.

28. *The Sporting News,* Apr. 8, 1972; *New York Times,* Dec. 12, 1973. See also the *Basic Agreement Between the American League of Professional Baseball Clubs and the National League of Professional Baseball Clubs and Major League Baseball Players Association,* effective on June 1, 1976, found in the office of Major League Baseball Players Association, N.Y.C., N.Y.

29. Rosenblatt, "Negroes in Baseball"; "The Black Dominance," *Time; New York Times,* Mar. 28, 1971; *The Sporting News,* Aug. 31, 1974; Siwoff, *Book of Baseball Records,* pp. 321–37.

30. Siwoff, *Book of Baseball Records,* pp. 342, 345; *Baseball Digest,* Mar. 1974, June 1974; *Philadelphia Inquirer,* Oct. 25, 1978; Angell, *Five Seasons,* p. 162.

31. *New York Times,* May 10 and 12, 1972, Sept. 21, 1973, Nov. 4, 1973, July 29, 1979; *The Sporting News,* Jan. 17, 1970; Kempton, "The Homecoming of Willie Mays"; Blount, "Yea, Mr. Mays."

32. *New York Times,* Dec. 2 and 12, 1973, Apr. 5 and 9, 1974, Nov. 13, 1978; *The Sporting News,* July 13, 1973; Buckley, "The Packaging of a Home Run"; Interview with Hank Aaron, *Playboy.*

33. Scully, "Discrimination: The Case of Baseball"; Eitzen, "Immune From Racism?"

34. *Baseball Encyclopedia* (3rd ed.), p. 1276; Siwoff, *Book of Baseball Records,* p. 352; *Baseball Digest,* Dec. 1977; *New York Times,* Dec. 8, 1971; Shecter, "Frank Robinson's Cool Assault."

35. *New York Times,* Sept. 26, 1974, Oct. 4, 1974, Apr. 18, 1978; Robinson and Blount, "I'll Always Be Outspoken"; Siwoff, *Book of Baseball Records,* pp. 318, 321–22, 352–53.

36. Durocher and Linn, *Nice Guys Finish Last,* p. 325.

37. *Official Baseball Register* (1978), p. 50; *New York Times,* Mar. 17, 1968, Aug, 7, 9, 28, and 31, 1977, Sept. 4, 1977, Mar. 8, 1978, May 7, 1979; *Philadelphia Inquirer,* Nov. 15, 1974, Aug, 28, 1977; *The Sporting News,* Oct. 20, 1979; *Baseball Digest,* Apr. 1971, Feb. 1972, Feb. 1974, Dec. 1976, May 1977, Feb. 1978.

38. *Official Baseball Register* (1978), p. 332; Ribowsky, "This Pitcher Makes Hitters Tremble"; *New York Times,* Aug. 12, 1980.

39. Olsen, "The Black Athlete—A Shameful Story"; *New York Times,* Jan. 24, 1967, Aug, 24, 1967, Dec. 17, 1967, Feb. 16, 1968, Dec. 9, 1971, Apr. 16, 1972; *New York Post,* Aug. 30, 1967; *The Sporting News,* Mar. 21, 1970, Mar. 4, 1971, Nov. 20, 1971; Hano, "The Black Rebel Who 'Whitelists' the Olympics."

40. *The Sporting News,* Dec. 26, 1970, Sept. 11, 1971; *San Francisco Chronicle,* Sept. 3, 1971; *New York Times,* Sept. 29, 1973, July 27, 1975, Mar. 21, 1979.

41. *Philadelphia Inquirer,* May 8, 1975; *New York Times,* Aug. 26, 1967, Nov. 15, 1970, Sept. 1 and 29, 1971, Feb. 28, 1973, Aug. 5, 1974, Apr. 6, 1975; Fimrite, "For Failure to Give His Best"; *The Sporting News,* Oct. 16, 1971; *San Francisco Chronicle,* Sept. 2, 1971.

42. *New York Times,* Mar. 1, 1978.

43. *The Sporting News,* Oct. 26, 1968, Mar. 21, 1970, Oct. 10, 1970.

44. Flood and Carter, *The Way It Is,* passim; *New York Times,* Apr. 12, 1973; Hall and Ellis, *Dock Ellis In the Country of Baseball,* pp. 140–52, 242–52.

45. *New York Times*, Mar. 26, 1972, Oct. 27, 1975, Sept. 15, 1976; LeFlore and Hawkins, "Stealing Was My Specialty."

46. Jackson and Libby, *Reggie*, p. i.

47. Ibid., pp. i–ii, 1–3; *New York Times*, Mar. 19, 1970, May 7, 1970, Nov. 30, 1970.

48. Jackson and Libby, *Reggie*, pp. 15–61, 81, 92–93, 101, 158–59, 203.

49. *New York Times*, Apr. 10, 1976, Nov. 30, 1976, May 24, 1977, Sept. 30, 1977, Oct. 21, 1977.

50. Lardner, "Operation Yanqui"; *New York Times*, Mar. 19, 1978; Povich, *All These Mornings*, pp. 183–84.

51. *Reading Eagle*, May 10, 1970; *Baseball Digest*, June 1969, Sept. 1970, Aug. 1973; *The Sporting News*, Apr. 17, 1971; *Baseball Magazine*, Apr. 1980; *New York Times*, Dec. 17, 1976, Mar. 6, 1977; *Baseball Encyclopedia* (4th ed.), p. 1656.

52. Granberg, "Baseball: It's Not a Game to Many Latins."

53. Wagenheim, *Clemente*, pp. 1–37, 132; *Reading Eagle*, May 17, 1970; *Baseball Research Journal* (1973), p. 102; Ways, " 'Nobody Does Anything Better Than Me in Baseball,' Says Roberto Clemente"; *New York Times*, Oct. 14, 1972, Jan. 2, 1973, Mar. 21, 1973, Apr. 1, 1973, Feb. 22, 1976.

54. *Baseball Digest*, Apr. 1970, Dec. 1975; *The Sporting News*, Oct. 26, 1968, Sept. 16, 1972; Leggett, "The Season of the Zero Hour"; Leggett, "From Mountain to Molehill"; Lardner, "The Pitchers Are Ruining the Game"; *New York Times*, June 22, 1975, Sept. 14, 1975.

55. Perry, *Me and the Spitter*, passim; Fimrite, "Every Little Movement"; *Philadelphia Inquirer*, Oct. 25, 1978; *Baseball Digest*, Aug. 1969, Sept. 1979; *New York Times*, June 25, 1979.

56. *Philadelphia Inquirer*, Apr. 7 and 28, 1968, Dec. 5, 1973; *Baseball Digest*, May 1968, Mar. 1971, Apr. 1973, Mar. 1974, Feb. 1975, July 1977.

57. Furlong, "Johnny Bench: Supercatcher"; *New York Times*, Oct. 20, 1972.

58. *New York Times*, Aug. 3, 1979; Stein, "The Disillusionment of Carlton Fisk."

59. Twombly, "Meet an Average Major Leaguer: Dirty Al."

60. *New York Times*, May 22, 1978, June 14, 1978; "Lelyveld, The Big Leaguer."

Chapter 9: Living the Dream

1. *Baseball Digest*, Aug. 1976; Haerle, "Career Patterns and Career Contingencies."

2. *Baseball Digest*, Aug. 1950, Mar. 1951, Sept. 1972, June 1978; *The Sporting News*, Feb. 5, 1972; *New York Times*, July 30, 1972; Roberts, *Fans!* pp. 20–21; Adamic, *What's Your Name?* passim.

3. Levy and Stevenson, "The Secret Life of Baseball."

4. Jackson and Libby, *Reggie*, p. 25; *New York Times*, May 1, 1974; *The Sporting News*, July 24, 1971.

5. Naughton, "Tension and Pressure of a Pennant Race"; *New York Times*, Sept. 30, 1979.

6. *Baseball Digest*, Nov. 1971, June 1976, Apr. 1977.

7. *The Sporting News*, Aug. 17, 1974, Aug. 9, 1975.

8. Ibid., Mar. 30, 1974; *Baseball Digest*, Apr. 1975; *Philadelphia Inquirer*, July 19, 1977; "The Pride of the Yankees," *Time*.

10. Duren and Drury, *The Comeback*, passim.

11. *New York Times*, Mar. 31, 1975; *Baseball Digest*, Apr. 1971.

12. *Philadelphia Inquirer*, Sept. 8, 1977; Conigliaro and Zanger, "Seeing It Through"; *The Sporting News*, Sept. 4, 1971.

13. *New York Times*, Oct. 7, 1972; *Baseball Digest*, Sept. 1959, Mar. 1970, Sept. 1977.

14. *Philadelphia Inquirer*, May 9, 1976; *Baseball Digest*, Nov. 1972.

15. Freehan, Gelman, and Schaap, *Behind the Mask*, pp. 19–21, 53, 61, 124; *Philadelphia Inquirer*, Sept. 8, 1977.

16. *Baseball Digest*, Sept. 1947, Feb. 1959, Sept. 1970; *The Sporting News*, Feb. 4, 1978; *Philadelphia Inquirer*, Mar. 5, 1978; *New York Times*, July 24, 1979.

17. *Philadelphia Inquirer*, Apr. 27, 1978; *Baseball Digest*, Feb. 1959.

18. *Philadelphia Inquirer*, Sept. 13, 1978; *The Sporting News*, Oct. 16, 1971, June 12, 1972; *New York Times*, July 19, 1971, Sept. 29, 1971.

19. *The Sporting News*, Oct. 9, 1976; *Philadelphia Inquirer*, Oct. 19, 1975.

20. *Parade Magazine*, Aug, 31, 1969; Parr, *The Superwives*, passim.

21. *The Sporting News*, Mar. 24, 1973; *Baseball*, Aug. 1979; Stump, "Dames Are the Biggest Headache."

22. Durham, "But Coach, It Helps Me Relax"; Weiss, *Sport: A Philosophic Inquiry*, chapter 2; Massengale, "Coaching as an Occupational Subculture"; Roberts, *Fans!* p. 132.

23. *Reading Eagle*, Oct. 24, 1978; Parrott, *The Lords of Baseball*, pp. 163–64.

24. Higbe and Quigley, *The High Hard One*, pp. 80–81.

25. Higbe and Quigley, *The High Hard One*, passim; Jordan, *A False Spring*, passim; Brosnan, "The Short Season."

26. Michelson, *'Sportin' Ladies*, pp. vii–xiv, 45–52, 63–68; *New York Times*, June 1, 1975, Aug. 12, 1979; *Sports Illustrated*, May 26, 1975.

27. Bouton and Shecter, *Ball Four*, pp. 33–37, 72–76, 124, 164, 252, 307–8, 365; Bouton and Shecter, *I'm Glad You Didn't Take It Personally*, pp. 1–3, 12, 67, 75–85, 133–53.

28. Veeck and Linn, *The Hustler's Handbook*, passim; Belinsky, *Pitching and Wooing*, passim.

29. Polak, "Ruthven: Balking When the Owner Advanced."

30. Gmelch, "Baseball Magic"; Voigt, "No Sex Till Monday: The Fetish Phenomenon in American Sport"; Browne, *Objects of Special Devotion*, pp. 115–35; *Baseball Digest*, Dec. 1974.

31. Gmelch, "Baseball Magic"; Louis, "Should You Buy Biorhythms?"; *Baseball Digest*, Aug. 1979.

32. Kahn, *The Boys of Summer*, p. 224; Blount, "Temple of the Playing Fields"; Roberts, *Fans!* pp. 109–11.

33. *New York Times*, Mar. 5, 1970, Oct. 20, 1974, Jan. 16, 1978.

34. Ibid., Apr. 9, 1978; Freehan, Gelman, and Schaap, *Behind the Mask*, pp. 102–3, 158, 189.

35. Personal interview with Curtis Simmons.

36. *New York Times*, Dec. 1, 1966, Feb. 28, 1971, May 21, 1972; *The Sporting News*, May 6, 1972; *Philadelphia Evening Bulletin*, Sept. 29, 1971.

37. *New York Times*, May 7, 1978, June 14, 1978.

38. *Philadelphia Inquirer*, Mar. 14, 1978; *Reading Eagle*, Sept. 29, 1970; *New York Times*, Mar. 9, 1970, Mar. 14, 1975.

39. Andreano, *No Joy in Mudville*, pp. 4–16; *New York Times*, Nov. 21, 1973.

40. *New York Times*, Aug. 24, 1970, May 15, 1978; *Reading Eagle*, Apr. 26, 1970; Roberts, *Fans!* pp. 84–85, 95, 122–28; *Philadelphia Inquirer*, Sept. 23, 1977.

41. Parrott, *Lords of Baseball*, p. 45.

42. Interview with Pete Rose, *Playboy*.

43. *New York Times*, Aug. 18, 1967.

44. Kirshenbaum, "Well Hush Their Mouths."

45. *The Sporting News*, Oct. 29, 1977.

46. "The Forty Million Dollar Body Shuffle," *Sports Illustrated*; *New York Times*, Mar. 19, 1978.

47. *Philadelphia Inquirer*, June 9, 1976, June 2, 1977; *New York Times*, Mar. 17, 1969, Apr. 21, 1969, Mar. 11, 1970, Feb. 3, 1978, Mar. 7 and 12, 1978.

48. *New York Times,* Aug. 4, 1972; *Philadelphia Inquirer,* June 4, 1971.
49. *Philadelphia Inquirer,* Sept. 11, 1977; *The Sporting News,* Oct. 21, 1978.
50. *New York Times,* Mar. 8, 1965, Aug. 4, 1972, Feb. 3, 1978, Apr. 1, 1978.
51. Ibid., July 3, 1978.
52. Freehan, Gelman, and Schaap, *Behind the Mask,* p. 118.
53. *New York Times,* May 31, 1966; *Baseball Digest,* Feb. 1959, Apr. 1959; *The Sporting News,* Jan. 26, 1971; *Sports Illustrated,* Oct. 4, 1976.
54. *The Sporting News,* Mar. 15, 1975, Sept. 3, 1977; *Baseball Digest,* Oct. 1979; Angell, *Five Seasons,* pp. 343–46.
55. Personal interview with Brandy Davis; Rooney, *A Geography of American Sport,* passim; Ordine, "Searching for Gems on Rough Diamonds." Obojski, *Bush League,* pp. 26–29, and *The Sporting News,* Nov. 20, 1976, sketches the declining attendance and dwindling number of leagues at the minor league level.
56. Obojski, *Bush League,* pp. 18–29; Veeck and Linn, "The Baseball Establishment."
57. *The Sporting News,* Dec. 14, 1949, May 31, 1969, Dec. 22, 1975.
58. *New York Times,* Mar. 6, 1978, Sept. 2, 1980.
59. Ibid., Mar. 6, 1978; Ryan, *Wait Till I Make the Show,* pp. 26–27, 72–75, 100–5, 223–31; *The Sporting News,* June 20, 1970, Nov. 20, 1971, June 24, 1972, Aug. 30, 1975, Dec. 13, 1975, Apr. 8, 1978. Klein, *On the Way Up,* pp. 11–23, 25–76, 86–106.
60. Klein, *On the Way Up,* pp. 11–23, 25–65, 67–76, 86–97, 99–106.
61. Jordan, "Big Sky, Big Dream"; *Philadelphia Inquirer,* Mar. 21, 1975; *The Sporting News,* Apr. 5, 1976, Mar. 25, 1978; *Sports Illustrated,* June 11, 1973.
62. Ferretti, "Down on the Farm With the Yankees' Gene Michael"; personal interview with Brandy Davis.

Chapter 10: Of Fans, Owners, and Other Non-Players

1. *Philadelphia Inquirer,* Oct. 8, 1971; *New York Times,* Feb. 1, 1972; *The Sporting News,* Feb. 26, 1977.
2. *Sports Illustrated,* May 18, 1970; *The Sporting News,* Mar. 5, 1977; *Philadelphia Inquirer,* June 8, 1977.
3. *New York Times,* Sept. 3, 1967, Dec. 4, 1967; *New York Post,* July 11, 1967; *The Sporting News,* Feb. 15, 1950.
4. Kennedy, "More Victories Equals More Fans Equals More Profits, Right?"
5. *Baseball Digest,* July 1959; Keith, "Beer is Out, Halters In"; *New York Times,* July 14, 1968, June 27, 1971.
6. Le Bon, *The Crowd,* passim; Klapp, *Currents of Unrest,* pp. 1–67.
7. Furlong, "Out in the Bleachers Where the Action Is"; *New York Times,* July 1, 1973, Jan. 30, 1977; *New York Post,* Aug. 1, 1967; Poe, "The Angry Fan"; Roberts, *Fans!* pp. 14–15, 50ff.
8. Einstein, "The New Breed of Baseball Fan"; *The Sporting News,* Jan. 29, 1972, Mar. 2, 1974; *New York Times,* June 6, 1974; Shaw, "The Roots of Rooting."
9. *Family Weekly,* Mar. 27, 1977.
10. *Sports Illustrated,* Apr. 25, 1977.
11. *New York Times,* Apr. 7, 1972, Aug. 14, 1972; Povich, *All These Mornings,* pp. 211–13; *Philadelphia Inquirer,* Mar. 12, 1975, Oct. 30, 1977.
12. *New York Times,* Jan. 27, 1967, Sept. 7, 1968; *The Sporting News,* Feb. 8, 1967, Oct. 26, 1968, Mar. 20, 1971, Sept. 4, 1977; Fimrite, "They're Beginning to Sound Like a Broken Record"; Bonventre, "The Ugly Sports Fan."
13. *The Sporting News,* July 24, 1976; *Washington Post,* July 8, 1975.
14. Le Bon, *The Crowd,* p. 174.
15. Deford, "Nobody Loves the Ruling Class"; *The Sporting News,* Nov. 17, 1973, Sept. 16, 1978.

16. *The Sporting News*, Feb. 16, 1974, Apr. 14, 1976, Nov. 5, 1977; *Baseball Digest*, Mar. 1951, June 1959; Gutkind, *The Best Seat in Baseball*, pp. 124–27.

17. *Baseball Digest*, Sept. 1950, Nov. 1950, Jan. 1951, Nov.–Dec. 1954; Gutkind, *The Best Seat in Baseball*, p. 97; *The Sporting News*, Oct. 19, 1974.

18. *The Sporting News*, June 9, 1979.

19. Gutkind, *The Best Seat in Baseball*, pp. 3–8, 18–36, 39–61, 77–80, 83–100, 205–9, 216.

20. *The Sporting News*, Sept. 13, 1969, Dec. 20, 1969, Dec. 2, 1972, Apr. 14, 1973, Oct. 6, 1973, Dec. 14, 1974, Dec. 13, 1975, Jan. 5, 1976, Feb. 22, 1977; *New York Times*, Mar. 2, 1977; *Sports Illustrated*, Sept. 4, 1978.

21. *The Sporting News*, July 15, 1978, Sept. 16 and 30, 1978; *Philadelphia Inquirer*, Aug. 26 and 28, 1978; *Philadelphia Bulletin*, Aug. 22 and 26, 1978.

22. *The Sporting News*, Sept. 9, 1978; *Philadelphia Inquirer*, June 28, 1979.

23. *The Sporting News*, June 2, 1979; *New York Times*, May 18 and 24, 1979.

24. *New York Times*, May 20, 1979.

25. Swift, "Odd Man Out on the Diamond."

26. *New York Times*, Jan. 3, 1979; Furlong, "At Last a Likable Ump."

27. Pope, *Baseball's Greatest Managers*, p. 165.

28. Brosnan, "The I's, We's, and They's of Baseball."

29. Angell, *The Summer Game*, p. 234; Linn, "The Meaning of the Game"; *New York Times*, Sept. 4, 1973, May 21, 1980.

30. Honig, *The Man in the Dugout*, pp. 251–52, 291–93.

31. *Reading Eagle*, Sept. 20, 1972; *The Sporting News*, Feb. 12, 1972; *New York Times*, June 9, 1978, July 30, 1978, Sept. 25, 1979; *Philadelphia Inquirer*, Sept. 13, 1978.

32. *New York Times*, Apr. 29, 1980; *Baseball Digest*, Oct. 1977; Wilner, "The Earl of Baltimore"; Linn, "The Earl of Baltimore, He's a Mouthful."

33. Bouton, "Reflections on Managing a Baseball Team."

34. *New York Times*, Sept. 12, 1971, July 26, 1972; *Philadelphia Inquirer*, Dec. 4, 1971.

35. Gorman and Holtzman, *Three and Two*, pp. 45, 85–91.

36. *The Sporting News*, Oct. 25, 1969.

37. Ibid., June 30, 1973.

38. Interview with Roone Arledge, *Playboy*.

39. *The Sporting News*, Feb. 14, 1976, May 21, 1977; Interview with Roone Arledge, *Playboy;* Parrott, *Lords of Baseball*, p. 265. Owner Galbreath of Pittsburgh judged baseball to be the only enterprise with partners who met twice a year.

40. Personal interview with Commissioner Eckert.

41. *New York Times*, July 18, 1975, Feb. 1, 1976, Dec. 9, 1977; *Sports Illustrated*, July 28, 1975; *The Sporting News*, Aug. 2, 1975, July 17, 1976.

42. *Philadelphia Inquirer*, Dec. 19, 1980.

43. Ibid.

Chapter 11: New Vistas for Baseball

1. *Time*, June 2, 1967, Oct. 20, 1967; *Sports Illustrated*, Dec. 20–27, 1976.

2. Johnson, "Television Made It All a New Game"; Johnson, *Super Spectator and the Electronic Lilliputians*, pp. 28–29, 215–25.

3. *New York Times*, May 28, 1969, Oct. 26, 1977, Sept. 30, 1979; *The Sporting News*, Feb. 22, 1969, Mar. 6, 1971, May 22, 1971, Mar. 24, 1973, Mar. 31, 1979; *Reading Eagle*, Apr. 16, 1981.

4. *The Sporting News*, May 22, 1971, Feb. 25, 1978; Smith, "Baseball Anyone?"

5. Welles, "We Have Seen the Future of Video"; *New York Times*, May 13, 1972, Oct. 26, 1974; Vaughn, "Ted Turner's True Talent"; *Reading Times*, Apr. 18, 1981; O'Connor, "Television on the Eve of Drastic Change"; *New York Times*, Nov. 13, 1977.

6. *Sports Illustrated*, Jan. 22, 1979; Chandler, "Television and Sports: Wedded With a Golden Hoop."

7. *New York Times*, Nov. 7, 1976, Oct. 30, 1977; Sugar, *The Thrill of Victory*, pp. 270–85, 317.

8. *New York Times*, Oct. 21, 1967; Kennedy, "Oh, What an Era!"; *Baseball Digest*, June 1968; *The Sporting News*, Oct, 23 and 30, 1976.

9. *The Sporting News*, Feb. 26, 1977; *New York Times*, Aug. 5, 1976, Sept. 19, 1976, Jan. 2, 1977, Nov. 12, 1980.

10. *New York Times*, Aug. 15, 1964, Nov. 3, 1964, Feb. 12, 19, and 24, 1965, Dec. 26, 1965, Nov. 20, 1966, May 21, 1967; Kowet, *The Rich Who Own Sports*, pp. 237–38.

11. Myrer, "The Giant in the Tube"; *The Sporting News*, Apr. 3, 1971, Apr. 8, 1972, Nov. 4, 1978; *New York Times*, Oct. 19, 1975.

12. *Philadelphia Inquirer*, Oct. 14, 1978.

13. Durslag, "They Can't Call Them as They See Them"; *New York Times*, Oct. 9, 1966, Nov. 12, 1980; *The Sporting News*, July 15, 1972; *Philadelphia Inquirer*, Nov. 6, 1975, June 8, 1978.

14. *Philadelphia Inquirer*, Nov. 6, 1975; *Sports Illustrated*, Oct. 7, 1968, May 15, 1978; *The Sporting News*, May 15, 1971, Dec. 15, 1973.

15. Marshall, "Howard Cosell Is Just Another Pretty Face"; Sugar, *The Thrill of Victory*, pp. 80–85, 276–88; *Sports Illustrated*, Apr. 17, 1978; *Philadelphia Inquirer*, Nov. 29, 1978.

16. *New York Times*, Mar. 24, 1980.

17. Sugar, *The Thrill of Victory*, pp. 318–22.

18. *The Sporting News*, Mar. 17, 1973; *Los Angeles Times*, Feb. 7, 1975.

19. *New York Times*, May 31, 1977.

20. *The Sporting News*, Mar. 11, 1978; *New York Times*, June 23, 1972.

21. Kahn, "Can Sports Survive Money?"; Blount, "How to Sportswrite Good."

22. Gumpert, "Eye on the Ball."

23. *New York Times*, Sept. 9 and 18, 1979.

24. Holtzman, *No Cheering in the Press Box*, pp. 144–68.

25. *The Sporting News*, Dec. 26, 1970; Baseball Writer's Association of America, *Constitution* (1967); Mendelson, "The Writers."

26. Holtzman, *No Cheering in the Press Box*, pp. 1–4; Lieb, *Baseball As I Have Known It*, pp. 36, 237–40, 265–71; *Philadelphia Inquirer*, June 6, 1980; *New York Times*, June 5, 1980.

27. *The Sporting News*, July 14, 1969, Mar. 17, 1973, July 12 and 19, 1975; *New York Times*, Aug. 12, 1980; *Philadelphia Inquirer*, July 2, 1975, Apr. 14, 1980.

28. *New York Times*, Aug. 29, 1969; Angell, *Five Seasons*, pp. 154–59; James, "Confessions of a Stat Freak"; Koppett, *A Thinking Man's Guide to Baseball*, p. 160. In 1968 a "Special Rules Committee" decided that "baseball shall have one set of records starting in 1876, without any arbitrary division into nineteenth- and twentieth-century data." They also accepted the principle that the "present is normal for all time." When taken to task for ignoring Willie Keeler's 1897 hitting streak, which Pete Rose's 1978 effort only tied, a noted statistician dismissed Keeler's effort as "stone age." For further information see Marc Onigman, *Northwestern University News*, Aug. 9, 1978.

29. Graber, "Baseball in American Fiction"; Roth, "The Great American Rookie"; Roth, "My Baseball Years"; Dillard, "The Wisdom of the Beast: The Fiction of Robert Coover." Ray Majors's *The National Pastime* is an example of a pornographic novel.

30. *Time*, Apr. 7, 1967; Grobani, *Guide to Baseball Literature*.

31. *New York Times*, May 3, 1967.

32. Ibid., Apr. 10, 1966.

33. "Sports and EDP," *Datamation*; Kerrane, "Plays About Play: Recent Sports Drama."

Chapter 12: Or, Striking Out in the 'Eighties?

1. *New York Times*, Nov. 2, 1979.
2. Ibid., Mar. 5 and 6, 1980, Apr. 6, 1980, May 13 and 24, 1980; *Sports Illustrated*, June 2, 1980; *The Sporting News*, Oct. 26, 1980.
3. *Philadelphia Inquirer*, Oct. 6, 1980; *The Sporting News*, Oct. 18 and 25, 1980.
4. *New York Times*, June 18, 1981.
5. Ibid., July 13 and 26, 1981.
6. *Sports Illustrated*, Mar. 9, 1981.
7. *New York Times*, June 22, 1981, July 2, 6, 9, 16, and 20, 1981.
8. *Time*, June 22 and 29, 1981.
9. *Sports Illustrated*, Oct. 5, 1981; *New York Times*, Aug. 21, 1981; *Time*, Aug. 31, 1981.
10. *Sports Illustrated*, Oct. 5, 1981; *Time*, Oct. 19, 1981.
11. *Sports Illustrated*, Oct. 5, 1981; *Time*, Oct. 19, 1981; *New York Times*, Sept. 28, 1981, Oct. 5 and 7, 1981.
12. *Sports Illustrated*, Aug. 17, 1981.

Bibliography

PRIMARY SOURCES

Unpublished Material

Allen, Lee. "Major League Recruits, Year by Year." MS, Office of the Historian, Baseball Hall of Fame, Cooperstown, N.Y.

Chandler, A.B. Papers. Library of the University of Kentucky, Lexington, Kentucky.

"Fines." File in Office of the Baseball Commissioner, New York.

"Former Commissioners." File in Office of the Baseball Commissioner, New York.

Public Documents

U.S. House of Representatives. *Organized Baseball.* Report No. 2002, 82 Cong., 2 sess. (1952).

———. *Organized Professional Team Sports.* Report No. 1720, 85 Cong., 1 sess. (1958).

———. *Telecasting of Professional Sports Contests.* Report No. 1087, 87 Cong., 1 sess. (1961).

Books

Allen, Maury, and Bo Belinsky. *Pitching and Wooing.* New York: Bantam, 1974.

Allen, Mel, and Ed Fitzgerald. *You Can't Beat the Hours.* New York: Harper & Row, 1964.

Alou, Felipe, with Herman Weiskopf. *Felipe Alou: My Life in Baseball.* Waco, Texas: Word Books, 1967.

Alston, Walter, with Si Burick. *Alston and the Dodgers.* New York: Doubleday, 1966.

Baseball Encyclopedia: The Official and Complete Record of Major League Baseball. Edited by Joseph Reichler. New York: Macmillan, 1969 (1st), 1976 (3rd), and 1979 (4th) eds.

Bouton, Jim, with Len Shecter. *Ball Four.* New York: Dell, 1970.

———. *I'm Glad You Didn't Take It Personally.* New York: Dell, 1971.

Brosnan, Jim. *Pennant Race.* New York: Harper & Row, 1962.

————. *The Long Season.* New York: Dell, 1961.

Cohen, Richard M., et al. *The World Series.* New York: Dial, 1976.

Conigliaro, Tony, with Jack Zanger. *Seeing It Through.* New York: Macmillan, 1970.

Conlan, Jocko, and Robert Creamer. *Jocko.* Philadelphia: Lippincott, 1967.

Duren, Ryne, with Richard Drury. *The Comeback.* Dayton, Ohio: Loring Press, 1978.

Durocher, Leo, and Ed Linn. *Nice Guys Finish Last.* New York: Pocket Books, 1976.

Dykes, Jimmie, and Charles Dexter. *You Can't Steal First Base.* Philadelphia: Lippincott, 1967.

Flood, Curt, with Richard Carter. *The Way It Is.* New York: Trident Press, 1971.

Freehan, Bill, with Steve Gelman and Dick Schaap. *Behind the Mask: An Inside Baseball Diary.* New York: Popular Library, 1976.

Frick, Ford C. *Games, Asterisks, and People: Memoirs of A Lucky Fan.* New York: Crown, 1973.

Gorman, Tom, as told to Jerome Holtzman. *Three and Two.* New York: Charles Scribner's Sons, 1979.

Gutkind, Lee. *The Best Seat in Baseball, But You Have to Stand.* New York: Dial, 1975.

Hall, Donald, with Dock Ellis. *Dock Ellis in the Country of Baseball.* New York: Coward, McCann & Geoghegan, 1976.

Higbe, Kirby, with Martin Quigley. *The High Hard One.* New York: Viking, 1967.

Holtzman, Jerome. *No Cheering in the Press Box.* New York: Holt, Rinehart & Winston, 1975.

Holway, John. *Voices From the Great Black Baseball Leagues.* New York: Dodd, Mead, 1976.

Honig, Donald, ed. *Baseball When the Grass Was Real.* New York, Berkeley: Medallion Books, 1976.

————. *The Man In The Dugout.* Chicago: Follett, 1977.

Houk, Ralph, with Charles Dexter. *Ballplayers Are Human Too.* New York: Putnam's, 1962.

Jackson, Reggie, with Bill Libby. *Reggie.* New York: Playboy Press, 1975.

Jordan, Pat. *A False Spring.* New York: Dodd, Mead, 1975.

Klein, Dave, ed. *On the Way Up.* New York: Julian Messner, 1977.

Lyle, Sparky, and Peter Golenbock. *The Bronx Zoo.* New York: Dell, 1979.

McGraw, Tug, and Joseph Durso. *Screwball.* New York: Signet, 1975.

Mack, Connie. *From Sandlot to Big League. Connie Mack's Baseball Book.* New York: Alfred A. Knopf, 1960.

McLain, Denny, and Dave Diles. *Nobody's Perfect.* New York: Dial, 1975.

Mann, Arthur. *Baseball Confidential: Secret History of the War Among Chandler, Durocher, MacPhail and Rickey.* New York: McKay, 1951.

Mantle, Mickey, and Bob Smith. *Mickey Mantle: The Education of a Baseball Player*. New York: Simon & Schuster, 1967.

Michelson, Herb. *Sportin' Ladies*. Radnor, Pa.: Chilton Books, 1975.

Oliva, Tony, with Bob Fowler. *Tony O!* New York: Hawthorn Books, 1973.

Paige, Leroy (Satchel), and David Lipman. *Maybe I'll Pitch Forever*. New York: Doubleday, 1967.

Pepitone, Joe, with Barry Steinback. *Joe, You Coulda Made Us Proud*. New York: Dell, 1975.

Perry, Gaylord. *Me and the Spitter*. New York: New American Library, 1974.

Povich, Shirley. *All These Mornings*. New York: Prentice-Hall, 1969.

Ritter, Lawrence. *The Glory of Their Times*. New York: Macmillan, 1966.

Robinson, Brooks, with Jack Tobin. *Third Base Is My Home*. Waco, Texas: Word Books, 1974.

Robinson, Jack, with Charles Dexter. *Baseball Has Done It*. Philadelphia: Lippincott, 1964.

Robinson, Jack, with Al Duckett. *Breakthrough to the Big League: The Story of Jackie Robinson*. New York: Harper & Row, 1965.

Robinson, Jack, with Al Duckett. *I Never Had It Made: An Autobiography*. New York: Putnam's, 1972.

Robinson, Jack, with Bill Roeder. *Jackie Robinson*. New York: A. S. Barnes, 1950.

Robinson, Jack, with Carl Rowan. *Wait Till Next Year: The Story of Jackie Robinson*. New York: Random House, 1960.

Robinson, Jack, with Wendell Smith. *Jackie Robinson: My Own Story*. New York: Greenberg, 1948.

Rosenthal, Harold. *Baseball Is Their Business*. New York: Random House, 1952.

Siwoff, Seymour. *The Book of Baseball Records*. New York: S. Siwoff, 500 Fifth Ave., 1978.

Tracy, David, Dr. *The Psychologist at Bat*. New York: Sterling, 1951.

Veeck, William, Jr., and Ed Linn. *The Hustler's Handbook*. New York: Putnam's, 1965.

———. *Thirty Tons a Day*. New York: Viking, 1972.

———. *Veeck-as in Wreck*. New York: Bantam, 1963.

Whitfield, Shelby. *Kiss It Goodbye*. New York: Abelard-Schuman, 1973.

Williams, Ted, and John Underwood. *My Turn at Bat: The Story of My Life*. New York: Simon & Schuster, 1968.

Woolf, Bob. *Behind Closed Doors*. New York: Signet, 1976.

Periodicals

Articles

Aaron, Hank. Interviewed in *Playboy*, May 1974.

Arledge, Roone. Interviewed in *Playboy*, October 1976.

Chandler, A. B., with John Underwood. "How I Jumped From Clean Politics Into Dirty Baseball." *Sports Illustrated,* April 26, May 3, 1971.

Conigliaro, Tony, with Jack Zanger. "Seeing It Through." *Sports Illustrated,* June 22 and 29, 1970.

Dark, Al, with John Underwood. "Rhubarbs, Hassles, Other Hazards." *Sports Illustrated.* May 13, 1974.

Flood, Curt, with Stu Black. "The Legacy of Curt Flood." *Sport,* November, 1977.

Jordan, Pat. "Big Sky, Big Dream." *Sports Illustrated,* June 11, 1973.

Krichell, Paul. Interviewed in *Esquire,* December 1957.

Lane, Frank, and Bill Madden. "Why I Traded Bobby Bonds . . . And Other Assorted Superstars." *Baseball Quarterly,* Summer 1978.

LeFlore, Ron, and Jim Hawkins. "Stealing Was My Specialty." *Sports Illustrated,* February 8, 1978.

Maglie, Sal, and Robert Boyle. "Baseball is a Tough Business." *Sports Illustrated,* April 15 and 22, 1968.

Robinson, Frank, with Roy Blount, Jr. "I'll Always Be Outspoken." *Sports Illustrated,* October 21, 1974.

Rose, Pete. Interviewed in *Playboy,* September 1979.

Smith, Red. "My Pressbox Memoirs." *Equire,* October 1975.

Telander, Rich. "The Record Almost Broke Him." *Sports Illustrated,* June 20, 1977.

Ways, C. R. " 'Nobody Does Anything Better Than Me in Baseball,' Says Roberto Clemente." *New York Times Magazine,* April 9, 1972.

Weiss, George. "The Administration Man." In *Baseball is Their Business,* edited by Harold Rosenthal.

Williams, Ted, and John Underwood. "Hitting Was My Life." *Sports Illustrated,* June 10–July 8, 1968.

Newspapers
Boston Globe. 1967, 1975, 1977–78.
Boston Herald-American. 1978–79.
Chicago Daily News. 1977.
Los Angeles Times. 1975–78.
New York Daily News. 1958.
New York Post. 1967.
New York Times. 1946–82.
Philadelphia Bulletin. 1971, 1978.
Philadelphia Journal. 1979–82.
Philadelphia Inquirer. 1964–82.
Pittsburgh Press. 1971.
Reading (Pa.) Eagle. 1964–82.
Reading (Pa.) Times. 1977.
San Francisco Chronicle. 1971.
Village Voice. 1975.

Wall Street Journal. 1976.
Washington Post. 1967, 1969–72, 1975, 1979.

Sporting Journals
Baseball. 1976–80.
Baseball Bulletin. 1978.
Baseball Digest. 1945–80.
Baseball Magazine. 1916 54.
Baseball Quarterly. 1977–80.
Baseball Research Journal. 1974–80.
International Review of Sports Sociology. 1968.
Journal of Sports History. 1974–80.
National Pastime. 1975–76.
Professional Sports Journal. 1979.
Sport. 1972–80.
Sports Illustrated. 1954–82.
The Sporting News. 1945–82.

Baseball Annuals
Baseball Dope Book. 1980.
Official Baseball Register. 1960–79.

Reports

Baseball Writers Association of America. *Constitution,* 1967.
Basic Agreement Between the American League of Professional Baseball Clubs and the National League of Professional Baseball Clubs and Major League Baseball Players Association. Effective, January 1, 1976. Office of the Players Association.

Other Sources

American Broadcasting Company. "Wide World of Sports," June 30, 1973.
A. G. Spalding Company. Brochure: "A. G. Spalding & Brothers—Cornerstone of American Athletics."
Frick, Ford, et al. "Race Question." Unpublished Report, August 28, 1946. In A.B. Chandler Papers. University of Kentucky, Lexington, Kentucky.
Voigt, David Q. Interview with Brandy Davis, National Scouting Director for the Philadelphia Phillies. January 19–20, 1977; July 13, 1978; January 14, 1979.
———. Interview with Commissioner William Eckert. August 10, 1967.
———. Interview with Curtis Simmons, baseball player and representative to the Players Association. November 12, 1967.
———. Interview with Lee Allen, historian of Baseball Hall of Fame, Cooperstown, N.Y. July 26, 1967.
Wiley, George T. "Data on the 1948 American League Stretch Drive." Unpublished MS. of Society for American Baseball Research.

Secondary Sources

Unpublished Material

Chalk, Ocania. "The Black Professional Athlete in Major Sports: A Study in Courage and Perseverance." Unpublished manuscript. 1970.

Detroit Tigers Press Release. January, 1968.

Haerle, Rudolf K., Jr. "Career Patterns and Career Contingencies of Professional Baseball Players: An Occupational Analysis." Unpublished manuscript. 1974.

Haerle, Rudolf K., Jr. "Member of the Team, But Uniquely Alone: A Sociological Analysis of the Professional Baseball Player." Unpublished manuscript. 1974.

Herrick, Theodore P., Jr. "Financial Controls for Minor League Baseball Operations." Ph.D. dissertation, Ohio State University, 1959.

Onigman, Marc P., and Daniel C. Frio. "Some Medicine for the Amalgamation Syndrome: Latin American Players, 1871–1946." Paper read before the North American Society for Sports History in May, 1976.

Riess, Steven. "Civic Financed Stadiums." Paper read before the North American Society for Sports History in May, 1980.

Books

Adamic, Louis. *What's Your Name?* New York: Harper & Sons, 1942.

Allen, Lee. *The American League Story.* New York: Hill & Wang, 1962.

———. *The Hot Stove League.* New York: A.S. Barnes, 1955.

———. *The National League Story.* New York: Hill & Wang, 1961.

Allen, Maury. *The Incredible Mets.* New York: Warner Paperback Library, 1969.

———. *Where Have You Gone, Joe DiMaggio? The Story of America's Last Hero.* New York: Signet Books, 1975.

Andreano, Ralph. *No Joy in Mudville.* Cambridge, Mass: Schenckman, 1965.

Angell, Roger. *Five Seasons: A Baseball Companion.* New York: Popular Library, 1978.

———. *The Summer Game.* New York: Viking, 1972.

Ball, Donald, and John Loy. *Sport and the Social Order: Contributions to the Sociology of Sport.* Reading, Mass.: Addison-Wesley, 1975.

Barber, Red. *The Broadcasters.* New York: Dial, 1970.

Bardolph, Richard. *The Negro Vanguard,* New York: Vintage Books, 1961.

Beard, Gordon. *Birds on the Wing: The Story of the Baltimore Orioles.* New York: Doubleday, 1967.

Beisser, Arnold. *The Madness in Sports.* New York: Appleton, 1967.

Berry, Henry. *Boston Red Sox.* New York: Rutledge Books, 1975.

Bisher, Furman. *Miracle in Atlanta.* Cleveland: World, 1966.

Boas, Max, and Steve Chain. *Big Mac: The Unauthorized Story of McDonald's.* New York: E.P. Dutton, 1975.

Boyd, Brendan, and Frederick Harris. *The Great American Baseball Card, Flipping, Trading & Bubble Gum Book*. New York: Warner Paperback Library, 1975.

Boyle, Robert H. *Sport: Mirror of American Life*. Boston: Little, Brown, 1963.

Brooks, John. *The Great Leap: The Past Twenty-five Years in America*. New York: Harper & Row, 1968.

Browne, Ray B., ed. *Objects of Special Devotion: Fetishes and Fetishism in Popular Culture*. Bowling Green University, Popular Press, 1982.

Clark, Tom. *Champagne and Baloney: The Rise and Fall of Finley's A's*. New York: Harper & Row, 1976.

Coffin, Tristram. *The Old Ball Game: Baseball in Fact and Fiction*. New York: Herder & Herder, 1971.

Condon, Dave. *The Go-Go Chicago White Sox*. New York: Coward-McCann, 1960.

Coover, Robert. *The Universal Baseball Association Inc., J. Henry Waugh, Prop*. New York: Signet,1968.

Donahue, James. *Spitballs and Holy Water*. New York: Avon, 1977.

Durso, Joseph. *Amazing: The Miracle of the Mets*. New York: Houghton-Mifflin, 1970.

———. *Yankee Stadium: Fifty Years of Drama*. New York: Houghton-Mifflin, 1972.

Eitzen, D. Stanley, ed. *Sport in Contemporary Society: An Anthology*. New York: St. Martin Press, 1979.

Galbraith, John K. *The Affluent Society*. Boston: Houghton-Mifflin, 1958.

Goldman, Eric F. *The Crucial Decade and After: America 1945–1960*. New York: Vintage Books, 1960.

Golenbock, Peter. *Dynasty*. New York: Prentice-Hall, 1975.

Graham, Frank. *The New York Giants*. New York: Putnam's, 1952.

Grobani, Anton. *Guide to Baseball Literature*. Detroit: Gale Research, 1975.

Harris, Mark. *Henry Wiggen's Books*. New York: Avon, 1979.

Hart, Marie, ed. *Sport in the Socio-Cultural Process*. Dubuque, Iowa: Wm C Brown, 1972.

Herzog, Arthur. *The B. S. Factor: The Theory & Technique of Faking It In America*. New York: Penguin Books, 1974.

Izenberg, Jerry. *How Many Miles to Camelot? The All-American Sport Myth*. New York: Holt, Rinehart & Winston, 1972.

Johnson, William O. *Super Spectator and the Electronic Lilliputians*. Boston: Little, Brown, 1971.

Kahn, Roger. *The Boys of Summer*. New York: Signet, 1973.

Keats, John. *The Insolent Chariots*. Greenwich, Conn.: Fawcett, 1958.

Kerrane, Kevin, and Richard Grossinger, eds. *Baseball I Gave You All the Best Years of My Life*. Oakland, Cal.: North Atlantic Books, 1977.

Kiernan, Thomas. *The Miracle at Coogan's Bluff*. New York: Thomas Crowell, 1975.

Klapp, Orrin E. *Currents of Unrest*. New York: Holt, Rinehart & Winston, 1975.

Koppett, Leonard. *The Thinking Man's Guide to Baseball*. New York: E.P. Dutton, 1967.

Kowet, Don. *The Rich Who Own Sports*. New York: Random House, 1977.

Kuenster, John, ed. *From Cobb to Catfish*. New York: Rand McNally, 1975.

Lasch, Christopher. *The Culture of Narcissism*. New York: W.W. Norton, 1978.

Le Bon, Gustave. *The Crowd*. New York: Viking, 1966.

Lewis, Franklin. *The Cleveland Indians*. New York: Putnam's, 1949.

Lieb, Frederick. *Baseball As I Have Known It*. New York: Grosset & Dunlap, 1977.

————, with Stan Baumgartner. *The Philadelphia Phillies*. New York: Van Rees Press, 1953.

Lowenfish, Lee, and Tony Lupien. *The Imperfect Diamond*. New York: Stein & Day, 1980.

Major League Baseball, 1973. New York: Pocket Books, 1973.

Manchester, William. *The Glory and the Dream: A Narrative History of America, 1932–1972*. Boston: Little, Brown, 1974.

Mann, Jack. *The Decline and Fall of the New York Yankees*. New York: Simon & Schuster, 1967.

Meany, Tom. *Baseball's Greatest Hitters*. New York: A.S. Barnes, 1950.

————. *Mostly Baseball*. New York: A.S. Barnes, 1955.

————. *The Boston Red Sox*. New York: A.S. Barnes, 1956.

————. *The Yankee Story*. New York: E.P. Dutton, 1960.

Michener, James A. *Sports in America*. New York: Dell, 1976.

Miller, D., and M. Nowak. *The Fifties: The Way We Reallly Were*. New York: Doubleday, 1977.

Minor League Baseball Stars. Cooperstown, N.Y.: Society for American Baseball Research, 1978.

Obojski, Robert. *Bush League: A History of Minor League Baseball*. New York: Macmillan, 1975.

Parr, Jeanne. *The Superwives*. New York: Coward-McCann, 1976.

Parrott, Harold. *The Lords of Baseball*. New York: Praeger, 1975.

Peterson, Robert. *Only the Ball Was White*. New York: Prentice-Hall, 1970.

Pope, Edwin. *Baseball's Greatest Managers*. New York: Doubleday, 1960.

Rabovsky, Mark. *The Namath Effect*. New York: Prentice-Hall, 1970.

Reamer, Verna, ed. *The Best of Red Smith*. New York: Franklin Watts, 1963.

Reich, Charles. *The Greening of America*. New York: Bantam, 1971.

Reichler, Joseph. *Baseball's Great Moments*. New York: Crown, 1974.

Reidenbaugh, Lowell. *One Hundred Years of National League Baseball*. St. Louis: *The Sporting News*, 1976.

Ribakove, Barbara, and Sy Ribakove. *The Nifty Fifties: The Happy Years*. New York: Award Books, 1974.

Roberts, Michael. *Fans! How We Go Crazy Over Sports*. Washington D.C.: New Republic Books, 1976.

Rooney, James F. *A Geography of American Sport*. Reading, Mass.: Addison-Wesley, 1974.

Rosenthal, Harold. *The Best 10 Years of Baseball*. Chicago: Contemporary Books, 1979.

Roth, Philip. *The Great American Novel*, New York: Holt, Rinehart & Winston, 1972.

Running Press Glossary of Baseball Language. Richard Scholl, ed. Philadelphia: Running Press, 1977.

Ryan, Bob. *Wait Till I Make the Show: Baseball in the Minor Leagues*. Boston: Little, Brown, 1974.

Sahadi, Lou. *The Year of the Yankees*. Chicago: Contemporary Books, 1979.

Schneider, Russell. *Frank Robinson: The Making of a Manager*. New York: Coward, McCann and Geoghegan, 1976.

Seaver, Tom, and Norman Smith. *How I Would Pitch to Babe Ruth*. Chicago: Playboy Press, 1975.

Shannon, Bill, and George Kalinsky. *The Ballparks*. New York: Hawthorn Books, 1975.

Shecter, Leonard. *The Jocks*. New York: Paperback Library, 1970.

Smith, Red. *Pressbox*. New York: W.W. Norton, 1976.

Smith, Robert. *Baseball in America*. New York: Holt, Rinehart & Winston, 1961.

————. *Illustrated History of Baseball*. New York: Grosset & Dunlap, 1973.

Sugar, Bert R. *The Thrill of Victory: The Inside Story of ABC Sports*. New York: Hawthorn Books, 1978.

Toffler, Alvin. *Future Shock*, New York: Random House, 1970.

Tuite, James, ed. *Sports of the Times: The Arthur Daley Years*. New York: New York Times Books, 1975.

Tutko, Thomas, and William Brown. *Winning is Everything and Other American Myths*. New York: Macmillan, 1976.

Vecsey, George. *Joy in Mudville*. New York: McCall, 1970.

Voigt, David Q. *American Baseball*. Vol. 1. Norman: University of Oklahoma Press, 1966.

————. *American Baseball*. Vol. 2. Norman: University of Oklahoma Press, 1970.

————*America's Leisure Revolution*. Reading, Pa.: Albright College, 1971.

————. *America Through Baseball*. Chicago: Nelson-Hall, 1976.

Wagenheim, Kal. *Clemente*. New York: Praeger, 1974.

Wallop, Douglas. *Baseball: An Informal History*. New York: Bantam, -

Weiss, Paul. *Sport: A Philosophical Inquiry*. Carbondale, Ill.: University of Southern Illinois Press, 1969.

Whiting, Robert. *The Chrysanthemum and the Bat: Baseball Samurai Style*. New York: Dodd, Mead, 1977.

Whyte, William H., Jr. *The Organization Man.* New York: Simon & Schuster, 1957.

Wind, Herbert Warren. *The Gilded Age of Sport.* New York: Simon & Schuster, 1961.

Woodward, Stan. *Sports Page.* New York: Simon & Schuster, 1949.

Zimmerman, Paul. *The Los Angeles Dodgers.* New York: Coward-McCann, 1960.

Articles in Periodicals

Anderson, Dave. "The Frustrations of Baseball's Greatest Hitter," *Sport,* August 1979.

Appel, Marty, "It's a Whole New Ball Game." *Baseball Quarterly,* Winter 1978–1979.

"Back to the Unfabulous '50s." *Time,* August 5, 1974.

"Ballparks." *Baseball Quarterly,* June 1979.

"Baseball 1974."*Sports Illustrated,* April 8, 1974.

"Baseball 1978." *Sports Illustrated,* April 10, 1978.

Bell, Marty. "The Reds' Winter of Discontent." *Sport,* May 1972.

"Big League Baseball." *Fortune,* August 1937.

"The Black Dominance." *Time,* August 12, 1979.

Blount, Roy, Jr. "Birds of a Feather Flock to Bob." *Sports Illustrated,* November 2, 1970.

———. "How to Sportswrite Good." *Esquire,* November 1976.

———. "Soil is the Soul of Baseball."*Esquire,* March 1978.

———."Temple of the Playing Fields." *Esquire,* December 1976.

———. "Yea, Mr. Mays." *Sports Illustrated,* July 27,1970.

Bonventre, Pete. "The Ugly Sports Fan." *Newsweek,* June 7, 1974.

Boorstin, Daniel J. "Television." *Life,* September 10, 1971.

Bouton, Jim. "Reflections on Managing a Baseball Team." *Esquire,* May 1971.

Boyle, Robert. "This Miller Admits He's a Grind." *Sports Illustrated,* March 1974.

"Braves Ride Again." *Business Week,* October 1953.

Brodsky, Jack. "Keep Your Head On." *New York Times Magazine,* July 31, 1955.

Brosnan, Jim. " Have the Hitters Really Gone?" *Look,* May 13, 1969.

———. "It's a Long, Long Season." *New York Times Magazine,* April 17, 1960.

———. "The I's, We's, and They's of Baseball." *New York Times Magazine,* July 3, 1966.

———. "The Short Season." *Playboy,* April 1976.

Bruce, Harry. "Rusty Staub: The Making of a Muscular Millionaire." *Maclean's,* July 1970.

Buckley, Tom. "The Packaging of a Home Run." *New York Times Magazine,* April 11, 1974.

Cartwright, Gary. "Confessions of a Washed Up Sports Writer." *Harper's*, March 1968.

Chandler, Joan. "Television and Sports: Wedded With a Golden Hoop." *Psychology Today*, April 1977.

Charnofsky, H. "The Major League Professional Baseball Player: Self Conceptions vs Popular Image." *International Review of Sport Sociology* 3(1968): 39–55.

Chass, Murray. "The Cubs: A Legacy of Losing Seasons." *New York Times*, August 11, 1980.

Christine, Bill. "An Official Scorer Who Has Lived to Tell About It." *New York Times*, July 22, 1979.

Daley, Robert. "The Man They Love to Hate." *New York Times Magazine*, September 1, 1974.

Deford, Frank. "Best Damn Team in Baseball." *Sports Illustrated*, April 12, 1971.

———. "Heirs of Judge Landis." *Sports Illustrated*, September 30, 1974.

———. "Move Over for Oh-San." *Sports Illustrated*, August 15, 1977.

———. "Nobody Loves the Ruling Class." *Sports Illustrated*, October 11, 1972.

———. "Watch on the Ohio." *Sports Illustrated*, September 29, 1975.

Devaney, John. "The Flaky Phillies Can Hit Like Crazy." *Sport*, December 1976.

Dillard, R.H.W. "The Wisdom of the Beast: The Fiction of Robert Coover." *The Hollins Critic*, April 1970.

Director, Roger. "Baseball—It's A Jungle Out There." *Sport*, October 1979.

Dries, Donald. "Iceman Musial." *Baseball Digest*, November 1946.

Durham, Richard. "But Coach, It Helps Me Relax." *Playboy*, January 1976.

Durslag, Mel. "They Can't Call Them As They See Them." *TV Guide*, November 27, 1971.

———. "When Will Sportscasters Be Allowed to Speak Up?" *TV Guide*, June 24, 1967.

Durso, Joseph. "What's Happened to Baseball?" *Saturday Review*, September 14, 1968.

Eck, Robert. "The Real Masters of Television." *Harper's*, March 1967.

Einstein, Charles. "Geopolitics of Baseball." *Reporter*, August 11, 1955.

———. "The New Breed of Baseball Fans." *Harper's*, July 1967.

Ferretti, Fred. "Down on the Farm With the Yankees' Gene Michael." *New York Times Magazine*, August 19, 1979.

Fimrite, Ron. "Ah, How Great It Is." *Sports Illustrated*, November 1, 1976.

———. "The Battle is Rejoined." *Sports Illustrated*, August 7, 1978.

———. "The Bringer of the Big Heat." *Sports Illustrated*, June 16, 1975.

———. "For Failure to Give His Best." *Sports Illustrated*, July 5, 1971.

———. "In Cuba, It's Viva El Grand Old Game." *Sports Illustrated*, June 6, 1971.

————. "No Place Like Home." *Sports Illustrated*, October 23, 1978.

————. "Of Fear of Flying." *Sports Illustrated*, April 12, 1976.

————. "Past 3000 and Still Counting." *Sports Illustrated*, May 15, 1978.

————. "Pinning down the Voodoo Ball." *Sports Illustrated*, August 27, 1973.

————. "Stress, Strain, and Pain." *Sports Illustrated*, August 14, 1978.

————. "Take Me Out to the Brawl Game." *Sports Illustrated*, June 17, 1974.

————. "They're Beginning to Sound Like a Broken Record." *Sports Illustrated*, September 26, 1977.

————. "Three Thousand: High Note of a Hit Parade." *Sports Illustrated*, August 27, 1979.

————. "Triple Crown to the Clown." *Sports Illustrated*, October 28, 1974.

————. "Wilbur's Knuckler is Alive and Swell." *Sports Illustrated*, June 4, 1973.

————. "The Yankee D Boys Did Double Duty." *Sports Illustrated*, October 30, 1978.

Flaherty, Vincent X. "Miracle Man of the Dodgers—From Flatbush to Fantasia."*Baseball Register*, 1960.

"The Forty Million Dollar Body Shuffle." *Sports Illustrated*, December 13, 1969.

Frazier, George, IV. "Courage is a High Pain Threshold." *Esquire*, March 1968.

Furlong, William. "At Last A Likable Ump." *New York Times Magazine*, February 25, 1979.

————. "The Boston Massacre." *Sports Illustrated*, September 18, 1978.

————. "How Specialized Can You Get?" *New York Times Magazine*, August 14, 1966.

————. "It's a Three Billion Dollar Business." *New York Times Magazine*, June 5, 1966.

————. "Johnny Bench: Supercatcher." *New York Times Magazine*, August 30, 1970.

————. "Out in the Bleachers Where the Action Is." *Harper's*, July 1966.

————. "P.K. Wrigley: Baseball Magnate." *Saturday Evening Post*, Summer 1972.

Gammons, Peter. "These Are the Boston Manglers." *Sports Illustrated*, May 1, 1978.

Gmelch, George. "Baseball Magic." *Transaction*, June 1971.

Golenbock, Peter. "1961—A Year to Remember—For Everyone Except Roger Maris." *Baseball Quarterly*, Spring 1978.

Good, Paul. "The Year the Mets Lost 'The Franchise.' "*Sport*, November 1977.

Graber, Ralph S. "Baseball in American Fiction." *English Journal*, November 1967.

Granberg, Mike. "Baseball: It's Not a Game to Many Latins." *New York Times*, August 30, 1979.

"The Great Carew." *Baseball,* August 1979.

Gumpert, David. "Eye on the Ball." *Wall Street Journal,* July 7, 1976.

Hano, Arnved. "The Black Rebel Who 'Whitelists' the Olympics." *New York Times Magazine,* May 12, 1968.

———. "Television's Topmost—This is America." *New York Times Magazine,* December 26, 1975.

Henderson, Cary S. "Los Angeles and the Dodger War, 1957–1962." *Southern California Quarterly,* Fall 1980.

Hicks, Jack. "The Total Gamer." *Sport,* August 1979.

Hoagland, Edward. "Where Have All The Heroes Gone?" *New York Times Magazine,* March 10, 1974.

Holway, John. "Japan in Big League Thrills." Tokyo News Service, 1955.

———. "Only the Hall was White." *National Pastime,* 1975.

Isaacs, Stan. "And on the Seventh Day He Was Still Talking." *Sports Illustrated,* October 29, 1979.

———. "The Orioles Play Stop the Music." *Sports Illustrated,* October 8, 1979.

Izenberg, Jerry. "The Odd Couple Plays Zaire." *Sport,* October 1979.

James, Bill. "Confessions of a Stat Freak." *Sport,* September 1979.

———. "How Old is Old?" *Professional Sports Journal,* September 1979.

James, Weldon. "Japan's At Batto Again." *Colliers,* August 2, 1947.

Johnson, William O. "Television Made It All A New Game." *Sports Illustrated,* December 22, 1969.

Johnston, Richard W. "Having a Ball at Midnight." *Sports Illustrated,* June 19, 1978.

Jordan, Pat. "Big Sky, Big Dream." *Sports Illustrated,* June 11, 1973.

———. "Pitcher in Search of a Pitch." *Sports Illustrated,* April 15, 1974.

Kahn, Roger. "Can Sports Survive Money?" *Esquire,* October 1975.

———. "Of Galahad and Quests That Failed." *Sports Illustrated,* January 31, 1977.

Kaplan, Jim. "Brock Still Has the Old Sock." *Sports Illustrated,* May 21, 1979.

———. "Do They Really Know the Score?" *Sports Illustrated,* July 24, 1978.

Keith, Larry. "A Bunt That Went Boom." *Sports Illustrated,* July 13, 1978.

———. "All the Champs Were Titanic Failures." *Sports Illustrated,* October 8, 1979.

———. "A Series Full of Flip Flops." *Sports Illustrated,* October 17, 1977.

———. "Beer is Out, Halters In." *Sports Illustrated,* July 18, 1977.

———. "He's Still Le Grand Orange." *Sports Illustrated,* August 21, 1978.

———. "They're Knocking the Stuffing Out of It." *Sports Illustrated,* June 13, 1977.

Kempton, Murray. "The Homecoming of Willie Mays." *Esquire,*October 1974.

Kennedy, Ray. "More Victories Equals More Fans Equals More Profits, Right? Wrong, Wrong, Wrong." *Sports Illustrated,* April 28, 1980.

————. "Oh what An Era!" *Sports Illustrated,* August 13, 1979.

————. "Who Are These Guys?" *Sports Illustrated,* January 31, 1977.

Kennedy, Ray, and Nancy Williamson. "Money—the Monster Threatening Sports." *Sports Illustrated,* July 17–31, 1978.

Kirshenbaum, Jerry. "Well Hush Their Mouths." *Sports Illustrated,* August 20, 1979.

Koppett, Leonard. "A Yankee Dynasty Can Never Come Back." *New York Times Magazine,* October 2, 1966.

————. "Busch, Beer and Baseball." *New York Times Magazine,* April 11, 1965.

————. "The Ex-National Sport Looks to Its Image." *New York Times Magazine,* December 20, 1964.

Kornheiser, Tony. "That Damn Yankee." *New York Times Magazine,* April 9, 1978.

Kostelanetz, Richard. "Understanding McLuhan (In Part)." *New York Times Magazine,* January 29, 1967.

Lahr, John. "Notes on Fame." *Harper's,* January 1978.

Lardner, John. "Mighty Robot at the Bat." *New York Times Magazine,* June 19, 1955.

Lardner, Rex. "The Pitchers Are Ruining the Game." *New York Times Magazine,* June 16, 1968.

Leggett, William. "Beware of the Boomerang." *Sports Illustrated,* June 3, 1968.

————. "The Big Leagues Select a Fan." *Sports Illustrated,* February 17, 1969.

————. "The Cincy Cannonball." *Sports Illustrated,* July 13, 1970.

————. "Court Martial For A General." *Sports Illustrated,* December 16, 1968.

————. "Digging in at Crooked Creek." *Sports Illustrated,* April 10, 1972.

————. "Mustaches All The Way." *Sports Illustrated,* October 30, 1972.

————. "Not Just a Flood, But a Deluge." *Sports Illustrated,* August 19, 1968.

————. "The Season of the Zero Hour." *Sports Illustrated,* June 17, 1968.

Lelyveld, Joseph. "The Big Leaguer." *New York Times Magazine,* August 7, 1977.

Levy, Maury Z., and Samantha Stevenson. "The Secret Life of Baseball." *Playboy,* July 1979.

Lincoln, Melissa. "First You Learn Where the Mound Is." *Baseball Quarterly,* Winter 1977.

Linn, Ed. "Ballplayers vs. Fans," *Saturday Evening Post.* August 12, 1971.

————. "The Earl of Baltimore, He's A Mouthful." *Sport,* July 1980.

————. "The Meaning of the Game." *Sport,* June 1977.

Looney, Doug. "Smile for the Birdies." *Sports Illustrated,* June 18, 1979.

————. "When the Odds Are Saying You'll Never Win." *Sports Illustrated,* August 6, 1979.

Louis, Arthur. "Should You Buy Biorhythms?" *Psychology Today,* April 1978.

Lowenfish, Lee. "A Tale of Many Cities: The Westward Expansion of National League Baseball in the 1950s." *Journal of the West*, July 1978.

Lukas, J. Anthony. "Down and Out in the Minor Leagues." *Harper's*, June 1968.

———. "How Mel Allen Started a Lifelong Love Affair." *New York Times Magazine*, September 21, 1971.

Mack, William. "Playing Hurt—the Doctor's Dilemma." *Sports Illustrated*, June 11, 1979.

Marshall, Joe. "Howard Cosell is Just Another Pretty Face." *Esquire*, October 1971.

Massengale, John D. "Coaching as an Occupational Subculture." *Phi Delta Kappan*, October 1974.

Mendelson, Abby. "Face to Face With Elroy." *Baseball Quarterly*, Winter 1977.

———. "The Writers." *Baseball*, October 1979.

Mulvoy, Mark. "Sore Spots in Big Arm Year." *Sports Illustrated*, August 26, 1968.

Murphy, Jack. "Ben Casey at the Ball Park." *New York Times Magazine*, August 23, 1965.

Myre, Anton. "The Giant in the Tube." *Harper's* November 1972.

Nader, Ralph, and Peter Gruenstine. "Fans: The Sorry Majority." *Playboy*, March 1978.

Naughton, Jim. "Tension and Pressure of a Pennant Race." *New York Times*, September 30, 1979.

O'Connor, John. "Television on the Eve of Drastic Change." *New York Times*, November 13, 1977.

Olsen, Jack. "The Black Athlete—A Shameful Story." *Sports Illustrated*, July 1–29, 1968.

"On the Difficulty of Being a Hero." *Time*, June 24, 1966.

Onigman, Marc. "Tom Yawkey: Gentleman, Sportsman and Racist." *The Free Paper*, 1980.

Opotowsky, Stan. "Take Me Into the Ball Game." In *Sport in the Socio-Cultural Process*, edited by Marie Hart.

Ordine, Bill. "Searching For Gems on Rough Diamonds." *Today*, April 26, 1979.

Papanek, John. "There's an Ill Wind Blowing For the NBA." *Sports Illustrated*, February 26, 1979.

Poe, R. "The Angry Fan." *Harper's*, July 1967.

Polak, Maralyn, "Ruthven: Balking When the Owner Advanced." *Today*, August 29, 1978.

"The Pride of the Yankees." *Time*, August 12, 1979.

Raskin, A.H. "What's Wrong With American Newspapers?" *New York Times Magazine*, July 11, 1967.

Reed. J.D. "Again, A Hub of Anxiety." *Sports Illustrated,* September 29, 1975.

Reed, William F. "He's Still Filling His Horn of Plenty." *Sports Illustrated,* May 19, 1980.

Ribovsky, Mark. "This Pitcher Makes Hitters Tremble." *Sport,* July 1979.

Rosenblatt, Aaron. "Negroes in Baseball: The Failure of Success." *Transaction,* September 1967.

Roth, Philip. "My Baseball Years." *New York Times,* April 2, 1973.

Schickel, Richard. "The Movies Are Now High Art." *New York Times Magazine,* January 5, 1969.

Schrag, Peter. "The Age of Willie Mays." *Saturday Review,* May 8, 1971.

Scully, Gerald. "Discrimination: the Case of Baseball." in Eitzen's *Sport in Contemporary Society.*

Shaw, David. "The Roots of Rooting." *Psychology Today,* October 1977.

Schecter, Len. "Frank Robinson's Cool Assault on the Black Manager Barrier." *Look,* May 5, 1970.

———. "You're Gonna Pay, Baby," *Look;* September 7, 1971.

Smith, Curt. "Baseball Anyone." *Baseball Quarterly,* Summer 1979.

Smith, Robert. "Baseball Needs a New Pitch." *Look,* February 18, 1969.

"Sports and EDP." *Datamation,* June 1, 1979.

Steiger, Gus. "Same Game . . . But Not Quite." *Columbia,* March 1964.

Stein, Harry. "The Disillusionment of Carlton Fisk." *Sport,* August 1977.

———. "Sportswriting's Poet Laureate." *Sport,* March 1978.

Stein, M. L. "Everything Changes: Even the Newsroom." *Saturday Review,* July 10, 1971.

Stump, Al. "Dames are the Biggest Headache." *Baseball Digest,* September 1959.

———. "On Deck for the Dodgers —O'Malley the Younger." *Signature,* August 1971.

Surface, Bill. "How Much are Sports Arenas Costing the Taxpayers?" *Parade,* November 27, 1971.

Swift, E. M. "Odd Man Out on the Diamond." *Sports Illustrated,* August 20, 1979.

———. "They're Out." *Sports Illustrated,* April 16, 1979.

Taubman, Philip. "Reggie Looks Back in Anger." *Esquire,* March 1, 1978.

Tobin, Richard. "When Sports Stars Broadcast." *Saturday Review,* September 13, 1969.

Trippett, Frank. "The '70s, A Time of Pause." *Time,* December 25, 1978.

Trumbull, Robert. "Japan: Baseball Fever." *Holiday,* October 1961.

Twombly, Wells. "How To Throw the Ultimate Fast Ball!" *New York Times Magazine,* July 25, 1971.

———. "Meet An Average Major Leaguer: Dirty Al." *New York Times Magazine,* July 16, 1972.

Vaughn, Roger. "Ted Turner's True Talent." *Esquire,* October 1978.

Veeck, Bill, and Ed Linn. "Back Where I Belong." *Sports Illustrated*, March 15, 1976.

———. "The Baseball Establishment." *Esquire*, August 1964.

Voigt, David Q. "Comiskey, Grace R." *Dictionary of American Biography*.

———"Landis, Kenesaw Mountain." *Dictionary of American Biography*.

———. "McGillicuddy, Cornelius (Connie Mack)." *Dictionary of American Biography*.

———. "Rickey, Wesley Branch. *Dictionary of American Biography*.

———. "Robinson, Jack Roosevelt." *World Encyclopedia of Biographpy*.

———. "Sex in Baseball: Reflections of a Changing Taboo." *Journal of Popular Culture*, Winter 1970.

———. "Spink, John George Taylor." *Dictionary of American Biography*.

Watts, Robert G., and Eric Sawyer. "Aerodynamics of a Knuckleball." *American Journal of Physics*, November 1975.

Weeks, Ed. "Goodby Gibby." *Baseball Digest*, December 1975.

Welles, Chris. "We Have Seen the Future of Video." *Esquire*, June 1980.

"Westward the A's" *Time*, November 22, 1954.

Whiting, Robert. "Where the Manager Tells You to Strike Out." *Sport*, May 1977.

Wiley, Peter. ' 'Inside the Front Page." *Human Behavior*, November 1978.

Williams, Ted, and John Underwood. "I Hope Carew Hits .400." *Sports Illustrated*, July 18, 1977.

Wilner, Barry. "The Earl of Baltimore." *Baseball*, August 1979.

Yardley, Jonathan. "Everybody Knew Me, Al." *Sports Illustrated*, August 29, 1977.

Yetman, Norman. "Immune From Racism?" In *Sport in Contemporary Society*, edited by D. Stanley Eitzen.

Index